ANOTHER MOTHER

A Cultural Critique Book

CESARE CASARINO, JOHN MOWITT, AND
SIMONA SAWHNEY *Editors*

Another Mother

Diotima and the Symbolic Order of Italian Feminism

Cesare Casarino and Andrea Righi, editors

Translated by
Mark William Epstein

A Cultural Critique Book

UNIVERSITY OF MINNESOTA PRESS
MINNEAPOLIS • LONDON

Copyright 2018 by the Regents of the University of Minnesota

All rights reserved. No part of this publication may be reproduced, stored in a retrieval system, or transmitted, in any form or by any means, electronic, mechanical, photocopying, recording, or otherwise, without the prior written permission of the publisher.

Published by the University of Minnesota Press
111 Third Avenue South, Suite 290
Minneapolis, MN 55401-2520
http://www.upress.umn.edu

ISBN 978-1-5179-0493-7 (hc)
ISBN 978-1-5179-0494-4 (pb)
A Cataloging-in-Publication record for this book is available from the Library of Congress.

Printed in the United States of America on acid-free paper

The University of Minnesota is an equal-opportunity educator and employer.

Contents

Acknowledgments — vii

Introduction: Another Mother, Another Introduction — 1
CESARE CASARINO AND ANDREA RIGHI

Part I. Metaphor, Metonymy, and the Politics of Sexual Difference

1. The Contact Word   IDA DOMINIJANNI — 33

2. To Knit or to Crochet: A Political-Linguistic Tale on the Enmity between Metaphor and Metonymy   LUISA MURARO — 67

3. On the Relation between Words and Things as Frequentation   LUISA MURARO — 121

Part II. On the Maternal Symbolic and Its Language

4. Maternal Language between Limit and Infinite Opening — 133
CHIARA ZAMBONI

5. Feminism and Psychoanalysis: The Dead Mother Complex — 159
LUISA MURARO

Part III. The Mother and the Negative

6. With the Maternal Spirit   DIANA SARTORI — 173

7. The Undecidable Imprint   IDA DOMINIJANNI — 211

Part IV. Thinking with Diotima

8. And Yet She Speaks! "Italian Feminism" and Language 237
   ANNE EMMANUELLE BERGER

9. Origin and Dismeasure: The Thought of Sexual Difference 277
   in Luisa Muraro and Ida Dominijanni, and the Rise of
   Post-Fordist Psychopathology   ANDREA RIGHI

10. Mother Degree Zero; or, Of Beginnings: An Afterword on 303
    Luisa Muraro's Feminist Inaptitude for Philosophy
    CESARE CASARINO

Contributors 321

Index 323

Acknowledgments

As this volume endeavors to show, the mother constitutes that primary relation—at once symbolic and real—that enables all other relations to self, others, and the world. To be in relation is always to be in exchange, is always to be in debt. As a book on the mother, as a book on the relation of all relations, thus, this volume was enmeshed inevitably in myriad relations, exchanges, and debts by definition from the very beginning and from beginning to end over the years. For such a rich debt, we are grateful. Among the innumerable people who have helped us think about and know the mother in her multiple incarnations, facets, and functions, and who have helped us with this book in very many different ways, we would like to thank at the very least Simona Antonacci, Irene Capitani, Zandira Capitani, Vincenza Casarrubea, Jason Christenson, Maria Costa, Silvia Divinetz, Susanna Ferlito, Domenica Impastato, Kiarina Kordela, Maria Liguori, Giuseppina Mecchia, Linda Medley, Dylan Mohr, John Mowitt, Thomas Pepper, Elide Righi, Iris Ruozzi, Simona Sawhney, Alan Serposs, Domietta Torlasco, Jason Weidemann, and two anonymous readers. Above all, we are immensely grateful to Ida Dominijanni: without her unwavering support—personal, political, and intellectual—we would have never dared to embark on a project on the mother.

Introduction

Another Mother, Another Introduction

CESARE CASARINO AND ANDREA RIGHI

MOTHER NAMES

Mother: it is difficult to pronounce this word, to utter her name, and be taken seriously nowadays. Within intellectual discourses and environments—including academic ones—invoking the mother typically elicits dismissive eye-rolling, or polite condescension at best, indicating the listener's immediate impatience or boredom with what is presumed to be a quaint throwback to various feminist debates of the 1970s (one thinks here, for example, of Adrienne Rich, of the investigation of the mother–daughter relation in the context of what she named "the lesbian continuum," of her influential *Of Woman Born: Motherhood as Experience and Institution*, etc.) Besides the fact that, we would argue, an intellectual as remarkable and complex as Rich has lost none of her power or relevance in and for the present, and hence that there is still much to be gained from continuing to return to her work and to the work of the other intellectuals who shaped that distinctive season of feminist politics (which goes approximately from the late 1960s to the mid 1980s and which is usually referred to as second-wave feminism)—besides all that, we believe that the question of the mother remains a crucial Gordian knot not only for feminist theory and practice but also for philosophy and politics *tout court*; we believe, in short, that we are never quite done with the mother. In this introduction, first we address who the mother is, what the mother names, why the mother matters in this context, and then we zero in on Diotima—the community of women philosophers that is the main focus of *Another Mother: Diotima and the Symbolic Order of Italian Feminism*.

If it is legitimate to ask why talk about the mother here and now, it is also legitimate to ask why and how it came to be that we do not talk much about her any longer, that a figure so important to some of the most influential intellectual discourses of the twentieth century (from psychoanalysis to feminism and beyond) has somehow fallen into desuetude and become unfashionable.[1] Arguably, the fact that the question of the mother is now no longer as central as it was for the last century is one of the many symptoms of the emergence of the contemporary post-oedipal order—which is no less patriarchal for being post-oedipal and to which we will return at a later point in this introduction. Be that as it may, we might begin with yet another and more fundamental question, namely, who, and what, is the mother? What nexus of discourses does she incarnate? What problematic does "mother" name in this volume? Though this too is not a question amenable to an easy answer, and though this question is what this entire volume aims to address, we will venture to offer a provisional answer as a heuristic device and starting point for the present investigations.

Mother is at once the woman who brought us into the world as well as that which gave us both life and language, thereby enabling everything else. Mother incarnates the chiasmus of language and life, speech and body, words and things. This mother, however, is not a static origin of all, a mute and inert wellspring from which everything comes forth; on the contrary, mother is a relational concept: mother names a primary relation. As Luisa Muraro—the thinker whose work constitutes the primary focus of this volume—puts it most incisively: "We learn to speak from the mother, and this statement defines both who the mother is and what language is."[2] It is crucial to note that in this sentence Muraro does not begin from the mother. She begins, rather, from a relation, from a teaching-learning exchange: "We learn to speak from the mother." It is this pedagogical give-and-take and back-and-forth between mother and child that defines and, indeed, produces both mother and language—and us. Muraro adds that this relation "does not separate being and thought and hence feeds on the mutual interest and exchange between being and language."[3] The problematic whose name is "mother" thus becomes clear: it is identified here as the nexus of relations between language and being as well as between thought and being, or, put differently, as the relation between epistemology and ontology. And the importance and originality of the way in which this problematic is posed and grappled with here also becomes clear. The implications of such an articulation of the mother, in fact, are momentous.

The *vulgata* of the history of twentieth-century thought tells us that this was the century of the so-called linguistic turn, starting at the beginning of the century with the different yet contemporaneous investigations of structural linguistics (Ferdinand de Saussure), of the Vienna Circle (Ludwig Wittgenstein), and of psychoanalysis (Sigmund Freud)—all thinkers with whom Muraro engages explicitly in her works. The story—including the rest of it—is well known, and there is certainly much truth to it. Inevitably, as it is often the case with historiographical clichés, this story also oversimplifies matters a great deal. Around the time that the three aforementioned thinkers and their attendant circles and discourses started to focus on and problematize the question of language, for example, a philosopher like Martin Heidegger could say that his time had forgotten the question of being and that contemporary philosophy exhibited a distinctive inaptitude for ontology—a declaration that spurred Heidegger for more than half a century of ontological investigations, which, importantly, were also centrally concerned with the question of language, and which exerted an immense influence on twentieth-century philosophy.[4] If this influence was so immense, that is also because—Heidegger's protestations to the contrary notwithstanding—the propensity for ontological inquiry was (or rapidly became) characteristic of his age. Just a few years before the end of the twentieth century another philosopher—Alain Badiou—would declare in his typically apodictic manner: "Our epoch can be said to have been stamped and signed, in philosophy, by the return of the question of Being. . . . When all is said and done, there is little doubt that the century has been ontological, and that this destiny is far more essential than the 'linguistic turn' with which it has been credited."[5] On the one hand, Badiou's assessment is a welcome corrective to historiographical clichés. On the other hand, it strikes us that Badiou is only half right, which is also to say that he is half wrong. It seems more nuanced and compelling, in fact, to argue that, from the later part of the first half of the twentieth century onward, the so-called linguistic turn rapidly prompted and merged with various ontological investigations, including the critique of ontology and of metaphysics (one thinks here of the likes of Jacques Lacan and, later, of Jacques Derrida and of Luce

Irigaray): in hindsight, the linguistic turn had been an ontological turn all along. (And if we mentioned Heidegger here that is because he was one of the first as well as one of the few philosophers in the twentieth century to understand with rare perspicacity that language posed a problem for any conception of being, that the question of language was indeed an ontological question in the first place.) Why can't or won't Badiou see "the century" as having been characterized in philosophy by a complex intertwining of the question of language and the question of being, and hence by an onto-epistemological nexus? Why does he counter a historiographical cliché (i.e., the twentieth century as the century of the "'linguistic turn'") with another just as oversimplifying story (i.e., the twentieth century as the ontological century)? It is at this point that the importance and originality of Muraro's approach—and of the approach of the community of women philosophers to which she belongs—becomes especially apparent (even though, as we will explain shortly, they do not put much stock in the value of originality, and with good reasons).

If Badiou is not willing and able to see how in the twentieth century the so-called linguistic turn produced and constituted an ontological turn in its own right, that is because he abides by a conception of language and being that is marked by separation. The temptation to say that only a man could abide by such a separation is very strong, but we will try to stay calm, be rational, and resist that temptation (though the words of Oscar Wilde's Lord Darlington in *Lady Windermere's Fan*—a play whose plot, incidentally, twists around the separation of a mother and a daughter—do come to mind: "I can resist everything except temptation."). Certainly, Badiou is not the only one to abide by such a separation and, in fact, he is in good and abundant company. One could add here a long list of otherwise very different modern and contemporary philosophers, ranging from Immanuel Kant to Michel Foucault and beyond, according to whom language and being, words and things, had been organically linked in a variety of ways in the premodern period, especially in the wake of Stoic philosophy, but became separated and started to follow their distinct paths with the onset of modernity.[6] Muraro is a rare exception in this nearly undifferentiated landscape: she is ex-centric with respect to this dominant current of modern and contemporary philosophy due to the fact that she considers the putative separation of language and being as the powerful story that philosophical discourses born and raised within, as well as at one with patriarchy need to tell themselves and others in order to function. Going against the grain of this founding myth of origin of so much philosophy, Muraro posits and starts from "the mutual interest and exchange between being and language": such a nexus, for her, is the beginning and condition of possibility of any philosophical investigation. For Muraro, further, *language and being do not function in separation from each other and indeed are not separate because thought and being are not separate in the first place* (the relation she posits "does not separate being and thought and hence feeds on the mutual interest and exchange between being and language"). Muraro's mother—or, more precisely, the triangular exchange that defines and produces at once mother and child and language—names the relation that keeps thought and being together. This mother constitutes nothing less than a radical feminist intervention into the most fundamental philosophical problematic of the twentieth century. And this is a problematic that has not disappeared with the advent of the current century. The emergence of a philosophical movement such as speculative realism, and its attendant critique of what Quentin Meillassoux calls "correlationism," for example, bears witness to the fact that this problematic is alive and well: in this context, Muraro's poignant description of the Kantian thing-in-itself as the mother's cenotaph is one of the many indicators of the ongoing relevance of this intervention.[7]

But what about politics? Muraro and the community of women philosophers to which she belongs, after all, maintain a safe distance from and a healthy skepticism toward philosophy and in the end are more interested in politics and in feminist politics especially, without, for that, ever ceasing to be philosophers and to do philosophy (and we will return to this apparent paradox later in this introduction). Why is it important and indeed urgent for politics to think and to foster a debate about the mother here and now? What is this "here and now"? We have learned from feminism, and from feminist writing and thinking practices, that one starts there, where and when one is—especially if this "there," as it is often the case, consists of many different places; that is, of many different spatiotemporal zones and subject positions at once. (Muraro, among others, taught us always to start from that mess which is given reality.)[8] Crucially, one of the places of this "there" for us was the most suffocating summer of 2016—when this introduction was being written—a summer that left a long trail of unspeakable horror, blood, and tears in its wake, and that bodes ill for many years to come. During this summer, it was very difficult to avoid the sense that the planet was spiraling down faster and faster toward an all-out, full-blown, and polymorphous global civil war. Among the many episodes of this global civil war, we want to focus here on two events that stand out, for us, as particularly emblematic and as particularly relevant to the matters at hand.

In the early hours of Sunday, June 12, 2016, a mass shooting took place inside Pulse—a well-known gay nightclub in Orlando, Florida— during the establishment's weekly Latin Night: forty-nine people had been killed, and fifty-three had been injured by the end of the night, in what was hastily called the deadliest mass shooting in U.S. history (and we say "hastily" simply because the definition of "mass shooting" must be problematized: as it stands, and as it is deployed in the media, this definition conspires in consigning events such as the 1921 Tulsa race riot or the 1890 Wounded Knee massacre or the 1857 Mountain Meadows massacre to the proverbial dust-heap of history). That the gunman responsible for this slaughter, a twenty-nine-year-old man by the name of Omar Mir Seddique Mateen, was a U.S. citizen born in the United States to Afghani parents who had emigrated in the 1980s, pledged (in his words) "allegiance to Abu Bakr al-Baghdadi of the Islamic State"[9] during a phone call to 911 half an hour into the shooting, used a legally purchased Sig Sauer MCX assault-style rifle and a handgun in the shooting, worked for the U.S.-based global security company G4S Secure Solutions, was said (by his father) to have been enraged at the sight of two men kissing, was said (by his ex-wife) to have been a physically abusive husband, was described (by ex-coworkers) as deeply racist and misogynistic,[10] was claimed (by Pulse regulars) to have frequented the nightclub and to have been spotted on several gay dating apps. That this, in short, was the shooter, and that his targets were primarily gay and lesbian Latinos and Latinas, marks this event as the cruel intersection of (at least) four especially vexed and especially central nodes of contemporary U.S. politics, namely, racism, gay and lesbian rights, gun control, and so-called Islamic so-called terrorism. (Predictably, the event was immediately dubbed and investigated as "an act of terrorism."[11] Why didn't anybody call it a gay hate crime?)

Let us rewind just a few days. On Friday, June 3, 2016, nineteen Yazidi women were locked in cages and burned alive in front of hundreds of people in Mosul, Nineveh Governorate, by soldiers of the self-proclaimed Islamic State of Iraq and Syria, as punishment for having refused to have sex with them.[12] Do you remember? Had you forgotten? Did you even read or hear about it at the time? These are not idle questions: assuming (undoubtedly presumptively) that the readers (much like the writers) of this introduction were not eyewitnesses to this atrocity, such questions point to and foreground the obscene imbalances of power in the current global civil war. (Obviously, eyewitnesses, as well as the loved ones of these women, among others, do not need such questions to realize the injustice and the imbalances at work here.) Had we not decided to highlight this particular event, it is likely we would not remember it. The atrocities that have taken place in Iraq since (at least) the end of the Cold War (i.e., since "Operation Desert Storm" in 1991) are legion—simply too many and simply too brutal for these privileged and distant observers (and perhaps for anybody) to think. Modernity had devised sophisticated tools to think the unthinkable and then come out unscathed and even reinvigorated from such an experience (e.g., the Kantian sublime, the Conradian horror, the Adornian declaration—eminently poetical in its deliberate and forceful terseness—that "To write poetry after Auschwitz is barbaric.") But it is becoming increasingly difficult nowadays to have one's cake and eat it too, or even simply to live and think.[13] To think in the absence of representation and its reifications, at any rate, is at once imperative yet increasingly difficult. Presumably, these fiercely defiant women and the soldiers who massacred them had names and faces (much like Mateen and all the people he killed, whose names and faces have now been paraded across millions of screens, for better and for worse). These are names and faces we shall never know—and never really think.

The jarring juxtaposition of these two apparently unrelated episodes from the summer of 2016 aims to draw attention to one crucial common feature that binds these events together, that reaches far beyond them, and that permeates the fabric of our violent present: aside from all the other connections that may be compellingly drawn between them, these two events share in a misogyny and a phobia for anything associated with the feminine that are endemic to patriarchal culture in all its different forms today. It is obvious and even banal, yet it bears reiterating that the perpetrators of the aforementioned atrocities and of innumerable similar atrocities (including all perpetrators of mass shootings in recent U.S. history) are men. Wounded masculinity kills. And violence against women is on the rise worldwide, a quotidian and most banal violence that—as Jacqueline Rose puts it in a recent, trenchant essay—is "a crime of the deepest thoughtlessness."[14] (Rose, who borrows and reelaborates the concept of thoughtlessness from Hannah Arendt, proceeds to argue, among other things, that violence against women "is a sign that the mind has brutally blocked itself.")[15] Protestations that patriarchy has been misogynistic and violent against women since time immemorial will not do: we will return later to the specificity of the contemporary post-oedipal order, but for the moment we will limit ourselves to pointing out that the fact that violence against women is increasing everywhere needs to be understood, among other things, as a reaction to the world-historical event of feminism in its various manifestations and movements and to the ways it has contributed to disturb previous regimes of power. This is why it is important and urgent to think and talk about the mother here and now, to think and talk about the ways—old and new—in which patriarchal culture exploits and then forecloses the power of the woman who gave us both life and language (as we shall see, this argument, variously made by the likes of Luce Irigaray and Julia Kristeva, among others, is one the fundamental starting points, rather than endpoints, of Muraro's work). The violence we have evoked here shall not stop without coming to terms with and breaking away from this patriarchal dialectic of exploitation and foreclosure of maternal power.

And, finally, another mother, of course, means also another family. Rethinking what we might call the mother function is tantamount to rethinking the ways in which the primary institution of reproduction and socialization of the human—the anthropogenic apparatus par excellence—functions and is practiced and lived. There is a theoretical and political discourse, of course, that has done much to rethink the family, with and beyond feminism, during the last three decades—and its name is queer theory. The theory and practice of queer kinship has produced much valuable work (including what is possibly one of Judith Butler's finest books to date, a book on that most fiercely defiant woman, the sister and daughter of Oedipus—*Antigone's Claim: Kinship between Life and Death*). Here, we want to invoke the work of Sara Ahmed. In the conclusion to her queer investigations into phenomenology, Ahmed writes: "The task is to trace the lines for a different genealogy, one that would embrace the failure to inherit the family line as the condition of possibility for another way of dwelling in the world."[16] Indeed. And this has been the task for a long time: In 1975, Gayle Rubin's rallying cry was: "feminism must call for a revolution in kinship"—(itself an explicit answer to and radical transfiguration of another and older rallying cry, namely, Karl Marx and Friedrich Engels's exhortation in *The Communist Manifesto*: "*Aufhebung* of the family!").[17] We believe that this task cannot be accomplished without addressing and being addressed by the mother function. In this sense, *Another Mother* is an invitation, an offering, "to trace the lines for a different genealogy" by rediscovering and rethinking the mother in queer kinship, where she had been all along.

Before we begin to undertake this task, a word of caution on the particular terminology that the philosophical writings collected in this volume employ. Much as the bare mention of the mother elicits boredom or disapproval, the term *sexual difference* may equally generate the annoying sense that this philosophy is steeped in old and superseded patriarchal divisions between man and woman. Diversity, after all, is today an indisputable accomplishment, as well as the buzzword for the market of ideas that promises to deliver a better society, from academia to the corporate workplace and beyond. How is it possible that these philosophers still name *difference* in the singular? It would take an entire book to answer this question (in fact, there is no dearth of books on the topic). For brevity's sake, we would like to remind the reader that, in these writings, sexual difference constitutes the ontological condition of possibility of several other sexual differences, which are historical forms based on specific social, political, cultural, and economic conditions. In other words, sexual difference is a category of potentiality. Sexual differences, on the other hand, belong to the realm of actuality. The former is unrepresentable (which does not mean inexpressible or unknowable), whereas the latter belongs to the realm of representation. Mother is the common name of sexual difference understood as the unrepresentable matrix of sexual differences. We return to the politics appertaining to sexual difference thus conceived in the final section of this introduction.

DIOTIMA'S MOTHER, AND HER COMMUNITY

This volume presents some of the most significant writings by four distinctive intellectuals of the Diotima community: the aforementioned Luisa Muraro, as well as Ida Dominijanni, Diana Sartori, and Chiara Zamboni. The Diotima community and these authors in particular are largely unknown to the Anglophone reader, for very little has been made available in English of the theory and practice of the Italian thought of sexual difference.[18] The most notable exception is the recent publication in English of Muraro's seminal work *L'ordine simbolico della madre* [*The Symbolic Order of the Mother*], originally published in 1992, which we encourage the reader to use as a companion to our volume, and to which we will return in the final section of this introduction.[19] Our hope is that *Another Mother*—along with *The Symbolic Order of the Mother*—will contribute to reversing this neglect.

The Diotima community was founded in the early 1980s at the University of Verona, but its members had already had a long history of involvement with other feminist political organizations and feminist philosophical collectives in Milan, Rome, Padua, and Parma, from the 1960s onward. Diotima is not so much a school or a current of thought, but rather a space for cultural debates and political activism, where theory always merges with practice, and where the thought of sexual difference philosophically brings together contributions from various strains and experiences of Italian feminism. Much like the mother is the common name of sexual difference, Diotima is the common name of an open set of philosophical and political relations. As the community writes on its website: "We are not a group; we are particular, specific women bearing the signs—at once singular and common—of a history of relations, starting from the relation with our mother and continuing with the relation that binds us together and whose name is 'diotima'—the common name of the relation among women involved in philosophical research."[20]

The legacy of Luce Irigaray, as well as the radical thought of Carla Lonzi, are central for understanding the general perspective that informs Diotima's seminars and publications.[21] This is particularly true for Muraro, who became Irigaray's first translator into any language in the early 1970s, but in general it is also true for the other members of the community. From Irigaray's thought, the Diotima collective draws, for instance, a genealogy of power based on the idea that the maternal represents the interdicted foundation of the social order—an interdiction that we described earlier as the dialectic of exploitation and foreclosure of the maternal. But the Diotima collective also reelaborates the basic tenets of what we may call Irigaray's epistemology, that is to say, the overarching theme of duality and metonymy as the deep structure that informs cognitive and emotional capacities and that is modeled after the feminine sex. For as she states, famously, woman's nonphallic economy is that "of two lips in continuous contact. Thus, within herself, she is already two but not divisible into one(s)."[22] To the extent that these traits occupy a central position in the thought of the Diotima community and constitute the core of a philosophy that is continuously rethematized, one could ask what critical novelty, what groundbreaking contribution these intellectuals bring to the table. For those who, having had an indirect exposure to the writings of Italian feminism, believe that the latter is simply a lesser branch of French feminism or a superfluous and not particularly innovative appendix of continental thought, we hope this volume will offer an opportunity to reconsider such a hurried verdict—and, in a sense, Anne Emmanuelle Berger's contribution to this volume addresses this question head on. Perhaps the first point to bear in mind is precisely that the passionate search for the theoretical new—today's surrogate for commercial innovation in the moribund state of corporate humanities—is not something that the feminist thought in question generally prizes. On the contrary, because of longstanding oppression, unearthing a distinctive feminist genealogy is a more essential goal for feminism. Within these genealogies, breaks, confutations, and other grand philosophical innovations are things that the thinkers under consideration in our volume gladly leave to the usual oedipal tradition of symbolic homicide. Such a tradition embodies what Muraro calls the "cannibal" tendency of intellectuals, "who believe they have invented what instead was simply transmitted to them."[23] The real question is instead to pause and reflect not on novelty itself but on the priority and centrality for today's debates of a series of radical insights elaborated by feminism, which bear testimony to a logical priority precisely because they go to the *root* of the problem, as the term *radical* signifies.

The thinkers we present in this volume, along with others who could not be included for reasons of space, retain a priority in contemporary philosophy that is first of all historiographical. Diotima, along with other Italian feminist thinkers not associated with the community, such as Leopoldina Fortunati, Silvia Federici, Carla Lonzi, and Mariarosa Dalla Costa, had begun in effect a philosophical investigation of the question of biopolitics long before anybody other than Michel Foucault—that is, Giorgio Agamben, Franco Berardi (aka Bifo), Roberto Esposito, Antonio Negri, Paolo Virno, among others—had begun elaborating this question further, as well as disseminating and popularizing it in Italy and elsewhere. Moreover, it seems to us that Diotima marks a clear discontinuity with and within that "Italian Theory," which, for better and for worse, is so in vogue in the Anglophone world, and that the primary discontinuity consists of the reelaboration of a psychoanalytic as well as feminist problematic to which most contemporary—and, not coincidentally, male—Italian thinkers are usually deaf.

What makes Italian feminism relevant for us today, among other things, is its deep understanding of the constitutive feminine elements of contemporary biopolitics—long before the concept was even named as such—and the comprehensive critical stance, more than the theoretical innovation, that Italian feminism elaborated over the course of four decades. In the terminology that Italian (male) philosophers used to popularize the concept, the biopolitical is broadly speaking a dimension in which the biological substratum of human life has become fully productive. It thus points to new possibilities of development of human potentiality as well as to the dangers of its manipulation and of its total submission into the circuits of production and exploitation. Yet, framed in this way, it is not difficult to notice how this ambivalence was something that women were accustomed to: it constituted indeed the very fabric of their existence since time immemorial. A mode of being in which the possibility of emancipation is always enmeshed with that of oppression is what defines the feminine experience precisely because women have been historically the agents that carried out the work of reproduction. Finally, this labor was characterized by a fundamental immaterial component that has now become hegemonic in cognitive capitalism. These productive practices recapitulate those same dynamics so that when discussing immaterial production the category "feminization of labor" is usually employed.[24]

The analysis and critique of the productive dimension of the work of reproduction, which until then was conceived of as something negligible because it was presumed not to create value, represents in fact the mainspring of Italian feminist thought. It was clearly articulated both in economic and theoretical terms by the first important Italian feminist group, Demau (Demystification of Patriarchal Authority), in its 1966 manifesto and, immediately after, it was given a more comprehensive philosophical organization by Carla Lonzi. In her seminal work "Let's Spit on Hegel," in particular, she isolated this point when she inquired why Marxism "overlooked that women play a part in the productive process through their work in reproducing labor-power with the family."[25] This deep awareness of a materialist analysis of feminine social conditions constitutes one of the compass points that orients Italian feminism in the critique of patriarchy, one that complements the more psychoanalytic approach that attacked the symbolic disciplining of the patriarchy. The feminist revolution against patriarchy was thus defined by an antimetaphysical effort that conjugated a critique of the patriarchal symbolic order and of the socioeconomic framework within which it operated. In short, this is a true materialism that embraced both the body and the mind of the women involved in the work of reproduction. And as such, the various currents that flowed into the sea of Italian feminism always stressed the need to produce political practices that would not only give voice to but also redefine feminine authority.

That this type of philosophical inquiry gives cause for reflection also for antiracist theory and practice will come as no surprise to the reader, for whom we assume it is no news that racism and patriarchy—along with patriarchy's attendant sexism and misogyny—are always intricately related. For example, Étienne Balibar is not alone in having noted the "amazing correspondence, almost interchangeability, of racism and sexism"—and, in effect, we were drawing attention to such correspondence and mutual imbrications when implying, earlier in this introduction, that it was not a coincidence if the women who refused sex with and were burned alive by ISIS soldiers in Mosul were members of an ethnic and religious minority and if the victims of the Pulse mass shooting were largely Latinas and Latinos.[26] It is true that the essays included in this volume and, in general, the feminist theory elaborated by Diotima do not specifically engage with the question of race (and there are historical reasons for this, including the ways in which the question of race, on the one hand, has marked indelibly each and every phase of the development of the Italian nation-state from its foundation in 1860 to the present day, and, on the other hand, has emerged as a crucial and highly contested cultural, social, and political issue in Italy only relatively recently). And yet, despite such undertheorization of race and racism, the theory and practice of sexual difference elaborated by the Diotima collective has much to offer to antiracist projects: this is the case not only because, generally speaking, it is hard to imagine a critique of racism without a critique of patriarchy (as the pioneering and still highly relevant work of black feminist thinkers such as Angela Davis, bell hooks, and others has shown); this is the case also because, in particular, Diotima's discovery and elaboration of the maternal symbolic constitutes an essential element in the critique of any system of domination, oppression, and exploitation to the extent to which such systems necessarily attempt, with varying degrees of success, to lay claim to the ownership of human reproduction. Obviously, the question of how the monopoly on the reproduction of human beings constitutes a crucial nexus between patriarchy and modern systems of domination, oppression, and exploitation—including, in particular, that foundational and paradigmatic form of biopolitical governmentality which is racial slavery—is a highly complex question, and a full investigation is beyond the scope of this introduction. Suffice it to say here that many a scholar who has grappled with the role played by patriarchal relations of domination and especially by the patriarchal control over human reproduction in the functioning of racial slavery has bumped up against the foreclosure of the symbolic order of the mother (without necessarily elaborating it or naming it as such). One thinks here of the path-breaking work of Colette Guillaumin, who already in the 1970s argued that the mutual imbrications of race and sex as well as the centrality of the control over human reproduction in racial slavery found their shared condition of possibility in the modern invention "of Nature, of our Mother Nature," of "the social idea of natural group," that is, in the modern invention of the naturalness of social relations of domination.[27] One thinks also of Hortense Spillers, who in the 1980s, when exposing the myth of the matriarchal structure of the "Negro Family" under enslavement as a racist and misogynist cultural fantasy, famously reaches the conclusion that, on the contrary, "the African-American woman, the mother, the daughter, becomes historically the powerful and shadowy evocation of a cultural synthesis long evaporated—the law of the Mother."[28] Although Spillers here is bearing witness to and grappling with not merely the foreclosure but the absolute destruction—or, as she puts it poignantly at one point, the "pulverization and murder"—of the maternal symbolic, her urgent exhortations to regain "the heritage of the *mother*" and to reclaim "the monstrosity (of a female with the potential to 'name')" as a form of "female empowerment"[29] strongly resonate with Diotima's emphasis on feminist practices aimed at establishing and fostering intense symbolic bonds (e.g., new languages, new political imaginaries, new ways of naming, new forms of community) between women (mothers, daughters, and sisters) and at elaborating a notion of feminine authority, rather than power, as a way to "articulate one's life according to the project of freedom."[30]

THE POLITICAL PRAXIS OF SEXUAL DIFFERENCE AND ITS SYMBOLIC ORDER

The radical and rigorous critique of both patriarchy and capitalism in all of its facets emphasized the necessity to produce a specific space of autonomy that would liberate women. And even if there were differences in the various currents of Italian feminism, it is fair to say that they all found their common horizon of meaning in a political praxis that would produce such a space of autonomy. Therein one finds one of the most significant differences between Diotima's project and Irigaray's lesson. What in Irigaray remains a theoretical possibility—for example, see her discussion of a feminine "divine potency" that transcends masculine definitions in *Speculum of the Other Woman*—for Italian feminism, and most certainly for Diotima, is from the start a concrete practice, the practice of sexual difference.[31] In time, this structural element would eventually mark a divergence from Irigaray, who has recently turned, for instance, to supporting gender equality and inclusionary policies typical of the co-optive State, which the Italian thought of sexual difference would never accept. The lesson of Lonzi still holds true: "Woman's difference is her millennial absence from history. Let us profit from this difference; for once we have achieved inclusion in society, who is to say how many more centuries will have to pass before we can throw off this new yoke?"[32] This is why Diotima continues to articulate a theory and a practice of sexed thought opposing any attempt to erase sexual asymmetry between man and woman.[33]

Due to their particular positioning in society, Italian feminists developed very early on an acute awareness of the link between the corporeal dimension of experience and its symbolic translation in term of social norms. Their struggle again was more distinctively biopolitical than that of their male counterparts, for they had to carry out a critique not only of capital relations of production but also of sexuality and the symbolic domain that regulated the social complex. Sexuality and the specific type of subjectivity that it generated was the obscure matter that defined, oppressed, but also disclosed the germs of liberation for a generation of women who were rapidly transitioned in the modern Italy of the postwar era. After all, the feminist slogan of 1968 "the personal is political" forces those who take it seriously to embrace life itself as a basis for action and thought. From its inception, Diotima decided to investigate the relationship between the mother and the daughter, basing its work on the notion of sexual difference as a *productive* structural asymmetry. The latter radically defies the centered, sovereign identity of the patriarchal order, where the male was the standard of measure and women its dependent variations. In this sense, and without fear of raising the objection of a precritical essentialism, we can speak of an ontological difference that cuts across subjectivity, specifically because the position occupied by woman under patriarchy is that of difference itself—the excluded, the subject whose identity is negated because it represents a property owned by man. It is that type of subjectivity that comes to the foreground when, as Dominijanni tells us, we speak of "an embodied and sexed singularity, born of tensions between reasons and drives, marked from and depending on relationships to others, first and foremost on the relationship to the mother as the matrix of life."[34] In the discovery of a radical autonomy for women, Diotima focused its attention on the symbolic placement deriving from the expression of the potentialities of the maternal order.

This is why this entire volume is organized as a debate, investigation, and further elaboration of one of Muraro's fundamental hypotheses, namely, the essential role played in the constitution of sexual difference by a process of symbolization that she refers to as the aforementioned "symbolic order of the mother"—a hypothesis that is related yet significantly different from the ones that other thinkers have put forth regarding the relation between sexual difference and symbolization, that is, Lacan, Kristeva, and Irigaray, all thinkers with whom Diotima has been in direct or indirect dialogue over the years. It is not our intention to impose our interpretation of Muraro's *The Symbolic Order of the Mother* on the reader. One of the deeper meanings of this work, after all, lies in the kind of response that it activates in those who encounter it. Here we will simply sketch the main features of this framework and leave the task of fuller interpretations and further elaborations to the attentive reader. We may begin from the idea that the symbolic force enabled by the maternal transcends that of the father, as it comes logically before but also goes beyond it. The symbolic order of the mother is not the specular counterpart of the masculine; it is not the oasis of respectability that eventually our society granted to women.

To use a Foucauldian terminology, the maternal manifested another order of positivity buried under the patriarchal censure. However, this order should not be conceived of as completely determined or as ideally perfected. On the contrary, the maternal is constantly being redefined and reworked through the social transformations occurring in society. Organized around a metonymic principle of signification, it displaces and undermines the verticality and uniformity of possession of the patriarchal order. While certainly involving the question of origin, the maternal is nonetheless a more general symbolic framework that patriarchy unfailingly obscures, devalorizes, or expropriates. After all, origin, if only for the drive to constant change that defines our mortality, is that shadow that does not abandon us once we are born, for it insists on our processes of growth till death. The maternal is what returns, but not as a mystical fusion, nor as the idealization of a complete positivity. In other words, we should not confuse the maternal with the role that the mother has taken up in patriarchal society nor, we may add, with the shiny image of the independent and free consumer woman projected by the post-oedipal order.

The maternal symbolic also occupies a unique position in post-1968 feminist debates, especially with regards to the deadlock reached by official feminism when rightfully denouncing the oppression of male society. As early feminist circles well understood, these representations of women's oppression tended to mirror the very logic that made that woman a victim so that, "caught in a vicious circle, the subject's political demand for recognition and reparation repeats, in the form of compulsion, the very experience of injury that subjugates (but also constitutes) the same subject."[35] The discovery of a space for an independent and logically prior maternal symbolic matrix represents instead the possibility for the political practice of freedom. This symbolic order offers a space of recognition and, most importantly, of authority that was previously foreclosed. The figure of the mother enables and thus also supports desire, for historically there has always been a "real difficulty which a woman encounters in acknowledging the immensity of a desire she has no way of putting forward, openly, in full sight of society, without the disguise of some female virtue."[36] In this sense, the idea of loving the mother innervating the political and theoretical practice of Diotima's feminism has far-reaching consequences. Within this type of mother–daughter continuum, for instance, standard conceptualizations of gratitude and indebtedness are turned around. From constraint and servitude, debt as social obligation mutates into the expression and the practice of freedom. This remark may seem paradoxical unless we are able to think ourselves as subjects in radically nonproprietary terms. The symbolic order of the mother constitutes an enabling structure that reminds us both of the lack of foundation for the subject and, thus, precisely because of the existence of this order, of its possibility to express its freedom. Here is how Muraro explains the difference between the symbolic order (as an enabling structure) and its common trivialization (the metaphoric qua the abstract):

> Many people confuse the symbolic and the metaphoric. In order to go over the difference rapidly, let us think about what bread means to the hungry or drugs mean to addicts. For them either bread or drugs are associated with everything and therefore acquire an enormous significance. This is not a metaphorical meaning, however, which prevails instead in the language of others, the well fed and the non-addicted.[37]

As a matrix the symbolic has an immanent force that is both material and logical. It is in this sense that it is a symbolic space; it carries with it the strength of a language that is world-forming. This is why for Muraro it is necessary to establish "a relationship that shows gratitude toward the woman who brought us into the world."[38] However, this debt is not associated with guilt and the need for material restitution. In reality, nothing is given back because what we own is not something we can appropriate and return. So what does learning to love the mother mean? The experience of this relationship—due to the fact that it is originary both in temporal and in logical terms—provides a schemata for our being; put differently, it defines the contours of our form of life, to use Wittgenstein's terminology. Conversely, "the advent of the law of the father (of patriarchy), which is superimposed on the positivity of the labor of the mother, severs logic from being and is a cause of our losing the sense of being over and over again."[39] This is the logical damage that the interdiction of the maternal propagates.

Muraro, in fact, reads the history of Western philosophy as the uninterrupted effect of the application of this law. She cites, for instance, two consequences. The first is duplication, that is to say, the doubling of being that occupied the work of generations of philosophers: being and nonbeing, the idea and its copy, the mind and the body, and so forth. The other is nihilism in its many forms, which again prescribes a certain severance and separation with being. All this may seem a reiteration of a belated essentialist philosophy. Yet, consider the case Muraro makes with regard to infancy and the symbolic competence we acquire then. Muraro argues that "children are capable of transforming a state of need into a veritable laboratory for the transformation knowledge of themselves and the world."[40] When confronted with the negative, children demonstrate an incredibly generative capacity to produce meaning, to play with reality, which adults usually take for naiveté at best. Growing up, in fact, means *growing out* of that fanciful pliability and finally confronting the gravity and *reality* of existence. But doesn't the paralyzing understanding of negativity sever the possibilities of being as well? Doesn't it freeze becoming, thus producing nihilism? Obviously, the theorization of a return to the playful, imaginative world that is typical of infancy is not a ruse to better dominate and thus manipulate existence. The early symbolic competence we develop as children is anything but a subject's absolute prerogative over reality. It is rather relationality and, we may argue, joyful reliance. The logical force of this operation involves both language and affect, interlocking them into a living dimension. This idea makes of Muraro's philosophy a contemporary form of monism.

The reader may appreciate here the significance of the term *symbolic* for Muraro, and thus also that of the expression "learning to love the mother." The roots of this philosophical conceptualization may be found in what feminists in Italy developed and practiced for many years with the notion of *affidamento* [entrustment], that is to say, the practice of relying on another feminine figure in order to support the expression of one's desire. As the Milan's Women Bookstore Collective argued: "authority is received originally from another human being who is in the position to give it, who has the authority to give it. But she cannot have it if the person who needs to receive it does not acknowledge it in her."[41] It is important to note the hermeneutical nature of the symbolic debt that mutually reinforces the two figures involved by providing recognition and thus a quantum of symbolic force for expression. In lieu of an economic transaction imbued with moral implications, what we have instead is the theorization and practice of an alternative form of social relationship. What a striking difference from the long shadow of guilt cast by the father, whose request in terms of reverence and duty is proverbial, and whose cult demands ceaseless expiation. And, conversely, what an empowering experience for women philosophers, and philosophers in general, whose thought is usually invalidated unless it pays dues to the tutelary deity of their forefathers.

From the start, for Diotima the practice of entrustment took a particular direction that, by *cutting across* the field of traditional theories, became a path for the production of philosophical work. As the founders of the community recall, two rules organized their discussion and theoretical practice:

> We envisioned the first six months as experimentation. In that phase, we believed it was best to produce the texts for discussion without using commentaries by other authors and without referencing philosophical positions that had been already defined; rather, we resorted to the knowledge produced by the women's political movement. In addition to the rule of not referencing external authorities, we also had another negative rule: not offering definitions of the terms we employed. Either those terms generated meaning through the discussion or they didn't at all. This meant that

that which was already said somewhere else was not to anchor us down, exception made for that which was able to re-present itself in a meaningful way and at a specific time.[42]

These authorizing mechanisms show a trust in the signifying capacities of discourse and of relationships that are reminiscent of creative manifestos. But the objective of sexual difference is not artistic novelty. Its work implies a symbolic cut that is assumed as it simultaneously constitutes a daily political practice, that is to say, a differentiating mechanism that engenders transformation in reality because it does not seek to seize the latter and turn it into some proprietary knowledge, and this is true also for the discovery of a particular feminine substance. Sexual difference is deeply rooted in specific singularities and their present relationalities. This practice "proceeds with the elaboration of difference itself by the same investigating subject" so that "difference from being a thought-object turns into thinking thought."[43] "Thinking thought" here means an immanent practice that does not produce a *thing* that can be defined and appropriated but rather a movement that disrupts the phallic paradigm of the Western rational subject based on sameness and on the progressive domination of reality.

Diotima's sustained effort in theorizing and practicing sexual difference is of significant impact when it comes to the analysis of postmodern, or neoliberal, society. It is also a good starting point for us to grapple with the particular time of our writing, as we mentioned earlier, a summer drenched in blood, with mounting waves of racism and sexism that, unfortunately, are likely to intensify in the near future. We are referring here to the rise of the current post-oedipal order that has come to regulate political practices and social norms in our society. From a political, economic, and socio-symbolic point of view, neoliberal governmentality moves from an exercise of power based on verticality to one that is horizontal. Openly biological racism, for instance, has been replaced by *cultural differentialism*, which "purports that each culture is different and noncommensurable," thereby constructing an ideology that is "not based on the verticality of the biological, but precisely on the postmodern horizontality of geographical and religious differences."[44] No less brutal than previous biological racism, the racism of cultural differentialism is deeply entrenched in the new modes of extraction of value. And insofar as domination and exploitation are the hidden core of racializing mechanisms, one should look at the unregulated and excessive environment of late capitalism to understand the reasons for the ferocity of today's wounded masculinities. As Paolo Virno writes, while post-Fordism engages in the production of collective knowledge it also "gives it a hierarchical, racist, despotic expression." He continues:

> It makes of socialization outside work a feral and deregulated sphere predisposed to the exercise of personal domination; it installs the myth of ethnic determination, of rediscovered roots, of "blood and soil" supermarket rhetoric; it reestablishes in its folds familial links between sects and clans destined to achieve that disciplining of bodies which is no longer provided by work relations.[45]

Neoliberal governmentality is based on privatization and exploitation of the common wealth in all its manifestations—that is, natural resources, social practices, rights and services of the public sphere, and so forth—and a tendency toward immaterial production and valorization that obscures its material base. Our post-oedipal society—no less patriarchal for being post-oedipal—is informed by a similar totalitarian logic. In the sexual domain, the disorder created by the predicament of the law of the father now incites transgression and enjoyment as principles that organize and direct the social field. Obviously, we have no nostalgia for the decline of an order that meant oppression and exploitation. But differently from certain current Lacanian approaches, Italian feminism makes clear that if this order has declined it is precisely because of the struggles feminism carried out. At the same time, Italian feminists also note that this struggle did not produce a total emancipation. Far from liberating, this new disorder has multiple consequences at the level of power. As previously argued, power has lost its vertical, hierarchical structure and is now disseminated in the fabric of society, not as a multiplier of freedom but rather as a micromechanism of noncoercive disciplining of the social body. While neoliberalism represents an unprecedented attempt at the valorization of the whole of reality, one that feeds on excess and on the breaking of boundaries, and thus also operates according to a logic that needs crises and emergencies in order to increase productivity, it is not surprising that acts of violence proliferate. As

Diana Sartori argues, "With the end of patriarchy also comes the end of its order; the result, however, is not the immediate establishment of a new order, but rather an increase in disorder, and the return of forms of ... action and emotion that are more archaic, increasingly often elementary and violent" (chapter 6 in this volume). To better understand the global civil war that is looming on the horizon, one should combine geopolitical analysis with a closer look at how the politics of life in neoliberalism and the politics of the symbolic in the post-oedipal order mutually reinforce each other.

The emphasis that Diotima puts on the historical dimension of the symbolic is thus a necessary resource for those who do not surrender to the horizontal disciplining of contemporary power. In Muraro we find a first attempt to dissect the molecular mechanism of power: she locates such a mechanism in what she calls the regime of hypermetaphoricity, which tends to homogenize the gendered division of labor within contemporary symbolic production, while the metonymic is for her the radical structure that cuts through a phallic uniformity and announces a new women's order. In Dominijanni, Sartori, and Zamboni, on the other hand, we find a further problematizing of the maternal in connection with the criticalities brought to the fore by our highly technologized "corpo sociale selvaggio" [wild social body]—that is to say, the post-oedipal body as it is controlled and mobilized through circuits of libidinal injunctions (chapter 1 in this volume). The primary dimension of desire that vitalist currents in contemporary theory sometimes depict as an oasis of potential freedom is in fact critiqued from the point of view of the transformations produced by post-oedipal society. Hence Diotima's interest in preserving a space for the negative as an inexhaustible gap that returns and that defies any effort to make of the mother a positive and self-centered entity or worse, that is, "an idealizing exaltation of the maternal as a palingenesis of politics" (chapter 6 in this volume). It is in the irreducibility of the maternal as an origin that always returns that we may find an opening to the deadlocks of contemporary society. Hence the idea of an-other mother, as a differentiator that is always *other* and that always repeats itself while transforming itself and while questioning her continuous return.

This volume follows a similar progression: from the impact of sexual difference and of the maternal on the understanding of language, to the notions of the maternal symbolic, maternal authority, and maternal negativity, and to the reappraisal of these notions in the wake of current theoretical debates and current transformations in the social and political domains.

In Part I, "Metaphor, Metonymy, and the Politics of Sexual Difference," we begin with "The Contact Word," by Ida Dominijanni. This essay was published as a preface to the 1998 edition of Muraro's book *To Knit or to Crochet? A Political-Linguistic Tale on the Enmity between Metaphor and Metonymy* (originally published in 1981); here, Dominijanni probes and elaborates further in a more explicitly Marxist vein Muraro's fundamental tenets of the maternal symbolic, particularly the importance of metonymic symbolization as a political tool against the identitarian politics based on quotas for women that institutional feminism has promoted in the last few decades. We then move to Muraro's "To Knit or to Crochet." This is an excerpt from the aforementioned book—that is, its first two chapters, which articulate the difference between the hypermetaphoricity regime and the metonymic one by engaging with a wide variety of thinkers, including Agamben, Freud, Irigaray, Lacan, Wittgenstein, as well as Lorenzo Accame, Paul Feyerabend, Alfred Sohn-Rethel, Jean Wahl, and, above all, with Roman Jakobson. And we close this part of the volume with Muraro's essay "On the Relation between Words and Things as Frequentation," which revisits the main themes of *To Knit or to Crochet* more than thirty years after the publication of that book by touching briefly on Virginia Woolf's work (*A Room of One's Own* and *Three Guineas*) and by offering further clarifications of the immanent relation between language and reality in its different forms: the masculine metalanguage that transcends the world, the metonymic system of significations that instead takes part in the world, and finally the latter's process of resignification through an open series of encounters between speakers.

In Part II, "The Maternal Symbolic and Its Language," we introduce the Anglophone reader to another key member of the collective: Chiara Zamboni. Her "Maternal Language between Limit and Infinite Opening" begins this part of the volume: this is a much revised and expanded version of an essay originally published in 1998 in Diotima's *All'inizio di tutto: La lingua materna* [At the beginning of everything: The maternal language]. This version of the essay capsizes the logocentric approach to language as a system of rules (and as a totality built on delimitations) by exploring its existential opening as a living but finite system, with its gaps and voids. Zamboni offers a thorough reexamination of the symbolic dimension of the maternal by focusing on the question of language while drawing on the works of Kristeva and of Françoise Dolto. We then continue with an essay by Muraro, "Feminism and Psychoanalysis: The Dead Mother Complex," which was originally published as the appendix to the 2006 edition of *L'ordine simbolico della madre* and which was not included in the English translation of this book. In this essay, Muraro reflects back on *The Symbolic Order of the Mother* by engaging briefly with André Green and Slavoj Žižek, and by arguing that the male symbolic standpoint always tends to conceive of the issue of freedom reductively as a necessary separation from the maternal.

Part III, "The Mother and the Negative," consists of two chapters of another book by Diotima, *L'ombra della madre* [The shadow of the mother] (2007), which is entirely centered on the maternal as figure of the negative. The first is Diana Sartori's essay, "With the Maternal Spirit," in which, besides engaging with many different feminist thinkers in the Anglo-American, French, and Italian traditions, Sartori offers a detailed analysis of and makes a distinction between what is productive in the maternal symbolic and the dark shadows that the masculine symbolic still casts on it. And the second is Ida Dominijanni's "The Undecidable Imprint." Here, Dominijanni offers a retrospective assessment of the political militancy of the Libreria delle donne in Milan, and develops a critique—friendly, though no less a critique—of Muraro's work, and, in particular, of Muraro's blindness to the question of the paternal and to the question of sexuality within the maternal symbolic.

We then move to Part IV, "Thinking with Diotima," in which we explore how Muraro's ideas resonate in contemporary debates both within and outside Diotima. Anne Emmanuelle Berger's essay, "And Yet She Speaks! 'Italian Feminism' and Language," contextualizes Muraro's work in the wake of the linguistic turn of the 1970s as well as illustrates the connections between Muraro's thought and more recent poststructuralist developments, particularly the critique of the androcentric view of the subject. Berger also recapitulates and reassesses some of the most important critiques of the thought of sexual difference offered by other feminist thinkers. In "Origin and Dismeasure: The Thought of Sexual

Difference in Luisa Muraro and Ida Dominijanni, and the Rise of Post-Fordist Psychopathology," Andrea Righi tests the efficacy of Muraro's feminism by addressing the problem of excess as it is posed by the injunction to enjoy typical of neoliberal society. In so doing, he also studies and provides a critical approach to another central element in Muraro's notion of the maternal symbolic, that of fixation. Finally, the afterword to the book, "Mother Degree Zero; or, Of Beginnings: An Afterword on Luisa Muraro's Feminist Inaptitude for Philosophy," by Cesare Casarino, completes our trajectory by returning to the beginning. As he details the intricacies of the problem of origin articulated in the first chapter of *The Symbolic Order of the Mother*, Casarino wants us to think not against or beyond but *together* with Muraro. The goal is to understand what is at stake when we discuss the question of beginning in philosophy, and to what an extent the dominant and patriarchal understanding of beginning obscures the ways in which, according to the maternal symbolic, origin is, in fact, always present in the plane of immanence. If we invoke here a Deleuzian terminology, a language that is key to our contemporary philosophical debates on ontology, that is because Muraro's particular perspective on the question of beginnings reveals unexpected and surprising connections between these two philosophers. But Muraro's perspective—unlike Gilles Deleuze's—is born out of an explicit acknowledgment and affirmation of the love of the mother: This *other* perspective is the true *differentia specifica* of Muraro's work and, indeed, of the Diotima collective. It is the result of an unrelenting and communal philosophical elaboration and political praxis of women's struggles. It is because of these struggles that we believe the following pages have so much to contribute to philosophy and politics today.

NOTES

1. We do note, however, a recent resurgence of interest in the question of the mother in Anglophone feminist philosophy: see, among others, Lisa Guenther's *The Gift of the Other: Levinas and the Politics of Reproduction* (Albany: State University of New York Press, 2006); Amber Jacobs's *On Matricide: Myth, Psychoanalysis, and the Law of the Mother* (New York: Columbia University Press, 2007); Lisa Baraitser's *Maternal Encounters: The Ethics of Interruption* (London and New York: Routledge, 2008); and Alison Stone's *Feminism, Psychoanalysis, and Maternal Subjectivity* (London and New York: Routledge, 2012). One of the aims of our volume is to foster a dialogue between, on the one hand, these current and

ongoing debates in the Anglophone world and, on the other hand, Italian feminist philosophical scholarship on the question of the mother.

2. Luisa Muraro, *L'ordine simbolico della madre* (Rome: Editori Riuniti, 2006), 46. Please note that since the English version of this work had not been published yet at the time when our book manuscript was being finalized, all quotations from this work are translated (a) by Mark William Epstein with Cesare Casarino in this introduction, (b) by Anne Emmanuelle Berger (from the French version of Muraro's work) in her contribution to this volume, and (c) by Cesare Casarino in his contribution to this volume. See also note 19 below.

3. Muraro, *L'ordine simbolico della madre*, 46.

4. Heidegger's famous declaration opens *Being and Time*. Martin Heidegger, *Being and Time*, trans. Joan Stambaugh (Albany: State University of New York Press, 1996), 1, but see also xviixix and 1–3.

5. Alain Badiou, *Deleuze: The Clamor of Being*, trans. Louise Burchill (Minneapolis: University of Minnesota Press, 1999), 19.

6. On this matter, see also A. Kiarina Kordela, *Epistemontology in Spinoza-Marx-Freud-Lacan: The (Bio)Power of Structure* (New York: Routledge, 2018).

7. Muraro, *L'ordine simbolico della madre*, 23.

8. For the question of "given reality" in Muraro's work, see "Mother Degree Zero; or, Of Beginnings" in this volume.

9. http://www.npr.org/2016/06/16/482322488/orlando-shooting-what-happened-update.

10. http://www.nbcnews.com/storyline/orlando-nightclub-massacre/terror-hate-what-motivated-orlando-nightclub-shooter-n590496.

11. "The FBI is appropriately investigating this as an act of terrorism." These were the words used by the (generally thoughtful) U.S. President Barack Obama at a White House press conference a few hours after the event. https://www.whitehouse.gov/blog/2016/06/12/president-obama-tragic-shooting-orlando. Despite the fact that investigations seem to have excluded the possibility of Mateen's involvement with so-called terrorist groups of any sort and that his devotion to any type of Islam has been proven to be very tenuous at best, Republican presidential nominee Donald Trump unsurprisingly called Mateen an "Islamic terrorist" in his nomination acceptance speech at the Republican National Convention in Cleveland, Ohio, on June 21, 2016.

12. http://aranews.net/2016/06/isis-extremists-burn-death/.

13. Many years after his 1949 pronouncement regarding poetry and Auschwitz in his "Cultural Criticism and Society," however, Theodor Adorno, in *Negative Dialectics*, modified his view in a passage that is highly relevant to the matters at hand: "Perennial suffering has as much right to expression as a tortured man has to scream; hence it may have been wrong to say that after Auschwitz you could no longer write poems. But it is not wrong to raise the less cultural question whether after Auschwitz you can go on living—especially whether one who

escaped by accident, one who by rights should have been killed, may go on living. His mere survival calls for the coldness, the basic principle of bourgeois subjectivity, without which there could have been no Auschwitz; this is the drastic guilt of him who was spared. By way of atonement he will be plagued by dreams such as that he is no longer living at all, that he was sent to the ovens in 1944 and his whole existence since has been imaginary, an emanation of the insane wish of a man killed twenty years earlier." Theodor W. Adorno, *Negative Dialectics*, trans. E. B. Ashton (London: Routledge, 1973), 362–63.

14. Jacqueline Rose, "Feminism and the Abomination of Violence," *Cultural Critique* 94 (Fall 2016): 6. In this essay, Rose cites the alarming statistics on rising violence against women. On this question, see also Gayatri Chakravorty Spivak's recent essay "Crimes of Identity," in *Juliet Mitchell and the Lateral Axis: Twenty-First-Century Psychoanalysis and Feminism*, ed. Robbie Duschinsky and Susan Walker (New York: Palgrave Macmillan, 2015), 207–27.

15. Rose, "Feminism and the Abomination of Violence," 6.

16. Sara Ahmed, *Queer Phenomenology: Orientations, Objects, Others* (Durham, N.C.: Duke University Press, 2006), 177–78.

17. Gayle Rubin, "The Traffic in Women: Notes on the 'Political Economy' of Sex," in *Toward an Anthropology of Women*, ed. Rayna Reiter (New York: Monthly Review Press, 1975), 199.

18. There are a few exceptions: *Italian Feminist Thought: A Reader*, ed. Paola Bono and Sandra Kemp (Oxford: Basil Blackwell, 1991); *Italian Feminist Theory and Practice: Equality and Sexual Difference*, ed. Graziella Parati and Rebecca West (Madison, N.J.: Fairleigh Dickinson University Press, 2002); and *Sexual Difference*, ed. Patrizia Cicogna and Teresa de Lauretis (Bloomington: Indiana University Press, 1990). While Dominijanni's work has been translated into English, and while Muraro's work has been widely translated into French, Spanish, and German, they do not feature prominently in the above-mentioned texts. Sartori's and Zamboni's works have never appeared in English.

19. Luisa Muraro, *The Symbolic Order of the Mother* (Albany: State University of New York Press, 2018).

20. Quoted in Vittorio Possenti, *Il nuovo principio persona* (Rome: Armando Editore, 2013), 66. Diotima's website may be found at this link: http://www.diotimafilosofe.it/.

21. Since its foundation, Diotima has published approximately ten books (i.e., Diotima appears on the cover as the name of the collective author of each volume; each of the volumes includes a series of single-authored essays by some of the community's members; and the essays are all on the same topic and in dialogue with each other. Many of the members of the community also publish their own books and pursue other projects).

22. Luce Irigaray, *This Sex Which Is Not One*, trans. Catherine Porter (Ithaca, N.Y.: Cornell University Press, 1985), 24.

23. Ida Dominijanni, "La madre dopo il matriarcato," interview with Luisa Muraro, *Il manifesto*, October 28, 2005.
24. See Cristina Morini, "The Feminization of Labour in Cognitive Capitalism," *Feminist Review* 87 (2007): 40–59.
25. Carla Lonzi, "Let's Spit on Hegel," in *Italian Feminist Thought: A Reader*, ed. Paola Bono and Sandra Kemp (Oxford: Basil Blackwell, 1991), 43.
26. Étienne Balibar, "Racism Revisited: Sources, Relevance, and Aporias of a Modern Concept," *PMLA* 123, no. 5 (2008): 1638.
27. Colette Guillaumin, *Racism, Sexism, Power, and Ideology* (London: Routledge, 2003), 136, 137.
28. Hortense Spillers, "Mama's Baby, Papa's Maybe: An American Grammar Book," *Diacritics* 17, no. 2 (Summer 1987): 80. When writing of the need to regain "the heritage of the mother," Spillers is referring specifically to "the African-American male"; however, this is argued within a general context of "female empowerment." For a reelaboration of Spillers's arguments in and for the present, see Alexander G. Weheliye's *Habeas Viscus: Racializing Assemblages, Biopolitics, and Black Feminist Theories of the Human* (Durham, N.C.: Duke University Press, 2014). We mention Weheliye's work also because, similarly to what we are arguing regarding the Diotima community, it shows how black feminist scholars such as Spillers and Sylvia Wynter, in effect, had been elaborating a theory of biopolitics (without naming it as such) well before Agamben and others gave it currency from the mid-1990s onward.
29. Spillers, "Mama's Baby, Papa's Maybe," 80.
30. De Lauretis, ed., *Sexual Difference*, 31. It should be noted that over the years Diotima has done much work to produce a concept of feminine authority that would be distinct from and altogether other than power intended as sovereign power, given the inevitably patriarchal connotations of the latter. See, for example, Diotima's *Oltre l'uguaglianza: Le radici femminili dell'autorità* (Naples: Liguori, 1995) as well as Muraro's recent book *Autorità* (Turin: Rosenberg & Sellier, 2013).
31. Luce Irigaray, *Speculum of the Other Woman*, trans. Gillian C. Gill (Ithaca, N.Y.: Cornell University Press, 1985), 319.
32. Lonzi, "Let's Spit on Hegel," 41.
33. See the point Muraro makes in "Feminine Genealogy," in *Engaging with Irigaray*, ed. Carolyn Burke, Naomi Schor, and Margaret Whitford (New York: Columbia University Press, 1994), 317–33.
34. Ida Dominijanni, "Venus's Strabismus: Looking at the Crisis of Politics from the Politics of Difference," *Iris* 2 (2010): 176.
35. Linda Zerilli, *Feminism and the Abyss of Freedom* (Chicago: University of Chicago Press, 2005), 100.
36. De Lauretis, ed., *Sexual Difference*, 115.
37. Muraro, *L'ordine simbolico della madre*, 3.

38. Muraro, *L'ordine simbolico della madre*, 3.
39. Muraro, *L'ordine simbolico della madre*, 27.
40. Muraro, *L'ordine simbolico della madre*, 127.
41. De Lauretis, ed., *Sexual Difference*, 115.
42. Chiara Zamboni and Luisa Muraro, "Cronaca dei fatti principali di Diotima," in Diotima, *Il pensiero della differenza sessuale* (Milano: La Tartaruga, 1987), 177, 179.
43. Cristiana Fischer et al., "La differenza sessuale: da scoprire e da produrre," in Diotima, *Il pensiero della differenza sessuale*, 32, 34.
44. Andrea Righi, *Biopolitics and Social Change in Italy: From Gramsci to Pasolini to Negri* (New York: Palgrave Macmillan, 2011), 161.
45. Paolo Virno, "Theses on the New European Fascism," *Grey Room* 21 (2005): 24.

PART I

Metaphor, Metonymy, and the Politics of Sexual Difference

The Contact Word

IDA DOMINIJANNI

When *To Knit or to Crochet* appeared in the summer of 1981, in the Feltrinelli Opuscoli series, I didn't read it and didn't even buy it. I was aware of the essay that had preceded it, which had been published by *Aut aut*, and which I had diligently read, as was customary at the time for militants of the heterodox left, who hungrily nourished themselves with heterodox journals.[1] Since I was a feminist militant as well, I paid attention to what Luisa Muraro wrote (although I didn't know her personally at the time). But I hadn't really taken it in, not because of a lack of interest or regard, but because of a sense of suspicion and also inadequacy to deal with a perspective focused on the symbolic, which someone like myself, who had been initiated to philosophy through a Marxian apprenticeship, was bound to feel. I really ought to add that whoever has had these Marxian foundations will sooner or later wonder whether the theory of language is not connected to the theory of capital and value, and whether the symbolic is not also constitutive of the social order. This was indeed my case, and yet this doubt was not the most urgent impulse in the revolutionary classrooms of the university I had attended in Florence in the 1970s.

Three friends brought me closer to this book, at three different moments in the development of the thought of sexual difference. First was Manuela Fraire, a feminist psychoanalyst, who showed me its relevance for the debate about the status of difference that was taking place in the pages of the journal *Orsaminore*.[2] The years situated at the juncture of the 1970s and the 1980s were times characterized by many theoretical and political uncertainties in feminism, which would soon be formulated more precisely as rigorous hypotheses and contestations; so that a discussion (which we did not then engage in) about *To Knit or to Crochet* would have indeed helped us to better formulate the issues at hand, and facilitated the dissemination of this text via the feminist circuits of the time. Instead, if memory serves, the text circulated less and with a lesser echo than it deserved.

The second was Rosi Braidotti around the mid-1980s, a time when the philosophical debate about difference was flourishing. As a precise surveyor of the maps that tie (or untie) Western theories of difference to the modern and postmodern break in the philosophical tradition, she was a careful observer of how this text incorporates and subversively reshapes the twentieth-century epistemological turn regarding the subject and the regime of representation.[3] The third and decisive push came from Paola Bono who, in 1991, gave me her copy of *To Knit or to Crochet* as an important reference for some research on the relation between the symbolic order and historical change. We were already in the midst of the full-blown Italian "transition,"[4] and Muraro's proposal provided many points to think not only about the status of sexual difference and the politics of the symbolic, but also about their relation to the decline of political representation and the explosion of media representation. This is the reason why, from that moment on, this book has become an indispensable compass for my movements among philosophy, women's politics, institutional politics, and mass media; the degree to which it has can be judged from the fact that Paola's copy is still in my possession (I never returned it to her), and is by now thoroughly thumbed and filled with annotations like those books, the few, to which one does not cease to return with a certain frequency.

After all, I could not have returned it to her. In the old edition the book has been impossible to find for some time, having met the same fate as a large portion of the important Opuscoli series, edited by Pier Aldo Rovatti, which incorporated so much knowledge of the theoretical and political movements of the 1970s: the senseless fate of being turned into pulp. Feats of our publishing industry, which has gone from being an active custodian of the living archives of knowledge to splitting into, on the one hand, the authorized museum of the sacred classics and, on the other, the iconoclastic arm of every "newfangled" turn in Italian political culture. And yet in the meantime a new season had opened for the reception of *To Knit or to Crochet*. Many of us had understood that the kernel of what Luisa Muraro had developed up to that point, as well as of what she did *not* develop, lay there, in that book. Not only. In the course of the next twenty years many issues that the book already saw or glimpsed have come to the forefront: from the complicity between symbolic order and social order to the centrality of the linguistic dimension in post-Fordist capitalist social formations to the mediatized politics of democracies in crisis at the end of the century. While at the time they were prophetic, those pages can now be reinterpreted along new paths. This is the reason why I repeatedly insisted with Luisa that she republish them; but without much luck since she is not fond of shepherding her work into the world, sharing the feminine tendency toward the dispersion of self she has repeatedly warned us against. It was necessary for me to act on my desire to present them anew to you rather than stimulating hers. And here we are, with this reissue, which is also a rereading of Luisa's text—a result of the manner in which we can work, engaging in dialogue with the others' thought and relaunching it. This I believe is one of the best results the practice of relations between women can achieve, even a bet on how this practice can mark, *autograph*, a feminist text in the period that decreed the end of the "sovereign solitude of the author."[5]

All this just to remark the metonymic dissemination of a text on metonymy that has a metonymic pace. A dissemination by contagion, by means of contingent contact between different but contiguous contexts. This is not a tongue twister. It is because of neither chance nor the lucid designs of history but precisely as a consequence of the infinite and unpredictable paths of contact and contagion that different contexts, histories, subjectivities, and intentions come into contact with one another. In presenting and re-presenting themselves on the minor social and cultural scenes, they weave more robust threads among themselves than those around which the *major* scene of official political history neurotically entangles itself. The seventies, the eighties, the nineties have flowed through the (scarce) collective memory as three decades that are so mutually remote as to lead to the virtual incommunicability of their respective political and demographic generations. And yet contact and contagion must have been established if today, while politics is agonizing, and while we witness social anemia and center-left neoconformism, we are republishing a text that first appeared in an issue of *Aut aut* devoted to the crisis of political rationality. An issue that dealt with the normative wrench that from the beginning of the eighties was squeezing the subjectivities of the seventies, and that was convinced that one had to protect the languages of that era from the alliance between the stereotyped vocabularies of official politics and media.[6] What goes around comes around, as a well-known refrain of the twentieth century tells us; or better, perhaps, different things come into contact, within new contingencies—first of all the political and theoretical event that has occurred in the meantime, the event of sexual difference, a sort of passage-bridge between two seasons of subjectivity which in *To Knit or to Crochet* is shown in its dawn, and therefore in all its potential.

Metonymic reception, I was saying, of a text about metonymy that has a metonymic pace. It is a peculiarity of Muraro's to practice in her writing the theoretical positions she espouses, and this makes her texts peculiarly mobilizing, as those of us know who are more used to letting ourselves be captured by the disequilibrium of rhythm than by the logic of the letter. Keeping faith with this practice, in *To Knit or to Crochet* the text proceeds by way of unforeseen combinations, spontaneous associations, heterodox slippages, undisciplined interdisciplinary border crossings, as it continuously shuttles between everyday experience and theory. These are all characteristics of metonymy, as the text itself explains as it unfolds. Metonymically, the latter refuses to reach any syntheses—to the point that it intentionally leaves argumentations incomplete—as in the last chapter, declaredly provisional—and refuses to rationalize the obsessions that drive it. These are returning obsessions of Luisa's, which can be found again in her later writings, and this text is in some way their catalogue: materiality and historicity of the symbolic; sexual difference; the relation between body and language, as well as between the wild social body [*corpo sociale selvaggio*] and the orderly social body; the nexus between power, knowledge, and pleasure.[7] In order to analyze them one by one I will be obliged to disassemble and reassemble her text in my own way, since I am not as gifted as she is in proceeding by way of effective metonymies. But following her, and perhaps even doing her one better, I will treat this text's subject matter as that which Luisa maintains it is: "a matter whose competence is for the non-competent" (chapter 2 in this volume).

The number-one obsession, the one behind it all, is the disquieting observation that one of the pillars of our culture is the separation of knowledge and pleasure, or better, following Michel Foucault, between pleasure and the regime of the true and the false. So that pleasure is never considered a source of truth although "it keeps quiet when it lies and says the truth when it speaks."[8] But when she wrote *To Knit or to Crochet* the author had not yet overcome that "difficulty of beginning an enterprise made of words" to which, ten years later, she will devote the first chapter of *The Symbolic Order of the Mother*, resolving it with a shift from patriarchal philosophical authority to maternal authority.[9] Hence she begins with a "renowned theory," that of the double generation of meaning first elaborated in the fifties by Roman Jakobson in his studies on aphasia in the wake of Ferdinand de Saussure, and then developed via Jacques Lacan's psychoanalysis and Claude Lévi-Strauss's anthropology (leading back in their turn to Martin Heidegger, Friedrich Nietzsche, Sigmund Freud, and Ludwig Wittgenstein).[10]

This renowned theory says that in order to weave the web of language one has to operate on two axes just as—hence the book's title—one needs two needles to knit wool yarn. One theorizes, conceptualizes, abstracts, substitutes, represents, and replaces things with words along the metaphoric axis. One combines, associates, finds relationships, passes from one context to another, alludes to and tells stories along the metonymic axis. Things and words acquire meaning through the references and associations that accompany them. The first axis can be configured as an ascending motion—"words instead of things, figurative meaning [*significato*] in place of the literal, the universal in place of the particular." The second, "foreign to this ascending motion, hinders it, cuts across it, prevents it from arriving at its logical conclusion—which would be that of gathering itself in a name, like the All, Being, God, and then silence" (chapter 2 in this volume). The structure is bipolar, but not symmetrical. Following Jakobson, Muraro repeatedly insists, her partisanship for metonymy notwithstanding, that the two axes are in competition, "in the sense of both collaboration and of rivalry," but not in a relation of complementarity or of peaceful alliance (chapter 2 in this volume). They may also collude or in any case signal the genetically unbalanced (and unbalancing) structure of language, "its constitutive dis-formity, its limping carriage, its insurmountable disequilibrium," which is the fundamental basis of its infinite generative possibilities.[11] Whether one pole will prevail on the other does not depend on the structure of language, which posits them both as interconnected, but on historical reasons that cannot be decided solely in theory.

One therefore has to explain why in our culture a *regime of hypermetaphoricity*, as Muraro defines it, has established itself, one in which the "metaphoric pole prevails and has ensured and established the exploitation of metonymic resources," so that between the two poles the "rival tension between metaphoric pole and metonymic pole is partially converted into a subordination of the second to the first" (chapter 2 in this volume). This results in an ever greater rarefaction of experience, or in its codification within preconstituted meanings that assume the value of a norm and of social normalization. Abstraction, generalization, rationalization, the duplication of the world into words and images defeat metonymic (auto)signification, while continuing to nourish themselves from it, within a large apparatus that promises—and largely achieves, since it can rely on projects, programs, schools, theories—"an integral re-presentation of the world," but risks ending like the sorcerer's apprentice: "it seems like the hypermetaphorical regime has become trapped inside its own game, namely, to replace things with figures, operating a substitution so to speak. The substitution instead runs the risk of being actual, effective, and irreversible," for "extra-linguistic reality, then, . . . seems to evaporate, one only exchanges signs in a language that revolves around itself, things disappear, transformed into signs in their turn, but signs of nothing" (chapter 2 in this volume).

Reality exterminated by its cloned double, that will be Jean Baudrillard's diagnosis in years closer to ours as he was reflecting on the completion of the Western arc of representation in the technology of virtual reality: "our culture of meaning is collapsing under the excess of meaning . . . the sign and reality sharing a single shroud."[12] As Jacques Derrida warns us in an essay that looks like *To Knit or to Crochet*'s twin brother, this a deadly fate that the Western arc of representation, precisely because it is based on metaphor, contains within itself from its origins. Within the statute of metaphorization itself—that is, "transporting to something—a name that designates something else" without ever reaching the proper name—we find both the potential and the limit of that movement of idealization that outlines the field of possibilities of metaphysics together with its fatal exhaustion. Genetically subjected to wear and tear, "metaphor . . . always carries death within itself. And this death, surely, is also the death of philosophy," the "white mythology" of Western man who has modeled his linguistic system and the form itself of the concept on this figure.[13]

However, under the hypermetaphorical regime it is not only a question of the death of white mythology. It is a question, and this is the point for Muraro, of everything which it is not able to restore, despite its promises of full representation: body, experience, nature, contingency, pleasure. It is a question of individuals and pieces of society, who/which are not contemplated under this regime, or cannot be expressed with its meanings, by its representatives and its interpreters; of those who, "caught in the movement of metaphoricization, end up living vicariously," left speechless or deported into imitation and conformity, passive or even rebellious, but of a rebelliousness without form or consequences (chapter 2 in this volume). These experiences remain inexpressible when censorship or repression bury them. Consider schoolchildren raised in the barracks-like high-rises of suburban ghettoes who in their class assignments write instead about green meadows, women on the edge between an insignificant existence and the glossy models of the feminine, micro and macro forms of violence that are inexplicable within the official code of conduct of democratic modernization. Recall the world of the defeated described by Nuto Revelli and that of the inhabitants of the "borgate" [city slums] described by Pasolini, and, quickly updating Muraro's list, the hordes of imitators in the antechambers of the palaces of power; Pietro Maso who, in the heartland of the Northeast, kills his parents for money; the revolts in Los Angeles black ghettoes; or kids who drop rocks from highway overpasses . . .

What is at stake in the hypermetaphorical regime, in other words, is that *wild social body*—obsession number two—which contemporary societies don't manage to either contain or translate. This wild social body is the tangible demonstration of a relation between symbolic and social orders, structure of language and structure of the world, in which Muraro sees, more than the correspondences of the structuralists or Wittgenstein's isomorphism, a veritable *complicity*. She writes: "between symbolic and social orders there is an opaque complicity: material servitudes that become logical exigencies and, vice versa, conditions of symbolic production that translate into social impositions" (chapter 2 in this volume). It is by underscoring this complicity, heeding both Lacan's discourse on the materiality of the symbolic and Jakobson's on its historicity, that Muraro grounds her wager. Once she has ascertained that the "symbolic . . . leaves its mark on social reality since it is implicated in it," it is necessary to invent a theoretical and political practice that is able to break the hold of the normative vise by means of which the two orders subjugate us, while mutually legitimating one another (chapter 2 in this volume). And who knows, the Western episteme may yet be open to other, less deadly, possibilities.

Ten years after the publication of *To Knit or to Crochet*, we are in 1991 and in the meantime the elaboration of the theory-practice of sexual difference has taken place, and we reencounter the kernel of this challenge in Muraro's response to questions posed by Teresa de Lauretis: "I realize"—Luisa writes—"more and more every day that it is difficult (impossible?) to transform a symbolic order and create freedom by political activism; but this is our gamble."[14] I will return to the developments of this wager in a little while. In the meantime, I want to underscore that reading *To Knit or to Crochet* allows us to see it in the context in which it was born, and therefore also to read its outcomes more correctly than has often occurred in the feminist debates of the eighties and nineties. These debates, for the moment let me just anticipate this point, have been obsessed with the suspicion that the proposal of sexual difference elaborated by Muraro and other Italian feminist thinkers is vitiated by essentialism, polluting the theory of the symbolic with rationalist and voluntarist accents, forgetting the decentering of the ego brought about by Freud with the discovery of the unconscious, and basically once more putting a prestructuralist, prepsychoanalytic, pre-twentieth-century—female—subject back on stage. *To Knit or to Crochet* is instead a demonstration that the exact opposite is the case, and this is also one of the reasons that I was bent on republishing it. The core of the theory of sexual difference is born—"is situated" to use a term invoked later by American feminism—precisely within the framework of the dialogue between structuralism and psychoanalysis and the debate on the epistemological turn at the beginning of the century. In any case, where if not there? That is where we were, men and women who didn't conform to the rules, at the end of the seventies, when the crisis of classical rationality and the labyrinths of a desiring subjectivity were not only debated in books but could be seen on the streets, in subversive movements, in the practices of daily life and sociability. There was no need to invoke Nietzsche, Freud, Lacan, or Foucault to support our faith in the end of metaphysics or to justify this or that academic strategy for women's studies programs.[15] These thinkers were among us whether we knew it or not; but we were also discovering, as women, that they didn't completely convince us.

In any case, Luisa knew this. And hence it is not in deference to an academic discipline that she begins with Jakobson but because of his thesis about the two axes of language—the *poor schema* [*schema povero*] of the crossed axes: in it, she sees and reinforces an epistemological intuition that reflects the moment of crisis in European culture between the nineteenth and the twentieth centuries. When the illusion of the mutual reflection between scientific and natural orders collapses, making room for an awareness that the first asserts itself as evidence of the will to control the casualness of the second, "at that point things found themselves in a new suspension. Previously their existence depended on their conformity with the 'true' laws of science. Now they are suspended between being there thanks to their giving themselves to experience, and a will to dominate that makes them be this way or that, which interprets them by adding something to them which they would be lacking."[16] Here they are, the metaphoric and metonymic axes. Dual generation of meaning, in which abstraction and rationalization don't quash the giving of things in their casual contingency, but instead let themselves be limited by it, according to a theoretical practice that unfortunately will not be followed subsequently by others.

Muraro arrives at her *defense of the poor schema* in the course of a tightly woven dialogue with its antecedents, its developments and its critics, taking us for a breathless ride around some of the most hair-raising and controversial paths of twentieth-century thought. During the ride we meet Nietzsche and his way of establishing the relation between metaphoricization, everyday language, and scientific language; Ernst Mach and Thomas Kuhn; the Wittgenstein of the *Tractatus*; the Foucault of *The Order of Things*; the Freud-Lacan and the Lacan-Kristeva axes, and behind them all, Heidegger; Marx, and Sohn-Rethel; but then also, Cubism and its "metonymic perspective," Gertrude Stein, and James Joyce. The result of the ride is that twentieth-century thought always asked the right questions, but every time its felicitous openings were boxed in by the return of the ancient oppositions (between body and language, things and words, reality and concepts), dominated by the obsession of death and the specter of the identical. And one cannot reach solid ground. From Heidegger onward, the prevalence of the discursive register in our existences is indisputable: outside of language there is nothing, there are no—Muraro repeatedly insists on this point—virginal things, authentic bodies, immediate experiences that are not already meanings, inscribed in the symbolic, marked by culture. True, but this truth doesn't take into account the fact "that there are many things of the great linguistic game that cannot be put into play" (chapter 2 in this volume). From the crisis at the beginning of the century onward, the paradigm of modern rationality has been dismantled and delegitimized, and yet its iron laws—"a selective truth and an existence in the conditional"—and its insurmountable divisions—rational, ordered, and normal, on the one hand, driven, excessive, and mad, on the other—return under another guise when we least expect them to, as in Noam Chomsky's generative linguistics or Julia Kristeva's semiotics.[17] Even Saussure's and Jakobson's structuralism wrecks against a rather massive reef. It is the illusion of the text's transparency, whereas the text is in reality inevitably opaque, as a consequence of its relation with time and body. A relation that structuralism, as a faithful mirror of the individual and social dematerialization of bodies that is a constant throughout the century, is unable to think about. The advantages of the *poor schema* therefore also stop at the threshold where modern rationality comes to a halt: our *being-having* a body, and the possibility of making this condition a matrix for consciousness (chapter 2 in this volume).

There is only one twentieth-century form of knowledge that crosses this threshold and that is psychoanalysis. For it was able to contain that process of dematerialization, opposing it on the one hand with Freud and the materiality of the impulses, and on the other with Lacan and the material efficacy of the symbolic. It revolutionized the status of the subject, giving it a sexed body and an unconscious. With only one move it changed our notions of body and language, showing that one always carries traces of the other; and finally it invented a practice—the analytical setting—that operates largely on the metonymic axis of symptoms, associations, contexts, and relations. In a philosophical culture like the Italian one, which continues to disregard it, the awareness and recognition of the Freudian-Lacanian epistemological turn are part of Muraro's important contributions in *To Knit or to Crochet*. Muraro knows "how to do justice to Freud," as well as to Lacan.[18] Not even the Freudian "tremor," however, has been sufficient to halt the hypermetaphorical drift of the regime of symbolic production. And not only because of the "belated recognition of psychoanalytic materialism," which has had, above all in Italy, reductive effects on that political culture that would have wanted to be materialist (chapter 2 in this volume). It was not sufficient because even psychoanalysis, the metonymic style of its practice notwithstanding, ends up, through the principle of symbolic castration, by confirming metaphor's domination within its theoretical statutes; and it even redoubles it by confirming that symbolic division of labor between men and women that reduces women "to the obscure task of gluing words to things" (chapter 2 in this volume). Meanwhile words fly along the metaphorical axis to build theory held together by the "eminent meaning" we all know, just like we all know to which sex it belongs.

We have reached the end of our ride. Where there is not the closure of an answer, there is the opening of a question:

> We are interested in finding a path that, *even in its form*, can account for that material reality that moves us and sometimes agitates us, almost without our knowledge. If there is a way of activating the symbolic productivity inherent in our being a body, woman, man, of our enjoying certain pleasures and interests rather than others, of finding ourselves here or there doing this or that. And being able to talk, addressing that material reality, and not always in flight, in substitution or cover-up. (emphasis added)[19]

It seems clear to me that the subject of this knowledge is a fully twentieth-century subject, post-Freudian and poststructuralist. From psychoanalysis it takes the decentering of the ego, the unconscious that interrupts the transparency of individual discourse and the social text, the metonymic practice of transforming oneself and the relation between self and reality. From structuralism it takes the wager of an epistemology that does not divide experience and theory and can read things the way they present themselves and not only through the imperialist filter of rationalization. But it is still missing something: a political intent, and the prism—the light Luisa would say—of sexual difference.

"Metaphorizing" Luisa's text, I have focused so far on the theoretical level of discourse. But if I were to give my opinion about the true spring that generates *To Knit or to Crochet*, I would answer that it is a political spring or, rather, to use a terminology that has by now become scandalous, a subversive will, one contrary to the ever-spreading conformism—Muraro's third obsession—and its very serious costs in terms of both knowledge and pleasure. One will say that here too there is a recognizable trace of the political and cultural context of the seventies, which echoes throughout the text. True, but only partially, because Luisa's discourse targets precisely the blind spots in available political discourses, also and perhaps first of all discourses that want to be—or wanted to be at the time—revolutionary. That is precisely the issue: what keeps on blocking the attempts at subversion of the social order from below? And why, since the *dispositifs* of the hypermetaphorical regime are powerful but also transgressible and full of holes, to most people "it doesn't even occur to disassemble the social text and to recombine it" (chapter 2 in this volume)? It is a question therefore of revealing not only the mechanisms of domination, but also the deeply rooted devices of its interiorization, the resistances to rebellion, the constraints of repetition, without which there is no politics but only rhetoric of change and reproduction of the status quo.

When Muraro writes *To Knit or to Crochet* she is already well versed in these matters, as the lucky few who own some surviving copy of *L'erba voglio* [The grass I want] can testify—this was the bimonthly started by psychoanalyst Elvio Fachinelli in 1971 in Milan, with a group of extraordinary freethinkers.[20] Commenting on the ritual declarations of left intellectuals after the Piazza Fontana and *Italicus* massacres, she had already noted how the transpositions of facts from their disturbing occurrence to the empyrean of democratic and antifascist rhetoric precluded the perception of the sources of daily fascism in democratic societies "at levels and in ways that politics is incapable of seeing and does not have the will to fight." She had already denounced professional politicians who assign themselves the function of "interpreters" whose intended function was to ensure "that people adapt to the political code, skipping over their daily experience."²¹ She had already deplored the legions of "experts" (psychologists in schools, sociologists everywhere, magistrates placed between mother and offspring, and so forth) whose purpose is to have common mortals renounce their control over their own lives and deliver themselves to specialized institutions. Finally, in contact with the young women of the student movement, she had already discovered that it is not only the social but also the sexual condition that puts women on the road to conformism and self-moderation, something that revolutionary theory doesn't know where to place in its scheme of the relation between structure and superstructure.

The discovery of the bond between patriarchal symbolic order and social order in *To Knit or to Crochet* illuminates these otherwise obscure phenomena: because it is precisely at the level of this bond that the "staging of normality" takes place and conformism is born, develops, and gradually becomes the norm (chapter 2 in this volume). This is where those who should have an interest in subverting a social or political text that does not consider or represent them are instead inclined to adapt themselves to it, conforming to behaviors, roles, and masks decided elsewhere, and adopting "a speech that resembles an attempt to guess what one should say, that searches for prefabricated meanings and words that might reproduce them, avoiding unusual associations for fear of giving rise to some irregular meaning [*significato*]" (chapter 2 in this volume). Luisa knows this from her experience as a schoolteacher. This is where social oppression is one with linguistic impositions, class assignments are filled with clichés like green meadows, the free movement of thought rooted in experience ends and the irreversible alienation in the territory of imitation begins. And this is where, we know from history's harsh answers, revolutionary political pedagogy fails—not to speak of proponents of reformist or democratic ones, who think that a tranquil, ordered, and rational "communicative action" is what is at stake in language. . . .²²

It is easy at this point to diagnose why this kind of pedagogy fails: it is because the language of traditional politics lies entirely within the hypermetaphorical regime, puts it to work in the schema of representation, and reproduces it in its own order of discourse. The representatives replace the represented, the universal transcends the particular, totality lords it over partiality (even in the traditions of the workers' movement, and we know with what tragic results), professionals interpret the needs of the common people, and worn-out metaphors—of "the Right" and "the Left": Order, Revolution, Equality, and many more—mobilize and simultaneously silence the social body. The extent to which that metaphoric process is immanent to that other "white mythology," twin sister of philosophy, which is politics in the West, is revealed by the fact that it is exercised primarily on that which politics, constitutively, has expunged from itself, from its Athenian origins to today: the body precisely, individual and social, removed and transcended in the metaphor of a "body politic," in its turn dominated by a Head. A not fortuitous metaphor that claims to bind rationality and sovereignty in a single destiny, relegating the social body within the opposite, also hardly casual, metaphor of viscerality.[23]

Thus twinned to the paradigm of a logocentric—or better phallogocentric, since originally it was a question of a virile rational head and a visceral feminine body—rationality, to its constitutive splits and its procedures of symbolization, politics traditionally understood can only enact, but never recognize, not to speak of break, the complicity between symbolic and social orders. One is tempted to say that in order to do so, it would need that same awareness of the limits of its rationality that moves the structuralist schema of the crossed axes. Politics is essentially nourished by fantasies of omnipotence, thus continuing to demote to irrelevance everything that makes us subjects (active and passive, à la Foucault) of the symbolic order: the imaginary, unconscious, emotiveness, dependence from language—everything over which politics does not rule, as is the case of reason over the heart in the popular proverb. The result is that the politics of change, and we are still talking about politics as traditionally conceived, cannot overcome that mechanism of repetition that nails the social order to the symbolic, subjecting it. Luisa will later observe "how useless it is to criticize what exists with the purpose of changing it. What exists reproduces itself not because it is considered good but because a mechanism stronger than our intentions and criticism propels it, no matter how justified those intensions and criticism are. The problem, then, is to break this mechanism of repetition."[24]

This mechanism does not pertain to the social or political order but to the symbolic: it belongs to the territories of the unconscious, where the struggle between the effort toward freedom and the compulsion to repeat takes place. It pertains to the *dispositifs* of language, where the struggle involving the regime of the sayable takes place, that is, where the space for the nonconventional representation of oneself and the world opens up or does not, which nonrepresentational representation is—a precondition, not an effect, of personal and political transformation. In order to break the mechanism of repetition it is therefore necessary to resort to a practice that is capable of acting at this level. One that is able to mobilize the factors that have been repressed by political rationality, to return the power of speech to those who are deprived of it, to return the "symbolic competence" that the hypermetaphorical regime assigns to the recognized experts to everyone, and to read experience as it presents itself, even when it displaces our prejudices. In other words, one has to interrupt the metaphorical drift by learning to speak and, first, to listen to metonymical language. And this proposal has little in common with the one that sees social aphasia as the virgin place for a possible palingenesis or a semiotic reserve of authenticity that irrupts into the social synthesis in exceptional circumstances.[25] The wild body cannot in fact be found elsewhere but within the social body, and it is not a prelinguistic body but is inscribed within the symbolic regime, and therefore, metonymically, capable of speech. The metonymic procedure is already language, one could say, recalling the slogan "it's already politics," with which Carla Lonzi consecrated the—metonymic—practice of feminist consciousness-raising.[26]

Lonzi was the foremost protagonist of the feminism of difference in Milan and among the first female thinkers about sexual difference. It is by chance that she comes to mind here. When Muraro wrote *To Knit or to Crochet* she already had ten years of political practice in the women's movement. That is where the idea of the metonymic wager comes from, as her text at times explicitly states and at times gives one to understand implicitly. The original intuition of the feminism of the seventies, that women were lacking not prostheses so as to resemble men, but needed the words to express themselves starting from their selves instead of from a male imaginary—in other words that the feminine condition is marked more by symbolic than social misery—had already provoked a break, sanctioning the primacy of the word in the politics of change.

When reelaborated in the first person, the practice of self-consciousness had already proven that a silent or muzzled feminine experience, or one forced into social conformism, or into the imitation of male models, acquires another meaning and opens up new perspectives of signification; this practice can therefore inaugurate new narrative strategies of female life, in which foreordained fates gave way to a free construction of the self. And the practice of the unconscious had already demonstrated that one could and should include fantasies, fears, repressions, and phobias in the linguistic and political game since they "constitute a nonsecondary aspect of reality through which both the repetition of the identical and the possibility of modification pass."[27] In addition, the richness and the contagious capacity of metonymic language had emerged, not only in its capacity of restoring experience, but also insofar as it acquires meaning in the relational contexts from which it originates, multiplying itself and them.[28] As it will be called in a collective text in which Luisa's hand is recognizable, *language-reason* is born from relationships among women and makes them function in their turn like a language:

> The horizon of female freedom widens thanks to the mediation of relationships among women and these operate like the signs of a language. The language of women articulates the, previously opaque, matter of women's experience of the world, into knowledge. . . . Women's political movement is distinguished by its constant attention to the word. Between us the word is an end, not a means. We turned to the word to find the true and free meaning of the difference of being women. The other things that circulate among us like money, ease, freedom of movement, jobs, health, and power—these things also are for us subjected to the primacy of the word. But not a word on which we could act as we want, on the contrary. Its primacy derives from its being the sense of a changing reality: that which things want to say.[29]

And the primacy of the word is exercised not only in calling and naming reality in a manner that is faithful to experience, but also in modifying it or, even better, in re-creating it—in "bringing the world into the world"— following the title of a book by the Diotima community.[30] Once more, this time from a more recent collective text:

> To name the reality that is changing, to name it with sufficient precision, is to invest in the world, opening the doors to its surplus.... Language and voice show hindrances as significant causes; defects are turned into occasions for improving the expression of meaning. Language is not a sum of words, but a multiplication, and more than a multiplication, a window open on and into this surplus, because—as linguistics well knows—a new word can put the meaning of all our past speech and life into play. Women's politics is a politics of the symbolic. It does not draw conclusions from the so-called data of reality without having interrogated their meaning, both that which they already have and the one they could acquire in light of my desire or yours.[31]

This is far different from a pure deconstruction of the place of women (or, worse, of Woman) in the patriarchal order, as the analysis of the symbolic is understood in much international feminist theory. In the Italian feminism of difference, the *politics* of the symbolic is configured as a continuous wager on the regime of sayability and on sense, in a game in which one continuously raises the stakes, as there are no limits to the creativity of language, or better, of maternal language [*lingua materna*], in other words of that language that does not surrender to the deadly primacy of the metaphoric, and keeps the relation between meaning and experience alive.[32] We have thus arrived at the heart of *The Symbolic Order of the Mother*, the book published by Muraro in 1991 that continues the obsessions of *To Knit or to Crochet*, while developing its presuppositions. Exactly ten years have passed, the most fruitful years for Italian thought of sexual difference, but also those that are most, so to speak, introflected. I believe I can see in these two texts by Luisa, at the beginning and the end of the eighties, the two moments in which it most fully shows its general hermeneutical and political capability—the two points of an arc from between which the thought of sexual difference extends itself and shoots its arrow into the present and the world.

It's not by chance that *The Symbolic Order of the Mother* is possessed by the same subversive tension and ends on the same nagging thoughts about the destinies of the wild social body as *To Knit or to Crochet*, but with the demeanor of someone who better knows how to show a path that was only outlined in the text of 1981 and that has in the meantime found confirmation in women's politics:

> There is the social body, which finds some kind of synthesis, and there is the wild body. I give this name to that part of human experience that goes beyond what a given socio-symbolic order can mediate and that, consequently, remains outside of the social synthesis or enters into it as object of interpretation and of other people's interventions. Before the politics of women, female experience was this wild body.
>
> I believe that for the type of human experience that is outside the social order, or is unhappily within it, there is only one possible symbolic order. This is the symbolic order that can refer experience to the authority of the mother. As a matter of fact, the authority of the mother represents the principle that has in itself the greatest capacity for mediation because it is able to put into the circle of mediation both our being body [*essere corpo*] and our being word [*essere parola*]. . . . We must fight to prevent the social synthesis of established power from substituting for the maternal principle. We must give a social translation to maternal potentiality in order to prevent social synthesis from closing up. We must fight to keep social synthesis open to anything we want to say, however distant or abnormal that may be.[33]

I will not discuss the merits of the theoretical-political proposal of the symbolic order of the mother here, except as it concerns us as the point of arrival of *To Knit or to Crochet*'s central wager: that of a metonymic symbolic order that doesn't split body and language, experience and word apart, but holds them together, and does not imprison the social text in the selective synthesis of the metaphoric chain, but keeps it open to "anything we want to say," especially for what it concerns, the wild social body. At the end of the metonymic axis there is the principle of maternal authority as the lever for the subversion of constituted powers in the existing socio-symbolic order. This point is as crucially important as it is misunderstood in the feminist reception of Muraro's proposal. What's at stake is not a metaphor of the maternal, but rather the real mother as figure of metonymic symbolization. Since the mother brings us into the world and teaches us to speak, she gives both life and speech, holding experience and language together in the earliest stages of infancy, in other words, before institutional knowledges and powers transform the learning of language into the learning of obedience and normality. Maternal language is the symbolic *dispositif* opposed to the regime of hypermetaphoricity and it can return the power of expression to the wild body, to the silent or silenced social experience of women and men. But to understand the valence of this figure, to avoid the misunderstandings that ascribe it to the "maternal imaginary" of much feminist psychoanalytical theory, it is necessary for us finally to approach more closely the status of sexual difference that *To Knit or to Crochet* outlines.[34]

In my opinion, *To Knit or to Crochet* discourages both any dichotomous reading of sexual difference and any identitarian notions of feminine difference. I understand identitarian notions to include both those that the Anglo-American debate defines as "essentialist" and those feminist theories that claim gender's representation and recognition (and which however do not coincide with the whole of "gender theories" of the Anglo-Saxon academic world), since both perspectives share, as should be obvious from the political outcomes, an emphasis on female identity that is contested by the notion of sexual difference elaborated in the Italian laboratory. If anything, the latter puts forth an anti-identitarian ontology of difference.

Certainly, a hurried reading of *To Knit or to Crochet* would instead seem to encourage these identitarian notions, perhaps due to the difficulties of some passages and the incompleteness of the text. At a first glance, it could be read as follows. Two sexes, men and women, are symmetrically distributed along the two axes of language: the metaphoric and metonymic respectively. In obedience and consonance with the law of the phallus and symbolic castration, men are assigned to the noble work of thinking, theorizing, representing, interpreting, exchanging. Women are subjected to the same law but are in the uncomfortable position of allowing its functioning from the outside. They are assigned to "the obscure labor of gluing words and things together" beginning with the phallus and the penis, and to the obscure destiny of making themselves into body-object, object and condition of possibility of masculine exchange. Along the associative chain logos-masculine metaphor and corporeal-feminine metonymy, the dichotomization of the human species, of symbolic labor, and of the social body would be guaranteed, and with it the identitarian definition of the two sexes, each with its own catalogue of attributes, the head and reason to men, the body and emotionality to women, and so forth. Dichotomization would be guaranteed and with no hope for change whatsoever, since not even the most powerful master-slave dialectic ever could win against this cast-iron structuring of the socio-symbolic order, in which one cannot see how woman could pass from the degree zero of negativity to degree one of individual and social existence (and in fact, together with Lonzi, we learned early on *to spit on Hegel*).[35]

But as we have already seen, this picture, which follows the Lacanian theory of the symbolic order, is, for Muraro, one of the points of departure, not of arrival. Not only because, as we know from Luce Irigaray, Lacanian theory is informed from the start, like the main tradition of Western philosophy, by the masculine imaginary. But because Muraro shares with Lacan the discovery of the connection between symbolic production and patriarchal regime, but not the diagnosis of its immutability. Moreover, unlike Lacan and many post-Lacanian feminist theorists who don't get this point, and in agreement with Jakobson, Muraro doesn't believe that the metonymic position is a presymbolic one and that it precludes access to the symbolic for women. As we saw, the metonymic procedure is already linguistic, "it is a mode of symbolic production" (and conversely no "literal" bodies, authentic and virginally untouched by meaning, exist, not even the female body). It is a mode that is neither the opposite of nor complementary to the metaphoric; it is, rather, its asymmetrical rival. It is capable of intercepting it, blocking it, disturbing it; it is capable of becoming a transverse barrier to the hypermetaphorical drift that the regime of representation has assumed in our societies. Capable of cutting it: feminine difference, in its metonymic characterization, is this *cut*—this "crossing that mixes" [*traversata mescolatrice*], as Luisa calls it, borrowing a figure from Irigaray, an author to which the reasoning in *To Knit or to Crochet* constantly refers.[36]

The symbolic order, thus, has within itself the principle of its own possible subversion. There is no need to look for it in an uncontaminated elsewhere, in an as-yet unexpressed semiotic reserve, in an authentic and original corporeality, in the infancy of the masses, or in some other place within the palingenetic imaginary of the political, because it can be found in a different principle of symbolization, brought by the feminine body, which traverses the whole social body. As we have seen it is the principle of contiguity between text and context, body and word, experience and language, which can open the social synthesis to anything we want to say, and leave it open.

It is also the principle of contingency and deferment, which breaks the logic of identity and disposes us to be open to all events. Metonymy, we read in *To Knit or to Crochet*, is the rhetorical figure that allows one to know difference "by moving from one thing to another, without passing through identity or equivalence," which is the basis of metaphorical substitution and, from there on up, of the entire construct of Western metaphysics (chapter 2 in this volume). And reciprocally—Muraro has developed this recently—difference manifests itself, metonymically, in contingency, "in that which happens to us and touches us," such as being born a man or a woman, and constitutively marks human identity.[37] Thinking sexual difference therefore means—here the path twists around between Heidegger and the tradition of female mysticism—thinking ontological difference in its contingent form: "God's contingency" as Muraro dared to say recently.[38]

In political terms the developments are just as relevant. The metonymic cut of the relation between body and word, experience and language—which, as we know, generates the practice of *starting from oneself* within the women's movement—leads, as I anticipated a little while ago, to a radical critique of identitarian politics. In other words, it leads to a decisive detachment both from a late metaphysical essentialism and from its postmodern overturning in the pluralist "identity politics" from across the pond. Far from overcoming the logic of identity, the latter simply fragments it in the geography of social, ethnic, and gender differences, each guaranteed by its own representation, in a public sphere that ever more closely resembles a cake divided into noncommunicating slices, shared democratic decorum notwithstanding.[39] Starting from oneself does not in fact mean remaining narcissistically attached to oneself, to one's own specificity and point of view; it means, rather, knowing how to separate oneself from them, "a way of thinking that is not tied to the logic of identity and is capable of walking in contingency."[40] This thought renews—pace the deathly fate of Western culture—the movement and the risk of birth: it is a "turning oneself into a beginning" [*farsi inizio*], the opposite of a regression into an identity (or into a community) lost or found that can be weighed on the market of the quotas of representative democracy.[41]

Sexual difference is in fact "original," but not in the direction of a return to a presumed origin, to the foundation or essence of being a woman, but rather in the opposite direction, of that which originates an opening of sense for being woman (and being man). As we have seen (and we are once more at the core of twentieth-century philosophies), sexual difference "occurs" in language (and in the historical-political conditions of relations among women). It is a rupture in the regime of sayability, an event of the symbolic order, which gives sense to a contingent fact, that of being born woman, which is otherwise silent.[42] Neither late metaphysical "thing" nor postmodern mere discursivity, but rather a notion both factual and pertaining to the order of events, sexual difference is an opening of sense in which it is not the identitarian fixation of gender but the multiplicity of meanings of feminine existence that can finally unfold.

This is not the only path along which the critique of political representation takes shape in the pages of *To Knit or to Crochet*. This critique is already advanced in one of the first pages of the text—another one of its political springs—but from a peculiar angle, which needs to be underscored quite particularly. Demonstrating the far-from-specialized nature of her topic, Muraro writes that "Jakobson's problem, the issue he posed about the historical modes of symbolic production, can be found again today as a political problem, posed by the women's movement and other movements that refuse the system of political representation" (chapter 2 in this volume). Another of the book's not insignificant merits is thus brought to the fore: repositing and reformulating the genetic link that binds juridical-political representation and linguistic-symbolic representation together in our culture, a connection which the classics of political thought were well aware of—let it suffice to mention Carl Schmitt—but which is often ignored by current political debates.[43] Reflecting faithfully the sickness-unto-death of their object—that is, the reduction of politics to technique—political analysts reduce the problem of political representation, and of its crisis, to a question of parliamentary quotas or to the proper functioning of an electoral law, thus losing sight of the complexity of the symbolic fabric that ties the representative to the represented since the origin of Western politics and the modern state. Only then to shed rivers of tears on the slippage from political representation to media representation; or, on the contrary, to celebrate the dissolution of the frictions of modern politics into the fluidity of a postmodern communication without borders or obstacles.

That a slippage of functions from politics to communication is ongoing, and the reasons for it, are well known. Upstream there is social complexity, the dissolution into mass culture and communication of those communitarian languages in which political identities and the capacity for symbolic mobilization of political parties were rooted, politics' legitimation and credibility crisis, the exponential growth of the media and both their technological and financial strengthening. Downstream there is the myth of direct democracy, where the transparency and immediacy guaranteed by TV exposure and the "real time" speed of the technologies of the electronic agora, and increasingly today also by the much more "democratic" horizontal character of the internet, would substitute for the opaque mediation of the parliamentary party system. These processes are occurring throughout the West, efficiently exemplified by the Italian laboratory and variously interpreted, on a scale that goes from catastrophism to technological optimism, and from nostalgia to rejection of the greatness of the modern paradigm of politics.[44]

And yet, it is precisely a closer look at the Italian transition—during which the transformation of the language and the forms of politics were obviously supported and amplified by the changes in the forms and language of the mass media—that suggests that there is no caesura between political representation and media representation, but rather a bond: an isomorphic mirroring, forms chasing each other that pass from the field of the political system to the media and vice versa, ending up constituting a single and perfectly conformed (and conformist) field.[45] The mechanism, in any case, is not new. Viewing the century in a long-term historical perspective, the relation between politics and media is marked more by alliance than by enmity; or better by a competition (intended, here again, as both collaboration and rivalry) in the construction of the public sphere in the era of mass politics and mass communication: birth, zenith, and crisis. This competition moreover brings us back to the roots the two fields share: the communicative function of politics and the political effects of communication. Politics *and* language, social order *and* symbolic order: we are back at the most important point.

Juridical-political representation *and* linguistic-symbolic representation are once more shown to be closely connected, an ironclad binomial that accompanies the history of politics in the West, and which is today certainly tipped in favor of the second term, but which as a whole tends toward a worrisome loss of sense and of a grasp of reality. Politics is losing that power of symbolic mobilization that made it powerful and that was based not only on the (metaphorical) "grand narratives" but also on communicative and linguistic practices (metonymic: all forms of participation, militancy, relation). Reduced to technique and administration, politics abandons this symbolic, linguistic, and communicative function to the media. But in the media this function is itself reduced to pure technique: stereotyped vocabularies, computerized formats, previously designed layouts, words with no sound, a representation that doesn't represent, and a language that doesn't speak of anyone or to anyone, in a regime in which anything can be said and it is no longer important *what* is said, but only *how* it is said. Politics and mass media, the two modes of representations, are traversed by the same, isomorphic tendencies (and today, not casually, by the same legitimation and credibility crisis), and above all by the tendency toward dematerialization, toward abstraction from both the individual body and the social body, toward self-referentiality: in a word, toward hypermetaphorization.

Luisa Muraro had already seen where things were going much earlier, back when the mass parties were still standing—the hurricanes of feminism, of 1968, of 1977, notwithstanding; when polls and ratings hadn't replaced consensus and social rootedness, reality TV hadn't been born yet, and Silvio Berlusconi was still in the construction business. Seen from the point of view of the bundle of phenomena that in the meantime has disrupted the relation between politics and communication, and has reconformed our existences, the figure of the "hypermetaphoricity regime" and the schema of the crossed axes have both proved to be very significantly ahead of their times and meaningful. They join both modes of representation together; they locate the problem of the media in the right place, in other words at the cusp of the arc of our civilization—a question of language and sayability that pertain to our social being, not of "tools" to be used "democratically" or to whose authoritarian use one resigns oneself. And they assist in orienting oneself in the contradictions that open up along the border between body (individual and social), communication technologies, and (crisis of) politics, which is revealing itself to be crucial in redesigning the public sphere at the end of the century.

The mass media civilization obviously fulfills, and perhaps even carries to implosion, the "great device of metaphoric substitution," which promises to restore everything while reducing everything to a sign of nothing, in a movement leading to reality's continued rarefaction. But this does not occur either univocally or pacifically (chapter 2 in this volume). As Muraro writes, the competition between metaphor and metonymy demands that bodies, contexts, and experiences must be continually evoked, visited, consumed, before they are annulled, translated into code, reduced to preformed meanings. Metaphoric translation feeds off this live matter. And the media in fact devour it, interrogate it, interview it, to then reassemble and restore it in their fashion: always closer to the social body, always more abstracted from the social body.

This is how one may explain the media's dual nature, both seductive and prescriptive; their advantage as compared to politics, since the latter does not manage even to brush against the social body; and the ever-increasing gap between the enormous amount of information that is available to us and the terrible reduction in meaning and significance that accompanies it. So that in newspapers and on TV one talks more and more about more and more things, while allowing them to say increasingly less, and above all nothing that isn't predictable: by every day repeating that the world is changing at a frantic pace, we are actually constructing a reality devoid of surprises. I don't know if twenty years after *To Knit or to Crochet*'s appearance students in Milan's suburban ghettoes still write that meadows are green in their class assignments, but I certainly know that in the newspapers the "Mezzogiorno" [Southern Italy] invariably remains backward and criminal, women are always oppressed or filled with revanchist instincts toward men, immigrants are invariably either a divine punishment or a great resource, and this notwithstanding the fact that Southern Italy is a nuanced reality and irreducible to a single adjective, that women for several decades have been, and still are, the protagonists of a revolution for freedom, that immigrants experience sexual, social, and cultural contradictions. And these are only three examples of how the *dispositif* of repetition—both intellectual (laziness, conformism, ideology) and technical (productive routines, market rules)—almost always seems to win against even the best subjective intentions. I am myself a living witness to how difficult it was to contaminate a left-wing daily like *Il manifesto*, conformed to the paradigm of oppression, with the perspective of female freedom. The result is that not only do experiences remain silent, as Luisa writes, but that we as "interpreters" also become ever more silent, blind, and deaf—and, appearances notwithstanding, not at all powerful—compared to what is occurring outside of these established meanings. In fact, the unease of those who work in communication and information is becoming ever stronger; but it does not express itself, since it buckles under when faced with the diktats of production. Or if it expresses itself, it accuses politics of the deafness and silence of which it absolves itself; and, reciprocally, politics accuses information, in a passing the buck of responsibilities that confirms the specular nature of the two fields, which at this point has become obvious even at the level of language: "the ugliness of politicians' and journalists' language is not only a mirror, it is the tortured substance of the loss of meaning of the political, so imminent that one almost doesn't dare denounce it for fear of making it fall completely," writes *Sottosopra* (from which we already quoted).[46] After all, the political-journalistic vocabulary is only the tip of the iceberg. Several years ago Italo Calvino had already denounced the sickness-unto-death that he thought had afflicted humanity's use of the word, "a plague that manifests itself in language as a loss of cognitive power and immediacy, as an automatic tendency to reduce expression to its most generic formulas, anonymous, abstract constructions and to dilute its meanings, blunt its expressive points, and snuff every spark that flies from the collision of words with new circumstances."[47] And it was once again Muraro who more recently highlighted the contradiction inherent in the fact that "an extraordinary explosion of technological power in human communication has occurred in an era of the absence of the word."[48]

Are there no antidotes? Are we irreparably squeezed between the virtual cloning of a dying reality mentioned by [Jean] Baudrillard and the aphasic condition of those who find themselves "as a historical task, this side of or below the necessary language"?[49] The metonymic key that Luisa proposes in *To Knit or to Crochet* opens onto a new possibility: the *political* possibility of a "linguistic guerrilla warfare" to be practiced daily inside the networks of the grand metaphoric device, putting the idea of starting from oneself and the maternal language to work, in order to interrupt, disturb, subvert the prescribed meanings and the conformist truths of the device itself.[50]

The contradiction that has already developed at the border between politics and new technologies expresses the need for a form of communication that differs from that of the old mass media, one both more individual and more relational, where the internet horizontality intercepts the sovereign's verticality as we have known it up to this point, in other words, in the two figures of political/state power and of TV-ocracy [*telecrazia*], both allies and competitors in the era of mass politics. The interactivity that connects solitary personal computer users via the internet alludes to the change that has already occurred, from the communitarian individual, who identifies with the group to which s/he belongs, to the deracinated individual who navigates in search of relationships, crossing the borders of traditional identities and modern states. Jumping over the ties and hierarchies of political representation to present her/himself directly to the other in the infinite perimeter of the electronic agora, the modern individual directly encounters the king's body, no longer two, sacred and secular, as [Ernst] Kantorowicz had described it, but one, extremely secular and more naked than ever, as we have all seen it, reading the Starr report on Bill Clinton on the internet.

But however new, it is indeed a contradiction, and one that is far from resolved, as those crooners of the "Californian ideology" would have it, who substitute the agonizing fate of politics at the end of the century with the magnificent destiny of the global village at the beginning of the millennium. Because, however direct, the communication that flows unhindered along fiber optic cables cannot and will not be able to overcome the limits of language and the opacities that interrupt the fluidity of the individual and social text. However accessible, the internet does not flatten out the differences and inequalities that continue to exist between the ordered and the wild social body. No matter how much they are facilitated by the electronic address book, relationships at a distance remain to a large extent imaginary. And to whatever degree it may be photographed, evoked, masked, dressed up, resignified by means of the thousand games on the internet, which—not casually—have it as its object, the body remains outside the internet. The body is translated into code, but out of context, and, divided once more, language online and physical presence at home, sight at work on the screen and touch in latency.[51] Paradoxically, in everyday parlance encounters on the internet are called "contacts." But touch, contact, and contingency return to present themselves as irreducible, inexpressible, and obscene residues, "off scene," in a virtual reedition of the hypermetaphorical drift of the end of the twentieth century. The process of dematerialization of the individual and social body, which traversed the century, is not stopping, and rather than becoming a measure of what's true and what's false, pleasure makes do with becoming virtual.

In the twilight of the modern saga of politics, the original alliance between the neutralization of the body, apparatus of political representation, and hypermetaphorical regime of representation returns in new clothing. Conversely, navigating in cybernetic space alludes to the need for contact and relationships that the traditional public sphere no longer satisfies, but which is lost in the illusion of a transparent and unhindered discursivity. The modern state of political representation and the postmodern state of virtuality are both shown as incapable of comprehending an incarnate and sexed singularity, open to relationship, to context, to contingency, in which body and language, experience and representation, materiality and the symbolic are not divided and do not disregard each other, the one aware of the potentialities and limits of the other. In a landscape crowded with confused and sometimes regressive attempts to overcome the traditional political paradigm, the thought of sexual difference has the advantage of having highlighted this nexus at the root of politics in a timely fashion, thereby bearing witness to the epistemological revolution of the beginning of the century at the century's end. Between metaphor and metonymy, to formulate it with a quotation from the years in which *To Knit or to Crochet* was written, *ce n'est qu'un debut*.

Translated by Mark William Epstein

NOTES

This chapter is the translation of a revised version of "La parola del contatto," originally published as the introduction to the second edition of Luisa Muraro's *Maglia o uncinetto: Racconto linguistico-politico sulla inimicizia tra metafora e metonimia* (Rome: Manifestolibri, 1998), 7–41.

1. See "Maglia o uncinetto? Metafora e metonimia nella produzione simbolica," *Aut aut*, nos. 175–76 (1980): 59–85. This first version also referred ("I was

asked to elaborate more fully," Muraro explained) to a previous essay "La verifica del piacere," *Aut aut*, no. 172 (1979): 148–54, as a comment on a text by Corrado Levi, *New Kamasutra: Sado-masochistic didactics* (Milan: Salamandra, 1979).

2. *L'Orsaminore* started in Rome in the summer of 1981 thanks to the initiative of seven women (including Manuela Fraire herself) and then others joined (including myself). Eleven issues of the journal were published, up to the spring of 1983. The debate I am referring to started with an essay by Rossana Rossanda, "Sulla questione della cultura femminile," *L'Orsaminore: Mensile di cultura politica*, no. 0 (1981): 65–71. In the following issues there were contributions by Lidia Campagnano, Gabriella Bonacchi, Franca Chiaromonte, as well as some collective essays.

3. See the recorded acts of the debate between Rosi Braidotti and Luisa Muraro on "Il tramonto del soggetto ed il pensiero della differenza," which took place at the Centro Culturale Virginia Woolf in Rome on May 26, 1992 (the recording is preserved at the center's archives).

4. [In Italian public discourse, the "transition" refers to the passage from the so-called first Republic (1945–1993) to the so-called second Republic (1993–on).—Eds.]

5. The expression comes from Jacques Derrida, *Writing and Difference*, trans. Alan Bass (Chicago: University of Chicago Press, 1978), 226. Starting with the theme of the death of the author in Derrida and Roland Barthes, Elizabeth Grosz asks herself what are the characteristics that ensure the feminine status of a text. She excludes that the author's sex and the content are sufficient: among the necessary requisites she lists are the traces of the political conditions in which it was conceived as well as "a feminist subversion of the patronym" (in other words of the male, authorial, position of the enunciation). See *Space, Time, and Perversion: Essays on the Politics of Bodies* (New York: Routledge, 1995), 23. The first path for the subversion I believe is the staging of the relation with the female other, which immediately exhibits a dialogic mode of intellectual work and a transgression of established genealogies and cultural authorities. To women friends who ask me why I spend so much time writing about texts by other women instead of writing my own books, I answer (also) in the following manner: because writing in a relationship with another gives me more pleasure than the satisfaction I derive facing myself, and because I see it as a form that better embodies the political and cultural enterprise we are carrying forward.

6. See the anonymous editorial "Premessa," *Aut aut*, nos. 175–76 (1980): 1–3. To give an idea of the political and cultural context, together with *To Knit or to Crochet* the issue contained contributions by Mario Vegetti, Gianni Vattimo, and Pier Aldo Rovatti on the collective volume *Crisi della ragione*, edited by Aldo Gargani (Turin: Einaudi, 1979), a subject of discussion at the time; by Giampiero Comolli on the experience of time in Elvio Fachinelli's works; by Luce Irigaray on analytical practice and sexual difference; by Gustavo Gozzi, Lapo Berti,

and Giovanna Procacci on power, state, and oppositional culture; by Hans-Dieter Bahr on terrorism; by Giorgio Grossi on the politicization of mass information; and by Giovanni Cacciavillani on [Jean-François] Lyotard. Just as a reminder to younger readers, the journal *Aut aut* for a long time managed to follow the movements and the breaks in subjectivities that didn't conform to the norm, working at the juncture of philosophy and political practice.

7. [Here and throughout the rest of this chapter, all the instances of the term "wild social body" translate the Italian *corpo sociale selvaggio*.—Trans.]

8. Muraro, *Maglia o uncinetto*, 172.

9. Muraro, *The Symbolic Order of the Mother*, trans. Francesca Novello (Albany: State University of New York Press, 2018), 1.

10. See Muraro, "To Knit or to Crochet," chapter 2 in this volume.

11. Muraro, *Maglia o uncinetto*, 189.

12. Jean Baudrillard, *The Perfect Crime*, trans. Chris Turner (London: Verso, 1996), 17.

13. Jacques Derrida, *Margins of Philosophy*, trans. Alan Bass (Chicago: University of Chicago Press, 1982), 271.

14. Muraro quoted in Teresa de Lauretis, introduction to *Sexual Difference: A Theory of Social Symbolic Practice* (Bloomington: Indiana University Press, 1991), 18.

15. [The term "women's studies" is in English in the original.—Eds.]

16. Muraro, *Maglia o uncinetto*, 131

17. Muraro, *Maglia o uncinetto*, 121.

18. Jacques Derrida, "To Do Justice to Freud: The History of Madness in the Era of Psychoanalysis," *Critical Inquiry* 20, no. 2 (Winter 1994): 227–66. This is an essay on Freud's legacy in the century's culture, written in a dialogue and polemic with the work of Michel Foucault. On the relationship between Freud and Lacan, and especially on the reception of psychoanalysis in the French Marxist philosophical context, see Louis Althusser, *Writings on Psychoanalysis: Freud and Lacan*, trans. Jeffrey Mehlman (New York: Columbia University Press, 1996). On the debt that the theory and practice of sexual difference owe analytical theory and practice see Dominijanni, "Il desiderio di politica," introduction to Lia Cigarini, *La politica del desiderio* (Parma: Pratiche, 1995), 7–46.

19. Muraro, *Maglia o uncinetto*, 135.

20. [The title refers to the Italian saying "l'erba voglio non cresce nemmeno nel giardino del re," which is roughly the equivalent of "the grass is always greener on the other side of the fence."—Eds.]

21. Luisa Muraro "Bombe sentimentali," *L'erba voglio*, no. 17 (1974): 7, 8. [The bombing of Piazza Fontana (1969) and of the train *Italicus* (1974) were part of a government strategy to defeat revolutionary movements through fear and a permanent state of tension.—Eds.] See Luisa Muraro, "L'anima a servizio," *L'erba voglio*, no. 11 (1973): 2–6; and "Le donne invisibili," *L'erba voglio*, no. 10 (1973):

2–6. See also the anthology of the journal, edited by Lea Melandri, *Il desiderio dissidente: Antologia della rivista L'erba voglio, 1971–1977* (Milan: Baldini e Castoldi, 1998).

22. In an essay published several years ago devoted to the university, reflecting on the aphasia of a female student who "starting from the first day of classes looked at me with a level of concentration that remained constant, similar to the look of creatures in front of the TV screen," Muraro notes: "In the silent and immobile mirror of that gaze, I was able to measure my loss. Mine, ours. For a century in philosophy we have done nothing but reflect on language. In that student's gaze I, like a beached whale, found the stable ground of a sure failure. When someone tells me: but have you tried reading the latest Habermas, just to mention one, I answer as one does in slogans: no, thank you. I believe in intellectual work, it's my profession, but there are defeats that need to be recorded." "Lo splendore di avere un linguaggio," *Aut aut*, nos. 260–61 (1994): 31.

23. See Adriana Cavarero, *Corpo in figure* (Milan: Feltrinelli, 1995). Even though they start from very distant epistemological presuppositions, I put in dialogue the reading of this book and of *To Knit or to Crochet* in my "Corpo politico," *Sofia*, no. 3 (1997): 38–49.

24. Muraro, *The Symbolic Order of the Mother*, 87.

25. See in *The Symbolic Order of the Mother* the polemical dialogue with Lotman, Agamben, and Kristeva.

26. Carla Lonzi, *È già politica* (Milan: Scritti di Rivolta Femminile, 1977). On Carla Lonzi, see Maria Luisa Boccia, *L'io in rivolta* (Milan: La Tartaruga, 1990).

27. Milanese feminists, "Pratica dell'inconscio e movimento delle donne," *L'erba voglio*, nos. 18–19 (October 1974–January 1975): 20.

28. For the relation between text and context in the theoretico-political elaboration of difference, see my reading of *Non credere di avere dei diritti*, in "Radicalità e ascetismo," *Memoria*, nos. 19–20 (1987): 142–55.

29. Libreria delle Donne di Milano, "Un filo di felicità," *Sottosopra Oro* (1989), available at http://www.libreriadelledonne.it/pubblicazioni/un-filo-di-felicita-sottosopra-oro-gennaio-1989/.

30. Diotima, *Mettere al mondo il mondo: Oggetto e oggettività alla luce della differenza sessuale* (Milan: La Tartaruga, 1990).

31. Libreria delle Donne di Milano, "È accaduto non per caso," *Sottosopra Rosso* (1996), available at http://www.libreriadelledonne.it/pubblicazioni/e-accaduto-non-per-caso-sottosopra-gennaio-1996/.

32. See Chiara Zamboni, "Le vie del simbolico," in Diotima, *Il cielo stellato dentro di noi* (Milan: La Tartaruga, 1992), 163–82; and chapter 4 in this volume, "Maternal Language between Limit and Infinite Opening." My debt to Chiara Zamboni in the writing of these pages is much greater than the references to these and other writings of hers might let one surmise. My training in putting the philosophy of language back on the feet of experience I owe to work done

with her during seminars at the University of Verona. A special thanks for some clarifications and suggestions also to Cristina Biasini.

33. Muraro, *The Symbolic Order of the Mother*, 98 [modified].

34. On the maternal imaginary see Teresa de Lauretis, *The Practice of Love: Lesbian Sexuality and Perverse Desire* (Bloomington: Indiana University Press, 1994) and the reading of it given by Manuela Fraire, "Oltre la parentalità," *Sofia*, no. 2 (1997): 15–22. I believe both are victims of the previously mentioned misunderstanding, which I have contested at greater length in my "Il desiderio di politica." On the figures of the maternal in feminist psychoanalysis see also Claudia Zanardi, "L'esperienza femminile nella psicoanalisi: Una ricerca di continuità," in *Psicoanalisi e identità di genere*, ed. Anna Panepucci (Rome-Bari: Laterza, 1995), 68–87.

35. "Let's Spit on Hegel" is the title of one the most famous and groundbreaking essays by Carla Lonzi. See "Let's Spit on Hegel," in *Italian Feminist Theory and Practice: Equality and Sexual Difference*, ed. Graziella Parati and Rebecca West (Madison, N.J.: Fairleigh Dickinson University Press, 2002), 40–59.

36. Muraro, *Maglia o uncinetto*, 113. The similarities between the reasoning Muraro develops in *To Knit or to Crochet* and the philosophical thought of Luce Irigaray are evident. Margaret Whitford, *Luce Irigaray. Philosophy in the Feminine* (London: Routledge, 1991), is very useful in this sense, and pays special attention to reconstructing the theory of the symbolic in French philosophy. These similarities notwithstanding it seems to me that Irigaray, unlike Muraro, ends up slipping into a dichotomous reading of sexual difference in several points of her development, points based on a sort of biological-symbolic realism that is closer to essentialism. It is not by chance that in her most recent work she argues for gender's citizenship and its being represented. I believe this slippage is due to the lack of that practice in Irigaray, which nourishes an investment in the *politics* of the symbolic as it is carried out in the feminism of sexual difference in Italy.

37. Muraro, "Partire da sè e non farsi trovare," in Diotima, *La sapienza di partire da sè* (Naples: Liguori, 1996), 17. See also Luisa Muraro, "Identità umana e differenza sessuale," in Diotima, *Oltre l'uguaglianza* (Naples: Liguori, 1995), 113–41.

38. Course on theoretical philosophy held at the University of Verona in the academic year 1996–1997.

39. See Diana Sartori, "Nessuno è l'autore della propria storia," in Diotima, *La sapienza di partire da sè*, 23–57.

40. See Muraro, "Partire da sè e non farsi trovare," 15.

41. Sartori, "Nessuno è l'autore della propria storia," 55.

42. See the reading by Salvatore Natoli of the genealogical analysis of Foucault in *Ermeneutica e genealogia* (Milan: Feltrinelli, 1981). Teresa de Lauretis very astutely relates the meaning of the origin of Italian thought on sexual difference

to Walter Benjamin's "leap in the open air of history," rather than to an essentialist vision. De Lauretis, *Sexual Difference*, 13.

43. See Carl Schmitt, *Roman Catholicism and Political Form*, trans. Gary Ulmen (Westport, Conn.: Greenwood Press, 1996), where it is obvious that within the concept of political representation, the technical-institutional device of representation joins its symbolic-evocative counterpart and would not be able to function without the transcendent and identifying horizon that the latter provides.

44. The bibliography on the subject is at this point boundless. See Giorgio Grossi, *Rappresentanza e rappresentazione* (Milan: Franco Angeli, 1985); Danilo Zolo, *Il principato democratico* (Milan: Feltrinelli, 1992); Stefano Rodotà, *Tecnopolitica* (Roma-Bari: Laterza, 1997); and Franco Carlini, *Internet, Pinocchio e il gendarme* (Rome: Manifestolibri, 1996).

45. For instance, the infatuation with the majoritarian electoral system as a mode of vote-counting in the political market was strengthened by the use of the electronic *agorà* as a market for opinions, the triumph of the myth of leadership by means of a televisual construction of the leader-character, the temptations of plebiscitarian appeal by the mobilization of "people" via TV opinion polls, the demand for transparency by TV visibility, etc. I have analyzed these dynamics in "Media, politica, antipolitica," *Democrazia e diritto*, no. 1 (1996): 335–53.

46. Libreria delle Donne di Milano,"È accaduto non per caso," 7.

47. Italo Calvino, *Six Memos for the Next Millennium*, trans. Geoffrey Brock (New York and Boston: Houghton Mifflin Harcourt, 2016), 68–69.

48. Muraro, *Lo splendore di non avere un linguaggio*, 33.

49. Muraro, *Lo splendore di non avere un linguaggio*, 33.

50. I steal this expression from Christian Marazzi, who studies the political relevance of the linguistic-communicative dimension in the conflicts of post-Fordist society. See Marazzi, *Capital and Affects: The Politics of the Language Economy* (Los Angeles: Semiotext(e), 2008) and "Passami il 23: Il passaggio dall'economia fordista all'economia dell'informazione," *Via Dogana*, nos. 38–39 (1998): 5–6.

51. See Tiziana Terranova, *Corpi nella rete: Interfacce multiple, cyberfemminismo e agorà telematica* (Genoa: Costa and Nolan, 1996). I believe Terranova's view is more productive than the by-now classic warning of Donna Haraway in *Simians, Cyborgs, and Women: The Reinvention of Nature* (New York: Routledge, 1991), namely, the warning not to trap feminist thought in an antitechnological perspective.

To Knit or to Crochet

A Political-Linguistic Tale on the Enmity between Metaphor and Metonymy

LUISA MURARO

FOREWORD

This text is the reworking, with the addition of a few new developments, of a brief essay, "Maglia o uncinetto? Metafora e metonimia nella produzione simbolica" [To knit or to crochet? Metaphor and metonymy in symbolic production], which appeared in the journal *Aut aut* in 1980.[1] That essay was in its turn an attempt to elaborate some ideas I had presented in an article that had previously appeared in that journal, "La verifica del piacere" [The verification of pleasure].

I have used the word "tale" in the subtitle because my discourse proceeds by following the succession of ideas as they gradually took shape. Truly to be a tale, however, it would have had to have a beginning, which it lacks. The text, in fact, begins with Roman Jakobson's theory of metaphor and metonymy, which was not the actual point of departure. I was driven to write on the enmity between metaphor and metonymy by an observation. In our culture, knowledge and pleasure are formally separated, even though many things lead one to suspect that intimate and secret relations exist between them. Spying on these relations and provoking them has been the primary motive of my research.

I thank those who helped me with critiques and appreciations.

I dedicate my work to my women friends of the Biblioteca in Parma.

Milan, April 1981
L.M.

TO KNIT OR TO CROCHET

Metaphor and Metonymy Are Not Twin Sisters

Hearkening back to a renowned theory that Roman Jakobson articulated in the fifties, I will state that speaking is like knitting. One needs at least two needles to knit. Jakobson says that when one speaks one operates on two fundamental axes: along one axis, linguistic units are selected; along the other, they are combined. A text, hence, is the product of a combination of signs one has selected, its meaning being determined by the crossing of the two axes. One axis—that of selections—is constituted by all the signs associated with the sign that appears in the text; these signs, however, don't appear since precisely that sign has been selected instead. [Ferdinand de] Saussure used to say: it is the sphere of in absentia relations, also known as paradigm. The other is the syntagm, namely, the axis of relations that are actually present, of those signs that appear in and constitute the text by entering into a variety of combinations.

So far nothing new compared to Saussure. Jakobson's theory became well known because of two additional developments. First, Jakobson hypothesized that the two axes correspond to the primary processes of all symbolic production. Second, he identified metaphor and metonymy as the two rhetorical figures he associated with the procedures that characterize, from the semantic point of view, the axis of selections and the axis of combinations, respectively. He spoke, therefore, about a *metaphorical directrix* for the axis of selections, and of a *metonymical directrix* for the axis of combinations.

In addition to provoking a resurgence of interest in rhetoric, Jakobson's theory was also taken up outside linguistics. [Jacques] Lacan recognized it as coinciding with his reading of Freud, of the unconscious as a language, thereby ensuring a sort of popularity for metaphor and metonymy. By now, they are a steady couple; one never finds one without the other, and I believe many no longer distinguish them very well—a typically metonymical mechanism that mocks theoretical operations being complicit in this state of affairs, as will become clear in what follows.

Such a confusion is precisely the opposite of what Jakobson had in mind: he had meant instead to differentiate as much as possible between two rhetorical figures that traditionally have been placed together near each other. I believe a contributing factor was that an important part of his theory was amputated, the part in which he says that the metaphoric and metonymic poles find themselves in a relation that is not one of pacific complementarity but one of competitive rivalry. This rivalry affects symbolic production, since it may manifest itself in the products as the prevalence of one of the two poles.[2] In other words, the mode of symbolic production is determined historically by the tension between these two differing principles—a tension that theoretical analysis, for its part, declares to be undecidable. This tension has various possible solutions that researchers register historically. Their science enters the play between the opposing symbolic principles, but it does not have the power to decide it.

There is almost no trace of this historical depth in the later developments of Jakobson's theory. And this has meant that, in effect, the traditional primacy of metaphor reestablished itself. In fact, in Jakobson's discourse, the space of symbolic action becomes historically dramatized because of the discovery of a production of meaning that may develop prevalently (and even exclusively) along the metonymical directrix, the obscure and obscured resource in signifying production.[3] To explain this point more clearly it is necessary for me to return to the level of explication of the theory, so as to clarify very simply what metaphor and metonymy are.

Jakobson calls the axis of selections the metaphoric directrix and the axis of combinations the metonymic. Such a denomination is justifiable if one keeps in mind what those two rhetorical figures are and in what they differ. They share in common the fact of being expressions that signify something other than their meaning, precisely by taking the place of the expression that would be the normal, habitual one. To speak of a "revolution" to refer to a radical change in society was a metaphor when the expression was normally used to indicate certain kinds of movements by bodies, especially celestial ones. To say of a woman that "she reasons with her uterus" in order to say that she reasons more according to her own emotions than to logic is a metonymy insofar as the power of disturbing rational thought may be attributed and has been attributed to the uterus. It is easy to discern the difference between metaphor and metonymy on the basis of these two examples. Those who invented the revolutionary metaphor didn't suppose there was any material connection between the motion of celestial bodies and radical social upheaval, but rather an internally perceivable resemblance. Metaphor reinforces the perception of a resemblance; indeed, it sometimes determines it. This is the reason it has been considered the poetic figure par excellence, since it enables the images of realities to vary indefinitely, inventing connections a prosaic mind would never have imagined. Without shunting poetry aside, one needs to add that the metaphorical procedure has other important functions as well. Since it makes us go beyond the descriptive level of existence as well as beyond the specificities of experience, it supports all forms of explanation, interpretation, and planning. Theories, including political ones, rely on it to give us a unitary and general representation of facts that, in concrete experience, may present themselves as unsewn, as fragmentary, or as entertaining relations which theory will demonstrate are irrelevant.

In metonymy the relation between figural sense and literal sense coincides with a material nexus, which may be spatial, temporal, causal, or of other type. To say that someone "thinks viscerally" is a figure of a metonymic type, either because the kind of thought that is strongly influenced by emotions is sometimes accompanied by truly visceral sensations, or because the intestine is part of the body, just like the head, to which one attributes the capacity for thought. By way of metonymic displacement, and by emphasizing the derogatory intention that derives from the superiority of the head over the rest of the body, one might reach the point of saying that someone thinks with his feet [*che uno ragiona coi piedi*].[4] Even the figure that Lacan uses for analyzing metaphor, "his sheaves were not miserly," is strictly speaking of a metonymic type: between the generous Booz and his sheaf, in fact, there exists a relation that the figure does not invent but refers to—a relation of property, of possession. Another rhetorical figure that is close to metonymy is synecdoche, an expression whose normal meaning refers to a part or a partial characteristic of the thing that is signified, such as "asking for the hand" of someone when one wants to have the whole body, or "black shirt" to refer to a fascist. (Jakobson always includes synecdoche in metonymy and I follow him in this usage.) The specificity of both metonymy and synecdoche consists in that they are formed by means of relations that are discovered, not invented. The connections may be of any kind so long as they are not established on the basis of a relation founded in pure thought, but on the basis of their presenting themselves to us as givens [*dati*].

While metaphor leaps out from an original thought [*pensata*], metonymy plods along the path of lived experience. Thanks to metaphor experience is reshaped as an ideal representation, while metonymy articulates experiences into its parts.

Their Competition in Symbolic Production

It is in these two rhetorical figures that Jakobson sees "the most synthetic expression" of the two directrices along which the process of signification is developed.[5] In the one, the meaning-effect derives from ideal references, in the other, the metonymical, from given, verifiable, practicable combinations. In the first, symbolic elaboration consists in defining things, in duplicating the world in a representation; in the second, things are signified by what accompanies them, in natural sequences or human usage.

When talking about archaic and classical Greek cosmology, Paul Feyerabend provides us with a good example of symbolic elaborations that are prevalently based on metonymic procedures (archaic cosmology), and on metaphorical ones (classical cosmology):

> The archaic cosmology (which from now on I shall call cosmology A) contains things, events, their parts; it does not contain appearances. Complete knowledge of an object is complete enumeration of its parts and peculiarities. Humans cannot have complete knowledge. There are too many things, to many events, to many situations . . . and they can be close to only a few of them.
>
> But although humans cannot have complete knowledge, they can have a sizeable amount of it. The wider their experience, the greater the number of adventures, of things seen, heard, read, the greater their knowledge.
>
> The new cosmology (cosmology B) that arises in the VII and V centuries B.C. distinguishes between much-knowing, πολυμαθίη, and true knowledge, and it warns against trusting "custom born of manifold experience," ἔθος πολύπειρον . . . In one version which played a large role in the development of Western civilization and which underlies such problems as the problem of the existence of theoretical entities and the problem of alienation, the new events form what one might call a *True World*, while the events of everyday life are now *appearances* that are but its dim and

misleading reflection. The True World is simple and coherent, and it can be described in a uniform way. So can every act by which its elements are comprehended: a few abstract notions replace the numerous concepts that were used in cosmology A for describing how humans might be "inserted" into their surroundings and for expressing the equally numerous types of information thus gained.[6]

The prevalence of one pole doesn't mean the other is absent, since what is necessary to symbolic production is their competition [*concorrenza*], in the sense of both collaboration and rivalry.

In this conception of language, the classic logico-philosophical problem of the relation between words and things is enriched with new aspects. If language is capable of reexpressing the world, if it is possible to relate words and things prior to their being placed in correspondence (whose definition has in any case always generated aporias) and prior to any intentionality (which is countered by language itself), that is due, perhaps, to that proximity of words and things that is established along the metonymical directrix. In its most elementary definition language would be a replacing of things with words. Well, this "substitution"—which the more sophisticated definitions do no more than elaborating further—pertains to language insofar as it is supported by the metaphorical process; in other words, it pertains to language insofar as, thanks to the expansion of meaning [*significato*], it can transcend its physicality and contextuality. In the metonymic process, on the other hand, the figurative meaning does not replace the literal one, since they are mutually supportive, nor do words tend to make things superfluous—one would in fact lose the meaning-effect if one lost sight of things. Those aspects of language that lead to its limiting itself, as well as going beyond itself, such as indicating or the integration of linguistic and nonlinguistic context, also belong to the metonymic directrix. And it is here, where syntagmatic combinations take place, that slips of the tongue, wordplay, and various accidents, willed or involuntary, also occur, and that, as a consequence, words are lightened of their meanings [*significati*], suspended between saying and not saying. Rhetoric also teaches us that metonymy supplies language with concreteness because it substitutes generic or abstract expressions with specific and descriptive ones, sometimes with reductive or ironic effects. In other words, something akin to the well-known expressiveness of slang and people's everyday language (*linguaggio popolare*)—an aspect of style in which, according to Jakobson, one sees the emergence of an essential aspect of symbolic work: the integration of words and things.

Insofar as it proceeds along the metaphoric directrix, the substitutive process of language, in and of itself, knows no limits: words instead of things, figurative meaning (*significato*) in place of the literal, the universal in place of the particular, in an abysmal progression since language itself can become that of which language speaks, and consequently one arrives at a metalanguage and so forth. The metonymic directrix, which is foreign to this ascending motion, hinders it, cuts across it, prevents it from arriving at its logical conclusion—which could be that of gathering itself in a name, like the All, Being, God, and then silence. Signifying production, therefore, is never only a substituting representation; it is always also proximity to things.

Language, Jakobson concludes, has a bipolar structure. This structure, however, is easily misrecognized and reduced to a unipolar schema in which the metaphoric pole is privileged. He explains this recurrent simplification by pointing out that the metaphorical procedure is homogenous with—and therefore also transparent to—the metalinguistic procedure one resorts to for the study of language, "while metonymy, which is based on a different principle, easily eludes interpretation."[7] The symbolic order better reflects (on) that which is homogenous with it, similar and conforming to it, while it does not grant recognition to what responds to "a different principle," even though this opaque component is necessary for its functioning.

We are at the threshold of what a theory, linguistic or not, can make explicit, and in fact Jakobson's problem, the issue he posed about the historical modes of symbolic production, can be found again today as a political problem, posed by the women's movement and other movements that refuse the system of political representation. This should not surprise us since what is in question is a problem that, as we have seen, is not limited to this or that specialized competence. And I intend to deal with it as such, that is, as a matter whose competence is for the noncompetent, because it is a matter that is decided there where theory does not reach, or, better, there where theory does reach but reaches while bearing the marks of partiality—marks that theoretical discourse finds difficult to tolerate, if one is to judge from the reactions to Jakobson that followed on these issues.

Theoretical Pacification

For starters, when passing from the structural linguistics, to which Jakobson's work belongs, to Noam Chomsky's generative linguistics, the schema with the crossed axes is abandoned because deemed inadequate to the theoretical tasks at hand—a grammar constructed according to that model would not be able to generate all and only those sentences that are grammatical in a given language.[8] A grammar cannot be built as the structuralists thought they could, disassembling the syntagmatic sequences and ordering the resulting entities into classes and paradigms. The model is therefore replaced by more complex theoretical procedures, preceded by a redefinition of the relation between linguistic theory and its object in a sense that conforms to that which already prevails in the so-called advanced sciences (physics): the theory, it is argued, does not deal with directly observable data but with theoretical entities that entertain a relation with observable data that must be reconstructed at a later stage. In the course of this passage the problem posed by Jakobson regarding the modes of symbolic production loses those terms that had allowed him to formulate it. Theory, in fact, is now able—thanks to a conceptual device[9] that it would take too long to examine here—to elaborate a single model of symbolic production that is applicable to each speaker and every language, possible and undeniable differences being considered as secondary and derivative with respect to the model.

> Here I would like to highlight a point that is perhaps minor but nevertheless instructive. One of the reasons that tell us to distinguish, in generative grammar, between "deep" and "surface structures" is due to phenomena of homonymy and synonymy: there are expressions whose signifier is identical but whose signifieds differ and, vice versa, expressions whose signifiers differ but whose signifieds are identical, without this becoming an obstacle for the functioning of language. As a consequence one needs to postulate a deep level and a level of appearance, with different structures and with complex relations of derivation of the second from the first. Meaning [*significato*] is constituted at the deep level, where the misunderstandings of the surface level don't exist: at the deep level synonymous

expressions have the same structure and, vice versa, homonymous ones have different structures.

Well, those aphasics that Jakobson recognizes as lacking the capacity for metaphoricization are not impeded by phenomena of synonymy and homonymy. For them the same word in different contexts is always a case of homonymy; the signified is always different though the signifier may be the same. To avoid the habitual inconveniences homonymy presents, they resort to periphrases or diversified terms; in other words, they change the signifier. By contrast, they don't recognize synonymy: when the signifier is different, the signified must also be different—a position that corresponds to the difficulty linguists themselves have in defining synonymy. The hypometaphoric aphasic thus overcomes the obstacle of homonymy and synonymy without it being necessary to postulate a deep level where meaning [*significato*] would be formulated separately from expression. The aphasic's activity of signification adheres to signifying materiality, which cannot be transcended in a metalanguage of unambiguous equivalences; the price paid for this adherence by the aphasic, however, is total dependence on particular contexts.[10]

In the end, Jakobson's problem is resolved via erasure, thanks to a decisive reinforcement of the metaphoric pole. Concrete data are substituted with theoretical entities, real processes are transposed into ideal models, and as it was previously the case for natural facts, it is established that for linguistic facts as well there is science only if they are subjected to an adequate interpretive system.

On the other hand, in treatises on rhetoric, metaphor and metonymy are not situated in the radical opposition Jakobson placed them in, not even in the case of theories whose development was influenced by his ideas.

I am thinking of one rhetorical treatise in particular, a collective work, which appeared in 1970, *Rhétorique générale,* which impressed me at the time because it classified rhetorical figures in a systematic fashion, so that all possible figures, invented or to be invented, were already theoretically included in it.[11] Up to that point, the rhetorical texts I had become familiar with were rather descriptive, and contained classifications that, however well-reasoned, remained open lists. Tzvetan Todorov has written that "rhetoricians are literally obsessed with the need to classify and reclassify."[12] I suppose that this obsessive need may become assuaged in an order of a systematic type whose criteria do not directly depend, for continuity or change, on the objects that present themselves for classification.

What the authors of *Rhétorique générale* write about metaphor and metonymy corresponds to their systematic approach. In fact they subsume both metonymy and metaphor under the logico-linguistic category of substitution, neglecting the notion of contiguity.[13] This notion, which as we know Jakobson uses for metonymy, is precisely the one that prevails in the order based on description and listing, where things signify because they are next to each other. Substitution, which Jakobson uses for metaphor, is the category of equivalence and identity: two things are equivalent or identical when they can be substituted for each other. As one knows, in reality they are no perfectly equivalent or identical things; however—the story goes—thought could not function if it could not think identity, and, on this basis, similarity, difference, etc. This is probably true, but it is especially true for theoretical thought, and let me note that many functions that today are commonly assigned to theoretical thought could be performed differently. For example, difference is also known by moving from one thing to another, without passing through identity or equivalence. It is true that in our culture this manner of thinking, although widespread, does not enjoy the same prestige, and has been relegated to the most trivial uses. Lists are considered inert. The typical instability of their criteria of classification is seen as a negative trait—whereas one could instead transform it into a plastic and dynamic adaptability, something that obliges the need for control just enough to be able to make one accept the new and the different as they present themselves.

In *Rhétorique générale*, the rhetorical dimension of language is treated generally as if it were a "deviation" with respect to a "degree zero" of speech, namely, literal speech, normal or normalized, that is, speech that strictly conforms to the norms of the linguistic system. Even though it is admitted that the definition of this "degree zero" presents not a few difficulties, and that in actual fact there is no speech devoid of figures, one insists that there is a need to postulate it if one wants to grasp the specificity of the rhetorical dimension.[14] And in fact the postulate is used successfully in the treatise. I will remind the reader that Jakobson does not postulate a "degree zero"; for him metaphor and metonymy in the strict sense, as tropes, replicate and exhibit, at the semantic level, the process of constitution of language itself, by means of combinations and substitutions. For the authors of *Rhétorique générale*, rather, the rhetorical dimension of language is nothing other than a type of speech that substitutes the "normal" type. They write: ". . . on the level of rhetoric, the message at degree zero is already implicitly issued."[15] Rhetorical operations become evident against the background of this normal or normalized speech. In particular, tropes, including metaphor and metonymy, consist in substituting, under given conditions, the semantic content of one expression with another,[16] a complete substitution in the case of metonymy[17] and a partial one in the case of metaphor.[18] Returning to our examples: the astronomers' revolution transfers something of its semantic content to the politicians' revolution, the idea of a complete overturning. Whereas the uterus of feminine reasoning has a completely different semantic content from the organ of gestation. The point is that in the case of metonymy the content is transferred, in practice, thanks to a combination of factors, something that does not occur with metaphor. This is an interesting point, our authors reply, but of no use since it contains a reference to things.[19] Once again, proximity as the unthinkable, and this time, further, unthinkable proximity of things and words.

Consequently metonymy loses what was one of its important characteristics in Jakobson, its being a replica at the semantic level of signs combining with other signs or things, and therefore its work in forming linguistic and nonlinguistic context. In *Rhétorique générale*, the context is no longer the work of metonymy; rather, insofar as the context contributes to form the background against which the rhetorical deviation is discernible, it is assigned to the degree zero.[20]

Degree Zero

Everything therefore seems to indicate that presupposing a degree zero, linguistic norm or normality, will subtract their specificity from metonymical operations, subordinating them to metaphorical ones. So the issue now is rather simple: it is a question of deciding for or against this presupposition. It is easy for me to imagine that readers who want to continue in the direction opened by Jakobson are favorable to agreeing:

let's eliminate this presupposition. I am not unreservedly in favor of this drastic solution, however, first because I would like to understand better that degree zero that scholars of rhetoric say, one way or another, one cannot do without. And second because I have seen mock abolitions of so many norms and presuppositions that I have become cautious in this regard. There are presuppositions in our reasoning that, once one has put them out the door, come back through the window. And the degree zero is one of these, as we shall see from the following case.

In a brief study of the relation between rhetoric and psychoanalysis, Lorenzo Accame rightly underscores how the importance of Jakobson's theoretical proposal is diminished by certain aspects of current studies of rhetoric. He is referring, quite precisely, to the postulate regarding the existence of a degree zero:

> It is significant, for instance, that, after Jakobson's theoretical proposal—namely, that one consider the opposition (or better the complementarity) *metaphor/metonymy* as the expression of the interplay of intralinguistic mechanisms (traceable to the activity of selection and combination of signifieds)—the opposite tendency has in fact developed. This tendency consists in the formulation of a theory of tropes and figures organized according to the typology of the *logical deviation* between "proper meaning" and "figurative meaning," producing explanatory models that are capable of accounting for "changes in meaning," starting from an ideal (logical) "norm" which would be immanent to all linguistic practice.[21]

According to Accame, if one wants to understand the *seductive* effects inherent in discourse, rather than postulating a deviation which the degree zero can account for, one needs to take this deviation for granted, and to consider it as proper to and constitutive of language itself. He writes that there is no perception of an event that is not also a staging of the event.[22] There is therefore no language as literal registration.

It seems to me one ought to agree; and yet there is a discrepancy between these statements—with which I fully concur—and what the author writes only a few pages earlier, where he provides a rhetorical translation of Freud's analysis of fetishism. The fetishist, Freud states, is someone who in order to deny reality to the perception of female castration invests some object that may be associated with the female body with phallic attributes. This is a rhetorical operation, Accame says, providing a detailed explanation in which among other things one reads:

> The fetishist responds to an assumption of reality through a psychic process that allows him to reduce the traumatic impact—and consequently to increase its reassuring meaning [*significato*]—by means of a metonymic concealment. This concealment enables the elision of the absence of the penis in women, surrogating it with the reference to and the overdetermination of an *in itself insignificant contextual element* (like the one that will take on the function of fetish).[23]

The presupposition the author would like to abolish thus makes its appearance once again. From this passage, in fact, one gathers that for the writer there does indeed exist a degree zero, namely, that in which the penis is given as "significant in itself," and that the reality of female castration is indeed registered, fetishism being the rhetorical operation that comes into view precisely against this background.

This position, however, is not in direct contradiction with the thesis according to which a registration of events is always also their staging. Let me just add that the "perception" of female castration is not the registration of a fact (even Jean Laplanche and Jean-Bertrand Pontalis say as much in the entry under "Denial" in their *The Language of Psychoanalysis*) and that not even the penis is significant in and of itself, its phallic effects being themselves the effect of a staging.[24] But then fetishism risks becoming almost irrelevant, a process among many others one may adopt in the process of constitution of sexual identity. There are those who give the penis importance, others give it to the nose, a shoe, hair, butterflies, and one thing is as good as another [*una cosa vale l'altra*]. I don't see any theoretical objections to drawing such a conclusion, but I see clearly that as a matter of fact this conclusion hasn't been drawn. Having a penis is not the same thing as having a nose or having hair. The penis is, if not the only, certainly the most important signifier of sexual difference *and* it has a highly valued meaning [*significato*]. One has to take this into account, whether one likes it or not.

But back to rhetoric. Rhetoric presupposes a "normal" speech against whose background a more elaborate rhetorical expression would stand out. The arguments in favor of this postulate are weak, those against strong. Even scholars of rhetoric recognize this. They warn, as we do, that to judge something on the basis of a norm or normality is to capsize the actual procedure that allows us to establish norms or to define normality according to what we may feel is strange or dangerous, for reasons that are often difficult to examine but that certainly precede the fixing of a norm.

If that postulate, weakly supported by arguments, continues to persist, there must be some hidden reason on its side, the same one that leads a scholar who theorizes about a general staging to think that, at the very least, not all stagings are on the same level. To idolize women's underwear, as those who hence are called fetishists do or did, is a stranger staging than that which leads an individual with male anatomy to assume a virile identity.

I had been reflecting for several days on this enigma of the degree zero, so much so that one night I dreamt I had resolved it: degree zero is nothing other than reality. Upon awakening I reexamined the "solution" and found it bizarre. Not in and of itself, since in fact there is an allusion to it even in *Rhétorique générale*, where at one point it is stated that language's degree zero is outside language, is a limit concept,[25] statements I had interpreted more or less as follows: if it existed, the degree zero would be things that signify themselves, reality that speaks for itself, that is, a speech that coincides exactly, for each individual, with that which is and which is experimented in the act of speaking itself. But it was strange that I had dreamt this, because this was, and remains, the position that I criticized, since it leads to an essentially metaphoric conception of language and, in particular, of rhetorically elaborated language: namely, a conception of language as that which substitutes itself for things or for the auto-signification of things. My preferences if anything went toward the position, maintained by Todorov, which argued that the degree zero was represented by self-sufficient language, a perfectly transparent speech that refers without ambiguities to what one intends to say—rhetorical speech constituting, by contrast, an opaque speech, which evokes the material density of language and therefore the presence of things.[26] But I remained uncertain. After the dream I found the enigma's solution, but outside the dilemma constituted by what were for me those two opposite solutions.

The degree zero does exist—this would be the solution—the rhetoricians are right to postulate it, even if then they don't manage to define it.

It is represented by the point of equilibrium or compromise that can establish itself—in symbolic production—between the metonymic and metaphoric directrices. The solution I had dreamt of was not wrong. When we say "these are the facts, this is reality, this is how things are," we appeal in effect to what we think is the case according to a representation that perhaps a dispassionate analysis would show is loaded with prejudices, presuppositions, etc., but which imposes itself on us as an insurmountable observation. Where does the constraining force of certain observations—a force that common sense tells us comes from facts, from reality—come from, when we inevitably find out (by way of reflection following a change) that reality and facts at best could account for part of our conviction? In other words, to stay in the realm of linguistics, what does the rhetorical expression that strikes us for its peculiarity diverge from? There is only one possible response: from that level where the metonymical procedure is welded with the metaphorical one. Even though this level is never definitely established, when it does constitute itself, things appear to signify themselves in an imperative manner that seems to prescribe the exact linguistic expression, from which one may diverge only due to ignorance or license. Degree zero would be that manner of signifying that neither exceeds nor reduces the movement that makes us pass from thing to thing, from sign to sign, from thing to sign to thing, a manner of signifying that is completely dependent on the reciprocal solidarity of syntagmatic proximities and paradigmatic choices. It would result in a text with a perfectly balanced strategy, whose syntactical elements don't jar with the overall meaning [*significato*]. "Rhetorical" would then indicate that form of speech that, due to either ignorance or license, does not remain within the circle that constrains things and words in a correspondence as fictitious as it is convincing, the correspondence we always believe we discern when metonymical and metaphorical resources are mutually supportive.

According to some scholars, scientific language would be a good approximation of language that is not rhetorically elaborated. One could counter this statement by saying that scientific language, at least in some of its decisive passages, performs some operations that are of an exquisitely rhetorical nature.[27] One can understand, however, how it might appear close to a degree zero if one considers that in scientific research metonymic and metaphorical procedures are articulated in a manner that is both elastic and stable, much more than in other signifying practices where ignorance and license reign unchecked. Centuries of discussions on induction and deduction to understand in the end that science is not confronted by such an alternative. I say it doesn't need such an alternative because the passage from the universal to the particular and vice versa is a practical operation that can be performed in all sorts of different ways, each and every time it is possible as well as needed. And it is possible as soon as one manages to invent a meaning [*significato*] capable of expressing and arranging the global sense of an exploratory movement, it doesn't matter of what kind or how extensive. Botanists work on large and detailed collections, Galileo concentrated on a few mental experiments, Freud fought with his and his patients' ghosts. Obviously, the sciences are not all the same, not even from this standpoint. A stable articulation of metaphoric and metonymic directrices exists above all in those sciences equipped with labs. The lab is the place that leads to metonymical explorations and that disciplines them in the form of the experiment, with selections and samples that are fundamental for the productivity of scientific discourse.

There is no language to say how things are, but there certainly are arrangements of the social-symbolic order for the staging of normality. When one has found the way, more or less felicitously, to make the exploratory tour one is capable of undertaking coincide with the words one is willing and able to use (or, vice versa, the tour one is willing and able to undertake with the words one is capable of using), it is then that things impose themselves on an objective registration, namely, that of the degree zero. At this point the rhetorical nature intrinsic to language becomes almost invisible: what stands out are only those rhetorical figures about which something is no longer apparent—either what relation they might have with the constitutive processes of language or whatever destabilizing [*squilibrante*] opposition might occur between them.

But one can also theorize and practice the rhetoricity intrinsic to language without surrendering to this destabilizing opposition. It is not clear if this is Accame's intention. But it is certainly Lacan's.

The Passion of the Signifier According to Lacan

As it was the case with the authors of *Rhétorique générale*, Lacan too repeatedly acknowledges Jakobson. There may well be reciprocal debt between the two, though I have not been interested in establishing that; due to reasons of presentation, I have decided to speak as if Lacan had followed Jakobson in his reasoning. What I am interested in showing is how Jakobson's theory of the bipolar structure of symbolic processes differs from Lacan's theory of metaphor and metonymy, the many points in common notwithstanding. I also wish to show that the first—assimilated by many to the second—is superior to it with respect to the analysis of signifying production seen as a historical reality whose modalities are not entirely dictated by its structural laws.

Lacan, and then many who followed him, identified metaphor and metonymy with the dream mechanisms that Freud called as condensation and displacement, respectively: a complete identity, exception made for the dream staging, which, as Freud teaches us, requires that thoughts be translated into images.[28] Once this correspondence has been established, the two processes, the metaphoric and the metonymic, are indeed shown to be clearly distinct, but one does not see opposition, not to speak of rivalry, between them. In dream work, in fact, condensation and displacement operate jointly in a relation of peaceful collaboration.

Jakobson also took an interest in *The Interpretation of Dreams*, though he reached a different conclusion. According to him both condensation and displacement operate on the metonymic directrix, while what is found on metaphorical one are identification and symbolism.[29] Here the competition between rivals, at least for symbolism on the one hand, and condensation and displacement on the other, is clear, although it was not systematically investigated by Freud. As it is well known, this theme will be part of the contrast between him and [C. G.] Jung, who derived the concept of the collective unconscious from dream symbolism. For Freud, dream work and the corresponding analytical work have to do with condensation and displacement, even though he does not deny the presence of symbols in dreams or the possibility of deciphering them. Following Jakobson's suggestions, one might perhaps look at psychoanalysis as a type of knowledge that developed by privileging the many specific paths of signifying production along the metonymic directrix, in opposition to the synthetic-theoretical-representational procedures of the metaphorical directrix. It is certainly not happenstance that its presentation(s) are in the form of stories and not treatises as in the case of other sciences.

To whoever asked him about his disagreement with Lacan, Jakobson would answer that it is explained by the fact that the concept of condensation in Freud is very imprecise, sometimes including some cases of metaphor, other times of synecdoche. Jean-François Lyotard, relating this answer, protests that one has no right to attribute to Freud a lack of precision that is such only for those who want to undertake a theoretical operation that Freud's text, says Lyotard, doesn't allow.[30]

In this context one should note that Freud, even if he didn't know Saussure, was aware however of the opposition established by James Frazer in *The Golden Bough* between "similarity" and "contiguity," an opposition that for Jakobson is analogous to that between metaphorical and metonymic poles. He refers to it at length in *Totem and Taboo*, writing among other things that ". . . similarity and contiguity are the two essential principles of the processes of association of ideas."[31] We would however search in vain for an analogy between these two principles and the procedures that he himself emphasized in relation to dreams. Which proves, if nothing else, that Freud was distant from Jakobson's as well as Lacan's later elaborations.

We do agree, hence, that Freud's text isn't that relevant to the disagreement between Jakobson and Lacan; the theoretical operation these two undertake, however, doesn't lose any legitimacy because of this, as Lyotard would have it, or, in any case, the arguments Lyotard resorts to—based as they are on distinctions between linguistics and rhetoric, as well as between linguistics and semiotics—don't detract from that legitimacy. When Jakobson establishes the metaphor-paradigm and metonymy-syntagm equivalences, we are not confronting an uncalled-for confusion between linguistics and rhetoric; we are confronting, rather, an affirmation of the intrinsic and constitutive rhetorical nature of language: there is no chasm between the most elementary processes of symbolic elaboration and the most daring symbolic inventions, such as in poetry and art generally.

It cannot be argued that either Jakobson or Lacan stick to Freud's text, but this is a fact that, due to its obviousness, I believe is less relevant than why and how Lacan is not a faithful reader of Jakobson. In the Lacanian version, the relation between metaphor and metonymy is not that polemically tense relation we find in Jakobson. Metaphor and metonymy are not even equal, since for Lacan there cannot exist a symbolic production characterized by the prevalence of the metonymic pole.

Here, it is necessary to add a clarification. Everyone knows of all the big talk about the signifier in Lacanian discourse. This is not without reason or consequences. The distinction between signifier (S) and signified (s) was introduced by Saussure to designate the phonic-acoustic (or graphic-visual) reality and the ontological-logical-psychological reality that meet and are structured in language according to differing structures, and hence without ever being fused together. Now, in linguistics it is the case that one deals with the signifier keeping its autonomy clearly in mind only if the specific object one is investigating is not the sign in its unity (signifier plus signified) and in its functionality (that is, the sign as a means of expression and communication). For a linguist a slip of the tongue is not a relevant fact, it's an accident whose examination can be left to the psychologist. Lacan, by contrast, is always aware of the arbitrariness of the relation between signifier and signified; that which language realizes—namely, their unity in the sign—is for him a precarious effect.[32] A slip of the tongue, hence, constitutes a linguistic fact as much as, say, the vowel system, because the autonomy of the order of the signifier is recognizable in both. One knows why Lacan prefers not to lose sight of the precariousness of the bond between signifier and signified: the fact that they are on two different levels as well as their unstable correspondence are for him Freud's essential discovery, which Freud did not express in these terms only because Saussure had not yet entered the scene.[33] Accordingly, he treats metaphor and metonymy as procedures that operate in the sphere of the signifier. He therefore states that metonymy operates on the connection between one signifier and another, while metaphor constitutes the substitution of one signifier with another. This is what makes his treatment different from the one we find in manuals of rhetoric or in Jakobson himself; and this is also what makes a comparison difficult, because the linguist does not deny the autonomy of the signifier. The linguist, rather, simply ceases to be concerned with it once dealing with entities for which language has realized the unity of the sign. In the case in question, the linguist explains what metaphor and metonymy are by means of the interplay of the spheres of the signifier and the signified, which are present simultaneously. This is also what I did above, without, for that, taking a position in favor of one or the other procedure. It was a question of convenience. (Spontaneously I sympathize with Lacan's "linguisterie"—the expression is his—which manages to hop over the separate competences established in the human sciences, without passing through the so-called interdisciplinary approach.)

I have drawn your attention to the discrepancy in the procedures because this is the only way one can understand the difference between Jakobson and Lacan. In the latter's texts one comes across statements that may lead one to think that there is a basic agreement. One reads repeatedly of "effects that are determined by the double play of combination and substitution in the signifier, according to the two axes for generating the signified, metonymy and metaphor."[34] But if we proceed to consider metaphor and metonymy separately, one immediately discovers that the *generation of meaning* [*significato*] is really the work of metaphor: "We see that metaphor is situated at the precise point at which meaning is produced in nonmeaning," or, "the synchronic structure is more hidden, and it is this structure that brings us to the beginning. It is metaphor insofar as the first attribution is constituted in it," etc., ". . . it is in the substitution of signifier for signifier [that is, in metaphor] that a signification effect is produced that is poetic or creative, in other words, that brings the signification in question into existence."[35]

In what is called the "passion of the signifier"—that is, of the signifiable that is subjected to the mark of the signifier, thus becoming the signified—the determining and inaugural function is metaphor's because it is only via metaphor that the bar separating S and s may be overcome and that something may be signified. The symptom is a metaphor.[36] To speak is, originally, to metaphorize. No production of meaning can occur along the metonymic directrix, because metonymy operates between signifiers without overcoming the bar, in a game of references that may either never end or become "perversely" blocked on the fetish, were it not for metaphor's intervention. Desire is a metonymy.[37]

This is where the divergence from Jakobson lies: for Jakobson, in fact, there is no hierarchical relation of importance between the two directrices when it comes to the generation of meaning [*significato*]. For Jakobson, even a language that avails itself only of a metonymical resource may exist: it may be an imperfect, laborious language—but language theorized as originating from the metaphoric principle would be no less laborious and imperfect, albeit differently so, if it didn't have the metonymical resource at its disposal.

Lacan doesn't deny that the latter is necessary to the symbolic process, but he states that its contribution is subordinated to the decisive intervention of the metaphorical operation. On its own the metonymic procedure would be a senseless wandering, a slippage either erratic or fixed, an enjoyment either frantic or blocked. In order for desire—which is a metonymy—to speak significantly, it is necessary for the metaphorical operation, by substituting an impossible literalness with the appropriate signifier, to tie the sequence of signifiers to an eminent *signified* (the "*signification*" of the phallus) and in this manner to the possibility of signifying as such.

> I have deliberately translated the French "*signification*" with "signified," avoiding the technical term "signification." There is an insoluble problem of translation here. Outside the technical language of linguistics "*signification*" is translated with "signified" and vice versa. In French, the technical term is "*signifié*." To say "the signification of the phallus" removes much of the original's meaning. In order for a term in the common language to lose its old meaning in favor of the specialized use (as for instance with the concept of "force" in physics), it is necessary for a separate specialized discourse to have been constituted and this is not yet the case with psychoanalysis whose language has developed and remains in a situation of osmosis with the common language.
>
> It is to be understood that "the *signification*/signified of the phallus" does not comprehend the abstract "*signifié*/signified" which is opposed to the signifier within the sign's unity. Hence the meaning [*significato*] of the phallus as active signifying. Moreover, this is true generally: what is the meaning of fear? That which the signifier "fear" signifies actively, that which it makes emerge from the limbo of the signifiable. But what does the phallus signify? It signifies active signifying; this is the reason it is also called the signifier of signifiers.

Only on this condition, which in psychoanalysis is equivalent to having symbolized castration, may the metonymic procedure exercise its proper function, already attributed by Freud to displacement, namely, circumventing censorship. The implication is that it also has a "more dignified function," that is, preparing the conditions for the decisive intervention of the metaphoric substitution within the discontinuity of the signifying matter.[38]

What Lacan says about metaphor and metonymy undoubtedly gives Jakobson's theory a radical quality it did not possess in its original version. As François Wahl has written: "It is one thing to find a principle for the organization of discourse in metaphor, to found it as one of the two functional poles of language, and to find it again in the processes of condensation of myth and dream; quite another to read, beneath the substitution of signifiers that constitutes metaphor's substance, a transport, a metaphor of *the subject*: thus recognizing the place of a subject (of the signifier, in other words of the unconscious) which is excentric with respect to that which, in this case the conscious Ego, claims to speak."[39] The subversive effect clearly depends on the procedure followed by Lacan, namely to consider the signified as something secondary as compared with the order of the signifier, even when they appear pacified in semantic unity.

It is thanks to the radical nature of this discourse that, among other things, the precise ties that connect symbolic production and patriarchal regime have come to light. Lacan shows how, before being regulated by society, relations between the two sexes are regulated by the symbolic order. Facts such as giving sons their father's name or female prostitution at masculine request, the banality of female frigidity as contrasted to the drama, tolerated with difficulty, of masculine impotence, man's easy betrayals, women's exterior faithfulness, their sentimental fixation, their incessant effort to appear beautiful, etc., are tied to determinations of the symbolic order.

But of a symbolic order that Lacan conceptualizes as necessary and unmodifiable, abiding by a single principle, that of metaphorization, which has no alternatives save mental illness. It has no alternatives but it requires certain conditions in order to function. We know, however, that the metaphoric principle is the one theories gladly recognize as being the one at work because it conforms to them more closely. And because, we add, it continuously gives them new reasons to grow in the task, by definition interminable, of overcoming the gap between themselves and the other-than-themselves. Within this other we must however suppose, following Jakobson, that there is also symbolic work of the metonymic type. Along the metaphorical directrix, discourse may develop toward its goal, which seems to be that of substituting the world with words—and thus silencing it—all the while, obviously, being comforted by the aristocratic certainty that there shall always be those who apply themselves to the obscure task of gluing things to words.

From Lacan one may glean that it is especially woman who is destined to do this job. Woman, in fact, does something strange: she makes a signifier correspond to a signified without passing through the appropriate metaphorical substitution, that is, without having symbolized castration. And not any old signifier/signified: woman turns her own body into an equivalent of the phallus for men, and she finds the signifier for her desire in the body of the man she loves, attributing the phallus to him. All work of the imagination, in the strict Lacanian sense. According to the rules of the symbolic order, we are dealing with a perversion, fetishism. The "defect of symbolic metaphor" led Judge Schreber to desire being a woman.[40] Crazy. . . Being a woman would be a little bit like being able to symbolize along the metonymic directrix. A man loses his mind there where a woman, instead, succeeds.

It is necessary that she succeed because the relation between the penis and the phallus, between the thing and the word, has to be established in some way or other; otherwise, what is psychoanalysis talking about, real men and women or theoretical entities? That women be what they are is a "logical exigency," says Lacan.[41] It is also a social exigency, because it is precisely the anomalous symbolization of which they are capable that makes it so "that, whether they like it or not, women in reality [réel] serve as objects for exchanges ordained by the elementary structures of kinship . . . while what is simultaneously transmitted in the symbolic order is the phallus."[42]

In Reason's Orphanage

Paradoxically, in the end it is precisely Lacan's discourse that forces us to think that between symbolic and social orders there is an opaque complicity: material servitudes that become logical exigencies and, vice versa, conditions of symbolic production that translate into social impositions.

Without a doubt, this is too happy of a coincidence—and it is difficult to understand whether it is entirely the effect of an extraordinary theoretical achievement or whether there is not also some manipulation. Lacan's disciples see the achievement; his critics look for the trick. I don't believe it is exactly either one or the other. When Lacan theorizes that everything is caught up in language's machinations—social institutions and individual behaviors, from sexual relations to the most fragile emotions, both in their normal and deviant development—it is almost no longer necessary for him to be correct in what he says because by means of his discourse he makes true what is occurring in any case.

From Freud to Lacan, and without excluding intermediate developments, psychoanalysis has stayed very close, as perhaps no other movement or school of thought, to the process of disintegration of the social body into a sum of individuals and to its reintegration through the pressure of words and images.

Some think that the fragmentation of society into individual atoms depends on the capitalist mode of production that entails a socialization based on the exchange of commodities and not on labor. This thesis was developed by Alfred Sohn-Rethel in *Intellectual and Manual Labor: A Critique of Epistemology*, where among other things one reads:

> As it assumes representation as the *ego cogito* of Descartes or of the 'subject of cognition' of philosophical epistemology the false consciousness of intellectual labour reaches its culmination: the formation of thinking which in every respect merits the term 'social' presents itself as the diametrical opposite to society, the EGO of which there cannot be another. Kant has the appropriate formula for this contradiction: "There is no ground in theoretical reason from which to infer to the existence of another being." Nothing could be wrapped in greater secrecy than the truth that the independence of the intellect is owed to its originally social character.[43]

So, already since the eighteenth century, it was clear to one philosopher, Immanuel Kant, that the existence of another being, mother and father included, was only a matter of faith (hence, perhaps, the religion of the family?). As is well known, in modern philosophy the problem of intersubjectivity will continue to return tormentedly, together with that of natural causality—which Kant thought had been solved. Ultimately in modern thought there is no way to affirm that between two things, two bodies, or two facts there exists some material relationship, except for those who have some kind of faith. This blind alley of modern rationality finds its most concise sanction in one of the initial propositions of Ludwig Wittgenstein's *Tractatus*, 1.21: "Any one can either be the case or not be the case, and everything else remain the same."[44]

So then, if we cannot say we have been generated by a woman and by a man, if the things we buy and use cannot prove the existence of those who produced them, if contact between bodies has no recognizable efficacy, what allows us to tell what makes us what we are? Simple, Lacan says so: the symbolic order.

Common sense revolts when faced with such a conclusion, but then it is precisely people with much common sense who offer its most glaring illustrations. In effect, physical generation, relations between bodies, natural causality, as they are imagined by common sense are mostly defensive fantasies gathered from the collective imaginary: words that try to fill the empty interval between bodies, things, facts, words in which there is nothing or little more than nothing of an implied materiality that autonomously is capable of producing knowledge.

In a society whose materialization is destroying the contents of social exchange, the polemical dispute between the two principles of symbolic production seems destined to be resolved with the prevailing of the metaphoric principle and the subsequent closure of language into a totality that is fundamentally without history, as presented to us in Lacan.

It is certainly true that Freud invented a language and a place, the analytical scene, where it is possible to know that the one who speaks, in addition to having a body, is a body, generated by a man and a woman, with an identifiable biography and a non-transcendable sexual specificity. Psychoanalysis therefore has established relationships between some individuals and some facts that is not simply the aggregate of one plus one, and it has given a body and a sex to the discourse about the rational subject. And it has, needless to say, shaken things up. Not sufficiently, however, to change either the mode of socialization or that of symbolic production. Rather than attributing this to an intrinsic lack or insufficiency of psychoanalysis, one should think perhaps of a complex configuration of circumstances, such as, for instance, the belated recognition of psychoanalytic materialism. Be that as it may, what has resulted from psychoanalysis, rather than the foretold subversion, has been a further contribution to the collective imaginary, circulating in the social body, operating for its symbolic reintegration.

Lacan wanted to remove psychoanalysis from its subordinate function as purveyor of illusions and imaginations so as to make it the theory of the inevitable dematerialization of relations between human beings and between humans and nature. It is clear that this is an outcome that in certain respects is far from if not the opposite of what Freud had in mind. One must add however that Lacan reached it via only a few transitions. As he himself has stated, he did no more than translate the Freudian discovery of the unconscious into the concepts of structural linguistics, an operation that is difficult to criticize in and of itself since it boils down to the elimination from Freud's discourse of the naturalist presupposition of a materiality operating according to laws that are independent of the symbolic order. The trick, if one wants to put it that way, consists in the fact that, together with dogmatic naturalism, one also lost sight of a material production that in our society takes place without knowledge.

Could the naturalist presupposition have been overcome with a different outcome? Probably so; but this—once again—depended and depends on circumstances that theoretical thought does not control or own. The insignificance of material relationships, the docile response of bodies to the interpretive word, the phantasmatic mobilization, these are not Lacan's inventions. They are, practically speaking, commonplaces of everyday life.

A BODY HERE, A BODY THERE

The Need to Have a Soul

It is difficult to undertake an exploration of symbolic space in terms of Jakobson's theory because, when it comes to symbolic production, we are in a regime that we could call of *hypermetaphoricity*—a regime in which the metaphoric pole prevails and has ensured and established the exploitation of metonymic resources. The characteristic of the hypermetaphoricity regime is that things, facts, bodies, specific experiences are caught up in a system of ideal relations that define and interpret them as well as rule their combinations, while in the opposite direction, when it would be the turn of things, bodies, and specific experiences to cut across the expansion of the metaphorical, we see that if this occurs (and it cannot not occur, since, at least in our culture, general meaning [*significato*] wants to encounter a specific datum somewhere), it occurs in well-defined and highly controlled conditions.

As a result, Jakobson's thesis needs to be modified. If theoretical relection prefers to highlight the importance of the metaphorical directrix, this is due to a disparity that is already present in symbolic production thanks to which the rival tension between metaphoric pole and metonymic pole is partially converted into a subordination of the second to the first.

The most evident aspect of subordination consists in the fact that bodies, things, signs, are prescribed the manner in which they may arrange and combine themselves, the consequence otherwise being disorder, misery, chaos, folly, etc.

One should not overvalue the power of this imposition. Just for starters, it's not true that if one moves out of place one fatally ends up in chaos, those who experience it know this—although it is true that their experience is submerged by an avalanche of discourses and mental associations of an opposite sign. On the other hand, the devices that regulate the social text have gaps: it's not true—and ultimately we know this—that in order to live one needs to produce, reproduce, educate oneself, talk, love, enjoy oneself in the prescribed manners.

All this notwithstanding, things proceed as if there was a rigid regulation. Those who experiment with significant combinations that don't conform to the dominant meanings [*significati*] seem to be few and are instead perhaps many, but their experience is not as contagious as one could expect—*diffusion by contagion* would be the mode of communication that best corresponds to symbolic production of a metonymic type, based on contiguity and on specific concatenations. At most it may occur that this type of diffusion is used to extract some meanings [*significati*], arguments, or images, which then will be put into circulation in the usual fashion. To most people it doesn't even occur to disassemble the social text and to recombine it according to their needs and specific form of knowledge. The political practices that have fought the impositions of the so-called social order discovered long ago that attempts at subversion from below easily give rise, in those directly concerned, to a sort of fear emanating from an internal origin. The fear of being out of place, in a pure state.

The fear of subversion exists also with respect to language. When I taught in schools at the compulsory level on the outskirts of Milan—in a modern neighborhood whose physical and human infrastructure was defended against the threat of an always menacing degradation by its proletarian families, fighting right and perhaps even more left—I was afflicted with the essays of students who were extremely faithful to commonplaces of every type. After having attempted, in vain, to have them take the measure of the high linguistic competence that should have been theirs, I had the idea of shaking them up with the dismeasure of poetic license, that of the avant-garde poets. And it worked, but only after they had seen *printed* poems with their own eyes. Obviously the authority of print was needed to counterbalance that associated with their stylistic norms, which, in addition to being cast in iron, were so detailed as to lead to meadows not being able to be anything but green and life anything but beautiful.

I must add that, in the midst of my efforts to dissociate the word "green" from the word "meadow" or other things of this sort, and to the extent to which I succeeded in doing so, I felt a certain unease. It was almost like a feeling that by doing this I was killing a soul—a stereotyped archaic soul, which for them was the figure of culture—and that, once this soul had fallen, others did not rise to prevent the walls of our classroom from stepping into the sad foreground, together with the high-rises of their neighborhood, quite visible through the enormous windows—modern schools have enormous windows. That neighborhood, always on the edge between dignity and degradation, which feared the initiatives of innovative teachers almost as much as it feared the vandalism perpetrated by thugs, has remained in my mind as the dead end of a blind alley, a cul-de-sac (in my village there was a small blind alley we called *Cul de saco*).

In some instances my unease was very strong. Years before working in the "cul-de-sac," I had taught in a school in the beltway around Milan, and one day one of my most beloved pupils—she had all the qualities: intelligent, workers' daughter, noncompetitive, sensitive, practical, and a bit rough—handed in a text for the class newspaper, which that week compared peasant labor and workers' labor. She was crying because in her contribution she had revealed that her mother, who worked in a factory that produced aluminum pots and pans, had to ask permission to go to the bathroom, with only a few minutes being allowed. She, her daughter, had wanted to respond to my insistence on a writing that was rooted in the concreteness of one's knowledge and she couldn't have done better, but she was deeply humiliated by it.

If the social order manages to obtain a consensus that is not directly proportional to the interests it protects, I think that in some measure the incapacity to invent autonomously the meaning of one's existence is involved. This meaning is received from outside. It can be obtained, for instance, by conforming to some models. The tiny spaces that were assigned to each family in the peripheral neighborhood I was discussing earlier were designed, like all modern lower-class housing, according to the image of large apartments, with ugly and uncomfortable results. And yet I am convinced that the builders correctly interpreted one of the residents' needs in this manner. The need to have a soul. The same can be said of small lower-class detached houses: there is a flood of them also around and inside my old village, one unlike the other and all made equally ugly by the effort to stand out, perhaps modeled on the appearance patrician families once gave to their palaces.

This is another aspect of the hypermetaphoricity regime: the lack (which for some things like cities and houses seems relatively recent) of a material capacity for combination, that is, the lack of capacity to combine the materials one actually has at one's disposal—including time, body, and space—into significant figures.

A Broken Spring

Things that don't contact one another, don't frequent one another, don't know about each other, are at risk of getting lost in a senseless heap. As a result one needs to metaphorize, to move from a blind and inert literalness to a plane where things are representable, where they can be placed in significant relations, organized, explained, interpreted, communicated. Thence the projects, the programs, the schools, the theories, the televisions, the fashions, and all the other devices to remake the world into words and images.

Let me repeat that, in my opinion, all this immense translation is less necessary than it is claimed to be. It does have, however, the characteristic of becoming gradually increasingly necessary because in the course of its movement it continues to consume live matter in the form of specific experiences and competences, thus accentuating the need to refer to some meanings [*significati*] that have already been constituted or to places deputized to the institutionalization of such meanings [*significati*]. Those who are caught up in the movement of metaphoricization end up living vicariously. Once upon a time, one wrote books to transmit knowledges or fantasies that readers in their situation were presumed not to have; now, the purpose of mass media is above all to tell us who we are, what we feel, what we want, and what we need.

One must add that the great device of metaphoric transposition gives everything back and even something more, sooner or later. It gives back further knowledge, self-awareness, new reasons to want, wider horizons for desire. And yet something is lacking, something does not come back. By now we are all aware that there is some loss in the passage from lived experience to its recomposition as mediated by cultural elaboration, regardless of how complete such a recomposition may be or how certain the relative gains may appear to us. To point to what is lacking I will avail myself again of what I was recounting earlier, namely the story of the humiliated girl.

I hope I didn't tell her there was nothing to be ashamed of, because there was something to be ashamed of, for her, for me, and for others. If anything one could defuse the situation by considering that, sooner or later, the workers' movement would successfully fight also for the recognition of someone's right to satisfy their needs without unnatural controls. Perhaps I actually did tell her something like that. But what is such a statement worth? Between the peasant, whose forms of servitude, as serious as they were, never included an externally imposed discipline on physiological functions, and the worker who has the right to go and stay on the toilet ad libitum (as much as she may want or care), there is a transition, that impersonated by my pupil's mother. Within this transition, an intolerable discipline was tolerated. After which, so that one may experience it as intolerable once again, it is necessary to argue and transform a bodily practice—with everything one might include in it, both general and particular, natural and artificial—into a generic right. The posthumous recognition of a right restores but doesn't reintegrate the body with its impulses, its pleasures, its peculiarities, its contingencies. (Without considering those cases in which the law does not remove a servitude but simply regulates it, as in the case of abortion for women.) In the course of that transition the body has ceased to speak for itself.

This is what is lost in the interval between a lived experience and its subsequent representation.

It seems, after all, that this is the path taken by the civilizing process in the relations between human beings and between them and nature: from savagery to servitude to emancipation to inalienable rights. Where, with each step, the bond between pleasure and knowledge, will and reason, and bodies and words is loosened irreversibly. Becoming aware of one's needs and desires is quite different from acting under their impulse, just as fighting for one's rights is quite different from rebelling with body and soul against intolerable impositions.

To which one could reply that without a certain distance and awareness, however, we would be captive of a blind agitation or that the revolt of the oppressed would fatally end in disaster. The objection is valid but only insofar as one denies, both theoretically and practically, any symbolic productivity to matter. Moreover, those who are very productive within the symbolic, thinkers and artists, know or should know that their performance would not be possible without a deep implication of the body, of desires, of biographical circumstances, in the movement of thought. An elaboration of the type that brings one from savagery to the affirmation of inalienable rights would make them into nothing more than banal imitators. If they are not, it means they have found the way of activating, in a civil manner, the symbolic productivity of matter. It seems that this way is not generalizable, for reasons that I believe are internal to the hypermetaphoricity regime, as I will try to explain further on.

I began to suspect there may be an unclear complicity between the social and symbolic orders when I was a schoolteacher with individuals, both children and adults, from subaltern classes. Ultimately, my greatest task was to prevent that social subjection (theirs but also mine) would be translated into an obstacle to the free movement of thought. And this is where I realized that, although I had no subversive intentions but only the honest goal of transforming the given situation—the one in which we, made of flesh and blood, found ourselves—into the beginning of an understanding of oneself and the world, well then, that is where I found that almost every step in the desired direction entailed a shock to the system of relations in which we were caught. There were moments in which it would have been necessary to put our hands on the social pact—by which I mean that tacit agreement that establishes the boundary between what is civilized and what isn't. For instance, it isn't civilized to take a piss among the machines of the factory section one works in, whereas going on strike, even a wildcat strike, is (the term "wildcat," however, signals that we are approaching the boundary here... so to speak). Moreover, in "advanced" societies the truly wild disruptions of the social pact are not rare. I think about the looting in the darkness of a blackout, brutalities and homicides without an apparent motive, and things of this sort. I could also add the incessant work of destruction that my "cul-de-sac" students subjected the school building and supplies to without being able to give a reason, destroying and regretting the destruction with the same monotony. A senseless production, separated from their symbolic production, which, as I said earlier, was distinctly conformist.

When looking at such events, I don't think about regression; I seem to perceive, rather, the wild body that our regime of civilization goes on building by its own side. Its protagonists are usually those individuals one calls mediocre, when one doesn't prefer to consider them crazy. For this reason one talks about exhibitionism, a simplifying label. Many cases aren't covered by it, and, in any case, one still has to explain why, due to the need to see one's existence recognized, one is driven to massacre ten people, shoot from the top of a skyscraper, jump out of a window, smash furniture, and similar actions. Ultimately, all those are mediocre—and they, or better, we are the majority—for whom no civilized forms to signify themselves, and to speak mobilizing their materiality, like body, drives, desires, and daily occupations, are provided; mediocre are those who cannot benefit from others' symbolic services like flattering attributions, valorizing imaginations, dependency. To sum up, those who in the civilizing process as it functions today risk losing not only their body but also an irreplaceable resource for any autonomous knowing and wanting. (I have written "resource" instead of "spring" [*molla*], which had come to me in a previous version. What I had in mind, actually, was "*susta*," a dialect word which corresponds to spring but whose etymology is almost opposite, since *molla* comes from *mollare, allentare* [to let go, to loosen], whereas *susta* comes from the Latin *suscitare*, to put in motion, to excite.)

The Unfaithful Narratrix

At this point someone will come and tell me I am fantasizing, as if things, bodies, and facts could be virgins, whereas they are always already marked by culture and hence cannot be opposed to its schemes. What does it mean to say that bodies could, should cut across the expansion of the metaphorical? Where are the bodies, the pleasures, where is the nature extraneous to the symbolic order?

I immediately recognize that my discourse has several characteristics of hypermetaphorical language, indeed of one that is uncritically hypermetaphoric; I am in fact neglecting its more recent and more sophisticated versions. I can do this because, by means of a rather conventional language, I am attempting to *indicate*. I indicate some things, and those who find them on their horizon understand me. Does this mean that I exclude others and offend language in its most human function? No, others will understand, only a little less. In any case, this is what always happens, people always speak themselves in addition to that which they speak about, that which they have in common, sex, money, food, culture, interests (exception made, as I will add later, for imitators). The "signifiable" is not an indeterminate limbo; in it we already find the detailed reality of our existence.

I have put forth Jakobson's theory once again because I believe it allows to take a step forward compared to the discourse that says: there is no immediate original experience, and hence it makes no sense to appeal to bodies, things, life as original instances that can be found beyond historically determined reality. This is absolutely correct so long as it is a question of refuting the procedures of a scientific rationality that entitled itself to suprahistorical truth by postulating the original character of experience. It is a little less so when this critique targets those who appeal to a reality that is not translatable into words because they find their own speech to be a mutilating translation.

There may be a constraint in the symbolic order such that we account only imperfectly for something in it, and there may be constraints in the social order such that some find themselves mutilated of that which the symbolic order doesn't account for. Jakobson's theory says that symbolic production (which obviously signifies all that is signifiable) is determined historically. The symbolic therefore leaves its mark on social reality since it is implicated in it. I will add that its nonsignifiable partiality remains unexpressed, but it exists and has effects. It leaves its mark on that which participates in the symbolic process without being able to signify in it. Alterity, extraneousness with respect to the symbolic order, is given by everything that is left without appropriate words by its constraints and that in the attempt to express itself comes up against its devices or falls into the void.

That there is something else going on, I believe, is revealed—negatively—by the apartments designed in an uncomfortable fashion, in the ravings of common sense, in the tricks of femininity, and every time the symbolic exercises its scheming power in detail. Because it is there, in its banal everyday triumphs, that one sees how symbolic production proceeds concomitantly with precise impositions of a social nature from which it is difficult to detach it without provoking ruptures of incalculable proportions. That is where one sees that there are many things of the great linguistic game that cannot be put into play.

In the tales that one of my grandmothers occasionally would tell of her life as a girl and as a married woman, here and there would be avoidances, small historical distortions, ad hoc explanations, etc., that made them conventional and a little boring. An intelligent listener, even without knowing the facts, would have easily been able to point out the adjustments that made the narration dull. But she, no, she couldn't. Between the historical truth—I repeat, easily reconstructed with the heuristic devices at our disposal—and her tales there was the barrier of everything because of which she could say of herself: this am I. For her to be able to narrate the simple historical truth, she would have had to pass through her children, the First World War in which two of them had died, the house of her marriage, her poor and submissive fellow villagers, to then shake them and beat them as one does with fruit trees, to achieve restitution . . . of what? For starters, her ability to remember and tell tales. The same, just so we can understand each other, that made Jean-Jacques Rousseau's *Confessions* splendid and Paul the Deacon's *History of the Langobards* important. Truth is not absolute, some will say, not even historical truth. I know that's what people say, but in a case like this the person speaking isn't attempting anything even resembling an approximation or transfiguration, but is instead proceeding in the opposite direction, in the sense of distancing themselves and erasing. By now nothing could bring that grandmother of mine to a site of narration that would be faithful to facts or desires, because the person who could have related events as they occurred, or transfigured them as one wants them remembered, no longer exists, as she has gradually turned into someone who only knows a mediocre convenient version of the same—for a metamorphosis that is part and parcel with the rest of her life. A perfect way of absconding, were it not for the trace of impoverished words. As if the structural division many theorize about, between the subject of the enunciation and the subject of the statement, had here become incarnated in a biography. Or vice versa, as if some circumstances of a historical nature had replaced a process of symbolic elaboration.

I believe it is something along the following lines: the symbolic and the social make their needs coincide mutually supplementing each other, and, in the blind spots where they bond, they determine a sort of impoverishment of symbolic production. A speech that resembles an attempt to guess what one should say, that searches for prefabricated meanings and words that might reproduce them, avoiding unusual associations for fear of giving rise to some irregular meaning [*significato*]: a strange irregularity of mixed nature, monstrous in the eyes of cultivated distinctions since it is inextricably linguistic, social, psychological, and even moral.

Wherever it establishes itself (and maybe it does have to establish itself somewhere so that society may reflect itself in its languages), this confusion erases entire chunks of experience, removes them from the signifiable, determining areas of unsayability in the social text, lacunae of meaning, silences.

Bodies, things, experience, nature, facts, are names of a blind and impracticable literalness under the hypermetaphoricity regime, since language, insofar as it is essentially metaphorizing, splits them into two: one the one side, chaotic matter, a deposit, on the other, meanings [*significati*], society, culture, history. Bodies, things, experience, as they are divided within themselves, have a double relation with language: on the one hand, a deposit of its signifying material, on the other, its representational contents. Therefore, one says, it makes no sense to appeal to bodies, to experience, to things, against culture, as if those were, in and of themselves, opposable to it. It makes no sense because the bodies and everything else either exist all mixed up in the deposit and as such they don't speak, or they exist in symbolic representation (common, scientific, historical, literary languages with their various mixtures) and as such it is culture that speaks.[45]

Before being a way of conceiving the relation between language and the world, whether right or wrong is really not that important, this is the action that the symbolic carries out practically when it is dominated by the metaphoric principle, with its own proper or self-attributed prerogatives. I have arranged them into a list, albeit an incomplete one, based on various treatises on metaphor: its prerogatives include transcending partiality, making certain associations significant (according to some, any and all associations), deciphering and translating, inventing the new, relating entities distant from each other, compensating mutilations, inserting the heterogeneous into communication.

Metaphorizing language, thanks to its prerogatives, promises an integral re-presentation in the form of meanings [*significati*], that is, of what we cannot say we are, have, or know literally, since the only existence we can recognize for ourselves is that of cultural translation, entirely implied in sociohistorical reality.

And this is where, they tell us, we must manage to read or inscribe everything we are or are not, and, possibly, would want to be. Turning backwards or sideways, toward a here that is either nonexistent or unnamable, is an illusion because we cannot be, have, know anything that is not transcribed in the there of symbolic existence. In the past and specifically in our culture, one used, it is true, to talk of things in themselves, absolute givens, natural laws, immediate experiences, but it was a dogmatic presupposition, now recognized and left behind. Therefore let us beware of undertaking, as a polemic against this culture, that which once was done to its advantage. One may still concede that things literally have a consistency of being that is lacking in our existence, but that plenitude is deadly, because living—when living also means to speak—is founded on some lack, the lack of being that is given us by symbolic existence. The symbolic is poorer in terms of being, but richer in terms of existence, etc.

It is useless to continue to expound on the many excellent arguments that have allowed the hypermetaphoricity regime to progress from the dogmatic formulations of the past—when bodies and things were ordered to assume this or that order in the name of presumed natural laws—toward the extreme rigor of which it is certainly capable. These are all very solid arguments, but we don't deem this to be sufficient because, from one progress to another, the promise of integral re-presentation has in itself become, in its turn, an illusion. The prohibition to appeal to something nonsignifiable was valid in conjunction with the promise of integral re-presentation. Without the latter—and by now we've understood we can no longer count on integrally reconstituting what lies in the deposit of confused bodies—without that promise, the prohibition can no longer claim to be valid as a criterion of existence. What is being devastated in terms of pleasure and knowledge is a visible lack. The nonsignifiable of our bodies, of our experiences, of nature, has become an extraneous silence of which it is impossible to say that "it does not exist."

Scholars of semiotics now recognize that society has languages at its disposal, which, even though they are many, do not manage to represent exhaustively all that society in fact is. There is always something that is on the margins or outside the semiotic systems with which society thinks and represents itself. Not in absolute terms, however, the scholars tell us, but relatively to that type of society and culture: a reality that is either misrecognized or excluded from recognition is part of that reservoir of dynamism that determines the modifications of society and its languages.[46]

I find this thesis, to which we owe an interesting view on the historicity of the symbolic and which is undoubtedly supported by many examples, to be in some respects accommodating. I am not convinced by the, how shall I put it, happy and neutral status assigned to that which, in a given society and culture, is rejected into insignificance. I ask myself, and I am thinking above all about women, but not only: how and where is that reservoir of dynamism maintained if in the meantime the social body uses it as matter for various speculations (the expression is borrowed from Luce Irigaray) to make sons, money, wars, empires, theories with it? Leaving it exhausted, deformed, stripped bare. . . . For example, did the peasants who were sent to fight on the fronts of WWI ever become a reservoir of dynamism for Italian society? More than sixty years have already passed, and how long will we have to wait before that blind experience may rupture the dominant languages and speak out? On the other hand, even granting that the reservoir somehow manages to be preserved, we need to ask ourselves whether the specific "nonsignifiable" of a certain society is limited to functioning exclusively as potential for the dynamism of that same society. If I think about our society, it seems to me that its "nonsignifiable" tends rather to become so distant as to be non-utilizable and destructive. In this manner, it joins the wild body that society builds alongside itself, a body or amorphous mass of senseless things and facts where those remains of its civilizing devices that cannot be integrated end up. By now I figure my grandmother is there too, sleeping in auto junkyards during the day, while at night zooming by on roaring motorcycles with the kids of the large, bleak suburbs.

The Division of Labor in Symbolic Production

A silenced world remains without words but not without work. In fact, there remains the job I previously referred to as that of gluing words to things.

Language, as we know, insofar as it proceeds along the metaphorical directrix, eliminates context and concentrates signification in the word. Consequently, the discourse that privileges the metaphorical pole tends to develop until it forms a closed and self-sufficient totality. The problem of its interpretation therefore arises, in the logical sense of the term: of its referring to something, of its having a relation with things.

In the natural sciences, for example, if one only deals with theory—and theoretical concepts are devised with an essentially metaphorical procedure—one cannot know what one is speaking of.[47] We saw that psychoanalysis, in its Lacanian version at least, solves the problem practically with the help of woman. Thanks to its confusion of penis and phallus, the concepts of "man" and "woman" immediately find referents in empirical reality, without the need of resorting to mediating models between theoretical language and empirical reality.

The problem of interpretation does not present itself for language that develops preferentially along the metonymical directrix, because this type of language gives rise to discourses that are markedly contextual, that are combined with things because they are there, in front of the eyes or in the skin of the speakers, or because the verbal expressions evoke their usages, characteristics, and vicissitudes.

Every schoolteacher dealing with children from subaltern classes is familiar with the problem of one of their verbal expressions jammed in the context. Teachers attempt to emancipate the language of these pupils from this form of servitude, and this is a good thing, were it not that their efforts are almost always undertaken ignoring that that manner of speech is like a sort of compulsory symbolic service which deserves all our respect, intellectual included. Children from subaltern classes, due to both age and social position, are great linguistic workers. Wittgenstein, after having written the *Tractatus*, was for six years an elementary school teacher among Austria's peasants.

Specific concrete experience is not present as such in hypermetaphorical discourses. And yet it is included as already interpreted, arranged, deduced, forecast. We are thinking about scientific and medical discourse, about law, public administration, psychology, pedagogy. Nature speaks in laboratories, people are supposed to express their political will in elections and by means of other devices of political representation, events and feelings are transmitted through mass media. Nature, people, events, and feelings "are what they are"; understanding them and signifying them would be the task of science, politics, and mass media.

And in the end the device through which voiceless entities speak appears as that which they need. Nevertheless without them the device would work to no end. But this elementary and ultimately not very mysterious fact—that without patients who suffer, masses who become agitated, interviewees who answer, substances that react, there would be no competent people to tell the truth about humanity, society, nature—we know has never been converted and, indeed, cannot be converted into power for those who emit signs, symptoms, or signals. Power is also an effect of accumulation and co-penetration; in the succession of specific things, added to other specific things, not much is accumulated, and still less is synthesized.

If every theoretical discourse tends to be speech about what it itself has defined, and if in the rounds of this tautological movement one may rest assured that things will be captured and comprehended in it, this is due first of all, as is well known, to the fact that these vacuous discourses gladly derive their weight from an already established power. But also always, to a certain extent, to the fact that a certain matter reacts, responds, involves itself, thus providing a meaning that is no longer internal to the discourse itself.

In the regime of hypermetaphoricity—this is its principal characteristic—the rival functions and the complementary functions of the metonymic and metaphoric poles are translated into a sort of division of labor. On the one hand, one invents words that are capable of condensing a maximum of signification, and one therefore works to overcome the fragmentation of specific experiences, to correct "false" links, to dissipate illusory appearances, to explain the enigma of synonymy. They have to be words with a great capacity to signify, never equivocal; and they succeed as long as they are together in the sky among themselves, yet there they are empty.

On the other hand, one works so that words may have context, efficacy, references. For this second type of job, those people turn out to be more adept whose materiality cannot be transcended to some extent, that is, those who do not forget—but not because they have a good memory or because they like it particularly—the terrestrial component of one's own existing. They don't forget it because it is something literal that is not fully substitutable, not translatable into meanings [*significati*] of value, nor can it be activated in civilized forms. To acquire meaning these people must stay in the presence of metaphorical figures, signify through them, dispose their existence in conformity with them. Along the metonymical directrix, one works without speaking. One doesn't elaborate an autonomous word, but one works so that meanings [*significati*] invented metaphorically may find contexts and references without running the danger of disintegrating, getting lost, or becoming corrupt.

This does not mean that the voiceless entities should be completely confused with the metaphorical figures from which they draw inspiration in order to signify themselves. The most efficient metaphorization, at least in our society, doesn't exclude the perception of a gap between what is represented as rational, true, just, and the actual experiences one lives. Let's take equality, for instance, the most glorious metaphor invented by the bourgeoisie. Proclaiming equality was and remains effective but not because such a proclamation would hide the fact of real inequalities. One doesn't ask that people ignore social differences. (God forbid!) One asks, rather, that they superimpose a figure of equality and its occasional symbolic realizations over the daily experience of social inequalities, and that they read experience by means of this figure. There follows, in addition to a great sensitivity to the promises of equality realizable in the most disparate manners (children, work, laws), a reasoning that implies, among its presuppositions, that "we are equal," with the mystifying effects that are easy to point out but not to neutralize. This is how the idea of equality gains life, by mobilizing people who perhaps don't even desire equality, taken literally.

The unfaithfulness of metaphorical figures is not an inconvenience; on the contrary, it is their game par excellence. They figure something that can never recognize itself completely in the figure. The inconvenience is due to something else, quite the opposite in fact, and consists in the fact that the game runs the risk of ending when the metaphorizing progression becomes irreversible and generates a cultural accumulation from which one cannot escape and when, hence, one knows nothing about things besides their depiction. At that point, one after the other the metaphors become what are called "dead metaphors." Dead and cumbersome. For example, we advance toward the realization of social equality, but the equality that has been realized no longer leaves room for the desire that existed when one said one wanted equality.

At the end of a small treatise on metaphor, Umberto Eco lists situations in which new metaphors may arise. Except for the case of artistic inventions, they are all situations in which cultural accumulation is nullified, the "rich cultural text(ile)" which Eco speaks of and of which metaphor would be a function. These are in facts states of cultural virginity, ignorance, or pure sensations.[48] Therefore, if it is true that the best metaphors—this is Eco's thesis—are those that show "culture in action," the resource of metaphoric invention, however, is not to be found inside culture, or perhaps it is, but then inside what we should call culture in passion, where one produces and one doesn't accumulate, "the other world" [Friedrich] Nietzsche speaks about, the world of first impressions.[49]

It seems that this other world is being extinguished. It seems that the hypermetaphorical regime has become trapped inside its own game, namely, to replace things with figures, operating a substitution in a manner of speaking. The substitution instead runs the risk of being actual, effective, and irreversible.

The subordinate labor that keeps the metaphorical figures alive is strongly encouraged and is the object of growing competition to the extent that one no longer competes for the quality but for the priority of interpretation. By now, to arrive before other interpreters means to arrive before the facts themselves, of capturing them as they are being born, before they have gathered some meaning for themselves. A minor example. In the wake of a journalistic scoop reporting the horrible malpractices going on in a certain hospital, the newspaper receives numerous letters of praise, all saying: well done, this is the press's highest mission, more of it. None of the letters, at least among those published, asked and questioned what was going on inside the heads of those doctors, nurses, employees, cooks, providers, relatives, and friends of the ill, who were either witnesses to or authors of the misdeeds: interested, afraid, indifferent, powerless ... another world of "first impressions" that vanishes behind the journalistic representation of a scandal that touches only naive readers and even then only slightly.

The division of labor in fact does not function the way it should. The providers of first impressions provide second impressions, since for them it is the interpretive grid—rather than facts, for which the grid has been substituted—that provokes those impressions that the grid itself claims only to interpret. Perplexity of the metaphorizers who see their resources being squandered search for more stimulating interpretations, return to old grids that, in their time, had provided good results, and so forth in a continuous escalation.

The world of first impressions is negated in the face of a symbolic production that practices the division of labor. Thanks to the latter, thought can develop to its extreme consequences without carrying the relevant burden. Freedom of thought, the famous freedom of thought, which comes along with a reduction of the real context, in a staging in which one can talk of anything and one does talk of anything, without any part of that which moves one to talk transpiring. A thought that wants to move without showing what moves it, the freedom of a thought that ignores its servitudes.

A discourse that has as its object even the most intimate human matters, such as the brains, the viscera, the sexual organs, but seems to come from a disembodied subject. This is how I manage to explain to myself that there are scientists who work to invent substances to be used in chemical warfare for the devastation of nervous cells. Their own nervous cells, obviously, don't realize what they are doing.

It is always the case, under the regime of hypermetaphoricity, that the concrete circumstances of thought and speech are considered extraneous conditions, which may possibly be taken into account in subsequent speech and reasoning; which reasoning, however, takes place in other circumstances that are themselves kept silent. It amounts substantially to a perpetual deferral that reduces those who are incapable of deferring to silence. Too bad for them (and luckily they do exist), one will say. OK, it's a problem that they will take care of on their own. But we are all the worse for it, if we are not allowed to be troubled and pained by the dissociation between what moves us to speak and what we speak about—discourse being able to rely only too easily on an automatic deferral that neutralizes the risk of an irruption of literalness: the silent and laborious matter that, rather than remaining devoted to its work, declares its extraneousness, declares its situation to be insufferable. In this regard, we still haven't moved beyond slips of the tongue.

By contrast, when those who do not have the credentials of superior competence speak, if they do not want to appear ridiculous, it is better that they refer to their material situation or follow lines of reasoning that closely adhere to it. And yet there exist rank-and-file soldiers, housewives, workers, or immigrants who would want to move beyond their obscure daily existence and instead be taken seriously as the authors of poems, philosophical theories, scientific discoveries, and social programs. What is wrong with this demand? The first answer would be that their most authentic knowledge is that of their own condition. This is true, but it's an incomplete answer. They are also embarrassing because they imitate strictly and unselfconsciously the vacuity of their model, which vacuity would however become manifest if this imitation were to become generalized.

Can One Always Imitate?

This notwithstanding, there is a deluge of imitation. They hypermetaphoricity regime is in crisis and that is one of its symptoms. The not-yet signifiable—"not yet" is, at least, how one would like to be able to consider it—is subject to the risk of wearing out due to constant imitation, when it is not removed into unbridgeable distances.

The proper functioning of the metaphorizing progression depends on its being crossed, under determinate conditions, by the literalness of given facts. We don't live in those Middle Ages that left things and bodies to their own affairs and commerce, destined to cease in any case upon the great appointment with death whose scrutiny was what every valid metaphorization had to go through. In our culture, one has always tried to stimulate interaction between a representational and planning order, on the one hand, and, on the other, the facts which that order should represent and modify with its plans, since it is firmly established that when the gap between the two levels increases too greatly and these levels begin to diverge, the representational-planning order needs to be modified. We find this schema, suitably adapted, in the sciences, in the law, in politics, in economics.

Imitative symbolic production tends to fill the gap on which the schema was based and which has always supported the augmentation of the interpretive order. As one knows, matter has its own capacity to respond to speech. One also knows that a certain matter, in order to have its existence recognized, may go as far as fashioning itself in complete conformity, to the point of expressing what options it is being given or what is imposed on it thus: this is me, this is my law. This is well known, and ultimately it's also okay, so that the process of assumption of the real into the symbolic may be completed. But it's okay "up to a certain point." It is still necessary both for the functioning of language and the dynamism of society that there be something else, something resistant and extraneous. But how can that point be fixed, which would be the border between "good" and "bad" imitation? Is it a question of aesthetic discernment, social convenience, or scientific strategy? Matter that has the capability of responding to the stimuli of the symbolic does not seem to have the capability of stopping at that crucial moment when its invaluable responsiveness decays into counterfeit.

Extralinguistic reality, then, when nothing else remains extraneous and resistant, seems to evaporate; one only exchanges signs in a language that revolves around itself, things disappear, transformed into signs in their turn, but signs of nothing. Apart from this, there are also enigmas, eccentric responses, voids, silences, occasional tremors. Perhaps because the "silenced experience"—that is, the process in which matter is articulated and becomes signifying, the moment in which there is a proximity between words and things that precedes their being placed in correspondence—is pushed back, and occurs in places we know absolutely nothing about.

I borrowed the expression "silenced experience" from Giorgio Agamben, *Infancy and History*, who takes it, polemically, from Edmund Husserl. Agamben writes: "For if the subject is merely the enunciator, contrary to what Husserl believed, we shall never attain in the subject the original status of experience: 'pure, and thereby still mute experience.' On the contrary the constitution of the subject in and through language is precisely the expropriation of this 'wordless' experience; from the outset, it is always 'speech.' A primary experience, far from being subjective, could then only be what in human beings comes before the subject—that is, before language: a 'wordless' experience in the literal sense of the term, a human *infancy* [*in-fancy*], whose boundary would be marked by language."[50]

Although there are points of contact between us, the way I use the expression "silenced experience" is undoubtedly not faithful to Agamben's discourse, in which we find a reference to the originary, the examination of which, unfortunately, means nothing to me. I agree with him that there is a limit to the translation of our cultural existence into languages, but, as far as I am concerned, I can't retrace a line back from the untranslatable to the originary because for me in that untranslatable there is deposited, in inextricable fashion, also that which is made insignificant due to historical violence. This is what I was talking about earlier in reference to my grandmother and the kids from the large, bleak suburbs.

Imitation grows and must grow, because the crossing of the interpretive grids by the given facts in their literalness risks being too lacerating, perhaps by now totally unimaginable. What do people want, literally, when they say they want equality? If the literal realization of social equality is depressing, what would the literal realization of that which is expressed in a will to equality unleash? Savage and remote matter even when one is dealing with common daily existence, through which then it is easier to pass as sleepwalkers or automatons. It seems impossible to make any sense out of it. Therefore it is better to think that, literally, one does not want, one does not see, one is not, and one knows nothing.

Speaking through internal references, without ever exiting the linguistic universe, is not a novelty in and of itself. This is how power speaks habitually. For curiosity's sake, I suggest rereading the events of Galileo's trial, which unfolded in such a manner so as never to allow the real stakes involved to transpire, and so as to deprive Galileo of any criteria regarding the behavior he may have needed to follow. The novelty is that imitation now tends to generalize that manner of speaking, obviously with different results. Speeches deciding about a war may be all wrapped around themselves, but then the tanks move anyway. The disquisitions of someone who is struggling with the problems of existence via the words of an interpretive discourse, on the other hand, usually don't move anything. Perhaps the difference in results depends on the entity of what is tacitly implied, the less power there is, and the fewer things are tacitly implied, all the way up to the despairingly empty explicitness of exhaustive analyses that spin on themselves and die.

In this situation, some point to the silence of the masses as a site of possible regeneration. Agamben speaks about infancy. Others, more banal and practical, try to give the good example. They say, in other words, that those who speak or write professionally, when they address the broader public should do so with clarity and simplicity, choosing concrete and direct expressions, and composing short sentences that contain a specific reference. This proposal has all the reasons of the world on its side, including the one that commands us to block imitation at some point (that is, in the transition from specialists to broader public), so that the separation between the level of theory and the language of common experience can be reestablished, if necessary with some trick or artifice. If for specialists the cat is a feline cataloged in their treatises, it is proper or rather necessary that for common speakers it remain the domestic or wild animal of their everyday lives and perhaps even of their nocturnal fantasies. The same goes for the dog, the body, work, time, money, love... Language actually needs the play of meanings [*significati*], which are synthesized and fragmented, which are generalized into abstraction and plunged into particularity. But under the hypermetaphoricity regime this play has been ensured by means of a division of labor that the proponents of "simple language," it seems to me, don't intend to touch. Ultimately they would want to restore, or institute *ex novo*, a fake language of a metonymic kind to be used by "simple folk," those, in other words, who in any case must remain devoted to the work of keeping words in relation with things and who risk losing themselves in the concentric circles of the transposed language.

At this point I had been thinking of writing a brief treatise in praise of imitation. I had three bullet points ready for the purpose. I have decided against it because, although I am an imitatrix and even derive some advantage from it, as soon as I attempt to present this situation, resentment together with a certain sense of humiliation start insinuating themselves. Actually there are also some comical aspects but I can't manage to portray them. To imitate, let that be clear, is not a funny matter on its own; it does, however, predispose one to laugh since there is really nothing, neither love nor science nor dignity, which the imitator doesn't ultimately suspect is some form of fakery, to be supported if need be with all one's forces, but this doesn't eliminate the suspicion, quite the contrary.

Women are notorious imitatrices. Their nonsignifiable dissimilarity [*diversità*] almost imposes imitation. As [Luce] Irigaray writes, "There is, in an initial phase, perhaps only one "path," the one historically assigned to the feminine: that of *mimicry*."[51] Perhaps the only one, but not an easily viable one even for us to whom imitation is nevertheless suggested in all sorts of manners. I remember I was around ten: one day, encouraged by my father, I tried on the clothes of a brother who was not home because he was studying with the Jesuits—among whom he then stayed. Dressed in this fashion I felt like someone else and, making good on my already established authority over my younger brothers, I led them in an attack against the first motorized means of transport that would pass along the road. An enterprise of this kind went beyond our usual kind of adventures. Finally a truck passed, and we hit it, I believe without consequences, with our slingshots. The truck driver, furious, stopped and went to protest to our mother. We had disappeared. She then focused her anger on me, and centered it on my male clothing, which she then harshly ordered me to remove. Just like Joan of Arc. And to think that it is precisely my mother who always kept and still keeps a print of Joan of Arc with her, in which one sees the French heroine in *male clothing* in front of the judges.

Imitation, as one can judge from these cases, entails also some inconveniences that directly affect the imitators. One of these is that imitators cannot share anything in common with each other. One would say that, evidently, between my mother's admiration for Joan of Arc and my adventure in male clothing there had to be some link, but if there was, it remained a dead letter between the two of us. This is really strange since the imitator is all bent on metaphorization (he is ready to highlight a recognized meaning [*significato*], a value), and the metaphor would be precisely that which facilitates communication—there does exist, I already mentioned it, a communication of a metonymic type, via contact and contagion, but it is probable that it is still aided by the spark of a meaning [*significato*] that is capable of connecting that which remains materially distant. It is not really so strange if one considers that the reverse is even more true, in other words, that communication also needs physical proximity, the so-called *medium*—which is much more considerable than is usually mentioned, air that vibrates, electromagnetic waves, etc.—and an autonomous articulation of its own. Well, this matter is not fully at the imitators' disposal, by definition. They have renounced it, they ignore it, or they have been expropriated from it. I would consider the latter an extreme case, even if not rare, which perhaps occurs among imprisoned slaves or those totally seduced. It is the case, more frequently, that they don't want to know and cannot know anything about it because their material being is insignificant in their eyes, and they don't know how to valorize themselves except by canceling their material being in imitation.

Imitators don't make love to one another, at best they are in solidarity with one another, they don't touch, and, naturally, they don't imitate one another. They have the cult of originality, creativity, and distinction. They despise their fellow human beings, they are alone. I couldn't write in praise of imitation if I think of the horror of finding oneself navigating among borrowed words, going and going—when one is without a body this can be done easily—having believed that those words would have led one somewhere, obviously not just anywhere but some place of value, the essential, and gradually discovering that one doesn't arrive anywhere, a deportation without end, lost.

The Mixing Crossing [La traversata mescolatrice]

While explaining that mimicry can be a path, that there is a path along which imitators can proceed without losing themselves, Irigaray has written: "To play with mimesis . . . also means to 'unveil' the fact that, if women are such good mimics, it is because they are not simply resorbed in this function. *They also remain elsewhere*: another case of the persistence of 'matter,' but also of 'sexual pleasure.'"[52] This makes me think of women's mimetic ability in the course of clandestine operations and the pleasure partisan women must have enjoyed in fooling fascists by playing the part of the pregnant woman with a belly full of leaflets, or playing the part of the prostitute, a family's mother, or a lover waiting for her love, depending on the situation.[53]

But how does one take the second step, which is affirming the knowledge and pleasure that are surely implicit in the game of mimicry? In the stories of partisan women I saw there was knowledge and pleasure, but they did not develop commensurately since then. Once the emergency that had favored the practice of that ludic mimicry, a liberated copying of female roles, ceased, the gain in pleasure and knowledge did not last.

The knowledge and the existence of that elsewhere Irigaray speaks about, I believe are in need of a symbolic elaboration of a metonymic type, of a language in which bodies and things become inscribed when no metaphoric substitution has made them yet superfluous, obvious, or sublimated. A language that would allow us to pass through the cleavage between a here that is blind and silenced, and a sublime and deporting other world. Not being (I am again quoting Irigaray) simply in a process of reflection or mimicry, neither in a here—opaque empirical reality, impermeable to all languages—nor in another world—self-sufficient infinity of the God of men. She speaks of a ludic and mixing crossing and by this I understand: from the deposit of confused bodies to the meanings [*significati*] these bodies acquire in their re-presentation—a mixing of those and these insofar as they are not yet or no longer divided by metaphoric operations, which does not correspond either to a zero of the symbolic or to pure delirium. Metonymic language is a mode of symbolic elaboration.

At its poorest level it will be a meager language, without sparks, without poetry, without élan, without the possibility of synthesis, pedestrian, illuminated by modest wordplay, rigidly contextual, exposed to all sorts of trip-ups. Those who have seen the film *Lacombe Lucien* by Louis Malle will easily understand what this is about; the protagonist in fact speaks a language of this type. But its elaboration may advance further and acquire, in opposition to the language of metaphoric translation, that expressive potential and that cognitive efficacy that the latter usually absorbs and exercises on its own. There is no word that does not depend on context to some degree, there is no meaning [*significato*] so condensed that it can detach itself totally from the combinations and situations that in actual fact originated it. Not all of that which is language, and not all of how language functions, is representable by language. To express and to know this limit is what metonymy is capable of, as it reveals the combinations and situations that words frequent in order to acquire meaning [*significato*], including the broader and more comprehensive meanings [*significati*].

Moreover, this is known to the "hypermetaphoricians" who, in order to potentiate their discourse further, expose it to metonymic dispersion. It is not an easy game, in which, among others, Lacan excels: His style is characterized, in fact, by a sort of discursive diffraction that demands much effort to those who want to understand his thought exactly and that, on the other hand, also ensures that he is not confused with the simplified versions of his students, even when they interpret him faithfully. Style is inimitable, as we know.

But behind the effect of style there is something more, a skillful *selection* at the level of the signifier, conducted in such a manner that that which the discourse asserts is that which itself results gradually from the specific sequences that include also accidental facts such as slips of the tongue, assonances, and wordplay. In this manner, the rival tension between metaphoric and metonymic processes is contained within a single process of the generation of meaning [*significato*].

Metonymic language, on the contrary, does not operate selections. It develops through a play of combinations and variations of data that acquire meaning in the moment. Or they don't acquire it, thus giving rise to a visible lacuna. Bodies, things, experiences, no longer confined within a blind literalness, autonomously produce a meaning of their own being there, a meaning that—when matched with the meaning [*significato*] that represents them in the symbolic order—has unpredictable effects. Verification, resonance, caricature, rift, deviation, irony—all may occur. Or an explosion of rhetoricity that demolishes the staging within which metaphor and metonymy were believed to operate in accord.

Translated by Mark William Epstein

NOTES

This chapter consists of the translation of the foreword and the first two chapters of *Maglia o uncinetto: Racconto linguistico-politico sulla inimicizia tra metafora e metonimia* (Milan: Feltrinelli, 1981).

1. Luisa Muraro, "Maglia o uncinetto? Metafora e metonimia nella produzione simbolica," *Aut aut*, nos. 175–76, (January-April 1980): 59–85.

2. Roman Jakobson, *Saggi di linguistica generale*, ed. Luigi Hellman, trans. L. Grassi (Milan: Feltrinelli, 1966), 39–44. In this regard the reader should also consult *Child Language: Aphasia and Phonological Universals* (The Hague: Mouton, 1968). Jakobson's research on metonymy started in the 1920s with some studies on realism and on silent cinema.

3. [Here and throughout this chapter, unless otherwise noted, "meaning" translates the Italian term *"senso"*; "meaning" may be used also to translate the Italian term *"significato"*; the latter, however, translates also the English "signified."—Trans.]
4. ["Ragionare coi piedi" (to think with one's feet) is an idiomatic expression in Italian meaning that someone does not think well, properly, rationally, etc. —Trans.]
5. Jakobson, *Saggi di linguistica generale*, 40.
6. Paul Feyerabend, *Against Method* (New York, Verso, 1993), 198.
7. Jakobson, *Saggi di linguistica generale*, 44–45.
8. Noam Chomsky, *Syntactic Structures* (The Hague: Mouton, 1965), 48.
9. [Here and throughout this chapter, "device" translates the Italian term *"dispositivo."*—Trans.]
10. Jakobson, *Saggi di linguistica generale*, 28–34. Oswald Ducrot and Tzvetan Todorov, *Encyclopedic Dictionary of the Sciences of Language*, trans. Catherine Porter (Baltimore: Johns Hopkins University Press, 1979).
11. Group Mu (J. Dubois et al.), *Rhétorique générale* (Paris: Larousse, 1970).
12. Tzvetan Todorov, *Littérature et signification* (Paris: Larousse, 1967), 107.
13. Group Mu, *Rhétorique générale*, 34, 92, 117.
14. Group Mu, *Rhétorique générale*, 35.
15. Group Mu, *Rhétorique générale*, 92.
16. Group Mu, *Rhétorique générale*, 92.
17. Group Mu, *Rhétorique générale*, 120–21.
18. Group Mu, *Rhétorique générale*, 106–7.
19. Group Mu, *Rhétorique générale*, 120.
20. Group Mu, *Rhétorique générale*, 95–96.
21. Lorenzo Accame, "Retorica e credenza: Alcune considerazioni di massima sul rapporto tra retorica e psicanalisi," *Quaderni del seminario di filosofia di scienze dell'uomo* 1 (1979): 92. Accame clearly does not see a competition between rivals in the relation of metaphor to metonymy but only a peaceful competition. This should not be attributed, as is frequently the case, to a reading of Jakobson filtered by Lacan since Accame clearly sees a divergence between the two (see 93n2).
22. Accame, "Retorica e credenza," 72. [Here and throughout, "staging" translates the Italian term *"messa in scena."*—Trans.]
23. Accame, "Retorica e credenza," 89; emphasis added.
24. Jean Laplanche and Jean-Bertrand Pontalis, *The Language of Psychoanalysis*, trans. Donald Nicholson-Smith (London: W. W. Norton, 1973).
25. Group Mu, *Rhétorique générale*, 35–37.
26. Todorov, *Littérature et signification*, 116–18.
27. Starting with Max Black's *Models and Metaphors: Studies in Language and Philosophy* (Ithaca, N.Y.: Cornell University Press, 1962), the rhetoricity of scientific language is both recognized and a topic of research, with, at least so far, an

exclusive preference for its metaphoricity. A partial but significant view: one recognizes and emphasizes the prevailing operation.
  28. Jacques Lacan, *Écrits: The First Complete Edition in English* (New York: W. W. Norton, 2006), 425–26.
  29. Jakobson, *Saggi di linguistica generale*, 44.
  30. Jean-François Lyotard, *Discourse, Figure*, trans. Anthony Hudek and Mary Lydon (Minneapolis: University of Minnesota Press, 2011), 246 and especially 256.
  31. Sigmund Freud, *Totem and Taboo* (London: Kegan Paul, 1930), 138.
  32. Lacan, *Écrits*, 418–19.
  33. Lacan, *Écrits*, 577–18 and 676–77.
  34. Lacan, *Écrits*, 578.
  35. Lacan, *Écrits*, 423, 682, and 429.
  36. Lacan, *Écrits*, 430–31.
  37. Lacan, *Écrits*, 430–31.
  38. Lacan, *Écrits*, 420–21, 428–29, 429–30, and 464–65.
  39. François Wahl, *Qu'est-ce que le structuralisme?* (Paris: Seuil, 1973), 131.
  40. Lacan, *Écrits*, 470 and 472.
  41. "The sexed being of these not-whole women does not involve the body but what results from a logical exigency in speech. Indeed, logic, the coherence inscribed in the fact that language exists and that it is outside the bodies that are moved by it—in short, the Other who is incarnated, so to speak, as sexed being—requires this one by one [*une par une*]." Jacques Lacan, *On Feminine Sexuality: The Limits of Love and Knowledge, 1972–1973, Encore: The Seminar of Jacques Lacan Book XX*, ed. Jacques-Alain Miller, trans. Bruce Fink (New York: W. W. Norton, 1999), 10.
  42. Lacan, *Écrits*, 471.
  43. Alfred Sohn-Rethel, *Intellectual and Manual Labor: A Critique of Epistemology*, trans. Martin Sohn-Rethel (Atlantic Highlands, N.J.: Humanities Press, 1978), 77.
  44. Ludwig Wittgenstein, *Tractatus Logico-Philosophicus* (London: Routledge, 1961).
  45. [In this paragraph and throughout, unless otherwise noted, "deposit" translates the Italian term "*deposito*," which can also be translated into English as "depot."—Trans.]
  46. Jurij M. Lotman, "Un modello dinamico del sistema semiotico," in *Testo e contesto*, ed. Simonetta Salvestroni (Bari: Laterza, 1980), 9–27.
  47. See the section "Metaphor and Science" in Andrew Ortony, ed., *Metaphor and Thought* (Cambridge: Cambridge University Press, 1979), 355–436.
  48. Umberto Eco, *Metafora*, in *Enciclopedia Einaudi*, vol. 8, 191–236. See especially 233–34.
  49. Friedrich Nietzsche, "On Truth and Lies in a Nonmoral Sense," in *The Portable Nietzsche*, ed. Walter Kaufmann (London: Penguin, 1976).

50. Giorgio Agamben, *Infancy and History: The Destruction of Experience* (London: Verso, 1993), 47.
51. Luce Irigaray, *This Sex Which Is Not One* (Ithaca, N.Y.: Cornell University Press, 1985), 76.
52. Irigaray, *This Sex Which Is Not One*, 76.
53. I am referring to Anna Maria Bruzzone and Rachele Farina, eds., *La Resistenza taciuta: Dodici vite di partigiane piemontesi* (Milan: La Pietra, 1976).

On the Relation between Words and Things as Frequentation

LUISA MURARO

While speaking about reality and about the symbolic order that keeps it together—at times well and at other times not so well—I asked myself: "What relation is there between words and things, between a text and the world?"

The answer I sketched started by saying that a relation between the two certainly exists. Whence such certainty? It does not come from demonstrations: it's one of those certainties that are not gained and secured through demonstrations because they are found already in ourselves (think of high-low, right-left). The certainty that words are in relation with being and not with nothing is a certainty that we find in ourselves because it comes into being with us qua speaking subjects. On this point philosophers and linguists agree: the subject is born with language. But the world too is born with language—the world intended as environment within which the I and the you of symbolic exchanges are situated. At first, this environment is the mother (I borrow this terminology from Donald Winnicott). Later, when the baby begins to have a relation with the environment that is not limited to the pure physicality of sucking, eating, spitting; when gestures, calls, and words that the mother understands and responds to enter this relation, in a crescendo that eventually will lead the baby to be autonomous, at that moment the world takes shape, is formed.

Such an invocation of infancy and of the maternal relation is my way of leading us toward an intuition of something that happens when there are words. The symbolic co-nascence of I-you-world is given every time that there are words, namely, when relations among human beings are symbolic relations rather than relations of force. The use of force—as Simone Weil insists—throws both those who exert it and those who are subjected to it into unreality.

Why do we say "exchange"? What do we exchange when we really speak to one another? Fundamentally, that which we exchange in the exchange with the other is the place of *subject-at-the-center-of-the-world*. The Latin etymology of the word *discourse* evokes the movement of coming and going, to and fro, much like the spool of the loom on which the threads of the warp are strung. The movement of being an I for a you and of becoming in turn a you for an other results in differences that are generated by the fact that, due to the other, the overlap between oneself and the all is missing, lacking: as this movement takes place, these differences turn into a common language. What [Ferdinand de] Saussure taught us about language is that it is made up exclusively of differences: significant differences rather than indifferent differences.

What is well known and commonly accepted about the relation between words and things is that it is variously configured according to different languages as well as that it changes according to the type of society and of culture even within the same language. (Whoever has read Michel Foucault's *Les mots et les choses* is familiar with this latter standpoint, which he introduced magisterially with his commentary on *Las Meninas*.)

Further, one needs to keep in mind that this relation is not at all as simple in itself as one might think and as philosophy itself led us to believe in the past; It is, rather, a complex relation, such that we might speak of several relations, even though such a plurality of relations is not always evident due to the fact that one type of relation is prevalent and prevails on the other relations, which do not manifest themselves for and through themselves, thereby remaining concealed in speechlessness [*mutismo*].

I will devote myself now to describing one of the ways in which words and things are in relation with each other. It's a way that borrows and foregrounds certain characteristics of metonymy—a rhetorical figure denominating the shift in meaning that occurs when going along certain already given and well-known concatenations. For example, "reading Virginia Woolf" or "drinking a glass" are metonymies: obviously, I drink what is in the glass and not the glass, and when I say that I am reading

Virginia Woolf what I mean to say is that I am reading the texts she authored.

Metonymy, thus, configures a relation between words and things that is akin to some kind of collaboration in which our practice of the world is called upon by words and contributes to signifying the world. And metonymy, hence, shows us that language has many resources: there is its tendency to constitute itself as a self-sufficient semantic totality, which is the tendency of theoretical language, and then there is the frequentation of the world that (female and male) speakers have—a frequentation that is at the foundation of practical knowledge.

We are dealing with symbolic procedures that are dissimilar from each other, and the one who discovered and investigated them—Roman Jakobson in his famous essay on aphasia—maintains that they coexist in the life of language but that they are not pacifically complementary.[1] The first procedure (which is of the metaphoric type) looks for differences that define meaning and looks for them in words and with words: it is metaphysical and metalinguistic. The second procedure does not allow the speaking subject to transcend, to go beyond its belonging to the world, namely, beyond its being part; the subject may say the true while moving, working, living, *and* speaking, namely, by adding information to what it already knew, little by little, as things go along. It is a procedure that does not define being and that, rather, recounts it, narrates it.

Language in which the resource of frequentation is more prevalent seems to be condemned to a degree of narrowness due to the fact that its capacity to signify depends on the relations among speakers as well as on the relations among speakers and their context. Such a language does not go as far as attaining universal value—or so they say. There is the world of drinkers, and there is the world of Virginia Woolf readers [*lettrici*]—partial worlds that usually do not overlap.

The charge of narrowness is understandable, and yet I do not share it entirely. In metonymy, meaning shifts through and over some important concatenations that are given by our being living bodies—sexuate, mortal, fragile, joyous, needy bodies. These are concatenations that take us into vast areas of experience that are common to all human beings.

In more general terms, I maintain that there is a universal that we may reach step by step, via partial proximities and commonalities that do not exhaust the entireness [*interezza*] of the world but that enable us to visit such entireness in some sort of inexhaustible voyage, helped by all that speaking subjects have materially in common, and, *in primis*, by our being body. Besides, I ask myself whether pure universal value—namely, the one that supposedly characterizes the word when the latter is posited in total symbolic independence from our being body, that is, from our being part of the world—might not be a chimera after all. If it is true that the relation between words and things is a complex one that avails itself of a plurality of modalities, and if one of these modalities is characterized by the metonymic mechanism, then even the most universal knowledge will always be indebted to our being body and our frequentation of the world.

Language in which the metonymic modality is prevalent does not lack a relative universality and is not devoid of creativity. There are inventions of the metonymic type that—either by themselves or in combination with others—move the imagination and open the world to new meanings.

For a conspicuous example of what I am saying, I think of Virginia Woolf's first political essay, *A Room of One's Own* (1929). Brilliantly conceived as a deviation following apparently secondary trajectories, this text gives free expression to that female revolt against patriarchal society which was seething within the English writer and countless other women. With this essay, as well as with the one that followed it and that is constructed in the same manner, namely, *Three Guineas* (1938), Woolf endowed an experience—which up until then had been caught and stifled in between terrified silence and hysteric protest—with language: there where there were only illness and speechlessness [*mutismo*], there she brought thought into being.

In fall 1928, she was summoned to Cambridge to speak to an audience of women students on the topic "Women and the Novel."[2] To this day, we still see double-headed titles such as this one, in which one head is "women" and the other can be just anything, from computer science to God. Woolf showed up and said that she would not approach this topic in these terms because she had nothing definitive to say either about the true nature of women or about the true nature of the novel. She would offer to her audience, rather, her opinion, which perhaps might have some truth in it, about both women and the novel, namely, that if a woman wants to write novels she must have money and a room of her own.

After this first move, she followed up with another one that concerned language: she would explain her opinion not with the intention to make it appear true but simply recounting—with the help of the art of the novel—how such an opinion had taken shape in her, letting us, a women's audience, look for whatever truth there may be in her words.

It was her discourse on method. Thinking is intended here as opening passages to the movement of the mind and as tracing paths through an experience that had no when and no where, that is, as a narration.

And so it happened that for the first time (for all that this manner of speaking is worth, I still like to say it) the world stopped mirroring itself in a tradition of thought that presented itself as universal but that corresponded to men's experience—a rich and varied tradition, but a fatally unilateral thought. And the world did *not* show itself as what it might be from the point of view of the other sex—a presumably complementary or opposite point of view. What the world showed of itself is one of its constitutive characteristics, namely, its possibility to be other, which is to say: a sum of differences that are continuously becoming—a sum that keeps itself together thanks to symbolic exchanges in a common language.

The two moves are complementary in that their result is to draw out the free sense of sexual difference. And yet they remain distinct. The first move produces a change in symbolic exchange: having abandoned the point of view of essence as well as the task of finding the right definition of woman (and of the novel), women begin to exist for themselves in an exchange between one who recounts "her stories" with words that resonate in the others who listen.

The second move concerns the possibility of the true. Is it possible to speak it? No—seems to be Woolf's answer—but in the void left by the unsupportable claim to know and speak the truth a trust emerges, a confidence in the fact that the other woman, whether she is reading or listening, would hear her voice and would make it resonate as such.

And this is what happened, historically, with feminist consciousness-raising [*presa di coscienza*] and the women's political movement.[3]

Years ago, at the end of the 1970s, I found in the feminist practice of self-conscientization the resources that enabled me to speak faithfully of my experience and to put an end to my imitation of the dominant philosophical language: Such resources led me to put forth a theorization of language that valorized the resource of the metonymic procedure. This is more or less how it went: we live in a symbolic order that privileges the metaphoric procedure (at the time, I called it: "hypermetaphoric regime") and that does not account for or hold in high regard those whose "work it is to glue words and things together." This formulation was meant to indicate those people who had been deprived of the symbolic competence necessary to interpret the world as well as themselves [stesse] in it, thereby fatally depending on the word of those others who arrogate symbolic competence to themselves and to others. And such an arrogation was always in the name and with the force of some power or other, including that which is given by political representation in our democratic system. Here is that symbolic debt I spoke about earlier—now unveiled. It is the debt that universal knowledge owes to the metonymic operation: this operation is demanded exclusively of those who live and are glued to their life context.[4]

I added, however, that this entire question could not end up with a theory: a theory is a construction made of words, and hence it is more apt to mirror totalizing symbolic procedures rather than those procedures which would adhere more closely to the human condition. The symbolic order reflects better upon that which is homogeneous with it and which conforms with it. But in practice—I wrote—it is precisely metonymic procedures that, their inevitable incompleteness notwithstanding, account for human condition better than any theory, as I had discovered myself thanks to feminist practice. We are at the limit of what a theory can explicate—I wrote back then—so much so that nowadays the question of the historical modes of symbolic production has returned as a political problem posed by the women's movement as well as by other movements that refuse the system of political representation.

My work as a woman thinker has continued to move in a double direction: on the one hand, endowing myself and other women with symbolic competence to interpret the world and themselves in it and, on the other hand, fostering the grafting of practice onto theoretical thought. I have always thought that, without this graft, the condition of being woman—in the wake of the fact that the price for this condition has been paid by so many women, starting from my mother, with an exhausting existence occasionally brightened up by meager victories—would have fallen into insignificance for me and would have destined me to the vacuity of a speculative effort wholly uprooted from my history and my very experience.

I have returned to that text I wrote more than thirty years ago for several reasons, one of which is that I would like to add something to it. As I continued my research on language, I came across a ponderous study dating back to 1934 in its original German and translated into Italian in 1983 after a second original edition in 1965: Karl Bühler's *Theory of Language*. The long third chapter concerns itself with the symbolic field of language and ends with a paragraph that I will quote almost entirely and that I will interpret in terms of my past research on metonymy as practical and theoretical wager.

Bühler writes: "Human language as a representative implement as we now know it has emerged from some developmental steps that can all be understood in the sense that it has increasingly freed itself from pointing and removed itself further and further from depiction."[5] In other words, properly human, verbal language is a system of representation of reality that no longer avails itself of the imitative forms found in reality itself and that does not avail itself very much even of index-signs, namely, those that are linked to the present state of things: I, you, here, now, etc. Such a language, in fact, is characterized by the fact that it *denominates* things and that, by means of names, it produces a symbolic representation of universal value (a representation that is neither imitative nor indicative). But, our author adds, there is something strange, something unclear in the type of representation that results from language. On the one hand, he explains, language has distanced itself from imitative reproduction, with which it has only an indirect relation—and this is how it is able to reach a high degree of universality. But when it comes to its primitive ability to reproduce by indicating the state of relations in which the speaker is immersed, such an ability has not been lost completely. I, Karl Bühler, have not been able to deduce why this is so on the basis of an adequate linguistic theory.[6]

This is followed by a problematic reflection that sheds much light on our theme and that confirms my earlier intuition regarding a "hypermetaphoric regime": "It may be that *we overestimate* the liberation from the deictic field, it may be that *we underestimate* the fact that such a verbal representation of a state of affairs is in principle open and in need of completion on the basis of knowledge of the state of affairs at issue."[7]

In other words—Bühler writes—there is perhaps a component that enters in all linguistically constituted knowledge but that emerges from a source that never integrates itself in the symbolic system and that "still produces genuine knowledge."[8] And, we add, the metonymic procedure solves the arcane mystery of a source that is in language but that is not in language and that nonetheless generates a true knowledge. Language limps, I wrote at the end of *To Knit or to Crochet*—the enigma derives from our being body and being word together. Beware, however, of the fact that language reproduces this enigma within itself and knows by its own nature our being body and our being word together. And I ended that work with these words: "We have yet to discover how much intelligence may derive from our body and how tight a link there may be between pleasure and knowledge."[9]

This conclusion is of no small help to those who search for the possibility of a knowing and an acting that would not be the mere expression of dominant power relations: to those who have in mind a political acting whose efficacy would be entrusted to the power of words.

Translated by Cesare Casarino

NOTES

This chapter is the translation of "Sul rapporto tra le cose e le parole: la frequentazione," *Per amore del mondo, la rivista* (online journal), no. 12 (Spring 2014), http://www.diotimafilosofe.it/larivista/sul-rapporto-tra-le-cose-e-le-parole-la-frequentazione/.

1. Roman Jakobson, "Two Aspects of Language and Two Types of Aphasic Disturbances," in *Selected Writings II* (The Hague: Mouton, 1971), 230–59.

2. I am inserting here a passage taken from my introduction to the Italian translation of Iris Murdoch's *Existentialists and Mystics: Writings on Philosophy and Literature*. Luisa Muraro, "Introduzione," in Iris Murdoch, *Esistenzialisti e mistici: Scritti di filosofia e letteratura*, trans. E. Costantino, M. Fiorini, and F. Elefante (Milan: Il Saggiatore, 2006), 11.

3. The literature on this topic is immense and to try and pin it down to just a few titles would be in vain. I shall limit myself, thus, to drawing the reader's attention to a book that clarifies what I have in mind when I speak of consciousness-raising [*presa di coscienza*] and the feminist movement: Libreria delle donne di Milano, *Non credere di avere dei diritti* (Turin: Rosenberg & Sellier, 1987).

4. Luisa Muraro, *Maglia o uncinetto: Racconto linguistico-politico sulla inimicizia tra metafora e metonimia* (Milan: Feltrinelli, 1981). This book was reprinted

by Manifestolibri in 1998, with a rich introduction by Ida Dominijanni (chapter 1 this volume).

5. Karl Bühler, *Theory of Language: The Representational Function of Language*, trans. Donald Fraser Goodwin in collaboration with Achim Eschbach (Amsterdam/Philadelphia: John Benjamins Publishing Company, 2011), 286.

6. Bühler, *Theory of Language*, 286.

7. Bühler, *Theory of Language*, 286.

8. Bühler, *Theory of Language*, 286.

9. Muraro, *Maglia o uncinetto*, 111. [This is the first sentence of the last paragraph of this work.—Trans.]

PART II

On the Maternal Symbolic and Its Language

Maternal Language between Limit and Infinite Opening

CHIARA ZAMBONI

When we are very young, we learn our maternal language like a carnal weave that is able to open us up to the names and secrets of the world. We learn it from our mother and from those around us. All of us can tell the story of their childhood language, the singular and contingent language spoken in the family. It has some concrete and sensual words and idiomatic phrases that are rooted in the memory of the heart. Nevertheless, the very fact of telling the story implies looking at it from afar, reflecting on it, without living it as we lived it then, as an authentic opening up to the world. Having learned the mutual language of the larger linguistic community at school, as well as many other specific languages, the story is continued but also interrupted. We no longer speak the substance of that first language, but that language functioned as a bridge so that we could learn other languages, other codes. In so doing, it incorporated itself into these languages, merging with them like a kind of vital emanation. It is just like water, which, given its transparency, once mixed with other liquids, can no longer be separated.

We feel the intensity of maternal language in the more creative moments of speaking, in poetry, in love, and in the more emotional moments, in the living experiences of the body, in old age, when words are in strict relationship with life.

I would like to talk about a sexual difference in terms of language, and this difference has to do with maternal language. The more sensitive and intelligent female schoolteachers are able to take children from the experience of an oral language, linked to use, to a written language codified into grammatical and syntactic rules, without humiliating the oral language of childhood, which students actually use as a privileged way to learn the written and regulated version.[1] However, this passage is not always a happy one. Something sometimes resists, especially among female students. What is it that resists?

I argue that this resistance and this rejection have to do with a sexed position in relation to symbolic law. I will explain this point through a quite well known short story in the form of a parable by [Franz] Kafka, entitled "Before the Law": "Before the law stands a doorkeeper. To this doorkeeper there comes a man from the country and prays for admittance to the Law. But the doorkeeper says that he cannot grant admittance at the moment."[2] The man from the country decides to wait outside the gate sitting on a stool that the gatekeeper lends him. And he ends up waiting his whole life to enter the gate. In the end, when he is fast approaching death, he asks the gatekeeper, "How does it happen that all these many years no one but myself has ever begged for admittance?" And the gatekeeper replies, "No one else could ever be admitted here, since this gate was made only for you. I am now going to shut it."[3]

Here, Kafka understands the gateway to the law as something different from individual laws. It is more like a symbolic event without foundation, but one that arranges the subjects in a certain way. In other words, it creates a space in which we are made to wait for a definitive and formal recognition of ourselves, which, however, does not happen. This hinders the fullness of life. Symbolic law is discontinuous—it is exactly an unfounded event—and it feeds on myth and history at the same time. The law has the desired effect when, without showing itself, it allows an entire life to live in the space that it creates between itself and human beings. That is, when we live in relation to it but without ever totally grasping the core of its meaning, which is taken from us. The latter always remains somewhere else.

Reflecting on the Italian language, Tullio De Mauro writes that knowing a language means knowing and controlling the rules that govern it. He distinguishes knowing how to control the rules from the use of the language, that is, a living language that is learned by speaking, and which has a lot to do with maternal language and orality, which is what characterizes it.[4] The gatekeeper of the law, who lends the stool to the man from the country who, in turn, sits and waits his whole life long, was effective due to the fact that he created a symbolic inversion. That which was material life was placed into the background while the wait in relation to the law became the main focus. Therefore, a paradoxical inversion occurs that puts the rules of language first—which are considered as something similar to grids that attempt to give order to the presumed chaos of life—and makes use drift into a secondary register, which is then presented as something that lacks measure and is still to be regulated. And which, in any case, comes after.

This inversion of value tends to hide that it is only with school education that we usually find what we first learned as linguistic use defined as the rule. But it is always use that helps us in material life: we rarely consult a grammar book when we have a doubt about speaking. We only have to remember the many phrases we have heard. Listening to the many voices in our memory gives us a measure for speaking.

It is hard to imagine that Kafka was thinking about a woman when he wrote about the man from the country sitting in front of the gateway to law for his entire life. A woman, we know, would have done a lot more. As the feminist thought maintains, a woman is both within and beyond the symbolic law, but this is a rather static formula. Let's imagine the situation a little more concretely.

I can imagine it from my experience as a university teacher helping students to write their philosophy theses. I remember one particular student and her degree thesis. The pages she brought me every week only contained very interesting intuitions if she found a precise rhythm in her writing. A rhythm that one appreciated by ear. We know that the first carnal weave of language is the body rhythm and that it is exactly this that is the most difficult thing to learn when we take up a foreign language. Even before birth, the rhythm of language is incorporated as a signifier in the bond with the maternal body.

When that student was guided by the pleasure of the text as she wrote her thesis, that is, without thinking of the content in the strict sense but taking the topic in relation to an interlacement of signs, according to a language flavor and a sensitive listening, she was then able to direct the text toward original intuitions. In the pages she brought me, she had unknowingly reinvented epic forms of parallelism, alliterations, and homophones: figures found in the great texts of shared culture rooted in orality.[5] However, the grammar did not always manage to remain on the same level as the rhythm and structure of the text. It was often bizarre.

If I restored the text to the grammar, that is, if I corrected it according to Italian language grammar rules, the writing lost its rhythm and she lost her intuitions. The intelligence of the topic became cloudy. The syntactic and grammatical rules took away her thoughts because she felt them foreign, doubly useless, and imposingly negative. She rebelled deeply. For her, grammar was an impediment. And yet, maternal language is immediately grammatical. It is a simple grammar whose forms are similar to those of dialects, even when the language of childhood is no longer dialect.[6] We can see this implicit grammar in action merely in the way a single word is pronounced. But in the grammar we relearn through a book, the pleasure of language is lost as the latter is doubled into objective rules. The competence that comes from the living language is lost.

How is the sexual difference in the aforementioned student's case in play? We find ourselves still within and outside the law, for this young woman took grammar literally and it was exactly for this reason that it became a burden to her rather than a framework on which to base her thinking. It was something impossible to bear. As a consequence, she rebelled against it. She withdrew from it, therefore even losing the simple grammaticality and life of the maternal language. She could only retrieve originality of ideas through phonic rhythm, the sound of linguistic structure. This is the way to reconcile oneself with that implicit grammaticality that language brings with it. It is the profound pleasure of linguistic structure in relation to the intention of meaning that can lead to a new acceptance of grammar dependence, but a dependence on the living grammar of affective, carnal, and rhythmic language, rather than the grammar that complicates living language. That would be an impersonal and conventional grammar, with no body and no unconscious.

Drawing on her practice and psychoanalytical intelligence, Françoise Dolto takes us a step further when she highlights a significant presence of passive pulsions [*Trieb*] in the experience of women that have to do with the pleasure of text. Passive pulsions are part of life impulses. Unlike active erotic pulsions that make up desire, for Dolto, sensual passive pulsions have a precise existential quality that is experienced during times of fluctuating attention to reality, times when realizing action is suspended. These are the first traces of a creative thinking-thought.

Dolto writes: "Girls find in themselves [after entering the oedipal] what they leave behind: the female power of their passive pulsions represented in the mother and in women. The role of the Father [symbolic] and the law is greater in males... The narcissism of boys is different to that of girls. Boys cannot get around the law."[7] With boys, the bond with the mother is accompanied by their progressive identification of themselves as masculine figures. Symbolic law digs its roots into this space, which gradually deepens and feeds on distancing. Something unphysical becomes the hidden source of regulated action. Boys therefore find no difficulty in doubling the regulations and rules of the living language learned from their mother or nurturers. There are few exceptions. Those men who have been able to get around symbolic law while not denying it are often writers. By crossing the law, they have creatively found the source of their writing practice in maternal language. I am particularly thinking of Elias Canetti, Marcel Proust, and Luigi Meneghello.[8]

That girls are more tied to the passive pulsions that they have in common with their mother is a leverage point for understanding their linguistic happiness when the space that opens starting from symbolic law has more of an instinctive, word-filled structure rather than just a pure void. Therefore, symbolic law, rather than arbitrarily double maternal language, creates a significant circle around one and the other. It is only when these pulsions are in play that linguistic rules are accepted as a vital part of this structure. Otherwise, as we have seen, these norms are empty and felt as foreign.

BETWEEN LIMIT AND INFINITE OPENING

It is said that learning how to speak during the initial years of life is dictated by a deep desire to communicate with the mother and other human beings in a verbal language. And this is true. We linger more rarely on the fact that the moment in which children truly access verbal language, which is an autonomous and self-referential structure, they renounce that intense communication with their mother, which is made up of exchanges, looks, touches, words spoken by the mother that the child takes as words of affective truth, whose sense rather than meaning is totally understood.

In learning to speak the shared language and to communicate, therefore, at another, more articulate, level of existence, children have to give up the pleasure of a unique and intense type of communication with their mother. Dolto maintains that this passage is neither mechanical nor deterministic. Not all children readily accept giving up the pleasure of a type of bodily and affective communication experience in favor of communication at the more complex and more impersonal level of a shared language, so much less bound to bodily presence.[9]

This is what characterizes human existence: any acquisition made on the level of being leads simultaneously to a loss. There is never any progress in our lives, but rather leaps of being. Learning to speak the language everyone uses is an example. We acquire the human sense of the shared word, which represents the enigma, the mystery that unites us. At the same time, we renounce the pleasure of a communication that came with no signifying mediation of words from the child, where the mother's words and those of other adults intermix with touch, smell, sound, and an emotional feeling with the entire body. In order to put this feeling back into play in the shared language, one needs an authentic linguistic creation. This creation will be something radically different compared to the wordless communication experienced in young infancy. A boundary has been crossed in the meantime: we have entered into the language that distinguishes subject from object, I and you, internal and external, past, present, and future. This leads to a metamorphosis of being. We have entered into the regime of a division between language and nonlanguage, but the benefit is an infinite wealth of expression. We have learned the maternal language, where words accompany things, but where they are also much more than the things themselves.

Crossing the boundary and abandoning the pleasure of wordless communication loads the words that one learns with extra reserve. What we lose is kept by a—let's call it—"memory" of the words. Words have a dense aura. It is as if they carry with them a potential of which they are the only contact, the hook on the surface of language. The visible of language bears an invisible in the communication exchange, which has the quality of an impalpable atmosphere. Words carry an involuntary memory like ripples on water bear the memory of a stone that has sunk to the bottom forever.

What I mean is, that the language we learn is not objectified precisely because it brings this reserve, this invisible, this atmosphere with it. And this is due to an expressionless, mute memory of something that sank to the bottom.

Paradoxically, we can actually find some theoretical formulas in Jacques Lacan that show what this memory means, this invisible of language kept in reserve in maternal language. In Seminar XX, Lacan designates maternal language as that language that maintains the relationship with the unconscious: it is language and unconscious together. It is for this reason, I add, that it cannot be the subject of an exhaustive study: it is always beyond definition, beyond the possibility of being *completely* understood and contained by the sieve of knowledge. It is no coincidence that, after speaking about maternal language with others, one comes away from the discussion slightly dissatisfied, as if everything can never be said. And that is exactly it. It is not possible to say everything because maternal language cannot be studied like any other language. It is not an objective historic fact. It seems to be a language like any other, but it is different because we are a living part of maternal language. We are grafted into it by speaking it. Which means that the unconscious lies between the words.[10]

In Seminar XX, Lacan refers to *lalingua*, or *lalangue*, as that language that is language and experience of the unconscious together, or as he states "Lalanguage, which, as you know, I write with two l's to designate what each of us deals with, our so-called mother tongue [*lalangue dite maternelle*], which isn't called that by accident."[11] Maternal language brings with it an unconscious relationship with the mother, which is cancelled, crossed out, not visible on the plane of meanings.

Women know more about it and stay stubbornly faithful to it. This is what Lacan seems to say when he notes in Seminar XXIII:

> It is no less the case that if there is something that may be supposed in history, then it is that what I have called lalingua is begotten by the set of women, faced with a tongue that can be broken down, Latin on this occasion, because this is what is at issue at the origin of our tongues. What is at issue is this fact of saying, examined with respect to what is involved of lalingua, with respect to what may have guided one out of the two sexes towards what I shall call the prosthesis of the equivoque, because what typifies lalingua among all the others is the equivoques that are possible in it.[12]

Here Lacan refers to religious groups of beguines in the thirteenth century who used French—the shared language, which was developing at that time—to speak about godly things in a time when male theologians continued to speak in Latin, a cultured language by then removed from experience, but with which maternal language was to enter into a vital circle.

It is interesting that Lacan refers to it as the "prosthesis of the equivoque." Reading "L'étourdit" one understands the sense in which he speaks of maternal language as *lalangue* and why ambiguity is one of its characteristics.[13] He means that, when considered from a *lalangue* viewpoint, speech is not only taken for its content but also for its assonances, homophones, rhythm, which take hearing the sense toward a fluid movement of signifiers. I will give an example of a recurrent figure in the writings of Hélène Cixous. I refer to her meditation of the French word *Orange*, which, for Cixous, reminds her of *Oran*, her native city in French Algeria, and *je*, the linkage to I in the shared language. In this way, for her, the word *Orange* bears as a signifier the root of her childhood city—unique and irreplaceable—and the presence of the grammatical pronoun "I," which concerns her. All this within the name of a fruit, the orange, which also happens to be a symbol of her native country.[14]

It is in this sense that maternal language is *lalangue*, the language of ambiguity, because one signifier leads to another, to a polysemy where the unconscious between signs is more in play than the objective reference and where, instead of totality, the nonwhole of language is given. However, this opens up to the real, that is, what Lacan defines as the impossible of the given symbolic order.

It is easy to see this by observing children. One can often notice a child in a corner repeating the words he just learned to himself, repeating the sound, the form, feeling the essence. Walter Benjamin also speaks about it in his *Berlin Childhood around 1900*. In the magical world of his infancy, since he understood wrongly and misunderstood them, the words he heard did not carry any objective reference. Nevertheless, through this involuntary deformation of the signifier, the words actually gave him access to a more authentic reality than that of the objective facts, because they dealt with the essence of life.[15]

BOUNDARY CROSSINGS

How does sexual difference play a role in this crossing of boundaries from a wordless communication to opening up to language? Which different subjectivization effects occur when one starts to give up one's own enjoyment of the corporeal and affective exchange typical of early communication?

Julia Kristeva describes the male position with respect to this existential cut in *Revolution in Poetic Language*. Kristeva considers two planes of signification. The more visible and organizing plane is that of symbolic language, which we pick up when we learn to speak. On this plane we are constituted as split subjects because it is true that we can say "I," but only in relation and opposition to "you," and always separated from "it," that is, from the reality that becomes a "non-I," in other words, an object. Lived time also becomes defined by language into the past, present, and future. When we begin to speak, the linguistic plane of symbolic order obliges us to "reject" the plane of passive-active pulsions that we experienced in the bond with the maternal body. "Semiotic" is what Kristeva calls the world of these passive-active pulsions.[16]

Kristeva describes the contradiction that emerges on learning to speak between the pulsional experience that took shape in the relation with the maternal body and the symbolic structure of a language that arranges and separates. The contradiction takes the form of a bona fide battle between symbolic and semiotic.

Only poets and writers know how to make the pulsional bond experienced with the maternal body emerge within the practices of text. They provoke an authentic revolution, not only in writing but also one with a political value. Kristeva maintains that the poetic transformation of language provokes a modification of the social codes that language brings with it and therefore affects behavior. The emergence of the semiotic on the symbolic, which occurs in poetical writings, transforms language, ways of thinking, and behavior.

I would like to suggest that Kristeva, in referring to poets and writers, really only alludes to the masculine position in terms of the loss of the pulsional bond with the maternal body. In fact, she only describes artists who have the ability to avoid the interdict of semiotic, transforming the symbolic into the practice of poetic text. It is no coincidence that she cites and comments on male writers and poets: [James] Joyce, [Stéphane] Mallarmé, [Comte de] Lautréamont, [Charles] Baudelaire, [Werner] Sollers, and so on. She never refers to female writers or poets. I thought that this was perhaps not coincidental and that her text should be interpreted exactly as the description of what happens to men in terms of crossing the boundary of language that marks the symbolic's rejection of semiotic. Kristeva's theory is not valid for women. With this statement I am offering an interpretation of *Revolution in Poetic Language*, since Kristeva does not explicitly maintain this. Nevertheless, it is an interpretation that is confirmed by the fact that her thought changes over time as she comes into contact with linguistic practices by women. It can be seen when, a few years later, she began her activity as a psychoanalyst.

As an analyst, she found herself having to listen to many women and began to pay attention to the modes and rhythms of their speech. Her own idea of semiotic was then transformed to become not so much what is rejected by the symbolic, but what accompanies it as the presence of voice, rhythm, acceleration, and slackening in speech, of all those aspects that I have called the dense aura of words, their carnal atmosphere, which forms in relations with the body of the mother. Describing this transformation in her language listening, Kristeva affirms that what became central for her at that moment "is precisely the concrete life of language."[17] The result was that she no longer considered the semiotic as in antagonistic opposition to the symbolic. Her linguistic theory changed thanks to listening to the living word of her female patients. She extended her view, which was no longer modeled on the experience of male writings. She realized how, for women, the daily experience of language is commonly marked by the signifying value of the semiotic, to which she, as an analyst, now paid particular attention. Therefore, in women's experience, there is a reciprocal game between semiotic and symbolic and no antagonistic conflict. There are, however, distortions at moments when the soul suffers.

In fact, in women's experience, some of the suffering of the soul show an unhappy relationship with the maternal language, which is always the symptom of something else.[18] We have seen how learning to speak means giving up emotional and corporeal pleasure with the mother's body, but the way we deal symbolically with this renouncement is different.

In women's experience, the semiotic has considerable value because it is felt as an indispensable element for living happily with the language. The essential point has to do with crossing that complex boundary that leads from emotional communication to really learning how to speak.

Linguistic happiness is achieved when a person manages to cross that boundary, putting into circulation words and affectivity, language and material reserve of sense, rules and living use of the language.

If this does not happen in a satisfactory manner, there are numerous experiences of linguistic unhappiness. In explaining this, I would refer to my experience as a teacher and to how young women spoke about their difficulties in writing a degree thesis.

For example, some confuse obeying the linguistic rules of grammar and syntax with the need to give up the pleasure of an emotional communication without words. They blame the rules for this loss, while is it an obligatory passage for accessing a new dimension of being.

Others, criticizing the implicit social codes that are contained in language as it is learned, refuse the entire language as an institution of power, and, therefore, cannot find their creative way to a space of freedom within the language, and through the language itself and its resources.[19]

There is also unhappiness in those who slavishly imitate the given language; they become mimetic, not in the theatrical and fun sense, but with suffering in that they are caught in a cage to which they adapt, showing the acute sense of the grayness and sterility of their communication.[20]

Many hint at body language and silence as a unique experience in which to find oneself and one's own pleasure. They accuse spoken and written language of being inadequate for expressing the intensity of such an experience. So that, feeling nostalgic for such a pleasant and apparently limitless communication, they are not attentive of the shared language, whose matrix nevertheless lies in maternal language. In their daily lives, they end up using ordinary words, words that are sloppy and without resonance.

The fact is, as Dolto observes, that women, more than men, experiment passive pulsions in the present and, for this reason, they are more greatly wounded by learning the structure of an orderly and objectifying language, one that separates the subject from the object, the symbolic language from the pulsional.

I remember the story of a friend of mine. When she was studying at university, she had to learn a series of specialized languages. It seemed to her, however, that those languages alienated her from herself and from a loving language that she imagined as a limitless extension of her own body. On the other hand, she felt obliged to learn those specialized languages because of a kind of command that she had given herself, thinking that she would otherwise have lost the relationship with her time and would have been pushed increasingly toward marginality. She therefore learned them, but resentfully. She expressed this refusal by using a simplistic language in her daily life, which, in her opinion, was supposed to give her back the immediacy she had lost. She deluded herself into thinking that she could refind the happiness of maternal language by taking refuge in a simple daily language. Her refusal of specialized languages gradually became a refusal of all language, even maternal language itself, which is rich and alive. She ended up adopting the term "thing" for every noun and "do" for every verb. Syntax was broken up. Verbs were only used in the infinitive and never declined. She no longer knew how to have a loving relationship with language and therefore neither with other people and vice versa, as the two things go hand in hand.

This is exactly the essential point: it is the loving bond with language that allows us to give life to the many languages that we come across during life, and to include within them that first vital impulse of opening up to the world that maternal language taught us. We know that women especially have a great love for language and this allows them to cross the boundary happily. It is therefore women who suffer the most when this does not happen.

I have often found myself facing the following question in regard to maternal language: is the latter the more daily language or the one of our roots, of the earth, kept and preserved within the sounds of poetry? Martin Heidegger gives an answer to this question, indicating that maternal language is the language of the mouth, the oral language, which is rooted in the earth. A language that is disappearing and that we find only in everyday speech. He metaphorically transfigures the language of the earth, maternal language, when he maintains in *On the Way to Language* that daily speech is like forgotten and worn-out poetry in which one can hardly discern the "sound of an authentic call," and he opposes poetic thinking to technical-rational thought.[21] I decided to refer to Heidegger's position here because it is a theory that has its own force of attraction, its own fascination. Nevertheless, it is a far cry from the position of maternal language that I am expressing here. Maternal language—what we learn in the maternal relationship—is no closer to poetic languages than it is to scientific languages. It cannot even be identified with daily language. It is, instead, the first opening up to the world through words that guide us within it sensitively and sensually. It is the condition that makes all languages accessible to us, from our daily oral language, with which there is usually convergence, to specific and foreign languages, learned inevitably from the phonic rhythms of our own language.[22] It is more a matter of seeing how much the sensual element and the vital impulse are creatively taken from specific languages. Certainly, poetry and literature are writing practices that owe much more to the phonic-material web of maternal language.

"FIDES" AND THE FABRIC OF THE SYMBOLIC

Maternal language teaches trust. Shouldn't it be the other way around? Wasn't it due to trust that, as "infants" [in-fans], we learned how to speak? A primary trust experienced from inside our relationship with our mother: a trust without proof? Of course, but sometimes we lose it. That trust is reborn when we listen to the words of people who know how to reawaken our desire for life and who we hear expressing a truth that touches us. Then we find it within ourselves, we relearn it, in the very instances in which we feel tired and suffocated by repetitive and falsely effective languages.

Trust is ferment, it is a lever and a necessary condition of symbolic language. It allows us to experiment and explore worlds in language that are still invisible. The feeling that accompanies it is one of happiness, which has to do with a premonition of imminent truth.

Suffering in language is, as we have seen, the symptom of something else. Nevertheless, it is good to know about it and reflect on it, because it indirectly teaches us where and how linguistic happiness can be found. There is a lot of suffering. For some, the difficulty of trusting in language leads to hearing words as firmly stuck to things in a kind of forced materialism. These words look like the skin of meaning. The world is then restricted to the smallest limits, all under control. There is no space between words and things: one lives in a suffocating prison, where there is no happiness, play, or even risk in speaking.

Coherence, which many see as a value, is one of the clearest signs. I refer to when coherence is not a choice but a compulsion, a constriction. There are some who, when they formulate a project, feel obliged to translate it into visible facts, because words are so binding for them that in no way are they able to go back on what they said. These people can only be "transparent." Sincerity is generally considered as an ethical behavior, but, as Dietrich Bonhoeffer taught, people must take into account the place and moment and who the interlocutors are in order for their words to be a truth that enlivens the context rather than destroys it in the name of a truth spoken at all costs, which could annihilate the other.[23] The symbolic capacity lies in considering the right words case by case.

It may happen then that, behind the coherence between saying and doing, between words and things, there is a suffering constriction that arises from a crack in our trust bond with others and the world, something that we should have learned in the interaction prompted by maternal language. Within the strictness of a rigid reflection between language and reality, the infinite possibilities of existence switch themselves off.

The stubbornness of achieving a desire, once declared, as if it were an absolute necessity, is a particular case. One does not realize then that, in expressing that desire in words as time flows by—that is, in following the expressive metamorphoses that change over time—the words of that desire can become the driving force for existential and political change.

However, in the claustrophobic attitude, the idea that what counts in speaking is what was said, is implicit; it is the content of the speech that is binding. It is a dangerous illusion to consider language as a tool that is totally subject to meanings to be expressed because it does not consider the gap between the world of language and the world of things that surround us—a gap that is only scary for those that had no trust in language in the first place. And yet, it is exactly this dynamic non-coincidence between words and things that gives birth to a renewed desire to find words that speak of experience, which is the very origin of expressive work.[24]

Language is symbolic because it endlessly weaves the world, relaunching the game of speaking and, through this, the experience of reality. Reality needs our linguistic creation to be known and to be dynamically created.

The world appears like one single profile when we stick to words already said. But then that profile becomes one of many when we explore the world with our experience and with the words at our disposal. The happiness of opening roads with words originates from the pleasure that the world is as it is and even more and different compared to what it appeared at first sight. It is a happiness that I would call philosophical: it accompanies the opening up of spaces of signification within the habitual space. It calls up visions.

The trust bond between words and things only needs to be installed once for us to know that we have had the experience. So that, when we lose it, we know exactly what we need in order to venture into the "great sea of being."

The first trusting relationship is the unequal one with our mother in very early childhood: an unbalanced relationship, given that dependence on the mother is at its maximum.[25] And yet a balance is created within the unbalance. Just as in our relationship with language, it is acceptance of depending on the language that gives us freedom within the language itself.[26]

The word "trust" has an interesting story. If we read the dictionary of *Indo-European Language and Society* by Émile Benveniste, we find that "trust" takes us back to the Latin word "fides," which also means credit in the sense of "I have credit with someone." Trust is not only the attitude toward opening that I have toward someone, but also the credit I enjoy with someone because that person trusts me. The Latin word "fides" therefore maintains what is essential in the relationship between mother and child, in that, since its Latin origins, the word brought with it the meaning of reciprocity and, at the same time, an inequality of conditions.[27]

The word "fides" also refers to believing in something whose existence cannot be demonstrated. It has a strong religious base, but we could interpret it more widely as the human capacity of having faith in what does not belong to the world of facts. We know that all symbolic production can show us unexpected meanings and illuminate imminent worlds that cannot immediately be verified.

Knowing how to endure emptiness: this is what faith is. It is the power to endure that words have no obligatory correspondence in the facts. Faith is also waiting: accepting the impasse of not having immediate answers to our questions about the world. However, it is also the opposite: knowing how to handle the leap across the void, when, due to a sudden burst, words throw light on a cloudy area of experience, beyond the given codes.

Paradoxically, a radical materialism is implied when we trust in the fact that words explore worlds of experience to which the established codes are blind. The counterproof is the following: when our bond with the world is weak, we cling to the codes at our disposal.

LINGUISTICS AND THE LIVING EXPERIENCE OF LANGUAGE

Language, which opens the paths to being, also opens to the world of specialized languages. These are modern-day global directions. On the other hand, it is evident that in order for a specialized language to follow its course, it must refer to creative inventions that can only come from the resource of maternal language. For example, just think how scientific discovery, founded on a partially technical language, needs images formulated in the words of daily experience.[28]

However, those involved in the discovery only consider the empiric side of the research and therefore only take as authentic the results expressed in a language that those on the outside see as alien. This is a language that has lost the infinite resource of language because it is anchored to the determining side of it.

In his book *The Crisis of European Sciences*, [Edmund] Husserl describes the process that took geometric physics from a ductile science to a language of general numerical formulas.[29] As the history of mathematics in the 1900s shows us, it is moments of crisis in a science that oblige scientists today to take another look at the fundamentals of their science and, therefore, to use a mother language.

Linguistics is the most paradoxical of specialized languages because it is the language that talks about language. Linguists study language and are also speakers and, therefore, have a living experience of the language.

There is always a moment in their highly specialized writings in which it is evident that what they are saying involves their experience as speakers, and these are the most interesting theoretical moments.

I take into consideration two linguists, [Roman] Jakobson and [Noam] Chomsky, and one psycholinguist, [Jean] Piaget, because they studied the genesis of language and would therefore seem to be close to the theme of maternal language. But that is not the only reason why I am analyzing them in this context.

My exact aim in writing about some of their contributions is to take a closer look at those reasonings in which it can be seen that they were aided by their own living experience of language. It is to maternal language that they owe those core concepts on language that really make one think.

In *Child Language, Aphasia, and Phonological Universals*, Jakobson shows how children lose something when learning to speak. Children restrict the range of sounds at their disposal to those required by the phonemes of the historical language they are learning. Every historical language has phonemes that do not coincide exactly with those of another. The way of organizing a phrase is also different as is the symbolism of grammatical genders and so, bit by bit, learning the language leads to an increasingly more complex differentiation between languages. But in Jakobson's opinion, just by going from sounds to phonemes, a child loses the infinity of sounds and immediateness of articulated expression in order to define and limit himself/herself in a precise language.[30]

Jakobson describes this process of learning to speak as being guided by two different forces: a "particularistic spirit" for which the child resists the unifying force of the language, and, on the other hand, the unifying tendency itself. The two forces oppose each other.[31] In this way, Jakobson points out what Dolto also demonstrated: a child does not learn to speak automatically. Children must, in fact, give up the pleasure of an affective wordless communication with their mothers in order to go on to a wider communication level. Contradictory powers come into play in children's lives.

Jakobson, however, when speaking of aphasias and the disintegration of the word that characterizes them, only refers to formal linguistic classifications that follow a linear route without affective gaps.[32] In this case, he loses the reference to the living experience of the language that, even in disintegration aspects, does not separate the affective side from the linguistic one and signals discontinuous moments of transformation. And yet it is Jakobson who, on reading the last poems by [Friedrich] Hölderlin, realizes how the poet's schizophrenia can be seen in his grammatical and phonetic choices within the linguistic structure: the loss of "you" and therefore of "I," the time and place indicators linked to a timeless present and a serene and inhuman nature. He sees a linguistic and affective gap: Hölderlin's very singularity, which is unconsciously replayed between before and after his illness.[33]

The living experience of maternal language is explicit in Jakobson when he demonstrates the intertwining of the grammatical, phonetic, and semantic levels of a poem. It is a symbolism that is not only cultural nor only natural. The resonance of the feminine and masculine, the jolliness of an open phoneme compared to the melancholy of dark phonemes, the speed of a verb in the future tense and the serenity of the present—these are symbolic echoes whose "rightness," according to Jakobson and those who follow the living experience of language, is not only a matter of culture. The contrast between nature and culture is foreign to the opening up to being that language allows. What Jakobson provides the most is the precise knowledge of these processes, while in speaking and writing, one proceeds with variable degrees of awareness.[34]

Chomsky also considers the genesis of speaking although in a radically different way to Jakobson.

Chomsky identified a limited number of linguistic principles. He calls them "universals of form." In his view, they are the conditions for forming every possible sentence in the language: from the most simple to the most creative.

He managed to define these few principles by observing the linguistic behavior of children. He wondered why children do not make certain types of error. Children do, of course, make a number of mistakes while learning to speak. However, they never make mistakes that invalidate the "universals of form," that it, these principles.[35] Why?

The answer for Chomsky is that every child, whether male or female, who comes into the world, has an innate schemata. And, over the course of time, with linguistic experience and education, this schemata is, so to speak, "activated."

In this way Chomsky shows the genesis of language: from a matrix of principles—the universals of form—an infinity of possible phrases is produced through precise rules.

Despite the enormous simplicity, and therefore, power of Chomsky's concept, the bond with the living experience of the language vanishes except—as we will see—in some significant points.

Although he only identified a few principles, Chomsky does not recognize that there is a limit in language—the loss of something—since he maintains that those principles are universal forms, which are the same for all languages in general. This is an aspect of his line of thought that, despite having been criticized in several ways, is still a cornerstone.[36] As a result language is seen as projected toward the infinite production of phrases. Yet, the great potential of language turns into the mechanical production of a matrix because it is not placed in relation to an effective limitation to be dealt with—along with all the emotional weight that that brings with it. It is a well-oiled machine without any glitches.

This has to do with the fact that Chomsky's speaker is a rational and normal individual: an abstract individual, in effect. Chomsky programmatically excludes any kind of individual difference.[37] Singularity in his epistemology could sound almost scandalous.

His research also impedes distinguishing the production of well-formed phrases from symbolic capacity, which, as we have seen, is something more than knowing how to formulate correct sentences.

And yet: even Chomsky, just like everyone else, is a speaker, and his experience of the language appears in having identified some linguistic principles and not others.[38]

Among these he introduces the fact that there has to be a subject. Of course, the subject of a sentence can be implied but even then its not-being-there is only apparent. Please note: the subject is already included in the grammar. But Chomsky proposes something much stronger: he includes the need for a subject among the very few language principles.

One could ask the question: why the subject? And if there were no subject, would there be chaos or something other than chaos in its place? Psychoanalysis touched on these questions when it placed the formation of the subject as the limit between conscious and unconscious.[39] On the existential and religious practice of "death of the ego," Western and Eastern literature has provided yet another answer to these questions.[40]

Chomsky does not ask himself these questions. He simply places individual experience as intuitive surety of this formal principle: he bases the need for a linguistic subject on the direct observation of speakers. He considers the behavior of children in order to maintain that nobody builds sentences without a subject. In my opinion, this is one of the best points in which Chomsky refers to his living experience of language. He wonders why children never leave out the subject. Trying to practice building incorrect sentences for them to be corrected by other people, as if you were a neutral researcher, goes against intuition. And, in fact, children never act in this way. The principle of subject is therefore innate. Adults intervene to correct children, but they never find themselves in the situation of having to correct a lack of subject in the sentence.[41]

Piaget, like Jakobson and Chomsky, also reconstructs the genesis of language. He speaks of a wider symbolic capacity than that of the use of language. This takes shape in children long before they learn how to speak. Moreover, it consists of imitation: young girls and boys not only imitate adult behavior but also that of animals and objects. They also know how to play in reference to situations not present at the time. One only has to think of a child running like a galloping horse or another making a hut out of two armchairs pushed close together. Another characteristic of symbolic capacity is being able to live in imaginary interior worlds, knowing how to keep the interior and exterior world separate and connected.

Later, this symbolic capacity will help to form verbal language, and this in turn, will lead to constructing logical thought at around seven years of age.

In this way, Piaget contributes to seeing maternal language not only as knowing how to speak, but also as symbolic knowledge in which many levels that cannot be reduced merely to linguistic skills intertwine.

Piaget, however, also proposes a mechanical succession between the various phases. Each phase frictionlessly includes the previous one. In this way, development is seen as an enrichment by determined stages. He certainly knows how to speak about the experience of abnormal children, but even in his studies, there is no mention of the fact that every symbolic step toward a richer situation also leads to the simultaneous loss of something else.

The different stories that little girls and boys and then women and men have with their mothers is totally ignored, as well as the fact that it is our mother who takes us by the hand and leads us beyond the limits of preverbal language in order to enter another level of being. And neither is there any trace of the different way of relating to the attitude of trust in the reserve of sense in words.

Reading Jakobson, Chomksy, and Piaget, one can observe how their texts become vital when they illuminate aspects of our habitual speaking. Something so normal that we cannot see through it. They bring them to our awareness, making us discover what we already do. The risk they run at all times is to turn language into a dead object. Something external and alien. While the reason language is alive is because it is internal and external at the same time.

Yet, those who maintain that living experience of language is an intimist and purely subjective experience are wrong. Language is immediately intersubjective even before we can think about "I." It is common to us and others without reasoning. This is why it can never be an instrument. It does not belong to us personally; we inherit it. It touches the body and soul without our will ever being able to stem it.

We live in the language. It is everyone's wealth, so much so that it belongs to no one. If we are surprised by the fact that the language in which we live and that surrounds us physically and intimately, like an extension of our bodies, is also the language of everyone and no one, then a feeling of wonder blocks us when considering its impersonality. Being foreign within our own language—intimate and foreign—makes us curious about its more than personal laws.

Language studies are one answer to this feeling of wonder, to this being at home yet, at the same time, alien within the language. They allow us to see the anonymous implication that involves us corporeally: something that our individual conscience cannot immediately arrive at.[42]

What the researchers often forget is that the relation between me as a speaker and the language I speak, if taken into consideration, leads to an awareness of the mechanisms of the language. The fact is, language is produced through me, even though it belongs to everyone. Personal testimony, through stories, autobiographies, letters, etc., illustrates an incarnation of language. An unrepeatable embodiment of everyone's language.

[G. W.] Leibniz's "monad" springs to mind. It is merely an expression of relations with others. It reflects the entire world starting from the relations that it has with it. It is a "perpetual living mirror of the universe."[43] The position it occupies, however, is unrepeatable because the time and place of its singularity are unique, "as one and the same town viewed from different sides looks altogether different, and is, as it were, *perspectively* multiplied, it similarly happens that, through the infinite multitude of simple substances, there are, as it were, just as many different universes, which however are only the perspectives of a single one according to the different points of view of each monad."[44] And just as, in order to know the world, one must pass through the singularity that it represents, in order to know the city of language, the perspective of an individual speaker already proves the potentiality of speaking. Linguists study the potentiality of language.

All too often linguists tend to look down upon the city from above, photographing the layout and forgetting that they themselves, as speakers, live in one of the houses.

And yet language studies train us to be impersonal. The fact is, that the living experience of language has something anonymous even in the singular juncture from which we can start. When, for example, referring to maternal language, one speaks of the pleasure that it preserves, one refers to something that is not personal, which is a pleasure in itself. Something that does not depend on us but which we trust in. An impersonal pleasure that helps us toward individual orientation.

Translated by Diane Lutkin

NOTES

This chapter is the translation of a much revised and expanded version of "Lingua materna tra limite e apertura infinita," in *All'inizio di tutto: La lingua materna*, ed. Eva-Maria Thüne (Turin: Rosenberg & Sellier, 1998).

1. For female schoolteachers and their mediation between childhood and scholastic language, see Luisa Muraro, "Lo splendore di avere un linguaggio," *Aut aut*, nos. 260–61 (1994): 29–30.

2. Franz Kafka, *The Complete Stories*, ed. Nahum N. Glatzer (New York: Schocken Books, 1983), 3.

3. Kafka, *Complete Stories*, 4.

4. See Tullio De Mauro, "Viva e vera," in *Dove va la lingua italiana?*, ed. Jader Jacobelli (Bari: Laterza, 1987), 68–69. The relationship between maternal language and living language is also developed by Andrea Camilleri and Tullio De Mauro in *La lingua batte dove il dente duole* (Bari: Laterza, 2013).

5. On the epic parallelism in languages with an oral imprint, see Roman Jakobson, "Grammatical Parallelism and Its Russian Facet," in *Language* 42, no. 2 (1966): 399–429.

6. On the relationship between maternal language and dialects, see Chiara Zamboni, "Lingua materna come risorsa per ricerche linguistiche interdisciplinari," in *Isole linguistiche?*, ed. Gianna Marcato (Padua: Unipress, 2000), 298–300.

7. Françoise Dolto, *L'immagine inconscia del corpo*, trans. Valeria Fresco (Milan: Red Edizioni, 2011), 343. From here on translation in languages other than English are by Diane Lutkin.

8. See Elias Canetti, *Tongue Set Free*, trans. Joachim Neugroschel (New York: Seabury Press, 1979); I also refer to Marcel Proust because he describes how initiation and love for language and literature is given by the language of the mother and grandmother. See Marcel Proust, *Swann's Way*, trans. Lydia Davis (New York: Viking, 2003). Lastly, the writings of Luigi Meneghello are essential, especially *Deliver Us*, trans. Frederika Randall (Evanston, Ill.: Northwestern University Press, 2011).

9. See Dolto, *L'immagine inconscia del corpo*, 78–80.

10. See the beautiful study by Jean-Claude Milner, *L'amour de la langue* (Paris: Éditions du Seuil, 1978).

11. Jacques Lacan, *On Feminine Sexuality, the Limits of Love, and Knowledge (1972–1973), Encore: The Seminar of Jacques Lacan Book XX*, trans. Bruce Fink (New York : W. W. Norton, 1999), 138. The French word *lalangue* is a wordplay on the *"lala"* sound that recalls a child's first attempt to learn a language. Lacan invented the word, which, in fact, cannot be found in the French dictionary.

12. Jacques Lacan, *The Sinthome, The Seminar of Jacques Lacan, Book XXIII*, trans. A. R. Price (Malden, Mass.: Polity Press, 2016), 98.

13. See Jacques Lacan, "L'étourdit," in *Autres écrits* (Paris: Éditions du Seuil, 2001).

14. See Hélène Cixous, "De la scéne de l'inconscient à la scène de l'Histoire: Chemins d'une écriture," in Hélène Cixous, *Chemins d'une écriture*, ed. Françoise Rossum Van Guyon and Miriam Diocaretz (Paris: P.U.V. Éditions, 1990), 15–34.

15. See Walter Benjamin, *Berlin Childhood around 1900*, trans. Howard Eiland (Cambridge, Mass.: Harvard University Press, 2006), 97–99.

16. On the symbolic see particularly Julia Kristeva, *Revolution in Poetic Language*, trans. Margaret Waller (New York: Columbia University Press, 1984), 46–51, 25–30. In any case, the two concepts are dealt with in an ample theoretical framework that we can read in the first chapter entitled "Semiotic and Symbolic."

17. For example, one reads how Kristeva describes the case of one of her depressed patients: "This distinction [between semiotic and symbolic] became central to my work starting from *Revolution in Poetic Language*. I currently develop it in the analytical field, that is, in situations that are not poetic writing, but those of analytical treatment. Hearing the semiotic in a situation in which the symbolic is suffocated or neutralized is, therefore, a way for the analyst to

give life back to the patient. In my first book, *Black Sun*, I give the example of a patient of mine who was in a state of depression and whose discourse was defensive. She affirmed that what she said meant nothing and often ended up not speaking at all. Now, this patient livened up when I turned my attention to her voice and when I interpreted the rhythm of her voice, its acceleration or slackening. In this case, I shifted my attention to a suprasegmental language level, as linguists would say, that is, a level that is no longer the one of signs but the one that regards (in a more elaborate way than echolalias since I was dealing with an adult) a use of prelanguage which, in my opinion, concerns the semiotic." Julia Kristeva, *Come prefazione: Intervista a Julia Kristeva (by Augusto Ponzio)*, only available in the Italian version of Julia Kristeva's *Il linguaggio questo sconosciuto*, trans. Angela Biancofiore and Augusto Ponzio (Bari: Adriatica, 1992), 15–16. This interview was carried out in 1992. During it, Kristeva added: "What the semiotic, as I intended it, did not want to avoid was precisely the concrete life of language" (20).

18. It is above all psychoanalysis that underlines how maternal language touches the body and soul and how suffering, in terms of maternal language, is a sign of an existential problem that goes far beyond a simple linguistic fact. A text that deals with this by comparing the position of various psychoanalysts on the bond between suffering and maternal language is Jacqueline Amati Mehler, Simona Argentieri, and Jorge Canestri's *La Babele dell'inconscio: Lingua madre e lingue straniere nella dimensione psicoanalitica* (Milan: Cortina Ed., 1990).

19. Judith Butler speaks of the maternal relationship as the beginning of a dependence on power in *The Psychic Life of Power*. Butler denies how, within this very maternal relationship, there is not only dependence but also a creative relationship with all its potential. The defect of her theory is that power is seen as something through which we can interpret all the facts of reality, while there is more to it. Judith Butler, *The Psychic Life of Power: Theories in Subjection* (Stanford, Calif.: Stanford University Press, 1997), 6–10.

20. For the double aspect of women's mimetism in terms of language—repetitive, static or playful and inventive—see Luce Irigaray, *Speculum of the Other Woman*, trans. Gillian C. Gill (Ithaca, N.Y.: Cornell University Press, 1985). Her theory is that playful women's mimetism leads to a new form of symbolization.

21. See Martin Heidegger, "Language," in *Poetry, Language, Thought*, trans. Albert Hofstadter (New York: HarperCollins, 2001), 205 [translation modified]. On the distinction between the poetic and the technical see "The Nature of Language," in *On the Way to Language*, trans. Peter D. Hertz (New York: Harper-Collins, 1982), 57–110.

22. On the capacity of maternal language to guide us toward learning foreign languages, see Elisabeth Jankowski, "Ascoltare la madre," in *All'inizio di tutto la lingua materna*, 11–36.

23. See Dietrich Bonhoeffer, *Ethics*, trans. Neville Horton Smith (New York: Simon & Schuster, 1995), 358–67.

24. On this theme of the dynamic noncoincidence between words and things as a driving force behind a constantly renewed and mobile desire to find words for experience, see Cristina Faccincani, *Alle radici del simbolico* (Naples: Liguori, 2010), 76–79.

25. Luisa Muraro, *The Symbolic Order of the Mother*, trans. Francesca Novello (Albany: State University of New York Press, 2018).

26. See also Diana Sartori, "With the Maternal Spirit," chapter 6 in this volume.

27. See Émile Benveniste, *Indo-European Language and Society*, trans. Elizabeth Palmer (Coral Gables, Fla.: University of Miami Press, 1973), 96–97.

28. To understand these statements on scientific discovery, see Imre Lakatos, *Proofs and Refutations: The Logic of Mathematical Discovery* (Cambridge: Cambridge University Press, 1976).

29. See Edmund Husserl, *The Crisis of European Sciences and Transcendental Phenomenology*, trans. David Carr (Evanston, Ill.: Northwestern University Press, 1970), 21–100.

30. Roman Jakobson, *Child Language, Aphasia, and Phonological Universals* (The Hague: Mouton, 1968), 13–44.

31. Jakobson, *Child Language*, 13–18 and 20–24.

32. Jakobson, *Child Language*, 36–38 and 64.

33. See Roman Jakobson and Grete Lübbe-Grothues, "Ein Blick auf 'Die Aussicht' von Hölderlin," in Roman Jakobson, *Hölderlin. Klee. Brecht. Zur Wortkunst dreier Gedichte* (Frankfurt am Main: Surkamp, 1976), 27–96.

34. On this linguistic symbolism, which Jakobson demonstrates in the intertwining of all levels of language, see Jakobson and Lübbe-Grothues, "Ein Blick auf 'Die Aussicht' von Hölderlin," as well as Roman Jakobson, "On a Generation that Squandered Its Poets," in *Language in Literature*, ed. Krystyna Pomorska and Stephen Rudy (Cambridge, Mass.: Harvard University Press, 1987), 273–300 and "Poetry of Grammar and Grammar of Poetry," *Lingua* 21 (1968): 597–609. But see also Roman Jakobson and Krystina Pomorska, *Dialogues* (Cambridge, Mass.: MIT Press, 1982), and Roman Jakobson, *Selected Writings, Volume 3, Poetry of Grammar and Grammar of Poetry* (The Hague: Mouton, 1981), 765–89.

35. See Noam Chomsky, "Le strutture cognitive e il loro sviluppo: Una risposta a Piaget," in *Liguaggio e apprendimento: Il dibattito tra Jean Piaget e Noam Chomsky*, ed. Massimo Piattini Palmarini (Milan: Jaca Book, 1991), 65, 156.

36. See, for example, Tullio De Mauro, introduction to J. Amati Mehler, S. Argentieri, and J. Canestri, *La Babele dell'inconscio* (Milan: Raffaello Cortina Editore, 2003), xxvii–xviii. De Mauro underlines that Chomsky problematized this abstract universalism but not enough to impair the fact that is considered as a cornerstone of his linguistic theory.

37. See Chomsky, "Le strutture cognitive e il loro sviluppo," 65.

38. Chomsky, "Le strutture cognitive e il loro sviluppo," 72.

39. Reference can be made, for example, to Lacan. Lacan maintains that the first nucleus of subjectivity is established in the mirror phase, i.e., when a child recognizes another similar to him or different from him outside of himself. The most important moment in the establishment of subjectivity is when a child learns language. Nominating the "Ego" according to precise and socially codified ways, language creates a split situation between everything that comes into what can be said in the language and everything that can be excluded from it. See Jacques Lacan, *The Seminar of Jacques Lacan, Book II*, trans. Sylvana Tomaselli (Cambridge and New York: Cambridge University Press, 1988), 51–63.

40. In Western literature, reference can be made to, among others, Simone Weil and her *Notebooks*. Here she describes the possibility that humans offer themselves as mediators in the world in front of God exactly in the moment in which the "Ego" ceases to exist. She writes, for example, that "water is inner death. Water image of pliant attentiveness . . . to wait is the extreme of passivity. It is to be obedient to time. Total obedience to time obliges God to bestow eternity." Simone Weil, *First and Last Notebooks*, trans. Richard Rees (London: Oxford University Press, 1970), 111. Here the possibility of opening to being and the dissolving of "Ego," as water would allow, is evident. In Eastern literature, this symbolic figure is present in Buddhism. For example, in the Zen version of Buddhism, abandoning the "Ego" takes the form of a leap beyond multiple relative awarenesses. See Daisetz Taitaro Suzuki, *Essays in Zen Buddhism (Second Series)* (London: Rider and Co., 1977).

41. See Chomsky, *Le strutture cognitive e il loro sviluppo*, 66–69. Chomsky also puts into play a reference to the intuitive behaviors of speakers when he states that the production of a sentence must be accepted by a native speaker, who then becomes a unit of measure for well-formed sentences.

42. On these themes, see Maurice Merleau-Ponty, *The Visible and the Invisible*, trans. Alphonso Lingis (Evanston, Ill.: Northwestern University Press, 1964), 181–82.

43. Gottfried Wilhelm Leibniz, *G. W. Leibniz's Monadology*, ed. Nicholas Rescher (Pittsburgh: University of Pittsburgh Press, 1991), 198.

44. Leibniz, *G. W. Leibniz's Monadology*, 200–201.

Feminism and Psychoanalysis

The Dead Mother Complex

LUISA MURARO

To write is good, to read is better: reading undoes the old weave and makes a new one, often a better one, because the mind of the one who reads, unconcerned with the work of writing, filters and at the same time expands in a generous welcome—the written work can be completed only by reading. But this cannot be done with one's own books: they cannot enjoy the benefit of our reading. One can do something else: one can "retract" them. One can retract them completely. Or one can criticize them, like Saint Augustine did in his *Retractationes*. Or yet again, one can go through them once again, retraverse them, like a landscape after many years of absence, as I will do.

L'ordine simbolico della madre [*The Symbolic Order of the Mother*] was published in 1991, immediately reissued, and after that was out of print. The first Italian edition can be recognized because of an enormous mistake on page 10, Euripides in place of Aeschylus, the author of the *Oresteia*. It was translated into German in 1993, and into Spanish a year later, and more recently, in 2003, into French. It was immediately commented on at length by Ida Dominijanni and Rossana Rossanda in the daily *Il manifesto*.

I derived the title from a text by Lia Cigarini and Maria Grazia Campari—which appeared in the journal *Sottosopra*—"La madre fonte del diritto" [The mother source of right], as well as from the developments given to their ideas by the research undertaken in the Diotima philosophical community and, more generally, by the feminism known as the feminism of difference.[1]

The mother is universally the name of the relation that is the *condition* of *human* life. By means of feminism we discovered that, in our civilization, the human condition was declined only in the masculine and entirely arranged around the mother–son relationship, in which the male child was presumed to be the realization of a woman's greatest wish and desire. There is therefore something that is unthought in the human condition—something enclosed in the mother–daughter relationship and present in some way in every woman's experience. This is the intuition the book attempts to develop, starting from two statements that are explicitly at odds with the doctrine of the structural necessity of the father: namely, that we receive at once both life and word from the mother, and that the symbolic order is made neither by power nor by the law but by language. Dominijanni, considering the book once again, recently wrote that it is precisely about "the symbolic order that the maternal language knows how to produce—namely, the ability to hold body and words together, the experience and the language that we learn in our primary relationship with the mother."[2] It is a revolutionary order, she continues, because the mother–daughter relationship is erased in the patriarchal order, "and to learn how to practice it in adulthood by substituting aversion for the mother with gratitude for the mother and for the other women who continue her work opens up the space for the sayability of women's experience, which is otherwise subjected to conformity to the norm and to male power."[3]

Francesca Solari (director and writer of the film *Addio Lugano bella*, in which she portrays herself while reading this book, a work dear to her) has written: in this book, the relationship with the mother starts to take place, a symbolic place in which a woman finds the resources to be in the world while following her own desire. She adds: "This is a philosophical work in the true sense of the word—the love of wisdom—written not to be right or to transform the world, but to bring the subtle truths of life closer; it's a book that reduces the gap between feeling and thinking, doing and being, thereby reducing the unease that this causes for both self and world: *a therapeutic work*."[4] I emphasize these last three words that, together with the generosity of the speaker, express an intuition that will return to make itself felt in my own words.

Later, Solari deals with a friend's objection—"And the father?"— to which she responds as follows: "The father: it was necessary that someone, a woman, would forget him for a moment, in order to begin moving closer to the mysteries, to the treasures, of the mother, in order to think without that mess of power and property that is all knotted up around the phallus."[5]

But there are those who believed it was not really possible to "forget" the father, and who did not see in the mother anything other than his equivalent or his lieu-tenant, so to speak.[6] Among the critiques of *The Symbolic Order of the Mother* that have been made by feminist thinkers, one that comes up frequently is that it substituted the figure of the mother for that of the father—i.e., the mother in place of the father without any guarantee of a substantial change.

What is my answer today, years later? To begin with I will complete my thought on the father: although I am critical regarding his presumed necessity, I am not at all opposed to his *possibility*, quite the contrary—I am favorable to it for a number of reasons that the book barely touches upon. Today, rather, I would dwell on this point because it concerns a topic that interests me, namely, the contingency of the real. In a sense, in the past one talked too much in terms of the necessity of father, taking for granted that he exists, that he has a function, that he has a place. . . . The father *and* the symbolic: what happened, in fact, is that when European thinkers (first) and American thinkers (later) appropriated the notion of the symbolic, this installed itself in their minds and expelled from them any thought of the contingency of the real—and by this I mean the awareness that things happen (and that anything may happen). These were often male thinkers to whom becoming pregnant never happened, who inhabited comfortable and solid structures like university campuses where it was easy to turn structuralism into a definitive horizon. It took 9/11 to reopen their minds: they had forgotten that the world continues to be made, remade, or unmade, much like and together with the language we speak. Paternity, especially, is not solid matter: Jacques Lacan—someone who knew what he was talking about—when talking about our era speaks of the "evaporation of the father," like water on a sheet that is hung out to dry.[7]

So, shall we place this book among the documents of an emergent society without fathers? No. If anything, the story it tells is situated at the beginning rather than at the end of the trajectory followed by patriarchy, in a sense that I shall elaborate on later. But ultimately its place is among the vicissitudes of the subject in that constant making and unmaking of the world to which I was referring earlier. This is a making and an unmaking that we have some inkling of, for example, by way of the experience of the uncertain and difficult relation we have to writing, when we ourselves are at stake in what we write—an uncertainty and a difficulty that no amount of practice, no métier, no ability, however great, allow us to overcome: only stupidity or folly do.

In the course of the recent research undertaken in the Diotima philosophical community on the topic of the negative (which resulted in *La magica forza del negativo*),[8] I found a text that sheds quite a bit of light on this book of mine from 1991. I am referring to "La mère morte" (The dead mother) by André Green, a text from 1980, published in *Narcissisme de vie, narcissisme de mort*.[9] The author gives the name of "dead mother" to a mother in mourning who is inhabited by pain due to a loss for which nobody can provide consolation, not even the newborn baby. Hence the kind of suffering the French psychoanalyst finds in certain patients, a suffering that is equivalent to an insurmountable attachment to the maternal figure. Due to this attachment to the mother, he writes, it can happen that the woman or the little girl cannot perform any investment in the figure of the father.[10]

Analogously, many women perceived that, in *The Symbolic Order of the Mother*, the mother had not been located in a place that had been the father's, because, as Francesca Solari's friend had sensed, there is no place of the father in the book. Francesca speaks of a "forgotten father," but one could also say: a father that has always remained in a volatile state.

The objection could then be: under these conditions, how can a woman write a book of philosophy? André Green informs us that, quite to the contrary, these types of patients are often productive on the artistic or intellectual level, where they try to "re-create the compromised unity of the Ego"—that's how he puts it. Their attempt fails, he states, but it doesn't fail there where they have moved their "theater of operations," and he sees no reason to deny "authenticity" to the products of their operations, in other words, to their works.[11]

I am struck by the term *authenticity* because it appears in my book in a formula that often recurs, *authentic sense of being*. . . . Some will say this is not so strange in a philosophy book, but perhaps it is since it is an expression that is abused in common parlance and is also regarded with suspicion by philosophy. So that in the introduction to the French translation of my book I criticized my use of this formula, saying that the use of the adjective "authentic" was redundant and that at this point I considered it a painful defect, a defect in the experience of being, a kind of lament that Green also gathers from his patients, almost in the same terms, as an interdiction of being, a loss of sense, an incessant search for sense.

At this point, a question emerges, namely, the question of learning what the "theater of operations" the author of *The Symbolic Order of the Mother* has moved to is. The answer is simple, it is us here, it is the women's political movement. The book was born thanks to the fact that she, the "patient," the one who suffers, had found a theater, which is still this one in which we find ourselves. I want to remind people about one of the fundamental characteristics of this theater, one that was underscored by Françoise Collin, a Francophone feminist and philosopher, who, when reviewing this book, writes that "the theme of the reconciliation of the mother with the daughter is a path for fertile reflections, a wager that lies at the foundation [*un enjeu fondateur*] of the women's movement, that of their ability to give sense, also, to themselves," where, you will notice, the issue of sense arises once more.[12]

Let me therefore get to the central idea of my *retractatio*: that book I wrote in 1991 is written on two strata, like a palimpsest, one scraped off and corresponding to the history of a passionate attachment to a mother who was wounded inside, and another layered on top of the first, occupied by the women's political movement.

What is the relation between the two texts of the palimpsest? And, implicitly, what is the relation between psychoanalysis and feminism?

In truth, these are highly simplified questions. For example: can we talk of two texts? If we go down this path, the texts will become ten, one hundred, like filo dough. Better not: *The Symbolic Order of the Mother* exists as a book to be read and not interpreted; in other words, it requires that it be "held together" in the mind of the ones who read it. It's (my) wager [*enjeu*] was—and I realize this more clearly now than I did then— to pass from the scraped-off text, the unconscious scene, that of monsters [*mostri*], that can only be shown [*mostrata*], to its de-monstration [*di-mostrazione*], without this passage leading simply to a result of mere senselessness, but, on the contrary, leading to its success in turning that which was only monsters on display [*mostro e mostra*], a circus-freak show, into something significant. I was attempting to stage, in other words, some part of the maternal potential that belonged to me, and I presumed that I was successful in doing so and that the effect was one of the highest possible sense and meaning, which took the form of a gain in philosophical intelligence. I had managed to accomplish something similar in the field of historiography by writing *La signora del gioco* [Lady of the Game], an essay on witch-hunting that was devoted to listening to what the defendants said about themselves and their world when put on trial.[13]

But there was also the risk and the fear of an overflow of the monstration [*mostrazione*] with respect to the de-monstration, and this can be felt in *The Symbolic Order of the Mother*. The book defends itself from the risk of this overflow (of senselessness) by resorting to a certain preconstituted philosophical culture, which sometimes becomes its mask and makes it unnecessarily convoluted. And this certainly caused some difficulties for a number of women readers, but less than one might imagine. Many were able to overcome this obstacle. Among them, I would like to mention the special case of Adriana Sbrogiò, who is now a friend of mine, who edited and published an abbreviated version of the book, distributing it in hundreds of copies, "purged" of the sections she found uselessly difficult and which often correspond to the convoluted sections, in the sense I already mentioned. Let me add that I have learned something since then, by attending the lessons of women poets: I am thinking of somebody like Amelia Rosselli, for instance, who comes close to saying nothing in order to say that which is pressing for her, that which presses her.

There is a myth, or, rather, a fragment of the great myth of Demeter, which succeeds magnificently in condensing my book's intent, both what is explicit and what is latent in it. After the abduction of her daughter Persephone, Demeter, the "dead mother" par excellence, wanders the earth refusing to eat, rest, or be consoled. The Orphics, however, do tell a story about her consolation. On the road between Athens and Eleusis, Demeter came across a poor house where she was welcomed hospitably. Baubo, the owner, offered her a restoring drink, which the goddess refused. Baubo then sat in front of her, spread her legs, and lifted her skirt showing her not very attractive body. At that point, the son she carried in her womb, Iacchus, started to laugh. The goddess also started to laugh and, laughing, accepted the drink.

André Green—who does not quote the myth and seems unaware of the mythological resonances of his own words—narrates that the patient he is treating did precisely this as a newborn, or does this now as a patient, toward the "dead mother": "to reanimate her, to distract her, to attract her interest, to give her back her taste for life, to make her laugh and smile."[14] Which is exactly what we see Baubo do in the Orphic tale about the consolation of Demeter. And which we might think the author of *The Symbolic Order of the Mother* is doing too: restoring to her mother something that has been taken away from her—freedom, joy, a daughter, or herself as woman.

I ask myself: in the society of women that is constituting itself, has it become possible to symbolically translate and to resolve the double grief of maternal mourning and of our impotence as living daughters?

Here the question that Solari raised when she talked about "therapeutic work" surfaces again. Green's patient, whether man or woman, did not, as a newborn, achieve the success that Baubo achieved, that is, the Orphic rite in honor of Demeter. But was the rite effective? Or was it an endlessly repeated liturgy, due to the awareness that there was nothing else to do but this repetition? Will the psychoanalytic therapy practiced by Green be effective? Is the writing-reading of this book, and are the political practices to which it refers, effective? Naturally, it is also a question of understanding this word, "efficacy/effectiveness," whose meaning cannot be left out from this issue.

I will seek help from the question of hysteria, which is dealt with in my book and which also recurs in feminist discussions. In the nineteenth century, the hysteric was a freak-show phenomenon, even though the spectacle had moved from convents and churches to the interior of hospital wards, for the benefit of a public all decked out in white coats. As we know, Freud, following the suggestions of his first women patients, redeemed hysteria by positing its truth and turning it into the cause (the thing) of the science and the practice of psychoanalysis. But the hysteric remained a prisoner anyway: psychoanalysis enclosed her within an interpretation, that of a presumed desire of the father, thus managing first to use and then to ignore the hysteric's intolerance for the regime of mediations, as well as her ability to say something other with respect to this regime and her ability to cause this same regime to say something other with respect to itself.

The liberation of the truth of the hysteric takes place with feminism, or, rather, with the feminism of difference and the primacy this assigns to the woman-to-woman relationship. This relationship is practiced within relations that are *not* ethically regulated by equality and reciprocity: they are unequal relations, of love and caring; often, they are conflictual relations; at times, they are obscured by the "shadow of the mother" (to quote the title of Diotima's latest seminar in fall 2005). It is precisely thanks to these irregular modalities that they manage to make the ancient mother–daughter relationship significant. In short, for the hysteric, feminism has been like a theater that gives some sense to symptoms by making sense emanate not from an interpretation that is produced by somebody else—who, thus, subtracts himself from the relation—but directly from the relationships that are in play on stage. The sense in question is the privilege of the daughter's proximity to the maternal body, a proximity without interdictions, and a privilege that, following the thought expressed in my 1991 book, only obtains for those "who know how to love the mother."

I am talking about possibilities. In my work, for me it is almost always a question of reconfiguring the landscape so that something else may occur. I work with my mind to open some paths for thought and some passages for women's freedom.

What I just called the privilege of proximity to the maternal body without interdictions is something that, as far as I am concerned, is allowed by women's politics, with all that this entails, which is to make something of maternal potential available. It is not allowed instead, and this is obvious, by the politics that men prefer to practice. (When I speak of "politics" I understand it in the broadest sense of the term, whereby to get married or not, to become a nun, to declare one's own homosexuality or, vice versa, to choose not to declare it, is also politics. As long as one thinks about what one does, and as long as what one does is done thinking also about others, in relation to others, women or men, there is politics.) It seems to me that men prefer—or, perhaps, need—to perform some separations, especially when the maternal is at issue (and the things associated with the maternal are numerous). This is well known but not negligible, first of all because a separation is a definition and modifies the entire field of meanings. Second, because women, who don't have the same symbolic needs as men, are increasingly less content to stay put in the place men had assigned to them, and all this creates problems that are raised to the nth power.

Let me take as an example two authors who are often quoted together, Judith Butler and Slavoj Žižek. In the course of his engagement with her in that large and convoluted tome entitled *The Ticklish Subject: The Absent Centre of Political Ontology*, I agree with him when he writes: "It thus seems more productive to posit as the central enigma that of sexual difference—*not* as the already established symbolic difference (heterosexual normativity), but, precisely, as that which forever eludes the grasp of normative symbolization."[15] But I don't agree with the path taken from there onward, where one finds, among other things, a tale of how freedom begins—a path that I find so typically "male," based as it is on a story of repeated separations from the maternal. He speaks, in fact, of "different logics" regarding, on the one hand, the primary dependency on, as well as awe or fear toward, the mother, in the form of a passionate attachment, and, on the other hand, the subjection to the socio-symbolic order, criticizing Butler for confusing these two forms of the constitution of subjectivity, the one that takes place in the theater of the unconscious, and the other that takes place in the socio-symbolic theater. His position is clear and, to those familiar with the issue, perhaps even obvious; but since the time one started studying women's history a bit better, the situation is no longer so obvious: think of witch-hunting, think of the *tricoteuses*, think of hysteria! These are all examples of the "confusion" that women make (provoke, are) between that which is most intimate and that which is most public. I doubt that women may aspire to symbolic independence in the terms that probably both Green and Žižek have in mind—an independence that is achieved via the separation from the mother and via the shift of a third level (which for Freud was the paternal, and for Green and Žižek I am not sure, perhaps also the paternal) into the symbolic. The separation that men practice and that is necessary, so they say, to their symbolic order would translate, for a woman, into a sort of deportation that deprives her of symbolic competence. It's well known that some women do become very successful in following this path, better than men as they say, to such a degree that we are afraid of her, but for most women this condition of deportees means that they (we) have problems, deficiencies in authority and originality. Let's be clear: if a woman cannot aspire to that type of independence, even when the impediment takes on the appearance of personal inadequacy or social discrimination, it's high time that we started thinking that the impediment really consists of her privilege, that of being born of the same sex as the mother.

Several times, even recently, I have heard people say that *The Symbolic Order of the Mother* is the text that constitutes the reference point of the so-called feminism of difference. Each and every time, I protested that this is not the case, because it is not. However, now I am inclined to think that there might be something right in that assessment. The feminism of difference, if one wants to use this label—namely, the feminism that promotes women's freedom not with laws but with relationships, not in the name of equality between the sexes but in the free sense of sexual difference—has basically accomplished this in these past years: it has saved the privilege of women's proximity with the maternal body. I don't attribute the merit entirely to the thought of difference; to the latter I attribute having kept in mind and having put into words something that existed in women's political practice, something that very much resembles the hospitality offered by Baubo, the peasant, to the terrible goddess.

Translated by Mark William Epstein

NOTES

This chapter is a translation of "Psicoanalisi e femminismo: Il complesso della madre morta," which was published as the appendix to the 2006 edition of *L'ordine simbolico della madre* (Rome: Editori Riuniti, 2006), 149–59.

    1. Lia Cigarini and Maria Grazia Campari, "Un filo di felicità," *Sottosopra* (1989), http://www.libreriadelledonne.it/_oldsite/news/articoli/sottosopra89.htm. ["La madre fonte del diritto" is a section of "Un filo di felicità."—Eds.]

    2. Ida Dominijanni, "La madre dopo il patriarcato," *Il manifesto*, 28 October 2005, 14.

    3. Dominijanni, "La madre dopo il patriarcato," 14.

    4. Francesca Solari, unpublished manuscript; emphasis added.

    5. Solari, unpublished manuscript.

    6. [Here, Muraro spells the Italian term *luogotenente* with a hyphen, i.e., *luogo-tenente*. In doing so, she is drawing attention to the etymology of the Italian

term *luogotenente*, which—just like the equivalent French term *lieutenant*, often used by Jacques Lacan—means literally "the one who takes place" or also "the one who takes the place of somebody else." This is why we have kept the hyphenation in the English translation.—Trans.]

7. Jacques Lacan, "Nota sul padre e l'universalismo," *La psicoanalisi: Rivista Italiana della Scuola Europea di Psicoanalisi*, no. 33 (2003).

8. Diotima, *La magica forza del negativo* (Naples: Liguori, 2005).

9. André Green, "La mère morte," in *Narcissisme de vie, narcissisme de mort* (Paris: Les Éditions de Minuit, 1983), 220–53.

10. Green, "La mère morte," 238.

11. Green, "La mère morte," 233.

12. Françoise Collin, "L'ordre symbolique de la mère," *Revue des lettres et de traduction*, Dossier "Le rapport mère/fille," no. 10 (2004): 517–23.

13. Luisa Muraro, *La signora del gioco: Episodi della caccia alle streghe* (Milan: Feltrinelli, 1976).

14. Green, "La mère morte," 235.

15. Slavoj Žižek, *The Ticklish Subject: The Absent Centre of Political Ontology* (London: Verso, 1999), 271.

PART III

The Mother and the Negative

With the Maternal Spirit

DIANA SARTORI

Hört, hört, hört! Rachegötter—hört!—der Mutter Schwur!

—W. A. Mozart, *Die Zauberflöte*, Act II

THE RETURN OF THE MOTHER'S SHADOW

There is something far from contingent in *returning* to the node of that which is obscure in the maternal after the work done with *La magica forza del negativo* [The magical force of the negative].[1]

First of all because the modality of the return is intrinsic to the relationship itself, one we can establish as prevalent with the maternal during our life, even when we have the good fortune of having a living relationship with our mother: we may always approach the maternal with a movement that returns, looks back, takes up again. We can only readdress it, we can only return to it, because it is something that has always already been, previously given: it was there from the beginning.[2] Secondly because the form of this *returning* is the same as that in which the obscure in the maternal manifests itself: it is the form of a shadow of the mother that re-presents itself, reappears, insists, may capture in the circuit of a reiteration, shimmers in the circle of a repetition.[3]

In this sense, one could suspect that this return to the theme of the negative, as linked specifically to the shadow of the mother, rather than being due to necessity is akin to a constraint and a repetition induced by the evocation of that same ghost. I don't want to deny the legitimacy of such a suspicion; I hope to show, however, how this captures some truth that goes beyond a possible obsessive fixation of ours.

When we published the book that emerged from the work we had done on the negative during the annual Diotima seminar, we published it above all because we noticed that as soon as we had named it there was a sort of liberating sense of recognition. Certainly, at that time it was above all a question of the necessity of naming the negative in our lives, and we started from that feeling even more than from a theoretical or political necessity. The latter soon followed, however, and that is when we decided to continue that work with the seminar devoted to *L'ombra della madre* [The shadow of the mother]. Additionally, there was a more precise and urgent motivation that convinced us of the need to continue to dwell in a zone as inhospitable as that of the obscure in the maternal: namely, the circumstance that, when facing the issue of the negative that is implied in relations and conflicts between women, we were forced to register their extreme difficulty and almost intractability. Our reflection on the experience of those conflicts led us to recognize how the shadow of the mother loomed over them.

The same long shadow that we felt descending upon us and casting a pall on our relationships seemed then to grow considerably larger: the shadow of the mother wafted around, and one could see how it loomed over the weave of reality, which was marked by it. It seemed to me I could almost follow it with my gaze while it projected a sort of shadow-line on the contours of reality, especially its conflicts.

The shadow of the mother outlines the contours of both these landscapes: on the one hand, the interior, intimate, deep landscape, the point of departure from which we move step by step down the singular path of our life, interlacing them with the paths of other steps and other lives, always followed by that shadow that we feel becoming intensely active during crucial transitions, in our relationships, in the politics of our relations among women, most powerfully when the latter is blocked.

On the other hand, there is the broader landscape of reality itself, traced by the interweaving of all these paths, by the forces that act within them, by their conflicts, their histories, their needs, by the meanings with which we attempt to give shape to all this and which also shape ourselves as well as, once again, that intricate web of steps. This landscape—of the lives we share in common and of politics—is also strongly marked by the maternal shadow.

There is, in fact, something intrinsically political about the node of the maternal shadow and of that which is obscure in the maternal: it is this facet, more than the first, which I intend to draw our attention to here.[4] I think it is crucial to focus on this question because I believe that it is precisely the maternal, and more specifically its obscure aspect, that marks and cuts across the conflicts of our present. The shadow of the mother may perhaps be made up of the substance of shadows, but it is the deep substance of the conflicts of our present. These conflicts are traced, even if not openly, on this thin shadow-line.

THE MOTHER KEPT IN THE SHADOWS

> Fu il padre tuo ch'estinse
> di lei la genitrice
> —G. Donizetti, *Imelda de' Lambertazzi*, Act I

The recent referendum on assisted reproductive technologies is perhaps the clearest example of how the maternal is today an object of political conflict.[5] As one can read in the introduction to the work prepared for the seminar, the blockage experienced when attempting to name this conflict constitutes the background for these reflections.[6]

This *eclipse of the mother*—to steal a felicitous expression from Maria Luisa Boccia—namely, her having been cast into the shadows by politics, is not at all a contingent fact.[7] It is instead a structural factor in politics, one of its deep, congenital traits. The definition of the political itself, in fact, is structured around the issue of the maternal. The exclusion of the mother from the political to a large degree overlaps historically and logically with both that of sexual difference itself and that of female exclusion. One should note, additionally, that over the course of time the maternal has proven to be the most irreducible and resistant core within the issue of the inclusion of women in the public and political spheres.

The very borders of the sphere of the political are designed in such a fashion as to keep the shadow of the mother away from its horizon, with the result that this shadow has thus become the shadow of politics itself. An obscure area that constantly follows its progress, its process of defining and redefining itself, much like a shadow.

A large number of feminist analyses have been devoted to this matter of politics intended as ban against a menacing and uncontrollable maternal, but at the same time intended also as hidden assumption of its nourishing foundation via the construction of a full-blown mythology of the maternal role.[8]

The reflections on these issues that are probably best known in Italy are those found in Luce Irigaray's analysis of original matricide: for her, the theme of the interdiction of the relation with the mother is central, and not only at the level of our political tradition.[9] Irigaray—who also draws from and links up with Johann Jakob Bachofen's lesson—develops the idea that underlying the paternal order, both symbolic and social, there is an erasure of the mother–daughter genealogy in favor of the father-son genealogy, which, in addition to the myths of Demeter and Kore, can also be found in the more properly political narration of the *Oresteia*, a veritable tale of the foundation of the law of the *polis*, of its right, and of its organizing principle.[10] It tells the tale of a transition, in this foundational event, from a maternal law to a paternal right. The first crime that is judged, but not condemned, by the city's first court is the matricide committed by Orestes in his father's name. The Erinyes, who represent maternal right and the blood bond, will not obtain the justice they invoke and finally, defeated and convinced through persuasion, they will move toward burial under the foundations of the Aeropagus, having at this point become innocuous and benevolent while still terrifying and capable of instilling that fear without which there is no law. Irigaray's reading underscores how the foundation of the city and its law rests symbolically on this original burial of the feminine connected with the legitimation of the killing of the mother, committed by the son with the daughter's complicity and sanctioned by Athena's decisive vote—Athena constituting a figure of "the daughter of the Father" alone—thereby indicating how the inscription of the feminine into the paternal order implies the rupture of the feminine filial bond with the mother.[11]

But in addition to Irigaray, many women political philosophers identify an analogous mechanism in the genesis of political thought, especially modern political thought. It's not possible to give an overview of the relevant studies here, but we can remind the reader of those who have provided the most significant contributions in opening up this perspective. Carol Pateman's theses, for example, are among the most influential: in addition to pointing out that the matrix and goal of the political order is to expel that which Jean-Jacques Rousseau stigmatizes as the "disorder of women," she finds also that the foundation of the original fraternal social contract is a sexual contract concerning the matrimonial rights of brothers on the wife, not that dissimilar from the paternal right on the mother.[12] Similarly, Hannah Pitkin found that the theme of the political control of "fortune" in Niccolò Machiavelli constitutes a symptom of an analogous fear of what is obscure in the feminine and the maternal, which is considered to be corrosive for the security of the civil order.[13]

Kathleen Jones has shown how contract theory of Hobbesian origin de-authorizes maternal authority while simultaneously attributing the function of protecting the maternal body to the sovereign, who represents the unity of the body politic.[14] In Italy, Adriana Cavarero too has investigated the tendency of politics to imagine itself as the creation of an artificial "body politic" in opposition to a natural corporeality thought of as feminine, thereby detecting the same device of metaphorization and negation of the body, and of the maternal body par excellence, which has constituted the foundation of both classical and modern political philosophy.[15] The theme of reproduction was also central in Mary O'Brien's work: in *The Politics of Reproduction*, by engaging also with Marxist–feminist understandings of the relation between the productive sphere and the reproductive sphere, she tackles the node of the function of reproduction, tracing its history and showing how the image of the public and of the political sphere is structured around the male need to construct a "second nature" in contrast to the female reproductive function.[16]

The foundational function of the negation of the mother in politics, and of the negation of her natural power of generation in the artificial masculine generation of the body politic—a function that prescribes a sort of "second birth" for the political subject in the public sphere—was then reconfirmed by an entire tradition of feminist thought that focused on the issue of the division between private and public.[17] These analyses have underscored how the traditional female reclusion in the private sphere and exclusion from the political sphere was intended primarily to turn the latter into the proper space for a subject who enters it precisely as an autonomous individual, namely, as an individual who has delinked from the sphere of dependency tied to the maternal world.[18] And they have registered, further, how it is the maternal that produces the feminine subject, whose body bears the inscription of maternal potentiality itself and of its being able to become two as well as of its not being fully one—a subject who is substantially not assimilable to the dimension of a separate and independent individuality for which politics is conceived.[19] Politics, in other words, has sanctioned the "impossibility of the maternal," thereby truly repressing it, as Patrice Di Quinzio has summed it up.[20]

This operation of repression has been underscored by Jane Flax in a manner that especially interests me here: in this regard, she states that in political philosophy one finds expressed what she defines as a "patriarchal unconscious," suggesting that one read what occurs on the philosophical plane as a "stream of social consciousness" on which infantile experience, as encoded in the construction of the gender system, exerts its influence: "The repression of early infantile experience is reflected in and provides part of the grounding for our relationships with nature and our political life, especially the separation of public and private, the obsession with power and domination and the consequent impoverishment both of political life and theories of it."[21] Philosophy in general and political philosophy in particular reflect the fundamental division of the gender system as it has been historically constructed, and consequently they also reflect "the fear and devaluation of women characteristic of patriarchal attitudes."[22] The political imaginary is shown, thus, to be imbued with a profound and pervasive maternal imaginary, which is perceived as obscure and dangerous and as perpetually threatening to politics, which must defend itself from it. It follows that a feminine perspective on philosophy and politics may come to represent "the return of the repressed, the exposure of the specific social roots of an apparently abstract and universal knowledge."[23] A "return of the repressed" that plays a key role in the spreading of maternal fantasies to which I will return at a later point.

Flax's perspective has been continued and developed by Christine Di Stefano in her work on the maleness of political thought.[24] The method Di Stefano embraces is particularly significant as she points to the best strategy for approaching the tradition of political philosophy—a strategy she defines as one of "space-off."[25] This is a rereading by means of the key provided by what political theory excludes from its field of vision. This constitutive absence is represented by the figure of the mother, which she refers to as *(m)other* to highlight its otherness: "As a figure of suspicion, of resistance and memory, the mother ((m)*other*) inhabits the 'other' side of the modern preoccupation for autonomous and active subjectivity, the modern drama of self-creation."[26]

And Julia Kristeva's well-known position on the presymbolic, semiotic dimension tied to the maternal body—a dimension she connects to the theme of abjection, of that which is constitutively rejected by identity and associated with the monstrous indistinction of the maternal—is a position that she herself has developed in a political vein, tying it to xenophobia and to the fear of that which is other and foreign, typical of an identitarian obsession that marks our political tradition.[27]

More recently, Judith Butler too has posited an original foreclosure of the first love bond with the mother as the origin of what she recognizes as the character of maternal melancholy that constitutes our vision of politics and power, or as she calls it, "the psychic life of power."[28]

All these analyses concur on the diagnosis: there is a mother kept in the shadow of politics. The maternal is the shadow-line that separates what may have access to politics from what may not, that defines both the border and the limitation of the political: the political keeps outside of itself both that which externally nourishes it and sustains it but also that which threatens it; the political defines itself through its difference from it.

It is this same shadow-line, furthermore, that marks a border of individuation within the political subject itself, who, in order to become such, a mature individual, must exit—as Joseph Conrad writes in his novel entitled precisely *The Shadow Line*—the world of infancy and the status of minor: "Yes. One goes on. And the time, too, goes on—till one perceives ahead the shadow-line warning one that the region of early youth, too, must be left behind."[29] On the one hand, that diagnosis is almost unanimous, as it is demonstrated by the history of feminism that has always focused on putting into question the limit(s) of the political—especially by means of the incessant contestation of the dualism of public sphere and private, familial, sphere—as well as on the node of the maternal role. On the other hand, however, one has also to recognize that the corrective political measures that have been proposed have been very different.

I cannot examine the various positions that have succeeded one another, and even fought each other: to do so would necessitate reviewing the entire history of feminism that has systematically found in the maternal (and I would say above all in that which is obscure in the maternal) that hard kernel which is irreducible to the pacific neutralizing inclusion of women within the confines of politics. It is sufficient to think of the eternal dilemmas of female citizenship, of the debates on equality/difference that always ended with a dispute on the maternal, of the debate on care, of so-called maternal thought, but even more recently of the political outcomes of the positions of Kristeva and Butler themselves, not to speak of the debate that is nearer to us.

During all these years, the political thought of difference, and the political practices that have supported it, have always had the mother at their heart. I believe that—considering the proximities and the distances from the various positions I just outlined—we can say that what has taken place are good words and good practices, or at least, words and practices that, in my estimation, are better able than others to avoid or limit the ambiguities that I believe are inevitably connected to a politics that refers to the maternal.

If, in fact, one has to acknowledge that the positions I have recalled possess somehow a common kernel—namely, that of considering the mother when thinking about politics, thematizing her either as a factor of disruption of the political patriarchal order or as a correction and transformation of the rules and models of politics—such positions have not been also without flaws, as well as without weak, if not negative, political perspectives and outcomes. I know I am being curt and hasty in my criticisms, and perhaps even ungenerous, but one has to admit that often efforts to preserve an awareness of the maternal in politics or to force politics by leveraging the maternal have become something quite different. Sometimes they have colluded with the inclusive strategy, sometimes with a differentiating tutelage, other times they have ended in an idealizing exaltation of the maternal as a palingenesis of politics.

Generally, I would suggest such defects are to be imputed to an undervaluation of the connection between female freedom and maternal reference, as well as between female freedom and that aspect of the obscure in the maternal that, somewhat provocatively, I almost would want to bless, since it acted as an obstacle to the process of an equalizing and neutralizing inclusion taken by the high road of modern politics. This is the case even in the form that it takes in Kristeva's position, who, in effect, proposes a political practice that leverages the negative, the abjection tied to the maternal, the semiotic and its possible expressions that irrupt into the paternal symbolic order. This is a proposal that, in my opinion, lacks political effectiveness and risks remaining subaltern to a distinctively patriarchal division of light and shadow—a division that would like to put the shadow of the mother back into play but that does not engage with the question of the displacement of the shadow-line itself.[30]

In many cases I would say that the flaws and weaknesses of the efforts undertaken have been due to an inadequate elaboration of the maternal that failed to thematize the difference between, on the one hand, reference to the mother, and, on the other hand, the image of the mother and its role in the paternal order—thereby delinking the affirmation of female freedom from the affirmation of the mother as a symbolic reference.

The politics of sexual difference as theorized and practiced in Italian feminism moved in a different direction: this politics was always careful to keep these two issues connected and always understood, on the one hand, how female freedom did not imply disavowing one's mother—quite the contrary—and, on the other hand, how the recognition of the mother was not to be confused with the glorification of the mother's traditional role.

But the point is: all these analyses were extensive, and we also went well beyond analyses. We tried to drag the mother out of the shadows, and in doing so we fully understood how this implied a radical symbolic conflict with that which has been called, precisely, politics of the symbolic. We conceived women's politics on this terrain, practices were invented, they were activated successfully, and yet there was a difficulty, a blockage, or a stoppage in the repetition. . . . Precisely the problem and the feeling we wanted to confront with the work on the negative.

STILL . . . THE SHADOW

Madre infelice corro a salvarti

—G. Verdi, *Il Trovatore*, Act III

Although I don't intend to repeat what I already argued in *La magica forza del negativo*, I do want to reassert here the conviction that subtended that reflection, namely, that to come to terms with the peculiar feminine difficulty with the negative it is necessary not to underestimate the power of the double patriarchal icon of the maternal: on the one hand, all luminous, beneficent, nourishing, and on the other, obscure, menacing, devouring, and uncontrollable.[31] That which establishes and constitutes the strength of the symbolic order of the father is the promise of making a break with the maternal, in both its aspects, through the paternal assumption of the negative that offers the third element, which allows for individuation and language. In order not to be continually trapped in the double icon of the maternal, one needs to carry the mother beyond the good and evil of patriarchy, exorcising her from the blinding and idealizing light of the fullness of good, as well as from the indistinct and annihilating obscure. This entails returning a bit of her own shadow to the mother, by facing the negative that exists in the ties with the mother, rather than the negative which leads one to separate from the mother by negating her. It entails recognizing what *already* performs the work of the negative in the ties with the mother and prevents the mother–daughter couple from becoming fused together, an indistinct redoubled identity, focusing instead on what inserts an opening, a surplus of transcendence into the bond with the mother.

This work on the negative in the relation with one's mother, as tough as it is, has a profoundly intimate aspect, singular and unavoidable for each woman, but it has also a symbolic and political aspect that is just as tough, unavoidable, and—this is my feeling about this issue at this point in time—even urgent.

I do not claim to confront both aspects of this work on the negative here: not only the place but even the act of expression itself would be fundamentally inappropriate. Though one certainly needs to confront the negative, to think that this is something one may confront in the form of a work is already rather dubious, and the same goes for the subject of this work, whether this subject is constituted by us or by the negative itself, which works on us.

I will limit myself to attempting to say a bit more, on the one hand, on the first aspect, where the feeling of blockage and repetition reasserts the limit of the work one can subjectively perform on the negative and vice versa, as we are the object of unceasing workings by the negative. On the other hand, I will discuss that symbolic and political urgency of the present moment, since in my opinion it illuminates something in both aspects, in their mutual relation, something that goes beyond the present conjuncture, although it is closely connected to the critical phase of change we are living through.

On the first front, therefore, the feeling one feels is that of a repetitive and inexhaustible return of the mother's shadow, and of the negative in the relationship with her, which seems to make the work of elaboration endless. The list of elaborations that have been proposed in this regard is also endless, but perhaps still unsurpassed in its lucidity is Jane Flax's famous essay that, already a long time ago, synthesized the typical nodes of feminine development under patriarchy.[32] Often, when they are under analysis, women feel as if they should first save their mother in order to be able to work on their problems and they develop a sense of guilt, as if they were betraying her in attempting to untie this symbiosis.[33] As a consequence of this tie with the mother, in a situation where the father is at the center of the symbolic and social order, women are therefore caught in this dilemma: either to remain tied to her, within her love, or to become autonomous so as to search for success on the outside, so as to be like a man. The result is that "there seems to be an endless chain of women tied ambivalently to their mothers, who replicate this relation with their daughters."[34] This reproduction of the maternal (to paraphrase the title of what is perhaps the most famous feminist book on the topic) is also a reproduction of patriarchy.[35] And until patriarchy exists the difference will inevitably be transformed into relations of dominion and subjection; that is Flax's conclusion, hoping that the repressed will become part of social discourse and realities, otherwise "there will be no one left to speak at all."[36] These are bitter words from the mid 1980s, after a decade of very important feminine reflections on the maternal.[37] This was a decade when, starting from the work of Irigaray, which went well beyond that diagnosis, our own phase of elaboration and political practice started here in Italy—a phase that is ongoing. It is superfluous to summarize the previous episodes: what was placed front and center in the thought and politics of difference includes feminine genealogy, relationship with the mother, payment of symbolic debt and gratitude toward the mother, maternal authority, symbolic order of the mother, as well as all those symbolic and political practices that have been activated in order to be able to speak and live beyond the deadly embrace of patriarchy.[38] And this has come to pass, in the singularity of our lives, which have acquired a meaning that exceeds the patriarchal order; but this has come to pass, moreover, at the symbolic level: feminine freedom has come into the world—we said—and hence we announced the end of patriarchy. Having said this, one still notes the difficulty and the negativity that prompted this research. The shadow of that which is obscure in the maternal returns: it insists, the reconciliation with the mother notwithstanding, and notwithstanding also the fact that the symbolic debt of gratitude toward her has been paid. Now, the feeling of suffering is legitimate and also inevitable, as is the activation of the desire to work to overcome those feelings and the situations that induce them. The feeling of frustration and disappointment that comes along with that suffering, as if an expectation had been inexplicably disappointed, is less so. As if one had become disillusioned with the hope that the symbolic recognition of the mother constituted the reconnection with the plenitude of that maternal place, understood as an irremovable good from which we have been treacherously separated in the name of the father. This is the shattering of that maternal icon that was all luminous and resplendent with goodness—a shattering that reveals how a fantasy of palingenesis and fulfillment was at work, a fantasy of a definitive and complete reparation with respect to our mothers that would be capable of removing any shadow from her, from our relation with her, and perhaps even from our lives themselves.

But it is precisely this search for total recognition—for a recognition without shadows, as Silvia Vegetti Finzi calls it—which feeds that endless chain of reparations.[39] Perhaps the shadow of the mother returns so darkly because her image is so devoid of shadow, and her return is all the more insistent the more the fantasy of a definitive reparation resembles that of definitively settling all accounts with one's mother.[40] But there is instead something *irreparable*: there is something that cannot be repaired in the original relation with one's mother, which is tied to the nonsymmetrical and nonequalizable nature of that relation itself: the irreparable here is precisely that which, in that contingent relation, gives us access to a surplus of transcendence in the relation, that which turns this relation into an opening that cannot be closed.[41] Just as there is something that cannot be repaired *in* the mother: the negative of her life, speaking of our real mother, and the offense which the mother, symbolically, has been subjected to.[42] There is an unredeemable wrong, which we cannot make right except via the justice that we will manage to bring into our lives. Walter Benjamin's tiger's leap into the past—the one motivated by the struggle for the oppressed past and by the awareness "that *even the dead* will not be safe from the enemy if he wins"—may save the living and their dead, but it doesn't resuscitate the dead.[43] This thought is hard to swallow for our politics, which I believe drew many energies from the desire to "repay a symbolic debt" to the mother: this is perhaps harder to swallow than the thought that there is something we cannot repair even in ourselves, or that something in the negative itself is beyond repair and perhaps cannot even be put to work.

The shadow of the mother, that which is obscure in the relation with the mother, returns to remind us of the impossibility of closure, of closing the circle. As in *The Ring* film cycle, an extraordinarily dark parable about the maternal relation and the negative, the well in which the mother has cast her daughter remains open: it is from this well that an evil that cannot be annihilated, only displaced, returns—not even reconciliation and recognition will be sufficient; its ghost will need to be crossed.[44] Less darkly than in this cycle, which is fully inscribed in today's climate of the return of the mother's ghost, and to which I will return later, there is a part of that shadow that, its obscure semblance notwithstanding, it is an evil, literally, to hurry to exorcise, imagining one will be able to make it vanish once and for all. Symbolic reconciliation, if it is truly reconciliation, is not the presumption of the closure of the circle on itself but a returning that twists the circle in an evolving spiral—and I am referring to yet another scene taken from the filmic imaginary, that of *Volver*. Well, then, if symbolic reconciliation is worthy of its name, it must recognize that which one cannot repair or close up once again. The infinite reparatory cycle of the repetitions of the history of the maternal does not close with a final repetition; perhaps it opens onto the infinite by recognizing precisely that which is beyond repair.

IN THE NIGHT OF THE LIVING DEAD

> Fuggi regal fantasima, / che Banco mi rammenti!
> La tua corona è folgore, / gli occhi mi fai roventi!
> Via, spaventosa immagine / che il crin di bende hai cinto!
> E altri ancor ne sorgono? / Un terzo? Un quarto? Un quinto?
> Oh mio terror! / Dell'ultimo splende uno specchio in mano,
> e nuovi Re s'attergano / dentro il cristallo arcano . . .
> È Banco! Ahi, vista orribile! / Ridendo a me gli addita!
> Muori, fatal progenie! / Ahi, che non hai tu vita!
>
> —G. Verdi, *Macbeth*, Act III

I come now to the second aspect. While is the case that neither the work of the negative nor the work we undertook on the shadow of the mother can be reduced to this contingent factor, I believe that part of the negativity we are facing, as well as of the goading confrontation with the shadow of that which is obscure in the maternal, should also be imputed to a profound change in the transformation of the present we are living through, as well as to the state of the symbolic conflict that is taking place precisely on the shadow-line of the maternal. If, as I have argued, the issue of the maternal and of the shadow of the mother defines politics, then, when one redefines politics, the shadow-line is shifted and vice versa. The relation with the mother is always in play: it is implied in the relationship between the sexes, it informs the structures of the social order, but even more it is a structuring element within the symbolic order, thereby acting in depth in the ongoing conflicts. It is therefore inevitable that in this phase when political, social, and symbolic relations are changing and being redefined, that shadow-line will cut across, intersect, interpret, and express these ongoing conflicts. The most obvious example is perhaps the way in which this shadow-line of the maternal cuts across the conflict on liberal individualism, but I believe it may be possible to trace something analogous in practically all the dimensions of current conflict, constituting their more or less hidden split. To ask oneself where the shadow-line of the conflicts of the present passes: this, I believe, is a good direction to take for understanding a reality that presents itself as already given and as already mapped out, first of all in the oppositions through which it represents itself.[45] The shadow-line of the maternal constitutes a key to capturing conflicts in politics and dissecting them differently, from the standpoint of political practice, which is intimately tied to sexual difference.

Attempts have been made to grasp the present transformation using different designations. Mostly people have spoken of globalization and postmodernity, and in recent years there has been above all a proliferation of analyses of that breach in the traditional borders of politics, which is fashionable to call biopolitics.[46] Whatever the respective explanatory capacity of these categories may be, they all appear under a different light if looked at from that angle, even when they present themselves as apparently more comprehensive. The case of biopolitics is perhaps the clearest: although the different analyses that have been proposed tend to fail to thematize this point, it seems obvious to me that the transformation of the form of politics from a sovereignty that above all possesses power of life and death to a power that administers life cannot be fully understood if one does not take into account, as I mentioned above, what an entire tradition of feminine thought has highlighted regarding the structuring function of the "separate spheres" for the definition of politics itself: a political sphere and a domestic sphere that is charged with the reproduction of life and entrusted to maternal care.[47] Without examining the question in depth, let this observation suffice: while a specification of its inception still remains controversial, the biopolitical transformation in question does not eliminate the conflict over the shadow-line of the borders of politics with respect to the maternal; it allows that line of conflict, rather, to be distributed and to reverberate across all conflicts, cutting across them and marking them, regardless.

If, in other words, we are faced by an unprecedented novel situation in which crucial aspects—be they conceptual, symbolic, or political—of the established order are changing, in all of these the issue of the relation between the sexes and of the place of the symbolic authority of the father and the mother is implied in a fundamental fashion. The various perspectives we may want to adopt to capture the outlines of the present can provide only limited intelligibility of such a present unless they are inserted in a more comprehensive framework: namely, the framework that is defined by the mutation of the practical and symbolic forms of regulation of sexual difference, which has brought us to the time of the end of patriarchy.[48]

As I said when the end of patriarchy was announced: let there be rejoicing for a welcome end, but there is not much to laugh about. Patriarchy may be dead, yet things are still not so simple: more than a century ago, a man, Friedrich Nietzsche, announced, in very virile fashion, that God was dead; this wouldn't mean churches would have less work, he predicted, and today, after an entire twentieth century of mourning, we must add that the nightmare of wars of religion is far from vanished. We shouldn't fool ourselves into believing that things will go any differently with the announcement of the death of the father, especially when the voice announcing it is female. So, yes, we are going forward, but it seems instead as if suddenly everything were going backward. Chiara Zamboni correctly observed as much: with the end of patriarchy also comes the end of its order; the result, however, is not the immediate establishment of a new order but an increase in disorder and the return of forms of regulation, conceptualization, action, and emotion that are more archaic, increasingly often elementary and violent—which fact places the question of the negative and of its expansion at the center of current politics.[49]

In women's politics, and also in the reflections of some men, the death of patriarchy, as well as the changes it entails in social relations between the sexes, in personal relationships, and in one's own ways of feeling have been the object of discussion and political practice for several years already.[50] Further, what is also widespread is a concerned awareness regarding the negative effects induced by the liberation of a patriarchal imaginary no longer ruled by the symbolic order of the father.[51]

Acknowledgments of the event in current intellectual discourse, on the other hand, are still too few, and the analyses are even fewer, and the readings that would underscore the relation between the death of patriarchy and the birth of female freedom and the feminist revolution are fewer still. It is true that there has been some explicit recognition that has contributed significantly to spread awareness of the event, such as that by Manuel Castells.[52] Generally, however, an understanding of the centrality of the event is still lacking, and it is registered instead as one element of the landscape, rather than, as it is, its more general horizon. What we have seen much of, rather, has been a series of reflections on the impact of the sharp decline of paternal authority, especially as it concerns the form of the family.[53] I don't think, however, that such reflections have had a sufficient feel for the radical nature of the political and historical consequences involved, or that they have had even the scope that the first diagnosis of the crisis of authority, as well as the announcement of the "society without father," by the Frankfurt School had in its time.[54] And, generally, such reflections have had even less of a feel for the fact that this crisis of paternal authority does not leave a world orphaned of authority, and does not abandon it to an obscure destiny without order, and witnesses instead the emergence of forms of order that can be related to maternal authority.[55]

This kind of (both male and female) blindness or speechlessness [*mutismo*]—in an environment that is remarkable for the competitiveness in registering events and for the prolixity in the analysis of minutiae—is a phenomenon that is worthy of reflection in and of itself, and that might shed some light on the nature of the patriarchal order itself.[56] Among the few explicit thematizations one should however note, if for no other reason because the author's celebrity has brought attention to it, the one put forth by Slavoj Žižek, who places the question of the death of patriarchy at the center of his analysis of the present situation, designating it as an issue of post-oedipal reality or as the "end of symbolic efficacy."[57]

The death of patriarchy is articulated by Žižek with reference to the sequence that the three different incarnations of the father's authority take in Freud: the oedipal father, the narration of patricide in *Totem and Taboo*, and the Father–God in *Moses and Monotheism*. The death of the father—which is equivalent to the realization that "the Big Other no longer exists," that is, the realization of the decline of the efficacy of the symbolic order—implies the death of all three of these fathers: the first, who is both the pacifying ego ideal and the superego of prohibition; the second, who is the "name of the father" emerged after the killing of the obscene archaic presymbolic father; and finally the third, the Father–God who incarnates the paternal authority of the will of an absolute "No!" as against the rigidity of a deceased, merely symbolic, order. To each of these deaths there corresponds a return of the dead father in phantasmatic form. The figure of the "humiliated father" returns, a father reduced to the role of impotent rival in barring the maternal object of desire, incapable of establishing a prohibitive norm that is replaced instead by "direct Super-Egoizations of the imaginary Ideal," both demanding and sadistic. The ghost of the obscene, archaic father also returns, along with the procession of his excesses—a father who is now merely despotic and devoid of authority. Finally, and this is the aspect that actually produces the contemporary decline of the force of the symbolic order itself, with the disappearance of the father of the "No!" paternal authority itself disappears. And with this, it is precisely the Nietzschean announcement that "God is dead" that is realized: the Big Other, the symbolic order no longer has any purchase; there is no longer any trust, and one loses the capacity to "believe"; the foundation of belief itself is undermined. The effects that Žižek correlates with these events are various, and they are all inscribed in an encompassing frame within which the decline of the symbolic order manifests itself as an "epidemic of the imaginary."[58] They range from new forms of phantasmatic harmony between symbolic order and enjoyment (the holistic *new age*), to the return of "neo-obscurantist

Jungian notions of archetypes of the male and female," and to the reemergence of the Big Other in reality and not as a symbolic fiction with the proliferation of fundamentalisms, a form of paranoia that is paired with cynical distance. And from a belief in an "other of the other" who pulls the strings, the conspiracy of an obscene and invisible power, to the spread of a culture of complaint and of legalism that is incapable of thinking a radical and revolutionary change, and again to the idea that we can reinvent ourselves freely and totally. And on and on we go, from the unrestrained power of money, to the decline of sexual desire, the impotence of analytical interpretation, the attachment to simulacra, the need for violence in the Real of the body itself (piercing, for example), the search for new subjecting "wounded attachments" in relationships (the example employed is that of lesbian couples who enact roles of domination).[59]

Žižek's description undoubtedly has the merit of hitting the mark both with respect to the crucial point of the present transformation, the end of patriarchy, and with respect to the outline of the wide spectrum of the effects it produces.[60] On the other hand, an awareness of what its determining factors are is really lacking: the events whose outcome it describes so unsparingly are in fact all internal to the arc of the modern subject, *ticklish* but still male—an arc that is reconstructed along the most canonical lines of the philosophical tradition and of Lacanian orthodoxy. One should not be surprised therefore if the actions of female subjectivity are absent from this developmental trajectory—in it, in fact, female subjectivity necessarily acts only as an absence—much like any influence of the feminist revolution on the decline of patriarchy is also absent, a patriarchy that therefore dies of natural causes. And without leaving any heirs, except for its ghosts that infest an exclusively posthumous reality that is prey to the plague of the imaginary. The paternal symbolic order can die, yes, but the problem with Žižek's vision is that it cannot be surmounted. What must be traversed, rather, is the ghost that is intrinsically tied to the imaginary and that supports the social fantasy, which fantasy presents itself as unviable and closed to any transformation. To traverse this ghost requires a particular type of "act."[61] This is an act that, by its nature, would be capable of retroactively revolutionizing its own conditions of possibility, given that the conditions of the order of the paternal are on the order of the impossible.[62] The nature of this authentic ethical act, and what a politics of the act might mean, is, truth be told, as central as it is problematic, as even an enthusiastic admirer of Žižek's like Jodi Dean has to concede: while attempting, from a feminist perspective, to develop the analysis of the postpatriarchal situation he proposes, she is forced to confess that in reality she does not understand what this might mean.[63] I am therefore not embarrassed also to confess my own difficulties in understanding many points of Žižek's position; the issue, however, is not really whether or not this incomprehension is justified: what is at stake, rather, is a more radical and legitimate suspicion.[64] The situation Žižek depicts of the contemporary decline of symbolic efficacy after the "death of the father" provides a clear picture of the present situation and of the flood of ghosts that torment it; but it is a picture that should be corrected by heeding Flax's warning: it is the irruption, by means of feminism, of female subjectivity and of the mother's return to the light of day after having been relegated to the shadows; it is this irruption that induces the return of the repressed of the patriarchal unconscious, thereby unleashing archaic ghosts that are no longer regulated by a paternal order that no longer orders.[65] All of this while the regulations that are currently in force are shown to be ever emptier and inefficient, even though they continue to proliferate with empty normative claims. These are claims that, on the one hand, are excessive, and, on the other hand, have no hold on life, except in an enforcing and ideological manner—and in the meanwhile there is no dearth of appeals to the need for values and ethics, at a time when thought of a postmodern orientation seems to undermine such appeals at their root. This picture seems so derelict, so adrift without the possibility of landfall: it is a world without anchor that seems to have lost trust even in the possibility of having some sort of grasp on reality. But it seems so if and when one looks at it and lives it from the (nostalgic, whether mournful or euphoric) point of view of a lost reference: that of the paternal order as the only possible frame for this picture. In sum, if and when one looks at it from the point of view of the narration about the constitution of the paternal order and about its interdiction of the first bond with the mother as a necessary access to the symbolic itself. And without the symbolic one is thrown back into a house infested by archaic and obscene paternal ghosts, or even worse, something that represents the most lethal threat for this perspective, by the manifestations of the mother's ghost, which the archaic and obscene paternal ghosts cannot contain.

Within this horizon, which is closed as well as built upon a constitutive maternal lack, what is lacking is precisely the perspective of the opening that the reference to the mother may enable. The paternal symbolic order, the so-called Big Other, prohibits such a reference, thereby forbidding itself from opening itself up to anything other, which would not be something totally Other of the Other. To think and to enact the transformation of an order that is conceived in such an ironclad fashion is truly tantamount to thinking a politics of the impossible.[66] Only that something along the lines of that impossible has indeed occurred. An event that goes unobserved while, precisely among those who devote themselves most passionately to thinking about a politics for the transformation of the existent, one furiously discusses if and how producing a radical change in the given order and in the normativity of its discourse may even be possible. A normativity that appears to be so pervasive in its forms of constitutive subjection that it seems to have left almost no opening to an instituting subjectivity, to authentic political action, and ultimately to freedom.[67]

Without becoming aware of this event—which is the rupture, the opening, of that claustrophobic order—the present condition really acquires the character of a nightmare of a house infested by ghosts, or of a horror film about the living dead, and politics comes to resemble survival, or the work of mourning, or even of a hunt for ghosts (Derrida called it *hantologie*), or the analytic practice of traversing the ghost.[68]

SHADOW, GHOST, SPIRIT

> La mamma morta m'hanno alla porta
> della stanza mia, moriva e mi salvava!
>
> —U. Giordano, *Andrea Chenier*, Act III

I stated above that it is necessary to bring the mother beyond patriarchy's good and evil by exorcising the ghosts and demons, by calling them by their name. One needs to add now that if there are so many ghosts in circulation it is because there are dead who are not dead, they haven't been buried, and we haven't worked through their mourning. The spectral atmosphere of this late or posthumous modernity has been noticed and diagnosed by many, sketched with different shades of color: from the somber ones of a closed horizon that casts its pall over an orphaned reality, a reality abandoned and inhabited by ghosts, to the phantasmagoria of a world of simulacra where the imaginary has exploded, shattering every residue of a grasp on reality to smithereens.[69] In any case, we still have a death behind us and, facing us, we are confronted with the urgency of dealing with it, especially with its undead residue. A name can now be assigned to the many deaths foretold that marked the course of the twentieth century: the deceased is the father, and the troubled times we live in are those afflicted by this death and by the returns of its restless specter.

But something is still missing from this (at least for some) bitter and despairing diagnosis: it is not only the patriarchal father who has died, the patriarchal mother died with him, and this death is still more difficult to elaborate, for both sons and daughters, for men and women. And this is a death, that of the patriarchal mother, which powerfully evokes its ghost, massively mobilizing the shadow of the mother.

Part of the return of the maternal shadow that goads us concerns the shadow of *this* mother, the mother of the paternal imaginary, her return is that of the patriarchal unconscious, to use once again Flax's expression.[70] The semblances of this ghost that comes along with the cohort of paternal ones have not been outlined in such detail, but its apparitions are overwhelming and numerous. There is, above all, the menacing omnipotent mother who undermines filial independence, but there are also the intrusive mothers, the protective and suffocating mothers, and then the demanding mothers, but there are also mothers who kill their offspring, and then the inept and powerless ones, those who are sick and depressed, those who love too much and those who don't love enough, the irresponsible ones who don't know how to be only mothers but also want to be women, those who want to be mothers at all costs, those who even want to have children on their own, those who don't allow sons and even daughters to grow up, those who don't step aside, and then again the fusional mother and the perfect mother, the one who is a custodian of the plenitude of goodness, the sacrificial mother, the one of care and the one who is totally understanding, the mother of love and protection, the mother of peace and that of natural harmony . . . and so on and so forth in the long theory of the various semblances of the "spectral mother."[71] Therein old and new fears become confused, while the traditional motherphobia and idealization of the mother and the more recent phobias and nostalgias triggered by the new female freedom can no longer be distinguished from each other.[72] All this during the time of a postpatriarchy that is taking the form of a *fratriarchy* dominated by unregulated conflicts, where, on the one hand, ghosts with vindictive intent against women agitate insistently, but where new hopeful questions directed toward women also emerge.[73]

This situation makes the task I was mentioning at the beginning much more complex and delicate, namely, the task of thinking the maternal in relation to politics without becoming entangled in the shadow that politics casts on the maternal. This task is the (political but above all existential) wager that it may be possible to constitute symbolic reference to the mother beyond the realm of the ghosts of the patriarchal mother. A wager that would make it possible for the reference to the mother to be that which symbolically cuts across reality's conflicts and defines them, while not being defined by them—the latter being a situation that instead would cut our ties to the mother and to reality itself for the nth time.

All this makes the game difficult and hazardous. Chiara Zamboni has suggested the following image: one is playing a card game, but it is as if the card representing the mother were no longer in the deck. To a certain extent this is true: in actuality, that card no longer has any real substance; perhaps it is only made of the substance that shadows and dreams are made of. It does, however, evoke the power of the maternal imaginary, perhaps only that of a shadow, but this shadow has real effects.

The situation can resemble those card games with figures, wizards, and monsters that evoke their own powers, those games that children have liked for some time now, and on which there is a famous Japanese cartoon anime (I believe it is called Yu-Gi-Oh! The protagonists challenge one another with cards, but the ghosts they evoke do actually fight each other in reality).

It's as if there were several levels to the game, but the game is only one, and we enter it together with our shadow: men and women in flesh and blood, and their shadows; an entire world of images and ghosts that also play their own roles, atavistic roles but also more recent ones, as well as those of fantasies and desires. But it is not a game, it is a multidimensional conflict, which itself comprises many conflicts that all lead back to the same match—the match in which we play for the modes and meaning of our freedom and of the life we share in common in the world.

And, as I see it, and as far as the essentials of my freedom are concerned, this conflict still presents the same front-line, that same shadow-line.

Are we then dealing with that same symbolic conflict for which we trained so much? Yes, but with an additional difficulty that, I believe, we might have underestimated: the difficulty of the imaginary's register and its game, with respect to which the card with the mother's image is continually requested, and thrown on the table. We find it in our deck without looking for it or wanting to play it: it inevitably comes along with us, much like we inevitably are followed by our shadow—the ghost doesn't leave us.

So, if this is where things stand more or less, how can we interpret the request Zamboni talked about? The one that comes from men who, having lost paternal regulation, ask us women to offer a sort of bridge to the maternal, hoping that the mother will be the one who is able to regulate this world lost in mourning. Should one, can one, answer this question? And how? I confess that I really don't have an answer on this issue: I have many doubts, as well as much suspicion that gives rise to even more questions.

Which mother, in fact, is that hope of salvation addressed to? Whom is the question addressed to? To us, as a possible contact with the maternal . . . yes, but, once again, which maternal? My suspicion is that the mother that is invoked might be the wife of that lost father. The benevolent face of the maternal icon, the nourishing mother. Whence the hope: that mother, after all, sustained that lost paternal world; it wouldn't be the first time that the male plea to save the world is addressed to women. Hence the question: should one respond, and, if so, how? Can that question also have another meaning? Which meaning, nowadays? Can we play the card of the maternal, knowing that the one we are asked to throw on the table is only the shadow of the mother?

Perhaps those of us who are cynical or who bluff would answer yes, but one would have to ask if they are only cynical and/or bluffing. Should we attempt some differentiations? The patriarchal mother is dead, but we are alive and so forth? But can we really make differentiations? Are we not always also accompanied by that shadow, really?

Many questions for which I couldn't honestly say I have an answer; I can only imagine some of the factors one should keep in mind if one has to play, which we have to do. Above all, we need to keep in mind that there are two registers in the game, but that the game, in any case, is played on only one table: the first register is the ongoing symbolic, but also imaginary, conflict, and I believe we have to play it with all the cards we hold, including the card of the shadow of the mother, which we cannot lay aside because it is part of the game and, in fact, it is even part of us. The second register is that of an intimate game, perhaps even a conflict, in which we ourselves have to deal with the shadow of the mother, and it is from the elaboration of this relationship that we might perhaps reach the lightness to freely play that game, knowing that ultimately we can risk no more than the shadow of the mother.

This elaboration on two registers, the intimate and the political, is vital if we don't want suddenly to find ourselves in a situation in which we have been played by shadows. . . .

It is inescapable, hence, that we settle our accounts with the shadow of the mother, but this doesn't mean we have either to exorcise her ghost or to embrace it. There is no doubt that some apparitions of the maternal ghost need to be averted, or at least we should expose ourselves to them with caution. I am thinking of the suspicion some women express regarding female political practices that invoke the maternal as compared with those that leverage the idea of women's freedom: the two are felt as contradictory, and the maternal is experienced as overwhelming or in any case as politically risky.[74]

I can't deny that the problem exists, and I share the concern, but I believe it can be imputed more to the ghost of the patriarchal mother than to a reference to maternal authority: these warnings are correct in saying that female freedom exceeds the maternal; they forget, however, that one can and one must think of a maternal potential that is itself free and is not entirely internal to the patriarchal horizon—which is precisely what we were attempting to do by speaking of the symbolic order of the mother and maternal authority.

In this regard, it is useful to think that the mother, obviously, is also a woman, and not only mother; that the mother is always also something other than our mother; that her desire is not only directed toward her children, it is directed toward the father, naturally, but also and above all toward herself and the world.[75] This reminder is useful for opening the mother–daughter dual couple up, which couple, thus, is not shut closed in an indistinct fusion. And without necessarily making a third entity, like the father, or the symbolic order of the father, intervene. It is true that freedom in its exceeding aspect also has this role, this capability, but the reference to the maternal, and especially to the shadow of the mother, has the advantage of reminding us of the weight, the gravity, which prevents the euphoria of freedom and the fantasies of a full voluntaristic control over the symbolic. The practices of freedom should not be opposed to those that refer to the maternal, quite the contrary; yet I believe that a certain dose of ambiguity is inevitable, which once again requires one to pass through the work of the negative and the shadow of the mother.

This passage through the shadow of the mother is not the same as accepting the invitation to traverse the ghost, namely, the invitation of the theoretical approaches I recalled above. Even though the crossing of the ghost, or of the fundamental fantasy, is evoked there to indicate the overcoming of that which it precludes or forecloses, to indicate the opening of the given order, of the social imaginary that presents itself as impervious to change, thereby determining the very conditions of subjectivity and of action in conformity with its disciplining normativity—all this is imputed to the hold of the imaginary rather than to the symbolic structuration of that (paternal) order whose persistence is itself supported by the hold of the imaginary in the first place. And this imaginary element is referred to the first relationship with the mother, in which the ghost that structures our desire and ties us to a particular modality of enjoyment is originally given. In this manner, for the nth time, what entangles us in repetition, what ties us to a forced dimension, one that is not free, what keeps us squeezed into conforming, what nails us to the forms of our subjection and hypnotizes us into "wounded attachments" that make us believe in regressive and comforting illusions of an identitarian nature, is our first bond with the mother. Simply put, the ghost is always tied to the mother. And once again it is a dangerous ghost, especially politically since all sorts of fantasies that shape the phantasmatic closure of our identity, as well as of community and of politics, are tied to it. This is a closure that involves an idealized belief in the illusion of the enjoyment of the "thing itself," which is the job of the paternal symbolic to forbid—that is, back when the paternal symbolic worked!—thereby carrying out the work of the negative, which is to say, the necessary symbolic castration. And so we are back to the traditional problem of our political tradition, namely, that it defines itself by reiterating the shadow-line of the maternal as its border. We should not be surprised that the person who has most developed this approach, Žižek, ends up by evoking Lenin's ghost as a political model.[76]

There is, however, something true (approach and results aside) in this tie between the ghost and the mother, following Freud and Lacan.[77] What is said about the ghost, about its ties to the imaginary, and about its role, may be useful to read the initial problem of a symbolic conflict on the shadow-line of the maternal at the time of the end of the paternal order and of the centrality of the level of the imaginary. This only on condition that one rereads this supposed tie in the light of the recognition of maternal authority and of its original function in the acquisition of symbolic competence, or, in other words, only on condition of performing a radical cut with the presuppositions of that image of language and the symbolic.

It is true that the mother is in the place of the ghost, if that's what we want to call it, because in one's relationship with her there is the first bridge between words and things, the first access to the symbolic that occurs thanks to a real relation, to a mediation incarnate. One may speak of ghost, of that first object of desire that passes through an actual enjoyment that gives us a way to desire, but many other names have been invented in the long history of philosophy to attempt to explain in another fashion what actually occurs in the first relationship with one's mother who teaches us how to speak. Ultimately this was what was being discussed in the classical and often abstruse problems regarding what functions as mediation, as concrete universal, as first paradigm, as empirical grammatical proposition, even as transcendental schema, and so forth....

What happens in the originary relation with the mother is that in that real relation access is given to that surplus of transcendence, necessity passes through that contingent relationship, the universal passes through a punctum-like particular, but much more simply what happens is that in those specific words which we learn we learn language, in that first object of desire we learn desire, etc.[78] But let me say it by means of a vision of language which I find more appealing, namely Wittgenstein's.[79] We learn language by means of a concrete practice in which we don't learn general rules but we go directly to particular judgments instead: we learn the deep grammar of our language—that which we may compare to the linguistic horizon that many see as a cage—with grammatical propositions that originally are empirical, and on the basis of the fact that we are entrusted to someone who introduces us into the word, normally the same one who has introduced us into life. The mother did the work of mediation that gave us our first point of support: there the word was the thing, they coincided; her word was in the order of truth by means of her. Extraordinary ordinariness. It is certain that this extraordinary aspect may establish the relation with the mother in a lost and mythical dimension of phantasmatic plenitude—due to the fact that what is essential in this passage has occurred once and for all time—and the imaginary component, thus, may assume this tonality. The ordinary aspect, however, consists in the fact that in this relation, in which the symbolic is provided with a foothold on reality and vice versa, we learn by means of symbolic competence to be ourselves, to be that point of intersection between the symbolic and the real, to be that which produces reality and which at once produces and may be able to change language itself.

Language is not a cage; it is modified and changes, even at the level of its deep grammar, much like our lives and practices, which are not merely a repetitive execution of norms: it happens, and it happens all the time. Similarly, reality is not a closed circle defined by symbolic norms and entirely surrounded by the inaccessible and nonsymbolizable Real (an idea that is complementary to that of a mythical maternal confined in inaccessibility and in lack of subjective freedom). Reality, rather, is a rough, disturbing, and infinitely fractured territory, where we ourselves become the bridge over the abyss between the Real and the symbolic. Reality is open to change: we can continuously speak it without ever shutting it down, luckily.

The shadow of the mother—even that obscure one that reminds us of that first passage of things into words via the incarnate mediation of an intimate relation not dissimilar from the relation that brought us into the world via a carnal passage from body into body—also returns to remind us that it is impossible for the linguistic dimension, for the order of the word, to close in on itself in a presumption of autonomy, both from the Real and from us as speakers.

It returns to remind us that that is not the word, that is not the thing. The numerous mediations that will replace her symbolically, despite all the preaching about the symbolic necessity of severing the bond to the maternal, can never replace it entirely.[80] If the maternal shadow possesses this irreducibility that says "this is not it," the maternal relation itself is the bearer of a non-identity in itself: the mother is always also something other than our mother; the relation in itself possesses something of the imaginary and the phantasmatic; the mother herself, on the one hand, is not that relation, and, on the other hand, as I have already stated, opens onto something that transcends the contingency of the relationship. In stating this I don't mean to say that the relationship with the mother fixes us into a position that one might define as hysterical. This is not the case because it is precisely in that relationship that she is the first to articulate the mediation and the passage through the negative of factual particularity by teaching us: "this is it!"

When viewing the shadow of the mother from this perspective it is perhaps possible to recognize it more as a *spirit* than as a ghost to be exorcised. Which does not imply that the shadow will vanish. But it may help us avert the fear that the shadow of the mother will appear only in the phantasmatic semblance of the double icon of the patriarchal mother, the dark and menacing one and the dazzling one, full of light and no shadows.

With this maternal icon divided between light and darkness I return in my conclusion to the issue I started from, namely, the relation between the shadow of the mother and the definition of the political. Traditionally its domain is represented as a public space, that of a full, solar, light, which ejects the shadow of the mother from itself and keeps only its nourishing and beneficent aspects. Due to this tendency to solar closure of the political space, the maternal—broken into the two icons, the functional and the irreducible—had the function of being at once that which was ejected and that which marked the limits of its territory: this function therefore prevented the maternal from imagining itself as total (albeit enclosed); it could imagine itself only as an external limit. That border was broken and opened by the cut of sexual difference brought by feminism. Perhaps precisely by listening to the mother's cry, women entered Sarastro's solar city, which in actuality was truly spectral, and they themselves are not Queens of the Night, but their bodies have brought sufficient shade to kill its sovereign. Confusion is great and there are those who shout that everything shakes, and that we are falling into the void. But one never falls into nothingness because it is not from nothingness that we came.[81]

The shadow does not let us precipitate into darkness; it allows us to see the depth of reality. The shadow-line is displaced and redefines the boundaries of reality, of politics, but above all it prevents politics from thinking of itself as completed and closed, as it has a tendency to do. That shadow that always returns and with which one cannot settle accounts once and for all, definitely, nor can one define it since it has to do with an opening that cannot be sutured and with that which always reopens the circle, comes to remind us that neither our individual life nor the space of our shared lives can be closed in on themselves.

The reference to the mother, also in its aspect of the obscure maternal, prevents the closure of politics: its shadow impedes the fiction of diurnal plenitude, undermines the constitutive fiction of the political, and in this manner demonstrates its capacity of bringing a truth factor to it.[82]

This can lead to a twilight dimension that moves the shadow-line inside the borders of politics, thereby making it traverse all the conflicts of politics and marking one of its intrinsic limits, beyond the shadow/light dualism itself. A shadowy but not indistinct dimension, where mediations cannot but always also be shadowed passages. A reality where the shadow reminds us of the impenetrability of our bodies under the full light of the solar reign of a politics, where the sun has become a prisoner of its own power and has forgotten its birth and the time of dawn, as Maria Zambrano defined it.[83] And this is another way of saying that we are not only at sunset.

Translated by Mark William Epstein

NOTES

This chapter is the translation of a revised version of "Con lo spirito materno," originally published in *L'ombra della madre* (Naples: Liguori, 2007), 33–64.

1. See Diotima, *La magica forza del negativo* (Naples: Liguori, 2005).

2. The expression is Virginia Woolf's, from *Moments of Being* (San Diego: Harcourt Brace Jovanovich, 1985). Anna Maria Piussi used it as the title of her contribution to Diotima, "Era là dall'inizio," in Diotima, *Il cielo stellato dentro di noi: L'ordine simbolico della madre* (Milan: La Tartaruga, 1992), 21–47.

3. Pedro Almodóvar had a good intuition that ties to these issues by giving his film the title *Volver* (2006), to return; in it he reaffirms a male gaze that is extraordinarily polarized on the maternal and the universe of female relations. Here there is a return of the ghost of the mother, the phantasmatic return of the

nondead, which in this case is to be understood literally since the mother embodies, when alive, the ghost of herself. There is also the return in the shape of the repetition of trauma, in the repetition of paternal violence for the new mother–daughter couple. But there is also the transformative, evolutionary, and salvific aspect of *volver*, in other words the sense of turning around, of becoming, of a turning point that is made possible by that return and the embrace between mother and daughter, which, more than the reconciliation at the end of a story, foreshadows a possible nonrepetitive opening of a new story/relationship.

4. I instead focused more on the first aspect in "La tentazione del bene," in Diotima, *La magica forza del negativo*, 9–33.

5. [The referendum in question took place in 2005 in Italy and was sponsored largely by a wide range of leftist political parties and NGOs. Its result was annulled due to the fact that—despite the heated debates leading to it, which involved numerous sections of Italian society, ranging from a particularly interventionist Catholic Church to feminist movements, from all political parties represented in the parliament to political organizations outside the typical institutions of representative democracy—the quorum of voters needed was not reached due to unprecedentedly low voter turnout.—Eds.]

6. The introduction can be found on Diotima's website: www.diotimafilosofe.it, where many of the contributions that appeared in the press can also be downloaded.

7. See Maria Luisa Boccia and Grazia Zuffa, *L'eclissi della madre: Fecondazione artificiale, tecniche, fantasie e norme* (Milan: Pratiche Editrice, 1998).

8. The many woman researchers in political philosophy who have examined the historical construction of our political tradition broadly agree on this point, around which different theoretico-political constructs all seem to revolve and which has been revealed as constitutive in the most diverse authors. The relevant bibliography is huge by now, and we cannot account for it here.

9. Luce Irigaray discusses this issue in many of her writings, particularly in *Speculum of the Other Woman*, trans. Gillian C. Gill (Ithaca, N.Y.: Cornell University Press, 1985); *Marine Lover of Friedrich Nietzsche*, trans. Gillian C. Gill (New York: Columbia University Press, 1991); *An Ethics of Sexual Difference*, trans. Carolyn Burke and Gillian C. Gill (London: Continuum, 2004); *Sexes and Genealogies*, trans. Gillian C. Gill (New York: Columbia University Press, 1993).

10. [Here and throughout this chapter, unless otherwise noted, "right" translates the Italian term "*diritto*," which may be translated also as "law" or "jurisprudence."—Trans.]

11. See Irigaray, *Marine Lover of Friedrich Nietzsche*, 101.

12. Carole Pateman, *The Sexual Contract* (Cambridge: Polity, 1988), 99. See also Pateman, *The Disorder of Women: Democracy, Feminism, and Political Theory* (Cambridge: Polity, 1989).

13. Hanna Fenichel Pitkin, *Fortune Is a Woman: Gender and Politics in the Thought of Niccolò Maccchiavelli* (Berkeley: University of California Press, 1984).

14. Kathleen B. Jones, *Compassionate Authority* (New York and London: Routledge, 1993).
15. Adriana Cavarero, *Corpo in figure: Filosofia e politica della corporeità* (Milan: Feltrinelli, 1995).
16. The deeper motivation O'Brien suggests for this need is that of constructing an artificial system that is capable of bypassing masculine uncertainty about paternity, instituting a modality for the recognition of patrilinear descent as against the natural matrilinear one. Mary O'Brien, *The Politics of Reproduction* (London: Routledge & Kegan Paul, 1981).
17. The dualism of the two spheres, the private-domestic and the public-political, is one of those issues that have been of most concern for both the thought and practices of feminism. For an exploration of the topic and relevant bibliography see my "Donne e uomini tra pubblico e privato," *Annali di studi religiosi*, no. 5 (2004): 367–88.
18. Many of the most interesting reflections that have derived from the ethics of care have focused on the topic of dependency. See Eva Feder Kittay, *Love's Labor: Essays on Women's Equality and Dependency* (New York: Routledge, 1999).
19. These observations are due above all to Elizabeth Wollgast's work on the atomism of modern politics and to those women scholars who have concentrated their efforts mainly on juridical analysis.
20. Patrice Di Quinzio, *The Impossibility of Motherhood: Feminism, Individualism, and the Problem of Mothering* (New York: Routledge, 1999).
21. Jane Flax, "Political Philosophy and the Patriarchal Unconscious: Psychoanalytic Perspective on Epistemology and Metaphysics," in *Discovering Reality*, ed. Sandra Harding and Merrill B. Hintikka (Dordrecht: Reidel, 1983), 255. Flax develops her own position in *Thinking Fragments* (Berkeley: University of California Press, 1990), and in *Disputed Subjects* (New York: Routledge, 1995).
22. Flax, "Political Philosophy and the Patriarchal Unconscious," 249.
23. Flax, "Political Philosophy and the Patriarchal Unconscious," 249.
24. See Christine Di Stefano, *Configurations of Masculinity: A Feminist Perspective on Modern Political Theory* (Ithaca, N.Y.: Cornell University Press, 1991). Di Stefano, together with Nancy Hirshmann, has also edited *Revisioning the Political: Feminist Reconstructions of Traditional Concepts in Western Political Theory* (Boulder, Colo.: Westview Press, 1996).
25. Di Stefano, *Configurations of Masculinity*, 18–19.
26. Di Stefano, *Configurations of Masculinity*, 191.
27. Julia Kristeva, *Powers of Horror: An Essay on Abjection* (New York: Columbia University Press, 1982), but her *Strangers to Ourselves* (New York: Columbia University Press, 1991), is also tied to this issue.
28. See Judith Butler, *The Psychic Life of Power: Theories of Subjection* (Stanford, Calif.: Stanford University Press, 1997). Wanda Tommasi reviewed this work in our online journal *Per amore del mondo*, no. 1 (2004), http://www.diotimafilosofe.it/larivista/.

29. Joseph Conrad, *The Shadow Line: A Confession* (Garden City, N.Y.: Doubleday, 1917), 4. Where is the light and where is the shadow here? The shadow is ahead of us, the light behind us in childhood and in the mother's light; the point is therefore to enter the shadow, which is unusual if compared with the usual narrative strategy, which sees the transition from shadow to light as the main path toward individuation on the male model. What probably counts here is the masculine assumption of the negative of reality.

30. For a critical analysis of Kristeva's position on this point: Diana Coole, *Negativity and Politics: Dionysus and Dialectics from Kant to Poststructuralism* (London: Routledge, 2000). My perplexity as regards Kristeva's position has been strengthened by the central role she assigns to matricide as access to the symbolic in her book *Melanie Klein* (New York: Columbia University Press, 2001). Manuela Fraire criticized her on this point in "Amare al cospetto della madre," *Il manifesto*, 29 October 2006.

31. [Diana Sartori is referring to her essay, "La tentazione del bene," in Diotima, *La magica forza del negativo*.—Eds.]

32. See Jane Flax, "Mother–Daughter Relationships: Psychodynamics, Politics, and Philosophy," in *The Future of Difference*, ed. Hester Eisenstein and Alice Jardine (New Brunswick, N.J.: Rutgers University Press, 1985), 20–40. Her essay in a historic monographic issue of *Feminist Studies* dedicated to outlining a feminist theory of the maternal was also important. See Flax, "The Conflict between Nurturance and Autonomy in Mother/Daughter Relationships and within Feminism," *Feminist Studies*, no. 2 (1978): 171–89.

33. In her opinion, this happens while expressing a desire for protection that often masks an anger for not having had enough.

34. Flax, "Mother–Daughter Relationships: Psychodynamics, Politics, and Philosophy," 37.

35. Nancy Chodorow, *The Reproduction of Mothering: Psychoanalysis and the Sociology of Gender* (Berkeley: University of California Press, 1978).

36. Flax, "Mother–Daughter Relationships: Psychodynamics, Politics, and Philosophy," 38.

37. This was a decade that had seen the development of other important and controversial positions: beyond those of Irigaray, Adrienne Rich, Chodorow, Flax, it should be sufficient to mention only Dorothy Dinnerstein, Julia Kristeva, Hélène Cixous, Sara Ruddick, Jessica Benjamin.

38. But since more or less youthful women continue to show an interest in the thought of difference it is not superfluous to recall at least the most crucial texts in this long itinerary: in addition to the books by Diotima, *Il pensiero della differenza sessuale* (Milan: La Tartaruga, 2003), *Mettere al mondo il mondo* (Milan: La Tartaruga, 1990), *Il cielo stellato dentro di noi: Oltre l'uguaglianza* (Naples: Liguori, 1995), *La sapienza di partire da sé* (Naples: Liguori, 1996), *Il profumo della maestra* (Naples: Liguori, 1999), *Approfittare dell'assenza* (Naples: Liguori, 2002), and *La*

magica forza del negativo, one must also mention Luce Irigaray's *An Ethics of Sexual Difference*; Libreria delle donne in Milan, *Non credere di avere dei diritti* (Turin: Rosenberg & Sellier, 1987) as well as Luisa Muraro, *The Symbolic Order of the Mother*, trans. Francesca Novello (Albany: State University of New York Press, 2018).

39. Silvia Vegetti Finzi employs this expression when discussing an inexhaustible demand directed at the mother. In the course of her entire life a woman will try to be recognized completely, without shadows, without reservations. See her essay "Paradossi della maternità e costruzione di un'etica femminile," in *Corpo a corpo: Madre e figlia nella psicoanalisi*, ed. Gabriella Buzzati and Anna Salvo (Rome and Bari: Laterza, 1995), 147–90. This volume is devoted in large part to the obscure aspects of the maternal.

40. Adrienne Rich in *Of Women Born: Motherhood as Experience and Institution* (New York: W. W. Norton, 1976) warned of this desire "to become purged once and for all of our mother's bondage" (236).

41. See Sartori, "La tentazione del bene."

42. I remember this terrible story that my teacher told me, perhaps the bitterest lesson I have had on that which is obscure in the maternal: each time a small girl does something bad, her mother adds a nail to the wall, then when the girl asks for forgiveness, she removes it. One day the girl tells her mother "but the wall is full of holes," to which the mother replies "Yes, like your mother's heart."

43. Walter Benjamin, "Theses on the Philosophy of History," in *Illuminations*, trans. Harry Zohn (New York: Schocken, 1969), 255.

44. The *Ring* film cycle has become the object of a veritable cult, and not only among horror enthusiasts, both in its original Japanese version and in its American ones. An interpretation close to the one I have proposed is provided by Matthew Sharpe, "Repetition: *The Ring* and the Diabolical Imaginary," *cinetext* (September 2003), http://cinetext.philo.at/magazine/msharpe/ring.html.

45. Chiara Zamboni has suggested a practice of this kind in "Il conflitto nascosto," *Il manifesto*, 15 October 2001.

46. The bibliography on biopolitics is vast at this point; for some guidance see *Biopolitica: Storia e attualità di un concetto*, ed. Antonella Cutro (Verona: ombre corte, 2005).

47. On this issue, see Tristana Dini, "Tra 'bìos' e 'zoé': Teorie femministe della biopolitica," in *Annali di studi religiosi*, no. 7 (2006): 29–52; and "'È già politica': Democrazia, biopolitica e singolarità sessuata," in *Biopolitica e democrazia*, ed. Adriano Vinale (Milan: Mimesis, 2006) as well as a book she edited on the issue of feminism and biopolitics, *La razza al lavoro: Femminismo e biopolitica* (Milan: Manifestolibri, 2012).

48. To the best of my knowledge I believe the announcement of the end of patriarchy, which at that time was greeted with perplexity and even a chorus of protests, also from women, can be traced to the monographic issue *La fine del*

patriarcato, Via Dogana, no. 23 (1995) and *È accaduto non per caso, Sottosopra* (January 1996).

49. In the course of the previous meeting of the Diotima seminar.

50. Diotima has devoted several annual seminars to the issue and Milan's Libreria delle donne has frequently returned to this problem in its journal *Via Dogana*. Some male groups have been formed who are working on the transformation of male identity both in relation to the end of patriarchy and to the feminist challenge. Among contributions in this vein let me mention Giorgio Cavallari, *L'uomo post-patriarcale: Verso una nuova identità maschile* (Milan: Vivarium, 2001).

51. I am thinking above all of the return, frequently observed, of violence against women, but many have pointed to the connection between patriarchy's crisis and the more generalized return of a climate of violence and the resolution of conflicts by force.

52. See Manuel Castells, *The Power of Identity* (Malden, Mass.: Blackwell, 1997).

53. There are many books on the issue, with a sociological or psychological approach; because of the perspective he chooses let me mention Marco Deriu, *La fragilità dei padri: Il disordine simbolico paterno e il confronto con i figli adolescenti* (Milan: Unicopli, 2004). For a historical reconstruction of the decline in paternal authority see Elisabeth Roudinesco, *La famiglia in disordine*, trans. Adriana Valle (Rome: Meltemi, 2002).

54. Max Horkheimer, "Authority and the Family," in *Critical Theory: Selected Essays*, trans. Matthew J. O'Connell (New York: Herder and Herder, 1972), 47–128; Theodor W. Adorno, Else Frenkel-Brunswik, Daniel J. Levinson, and Nevitt Sanford, *The Authoritarian Personality* (New York: W. W. Norton, 1969); Alexander Mitscherlich, *Society without the Father: A Contribution to Social Psychology*, trans. Eric Mosbacher (New York: Harcourt Brace & World, 1969). Let me also mention Herbert Marcuse's essays in *Psychoanalyse und Politik* (Frankfurt: Europäische Verlagsanstalt, 1968).

55. A transformation which instead Alain Touraine seems to understand in his *Le monde des femmes* (Paris: Fayard, 2006).

56. The prevailing male myopia and silence may not be surprising, but I am struck by the female and feminist ones. I attribute the latter, on the one hand, to the fact that those who espoused critical and remonstrative positions and who embraced the political perspective of women's oppression at times rest on their laurels, and on the other to what seems to me an inability to perceive change—an inability due to having embraced a position that considers the symbolic order of the father as an enclosed horizon that turns female difference precisely into its impossible other.

57. Žižek deals with the issue in several places of his endless oeuvre, but the crucial points are summarized in his *The Ticklish Subject: The Absent Centre of Political Ontology* (London: Verso, 1999).

58. Žižek devotes another text to the various aspects of this, which he considers a veritable contemporary plague, *The Plague of Fantasies* (London: Verso, 1997). See also his *The Metastases of Enjoyment: Six Essays on Women and Causality* (London: Verso, 1994).

59. The expression "wounded attachments" which Žižek borrows from Butler actually belongs to Wendy Brown, who used it as the title of one of her chapters in *States of Injury: Power and Freedom in Late Modernity* (Princeton, N.J.: Princeton University Press, 1995). She is also the origin of other frequently borrowed analyses on the characteristics of the present crisis, especially the critique of the left's legalitarian drift. Together with Janet Halley, she is the editor of *Left Legalism/Left Critique* (Durham, N.C.: Duke University Press, 2002).

60. The types of concern Žižek expresses, especially insofar as their political repercussions are concerned, seem to exhibit many continuities with those that were characteristic of Frankfurt School critical theory.

61. This concept of "ethical act" is borrowed from Jacques Lacan, *The Seminar of Jacques Lacan: The Ethics of Psychoanalysis Book VII*, trans. Dennis Porter (New York and London: W. W. Norton, 1997). For the political relevance of this concept, and more generally of the Lacanian perspective, see Yannis Stavrakakis, *Lacan and the Political* (London: Routledge, 1999). As far as I am concerned I believe that an understanding of what this concept means is quite clear for anyone who has lived the feminist dimension.

62. The authentic ethical act goes beyond good and evil, and in this perspective this raises a question of a choice of the "worse," as Žižek says, which requires one to focus attention on the negative. This explains Žižek's attention to the negative in *Tarrying with the Negative* (Durham, N.C.: Duke University Press, 1993) as well as to the return of the Kantian theme of "radical evil," for whose interpretation he gathers inspiration especially from some women who have worked on this topic in the last several years: Alenka Zupancic, Joan Copjec, and Renata Salecl, *Ethics of the Real* (London: Verso, 2000); *Radical Evil*, ed. Joan Copjec (London: Verso, 1996); Joan Copjec, *Read My Desire: Lacan against the Historicists* (Cambridge, Mass.: MIT Press, 1989) and *Imagine There's No Woman: Ethics and Sublimation* (Cambridge, Mass.: MIT Press, 2002); and Renata Salecl, *Perversions of Love and Hate* (London: Verso, 1998). I have discussed Žižek's position on this choice of the "worse" in "Meglio un uovo oggi," *Per Amore del Mondo*, no. 1 (2004); the proverbial need "to break some eggs to make an omelet" returns in Žižek's recent work *The Parallax View* (Cambridge, Mass.: MIT Press, 2006).

63. Jodi Dean, "Feminism in Technoculture," *Journal Review of Education, Pedagogy, and Cultural Studies* 23, no. 1 (2001): 23–47. Dean compares postpatriarchy to contemporary technoculture and asks herself why, if feminism has won, there seems to be something missing: we don't have what we want. She analyzes the female repercussions that she sees articulated in fear, in the nourishing of desire, and in the search for perfection. She looks with favor to existent

"multiple feminisms" but she raises the problem of how we are forced to choose even though there is no real choice; gathering inspiration from Drucilla Cornell and Rosi Braidotti, she makes some political proposals among which are: take the system literally, not with irony or parody, and defend imagination. Dean is the author of *Žižek's Politics* (London: Routledge, 2006).

64. A similar suspicion has been articulated in the criticisms repeatedly made by Judith Butler (her position is criticized by Žižek in *The Ticklish Subject*) who engages in a discussion with Žižek in Judith Butler, Ernesto Laclau, and Slavoj Žižek, *Contingency, Hegemony, Universality: Contemporary Dialogues on the Left* (London: Verso, 2000). Rosi Braidotti also takes her distances from this approach in *Metamorphosis: Towards a Materialist Theory of Becoming* (Cambridge: Polity, 2002). On the limits of Žižek's analysis of the post-oedipal future, see Ida Dominijanni, "Ma di che sesso è il soggetto post-edipico?" *Il manifesto*, 22 July 2003. She also tackles the issue of the fall of symbolic efficacy, in an analysis that starts from the history of Italian feminism, in her "Eredi al tramonto: Fine della politica e politica della differenza," in *Politica e destino*, ed. Mario Tronti et al. (Rome: Sossella, 2006), 125–43.

65. Flax, "The Conflict between Nurturance and Autonomy."

66. The limits of the Lacanian view of the symbolic and language have been cogently highlighted starting from a Wittgensteinian and feminist approach by Toril Moi, "From Femininity to Finitude: Freud, Lacan, and Feminism, Again," *Journal of Women in Culture and Society* 29, no. 3 (Spring 2004): 841–78. For a general picture, see Elizabeth Grosz, *Jacques Lacan: A Feminist Introduction* (New York: Routledge, 1990).

67. This is a common condition in the contemporary philosophical debate about politics, but here I am thinking above all about the example given by Butler, Laclau, and Žižek in their *Contingency, Hegemony, Universality*.

68. See Derrida, *Specters of Marx: The State of the Debt, the Work of Mourning, and the New International*, trans. Peggy Kamuf (New York: Routledge, 1994), a text that plays out on the meaning of the specters that infest the present. Strangely enough even though he returns to the key figure of the specter that announces itself in *Hamlet* with the words "I am thy father's spirit" Derrida doesn't consider the father's actual specter.

69. The analyses of the present that focus on the crucial position of the imaginary are legion; among the many see Cornelius Castoriadis, *The Imaginary Institution of Society* (Cambridge: Polity Press, 1987). Fulvio Carmagnola insists on this aspect in *Il consumo delle immagini: Estetica e beni simbolici nella fiction economy* (Milan: Mondadori, 2006).

70. Andrea O'Reilly has insisted on this distinction between *mothering* and *motherhood*; see *From Motherhood to Mothering: The Legacy of Adrienne Rich's "Of Woman Born,"* ed. Andrea O'Reilly (London: Women's Press, 2004).

71. The definition is from Madelon Sprengnether, *The Spectral Mother: Freud, Feminism, and Psychoanalysis* (Ithaca, N.Y.: Cornell University Press, 1990).

72. Among the many examples one could mention, one that I find particularly disquieting is that which emerges from the films of Park Chan-Wook in his cycle on vengeance. Particularly *Old Boys* (2003) poses worrisome questions regarding daughters' accessibility to their fathers in a post-oedipal situation in which maternal authority is absent.

73. This fratriarchal nature of postpatriarchy has been underscored from many sides, in Italy most forcefully by Dominijanni. Some useful reflections on the "regime of the brother," even though they start from modernity itself, can be found in Juliet Flower MacCannell's *The Regime of the Brother: After the Patriarchy* (London: Routledge, 1991).

74. I am not alluding to positions such as that expressed with great resonance by Mary Dietz with respect to theories of care and maternal thought—many of the most important essays are now collected in *Turning Operations* (New York: Routledge, 2002)—and which belong in the tradition of emancipation; I am alluding, rather, to warnings of this kind that come from the thought of sexual difference: for instance, a warning of this kind was brought to the Diotima seminar by Maddalena Spagnolli.

75. As far as this non-identity is concerned let me refer to my "La tentazione del bene."

76. See Slavoj Žižek, "Afterword: Lenin's Choice," in V. I. Lenin's *Revolution at the Gates: A Selection of Writings from February to October 1917*, ed. Slavoj Žižek (London: Verso, 2002).

77. For the meaning to be attributed to this much debated concept I believe it is still important to refer to what Jean Laplanche and Jean-Bertrand Pontalis write in the "Phantasm" (or Fantasy) entry in *The Language of Psycho-analysis* (New York: W. W. Norton, 1974) and in *Fantasme originaire, fantasmes des origines, origines du fantasme* (Paris: Hachette, 1985).

78. And perhaps even by a mother who is taken by her nonfreedom, freedom.

79. The vision expressed in the works of the second part of Wittgenstein's production *Philosophical Investigations*, trans. Elizabeth Anscombe (Oxford: Blackwell, 1997), but above all in *On Certainty*, trans. Denis Paul and Elizabeth Anscombe (Oxford: Blackwell, 1969) as well as his *Remarks on Color*, trans. Linda L. McAlister and Margarete Schäte (Berkeley and Los Angeles: University of California Press, 1977).

80. For this point in particular, but more generally for what I am saying, I am obviously indebted to Luisa Muraro's position(s) in *The Symbolic Order of the Mother*, and also to the work on maternal language done by Chiara Zamboni. See Zamboni, *Parole non consumate: Donne e uomini nel linguaggio* (Naples: Liguori, 2001); *Il cuore sacro della lingua*, ed. Chiara Zamboni (Padua: Il Poligrafo, 2006); and *All'inizio di tutto la lingua materna*, ed. Eva-Marie Thüne (Turin: Rosenberg & Sellier, 1998).

81. This great fear of destruction reminds one once again of an answer given by Wittgenstein, who, to those who accused him of destroying everything which

is "great and important" and leave only "bits of stone and rubble" behind, he calmly observed that "what we are destroying is nothing but houses of cards and we are cleaning up the ground of language on which they stand" (*Philosophical Investigations*, §118). The premises for certain collapses can be explained by a statement such as this: "Remember that we sometimes demand definitions for the sake not of their content, but of their form. Our requirement is an architectural one; the definition a kind of ornamental coping that supports nothing" (§217).

82. Thinking about that male request for a bond with the maternal I am tempted to look with favor to the keeping of the maternal shadow in the game, even in its most obscure and irreducible aspect. If in fact that request is addressed to the nutritional maternal, to only respond in that sense would collude with politics' tendency to close in on itself in its presumption of totality.

83. "Unlike the reign of Aurora, when the sun appears—that unique celestial body, powerful, potent, and decisive—with it appears its reign, the reign of power. Power which when it ceases to be of the dawn is converted into imperative, reigning, unique, without bothering about establishing prolegomena, the foundations of its unique reign; never turning back to contemplate its own apparition or birth. One would say that the sun is, without being born. . . . Only in the penumbra does liberation from its own reign, even for the sun itself, lie hidden; a reign in which the sun itself remains prisoner of its own power." María Zambrano, *Dell'aurora*, trans. Elena Laurenzi (Genoa: Marietti, 2000), 133–35.

The Undecidable Imprint

IDA DOMINIJANNI

I first started writing about feminism with two articles in *Il manifesto* that talked about the "discovery of the mother" in consciousness-raising groups [*gruppi di autocoscienza*].[1] It was 1979, dark times after Aldo Moro's assassination, when mainstream political discourse tied feminism to the decline of the movements of the 1968–1977 period, just as initially it had tied it to their ascent, in both cases considering it merely a supplement to male politics.[2] In those two articles I instead argued there was no retrenchment but a transformation of the feminist political laboratory, and that a crucial role in this transformation was played by a shift in emphasis from the analysis of the woman-man relationship (as well as that of woman–law of the father) to that of the woman-woman relationship (and that of woman–maternal-phantasm). I thought this shift would be decisive in removing certain obstacles (symbiotic temptations and difficulties in the process of individuation, rivalries, difficulties in channeling creativity toward a project or a product), which referred back to an unelaborated relationship of women with the real mother, or to forms of idealization of the maternal, or to a lack of awareness in the reproduction of the roles of daughter and mother in relationships between women. I was writing on the basis of a limited experience—Florentine feminism, and the "Rosa" collective specifically, which was traversed in peculiar ways by these sorts of dynamics—but I was not the only or the sharpest person to write about this.[3] One can find a plethora of references to the "problem" of the mother in the movement's archives in the second half of the 1970s, and if I am beginning from those two articles it is only to remind us, and me first of all, how long the history of the "maternal obscure" that this book by Diotima wants to thematize again actually is.

Although especially central to the path taken by Milan's Libreria delle donne [Women's Bookstore], the issue will soon find a significant turning point in the bookstore's own *Catalogo giallo* [Yellow catalogue]. These are the years 1980 to 1982, when a group from the bookstore meets several times, the very first in a hotel in Caspoggio, in order to read their most beloved women authors with an eye toward sexual difference, and it immediately finds itself confronted with the usual problem of the mother. Yet something in one of the next meetings shines some light on this repetition:

> I have thought again about the discussion in Caspoggio. Why do discourses about the mother always end up at the same point? Arguing that the mother is to blame, that no, she is innocent, in other words saying nothing. This occurs when we speak about our experience with our real mother or with women we know and immediately there are two sides, those who argue innocence and those who argue guilt. This doesn't occur when we talk about our favorite female author, about her texts, her original language. In this case there is a recognition for a woman and a language that occurs independently of the rules of a male society. We are free (we are not oppressed internally by the experience of the relationship with our mother) and we use her words with pleasure, we suggest others to her, we do some things, guaranteed by her existence. . . . However, for me rereading the accounts of that experience has not been useless. The word mother that was evoked there allowed me to analyze the group's work following a lead [*traccia*] that previously wasn't as clear and was now becoming evident. We chose a female author (mother) whom we liked; we got together in a group to discuss some texts by women authors (mothers) not because of a literary passion but searching for words by women that were not tied to the rules and expectations of a male society (of the father), on a search for original languages (languages of origins). We each gave the other the word, they to us and we to them—beyond recriminations against the mother, which does however leave a residue . . . which should not be erased since that too is a reality. That residue—which becomes visible when we are in trouble and our defeat in a patriarchal society comes back to weigh on us—evokes phantasms that are definitely present in our imaginary. But it

didn't prevent our relationship with the maternal text, in other words the work of the *Catalogue*.[4]

Between the "Caspoggio debate" and the final compilation of the *Catalogue* a decisive transition had occurred: the symbolic figure of the mother became detached from the infantile experience with the real mother, but without forgetting or negating her; keeping her in mind instead. That originary imprint is inerasable, but it can be elaborated into a larger figure, which includes it and goes beyond it, clearing the field of the division between those who argue "innocent" and the others who argue "guilty." The phantasm of the originary is resolved, even if not dissolved, in a symbolic construction, by means of a practice of transference from the mother to the writers-mothers we freely chose. From the outlines of a "symbolic mother" as a "sexed figure of origin" to the invention of the practices—entrustment, disparity, authority—which will give shape and rules to the politics of the symbolic in the feminism of difference, the continuation of this story will be narrated a few years later in *Non credere di avere dei diritti*.[5] But rereading the Caspoggio narrative is useful in order to focus on the dialectics between the lived experience of the relationship with the mother and its elaboration in the lived experience of relationships with other women; or, in other terms, between the imprint (real and phantasmatic) of the primary experience and the construction—also experiential—of a symbolic form. This is a dialectic that I believe is crucial to bear in mind if today we want to think about the "maternal obscure."

Why then should we think about it? This time I confess I have some questions on the topic for this book chosen by Diotima, or about its presuppositions, as if on it there converged, or, rather, diverged, different paths of political and theoretical practice that it would be useful to somehow make explicit.[6] Insofar as my path is concerned, I believe that the discovery of the mother's symbolic dimension, and the invention of the correlated political practices, has been and remains a turning point of extraordinary import for women's politics, with extraordinarily significant results, which we should endeavor to reassert and to make our own as much as possible. Let me recapitulate these results: the introduction of that dimension of transcendence, genealogy, verticality, and authority in relationships between one woman and another as well as in relationships among women, which has given freedom and autonomy to female thought and action, which has broken the paradigm of oppression, shattered the paralyzing regime of mutual recognition in a shared misery; the reconversion of envy into gratitude; the opening of a regime of exchange among women that has overcome the symbiotic and inconclusive drift that blocked it; the establishing of relationships between one woman and another as well among women that are ordered and ordering, which resolves the conflictuality and microrivalries that traditionally traversed them. All of Italian feminism, including that part which has always been hostile to this path, has gained from this positive paradigm, which has displaced the traditional narrative of this kind, that of the victim. This positive paradigm has in its turn accompanied, perhaps promoted and certainly interpreted, a social and cultural change whose traces can easily be found within us and around us, in both private and public life. This is seen in relationships between today's adolescents and their mothers that are more settled than they once were, in the relations of trust between women which nourish and organize workplaces that are otherwise under the sway of power and money, in the female authority that marks schools and universities, in the battles we engaged in with psychoanalysts to resist their commandment that we should reach individuation by "forgetting" the mother and leaving her behind.[7]

However, the importance of the results notwithstanding, or perhaps precisely because of this, I never thought that the "positive" horizon of the symbolic order of the mother would resolve every kernel of negativity, nor that it had been conquered once and for all. I have known since the days of my consciousness-raising [*autocoscienza*] practice to what extent that "residue" which the *Catalogo giallo* spoke about is strong and tends to reverberate in relationships between one woman and another as well as in relationships among women; hence, it has always seemed obvious to me that that order does not eliminate the negative, but needs to continuously reelaborate and rework it. And since today we are confronting evidence in the news that is contrary to the traces of positive change I just quoted, it also seems obvious to me that in a society that is increasingly maternalized, there are always new impulses toward death and destruction both *against* and *within* the maternal. Consider that at least four of the significant crimes that have bloodied the provinces of Northern Italy in the last ten years and fed the collective imaginary have a mother accused of having killed a son, or daughters who have killed their mother, or failed mothers who kill a fulfilled mother at their epicenter.[8] These are the reasons I read *La magica forza del negativo* by Diotima, a book moreover that I consider excellent, with a mixture of satisfaction and amazement. It is as if one discovered something in it, the negative in our lives and our relationships precisely, that for me has always been there as something not completely resolved or not completely resolvable within the order of the mother.[9]

Why then does the negative return? What does it have to do with the permanence of an obscure side, not enlightened and perhaps not enlightenable, of maternal potential and the primary relation? And to what degree are the transformations of the social, the symbolic, and the imaginary interpretable today, for both good and bad, also as effects, as reverberations, of the resignification of the mother that feminism has propounded? In my attempt to provide some answers I will once again start from that "residue" of the *Catalogo giallo*, but in order to change its name. In the course of time, by observing our political practice, I have reached the conclusion that in women's relationships oriented by the symbolic order of the mother the imprint of one's relationship with one's real mother remains and never ceases to re-present itself, like a wound that reopens, if the relationship was a unhappy one, or like a symbiotic enjoyment that closes once again, if the relationship was a happy one. This is an imprint that awareness, psychoanalytical work, linguistic elaboration can bring into focus, but not erase, one that the symbolic procedure of "knowing how to love mother" suggested by Luisa Muraro helps to treat, but while leaving all its ambivalences open.[10] It is not a question of a *residue*, however, but precisely of an imprint, of an *impression* of the constantly returning origin.[11] It therefore should not be thought of as a remainder, which one can sooner or later eliminate, dispose of, or dissolve during the process of symbolization, but rather as an uneliminatable excess, which resists and complicates the process of symbolization itself. It is something *undecidable*, which one never stops coming to terms with, and with which one can never settle accounts completely. Psychoanalytic literature has been dealing with this excess since it attempted to oppose the secondary place that the mother occupies in the Freudian system, and it provides ample proof, confirmed by our political practice, of how the sign of the relationship with the mother is particularly marked and "exceeding" [*eccedente*] in the process of female subjectivization, to the extent that it connotes the very structure of sexual difference.[12] But what does thinking this undecidability of the maternal imply, both with respect to politics' traditional paradigm and with respect to the politics of the symbolic? And prior to that, what does it tell us about the process of symbolization itself?

Luisa Muraro's *L'ordine simbolico della madre* is the text we should turn to with these questions in mind. She shares with other female authors, first of all Luce Irigaray, the project of bringing the figure of the mother and the mother–daughter relationship, both imprisoned in the patriarchal imaginary, to the light of the symbolic.[13] Yet, it is her proposal that most systematically places a wager on the possibility of turning the mother into the logical and epistemological principle of a process of symbolization that is other than that of the paternal Logos. Returning the mother to her function of giving both life *and* speech, the one inseparably from the other, Muraro reconnects body and language metonymically and brings access to the symbolic back within the maternal relationship. It invalidates the oedipal and symbolic castration theorems as a posteriori legitimations of patriarchal dominion; it reformulates the maternal relationship as a socio-symbolic form, no longer confined to the private sphere, but charged with implications for the public sphere: on the political level insofar as it is the shape of an unequal relationship that takes dependency as a constitutive given, and on the linguistic-communicative level since it is the shape of a relationship between being and language that modifies the devices of authority and sayability, and in this fashion also those of historical and political change.

There is no need to underscore, even less in a book by Diotima that has been its most fertile interpreter, the political and theoretical fecundity of this proposal. The latter has given coherence and greatness to the politics of the symbolic, bringing the originary feminist practice of putting experience into words and modifying reality through language to its point of greatest tension and expansion, within the "circle of body and word" mediated by maternal authorization and gratitude for the mother.[14] I remember with clarity—and gratitude—the sense of lightness and empowerment that the logical proceeding from the "difficulty of beginning" to the maternal principle of the speakability of female experience, or rather of "anything we want to say," gave me.[15] I would no longer be able to give this up. It is therefore starting from a given fact that today I ask myself if something, and what, has been lost in the great gain of the maternal symbolic; if something, and what, resists symbolic translation, even if metonymical, remaining nonsymbolized and nonsymbolizable, unsaid or unsayable. And if there is a limit, and which, to the potential of the symbolic, and the politics of the symbolic.

Some thought should be given once again to two voids in *L'ordine simbolico della madre* (but from here on I could avoid italics, because the argument regards both Luisa Muraro's text and the work, both theoretical and of political practice, that is tied to that text), and to an objection that Angela Putino stated to it in the past. The first void is the place of the father, who doesn't appear and is not contemplated. This absence, Luisa explained to me when talking about it, does not preclude the *possibility* of the paternal figure, but contests the *necessity* of the law of the father.[16] I think she should be given credit for this position, because it allowed us to think of the mother, the daughter-mother genealogy, and access to the symbolic *independently* of the oedipal triangulation. A triangulation in which other feminist treatments remain inexorably entangled, although they, like us, also consider the mother–daughter relationship a principle of subjectivation and social bond that differs from those modeled on the modern individual.[17] However, that absence leaves some things unsaid, both as regards the structure of the symbolic and the relation of the maternal genealogy with the other. As for the structure of the symbolic, in *L'ordine simbolico della madre* metaphor and metonymy, contiguity and substitution, relationship and law don't cross one another anymore, while *Maglia o uncinetto*, a previous and pertinent text by Muraro, left a movement between metonymical and metaphorical axes of symbolization open.[18] As for the relationship of the maternal genealogy with the other, when the father is omitted from the argument the daughter's love for him is omitted as well, which is a relevant factor for both infantile and adult female sexuality. Not to mention the mother's desire for the man—it is almost as if the sexual act, which is at the origin of procreation, had become secondary or something not worthy of consideration, just as it becomes secondary and unworthy of consideration in today's technologically assisted procreation.

Let me now turn to the second void: within the order of the mother female sexuality has been gradually dissolving. The more the mother became a sexed figure of origin, of female speech and authority, the more her sexuality vanished. This is a paradoxical outcome, which was not part of the argument's premises. For example, it was not in Luce Irigaray's first texts, where the project of bringing the mother–daughter relationship foreclosed by the patriarchal symbolic to representation was not distinct from that of making room for women's sexuality. It was precisely female sexuality—the labia that touch, the sex which is not one—that inaugurated the metonymical economy of contiguity as against the metaphorical and patriarchal one of substitution and sacrifice.[19] Subsequently, might it have happened that the "ontological desire" that supported our theoretical and political research once again veiled erotic desire? May language, even though tied metonymically to the body and experience, have silenced sex? Or the maternal symbolic once again reproduced the desexualized imaginary of the mother? It seems to me that sexuality once again questions us along this divide, which on the one hand concerns the limits of the symbolic, on the other the relationship between symbolic and imaginary. Sexuality, in fact, exceeds the process of symbolization: it underlays it but cannot be reduced to it, it nourishes the desire to know and speak but it lives beyond language, when language retreats or collapses. And, vice versa, it has been silent, for too long, in our discursive practices. When sexuality is silent, however, we know that something, in the "circle of body and word," is blocked, or returns in unforeseen ways.[20] And, in fact, I fear that it may return, against our best intentions, in the form of a female desire that has been silenced once again, or in that of a maternal potential that has been once again desexualized.

I still have to consider the objection formulated by Angela Putino in *Amiche mie isteriche*.[21] This is a text that I rejected when it first appeared because it seemed to me to constitute too harsh an attack on our practice, but whose theoretical core I believe should be reconsidered today as a critique of the role played by the "hysterical position" in *L'ordine simbolico della madre*. The figure of the hysteric does indeed play a key role in Muraro's text.[22] It expresses an attachment to the *maternal continuum* that cannot find expression in the patriarchal order, but can instead find mediation in the maternal order, by means of the reconversion of resentment toward the real mother into gratitude, by means of relationships between women or the mother language. According to Putino, however, this is not a strategy for elaboration but rather the repositing of the hysterical position, in the sense that the maternal model, wanted by the hysteric especially when she opposes it, unifies differences among women on the basis of the fear of loss. This manner of engaging in relationships, she argues, becomes an immunizing process with respect to the risks of becoming. Metonymically bound to the context, the mother language does not leap into the symbolic, into the necessary tension of abstraction, and into distinction and separation, but always produces a word that is entangled in the imaginary, always close to the origin. In other words, for Putino, the hysterical attachment is reproduced in relationships among women as a defensive structure toward the divergent becoming that characterizes the "event" of sexual difference in the twentieth century. The symbolic order of the mother remains tied to the maternal imaginary.[23]

Personally, I didn't share Angela's critique at the time and I don't share it today, nor do I agree with the alternative she proposed of a becoming-woman entirely based on the improper and on divergence, and not at all on what is shared and on convergence, nor on her reiteration of the superiority of the metaphoric over the metonymical in the process of symbolization. And I remain convinced that the reinterpretation of the figure of the hysteric has actually had therapeutic effects, contributing to a modification of the sense of many "hysterical" female behaviors. Nevertheless, it is true that reproposing the primary relation produces inhomogeneous, and sometimes opposite, effects in the political order constituted by the relationships between one woman and another as well as among women. (In my opinion, this primary relation is also based on one's experience of the relationship with one's real mother). Consider claustrophilia and claustrophobia, ease and intolerance, satisfaction and lack; and too often, together with claustrophilia and ease, an unbeatable tendency toward self-moderation, which invariably lowers the target of the shared political wager. But there is more. Precisely insofar as the reinterpretation and the "political therapy" of hysteria have efficiently modified female discontent, to what degree and until what time is it right to repropose them? Looking at the negative in relationships between women, are we still sure that hysteria is the symptom we should be focusing on and on which the artillery of practice should be concentrated?

We are here entering difficult terrain, but one that I believe it is important to till. Both the clinic and common sense today converge in telling us that in the course of a century, in the female population of Western societies, the hysterical symptom has been largely replaced by the anorexic one, while the former has in the meantime largely shifted onto men. The ordinary exercise of biopolitical government confirms this diagnosis. Today it is no longer the hysterical body that constitutes the public danger that must be interned, surveilled, and punished, but the anorexic body, its capacity to resist, its power of blackmail, its self-destructive determination, its uncapturable lightness, its fleeting thinness, its androgynous sexuality. Ministers, prime ministers, anchormen and anchorwomen, well-to-do women whose curves have been reshaped with silicone furiously attack size two with an ardor that is certainly not inferior to that of the doctors and nurses of the Salpetriére.[24] In their paterno-maternalistic victimization strategy of unappetizing adolescents, treated as stupid and passive prey of the aesthetic canons of high fashion, the illiberal mark of the control and discipline of the female body returns in a very recognizable fashion; and so does the cynical mark of the inability to listen to that which the female body is telling us by way of a symptom. Compared to the media gossip, psychoanalytic knowledge proceeds with caution: the anorexic renews the challenge that Dora represented for Freud when she closed his study's door behind her in 1900. The principal suspect is the mother once again: the mother who narcissistically invests a perfectionist commandment on her daughter, or one that is too conventional and conformist, whom the anorexic adolescent will rebel against; a mother who is not very communicative or incapable of responding to her daughter's desire to communicate; the mother as one half of the parents' couple who is confused and confusing and doesn't know how to transmit sexual difference to her daughter; the mother as a mirror that doesn't smile, or responds with a grimace, to the daughter's need to receive a symbolic contour to her image from her gaze.[25] The hypotheses about what the anorexic symptom (or the bulimic one, which is unanimously considered its flip side) reveals about the daughter's bonds with the mother are more uncertain: a desperate attempt to defend herself from fusionality and dependence;[26] a request for love which does not find and does not want to find fulfillment in the food offering given by the mother;[27] a desire for differentiation and subtraction from the mother;[28] or, on the contrary, a mourning for the detachment from the bond with the mother required by the patriarchal economy.[29]

But even if this last one were the most fitting hypothesis, it would be the only sign of continuity between the hysterical and anorexic symptoms, within a situation of complete discontinuity. In actuality the two symptoms are inscribed in two completely different symbolic orders, or disorders, marked by a historical change promoted also, if not primarily— this is the point—by the female-feminist revolution. While the hysterical female body expressed a sexuality that was interdicted by the law of the father and was trying to find words to signify itself—and found them in the psychoanalytic *talking cure*[30] and in the feminist linguistic practices— the defeminized, dematernalized, and desexualized body of the anorexic does not ask for and does not offer signification either to the analyst or to the mother or to the other woman. It presents itself as an identitarian given, a nonsymbolizable return of the real, a body-fetish that exceeds discourse and that the ego entirely depends on. The *talking cure* risks a checkmate, and the symbolization process reveals its limits.[31] This transition does not occur in a void. In the meantime, the feminist revolution reinterpreted the hysterical symptom in response to the hysteric's demand for meaning subtracting it from the disciplinary knowledge of medicine and the experts. This produced an excess of meaning, a female knowledge of women that the anorexic refuses as a "circuit full of word(s), too full." Therein the anorexic is no longer the prisoner of male disciplinary action but of "the reality of her own body."[32] If hysteria is the symptom that accompanied women's entry into modernity and which feminism responded to politically, anorexia can then be seen as not only the symptom of a female resistance to a hedonistic and consumerist postmodernity, but also as an unforeseen and paradoxical effect of female change, of the female knowledge of woman, of the feminist symbolic revolution.[33] From the neurotic symptom of female oppression to the perverse symptom of female freedom?

I will return to this change of scenario in a little while. However, not before asking myself if and how this symptomatic shift emerges within our practices, generating conflicts and dynamics that are uninterpretable in the "hysterical" lexicon and are not treatable by means of the "therapy" of gratitude for the mother or by the practice of authority and disparity. I am thinking for instance of ways in which the relation with the other-woman is attacked, which appear *within* the symbolic order of the mother and have nothing in common with either the hysterical or the oedipal scene. They present themselves instead as calculated subtractions, determined and anesthetized, whose intent is directed toward sabotage or matricide of the "symbolic mother," rather than toward real mothers; that is, directed toward a symbolic mother who represents the very stitching together of relationships between one woman and another as well as among women. Further, this is a mother who has been internalized as powerful and indestructible, to whom one can always return, like a strong net that is no longer subject to either the law or the tantrums of the father.

What I mean, in any case, is that we also owe the anorexic symptom an attempt at a sympathetic hearing, at the sort of reinterpretation that we dared with the hysterical symptom. If in the hysterical conversion against the mother we saw the need for the maternal *continuum*, could the subtraction of the anorexic body from the mother not represent the opposite need of discontinuity from the maternal, a female difference from the mother to which space and meaning should be given?

Up to this point I have kept the argument within the boundaries of the theoretical and political practice of difference; but as always the latter speaks of wider tendencies and interprets them. The questions on the fate of female genealogy, of the symbolic order of the mother and the mother–daughter relationship are in fact, obviously, tied to our present, to its political anthropology and criteria of interpretation. Post-Lacanian literature on anorexia can act as a bridge for a reading of the present in terms that affect feminist thought, as often happens, tangentially: by way of consonances and dissonances, convergences and divergences, admissions and omissions. Here, the anorexic-bulimic symptom, in fact, appears within a constellation of symptoms related to practices of enjoyment (perversions, drug addictions, bulimia, alcoholism) or of the stagnation of enjoyment (anorexia, depression, panic), which, compared with the Freudian era, signals a change in the socio-symbolic order and requires a change in the theoretical-clinical paradigm. In Freud's time "civilization's discontent" was referred to the repressive imperative of a social super-ego, which required the interdiction of enjoyment and the renunciation of the impulse to satisfaction ("you must/you must not") from individual subjects, in exchange for access to the community.

Today, on the contrary, it seems to be referable to the imperative to enjoy ("you must enjoy"), which characterizes the late-capitalist and postmodern social super-ego and the contemporary narcissistic personality.[34] Freud conceived of psychoanalysis as a "symbolic clinic," a *talking cure* based on the hypothesis that the symptom expresses the coded return of the repressed desire in the language of the unconscious. Today, on the other hand, the new symptoms associated with compulsive actions, lack of inhibition, the use of the object for one's enjoyment, do not appear to be referable to the dialectic of repression–return of the repressed. As manifestations of the Real rather than coded messages to be interpreted, these symptoms simultaneously signal a crisis in symbolization capacity in their bearers, of the "symbolic virtue of the word" in the *talking cure*, and a limit of the symbolic as such.[35] In Freud's time, as a symptom-synthesis of the neuroses of the era, the hysteric's expressive body demanded language and symbolization. Today, as a symptom-synthesis of the "perversions of enjoyment," the anorexic's body, refuses them, or doesn't know what to do with them.[36] Last but not least: while in Freud's time the father guaranteed subjectivation and the hold of the symbolic order, today the crisis of the Big Other, of the moral subject, and the symbolic order is condensed in the father's decline.[37]

Where is and what role does the mother play in this still rather interesting picture, and who set off the crisis of the father's ordering function? Just as in Freud's time she is nowhere and doesn't play any role, except as the number-one suspect behind every pathology. Neither she, nor the daughter or woman are considered as active participants in the crisis of the law of the father, just as they are not traditionally considered in the vast literature which, from Max Horkheimer onward, denounces the dismal fate of the "society without father" in recurring waves.[38] This removal is even more astonishing after forty years of feminism and casts a shadow of suspicion that stretches from today's psychoanalytic theory to that of its origins. Elizabeth Roudinesco, in fact, who is also following in the tracks of post-Lacanian reflection, but with a gaze longer than others', questions the entire trajectory. Accordingly, the "crisis of the father" is coterminous with modernity, in other words with the secularization of the institution of the family and the State. Its alarmist denunciations punctually return each time that the fear of a feminization of society, women's autonomy, the uncontrollability of female sexual desire, and the growth of maternal potential increases. The Freudian invention of the oedipal paradigm is already an answer to the decline of the father: it reorganizes the symbolic order no longer around the omnipotent figure of the Father–God of traditional societies nor on the already less powerful one of the pater familias of the bourgeois era, but around that of "a son who became a father as the heir to the great, destroyed, figure of a mutilated father."[39] Oedipus and Hamlet, the unwitting patricide and the failed one, both guilty of desiring the mother, are the two figures of this transition. This is a transition that at once relaunches the institution of the family and male genealogy at the price of the sacrifice of the father and the guilt of the son, and opens the way to female emancipation at the price of channeling female sexuality into maternity, while reconfirming the mother–daughter rivalry. All conditions that the unfolding of historical events, in the second half of the twentieth century, will undermine: with legislation that accompanies the dissolution of the family and the biparental bond; with the anti-authoritarian movements that give the final shove to the "mutilated patriarch"; with female sexual liberation that, supported by medical and scientific innovation, separates sexuality and procreation, subtracting the female body from patriarchal control. And, I would add, with the feminist reintroduction of the mother and of female genealogy into the world, which also deprives the "mutilated patriarch" of his advantage of reigning over the rivalry between mother and daughter, woman and woman.

Straddling the history of Western society and of psychoanalysis, Roudinesco sees and follows all these transitions, except for the last one. On the male front she follows the extreme rebellion against the father of the anti-authoritarian movements of 1968 and she embraces the libertarian demands put forward by the "anti-oedipal" and anti-Freudian revolt of [Gilles] Deleuze and [Félix] Guattari to then notice—in my opinion correctly—that their outcomes are somehow complicit with the narcissism and individualism of the late twentieth century. On the female front, she reconstructs the progressive "maternalization" of the family over the course of the last century, up to artificial procreation, which brings the split between sexuality and maternity to its ultimate consequences. Even though with many ambivalences, artificial procreation sanctions female control and male marginalization in the reproduction of life. Reduced to the role of anonymous sperm donor, the father loses that power of symbolic naming that was constitutive of his authority, and once more blames women for this loss. According to Roudinesco, it is here, in this "overturning of the procreative order," that one can find the key to measure the destiny of the relations between the sexes: caught between the crisis of paternal authority and the "separating Logos" on the one hand, and a potential "not so much female as maternal" on the other, its outcome is tied to "the emergence of a new symbolic order" that will arise from the conflicts of the present.[40]

Is the new symbolic order therefore all yet to come? Has the feminist revolution only demolished the patriarchal order, without bringing another into the world? Without the "separating Logos" of paternal authority and phallocentrism are we all destined fall prey to indifference, narcissism, and commodification? Has maternal potential swallowed female sexuality once again, and is it once more the source of processes of phantasmization and criminalization of women? The onus of the response, clearly, rests with us and not with Roudinesco. We are the ones who rethought the mother as the principle of a symbolic that does not separate but unites, wagering on its ability to perform a social regulation that does not depend on the law, testifying to a process of subjectivization that does not pass through the sacrificial act of patricide or its matricidal analogue. But in order to respond it is necessary to couple theoretical and practical imagination with social analysis, attempting to identify signs of what the mother is and will be after patriarchy in the present, in her lights and shadows, in her real and phantasmatic aspects.

Along this line, I believe the post-Lacanian perspective should be accepted for what it says about the "death of the father" (after and in sequence with the death of God, metaphysics, politics, and whatever else), and simultaneously overturned for what it does *not* say about the case of the mother. It could also be legitimate to liquidate it as simply a repetition of the foreclosing of the primary relationship. In this regard, it is sufficient to reread "*Mater mortifera*," a text by Lia Cigarini, which she wrote in the course of a polemic with Elvio Fachinelli in the by now distant 1974. It highlights the repetitiveness of the combination of crisis of the father and phantasmization of the mother, and the way it is reproposed in a society in which "virile parades and endemic fascism" are always lurking.[41] As the history of the West teaches us, and as the previously mentioned authors, from Horkheimer to Žižek to Roudinesco, are aware of, the returns of arguments about the crisis of the father always accompany or are a prelude to repetitions of the attempt to restore patriarchal authority and traditional masculinity, which are today obvious everywhere, from the West to the East of the globalized world.

But as is always the case, it is crucial to focus on what in the repetition makes a difference. And difference today is not due only or especially to the sharpening of the crisis of paternal authority and a masculine narcissist syndrome. It is given by what we have brought or rebrought into the world about the mother, about her potential or impotence, about her reality or phantasmaticity, beyond the traditional declensions of the maternal. After forty years of feminism, the mother is not behind us: As far as the social imaginary is concerned, we are the mothers. The real or phantasmatic perception of the mother directly concerns the real or phantasmatic perception of what we have said or done within feminism. This is the reason why it is important and difficult to attempt to decipher it.

In reality, it is not so difficult to map the removal of the mother in political thought and in the crisis of politics. As I previously mentioned, the mother and the relation with the mother have played significant parts in feminist political thought, in Italy and abroad. They are figures of the critique of the individual, the body politic, and the modern social contract, of sovereignty and power, of politics' and democracy's legalistic-juridical drift, of the modern qualifications of equality and fraternity and the modern and postmodern qualifications of freedom. By reinterpreting the exclusion of the mother and sisters from the social pact we denounced its patriarchal-fratriarchal character as well as its egalitarian fiction. By analyzing the maternal relationship as a social form, we contested the liberal individual's absolute claims to autonomy and independence, and we made room for a subjectivity that is aware of fragility and dependence, and a freedom that is aware of its bonds. By interpreting maternal authority as a source of symbolic authorization we showed that power is not a measure of all things and that juridical mediation can be substituted, or at least paired, with linguistic and relational forms of mediation.[42] By putting forth the undecidability of the maternal, as I am here proposing, we are asking politics to confront the limit of its claim to decide everything as well as the theoretical axiom that identifies politics with decision. One cannot say that we were not of our time, or that we were outside this world, since this feminist critique of modern politics insists precisely on its clearest points of crisis, and since it goes beyond the crisis in conceiving unheard of and efficacious political forms and practices. When these forms are not taken into account, politics—both theory and praxis—demonstrates not only a deafness but also a melancholic and nihilist grieving, which is complacently happy to pause near the specters of what has ended rather than opening up to what has been born.[43] Biopolitics, as well as the contemporary biopolitical paradigms, can do even worse: at the level of theory, by retracing the relations between politics and life without considering feminist thought and the mother's work for life; at the level of praxis, by resuscitating the power of the law (of the father) against maternal symbolic authority.

And it is precisely where the law reappears with its claims to transparency and rational regulation that the maternal phantasms also reappear at their strongest. There is nothing better than the lengthy succession of events tied to the Italian law on medically assisted procreation to demonstrate this incestuous nexus between the totem of the norm and the taboos it refers to, between a will to regulate and panic for something that doesn't allow itself to be regulated.[44] After all, what was the intended objective of that prohibitionist and misogynist law?[45] Not the generating potential but the symbolic authority of the mother. Not her body, but her talking body; not her natural capability but her right to decide about it; not the uterus, but the relation with the other that is implanted in the uterus. There was instead an unrestrainable nostalgia for the mother's generating potential, for her biological and affective womb, both in those who wanted to appropriate it technologically and in those who felt expropriated by technology. What wasn't tolerable was the mother's freedom to deliberate about it, in a negotiation with medical-scientific knowledge and the criteria of good and evil, of the licit and the illicit, which cannot be established and put in the form of a law once and for all, but is handled within a given situation, one instance at a time, independently from male desire, and oriented by the desire for maternity.

Consider the fear of the undecidability of the maternal and of its excess with respect to the form of the law, and the fear of the dislocation of the mother's symbolic authority from the traditional potential of the maternal. On both sides, the events of the "Legge 40" appear to be emblematic of the imaginary about the mother that we are dealing with today. As an effect of that dislocation, a confused phantasmatic match is played, both in the personal and in the public spheres. A match in which nostalgia for the patriarchal mother is confused with a fear of the mother as resignified by feminism—and both the one and the other, nostalgia and fear, share in the desexualization of female difference. On the male side this often leads to a contradictory entanglement of demands and suspicions, which is indeed difficult to decipher. There are requests for care and nourishment, often transferred from the realm of material care to that of psychological and intellectual care, as well as suspicions toward the unprecedented manifestation of an exacting and scarcely complicitous maternal, generous but not very caring—as mothers, let's say this frankly to one another, we are not at all reassuring and for this reason not very recognizable. Luckily, I say. In any case to meander among other people's ghosts wouldn't take us very far. Rather we should ask ourselves: in what way are we accomplices in this dance of ghosts? To what extent do we also give in to this nostalgia for an ancient and blackmailing maternal power? How much did we concede, in exchange for a recognition of authority, in terms of loss of sexuality, thus placing ourselves on the slippery slope toward a replication of the traditional maternal figure? To what extent did the focus on the mother–daughter relationship distract us from asking what the relationship between the mother and the narcissistic sons of the mutilated and declined father is? Orphans of the father's law, they double and open up requests to the mother. On the one hand they ask for an archaic reassurance and on the other for original and breakaway responses to today's blind spots. In the game of apportioning power according to fixed rules, they are always counting, however, on reaching an integration of this unforeseen, dislocated, maternal obscure.

With the candidacies and elections of women to premierships and presidencies in Europe, the United States, and Latin America, the symbolic match of the political resignification of the maternal becomes more urgent: "I want the same things for French citizens that I want for my children," Ségolène Royal stated while presenting her electoral program.[46] If the long path of disinterment of female genealogy from the repressed of politics were to close completely—that it will do so partially is certain—with an egalitarian integration and the exercise of a reassuring and "therapeutic" political function for the crisis of the phallocentric political order, this would be a lost match for us. It is up to us to reconfigure it and to relaunch it, wagering on the possibility that the era of the "end of the father" will not come to a close with the disintegration of the symbolic order but open onto a female surplus [*eccedenza*] that can transform it. The wager with which Muraro concluded *L'ordine simbolico della madre*—"We must fight to prevent the social synthesis of established power from substituting for the maternal principle. We must give a social translation to the maternal potential in order to prevent the social synthesis from closing up. We must fight to keep social synthesis open to anything we want to say, however distant or abnormal that may be"[47]— should therefore be reaffirmed and relaunched. If resignified as the figure of a Logos that doesn't separate but unites, of a subject that is not closed within atomism but is open to relationships, of a disparity that is based not on hierarchy but on desire, of a mediation that doesn't make the law into its prosthesis, of an undecidable that marks the limit of the will to power—if resignified in such a way, the mother can disrupt the zero-sum game of today's democratic politics and the horizon of mourning of the end of the law of the father.

Diotima's book also discusses whether in order to relaunch this wager it would also be necessary to open the obscure side of maternal potential onto the public space, without the mediation of the practices of relation, disparity, and authority of which we have availed ourselves so far in order to resignify it.[48] Here I would be cautious. These practices are not means to affirm an enunciation or a meaning, they are performative actions by which meaning emerges, showing itself and becoming intelligible. To unhinge the maternal principle from the practices that allowed new meanings to be read in it could mean to expose it, defenselessly, to the returns of a patriarchal imaginary and a female hysteria from which it has not been immunized once and for all.

Compared to when we turned the mother into a symbolic principle of order centered around some practices, I do believe that we have some other elements to consider. Even though it is more open than the paternal Logos "to anything we want to say," not even the mother language has the power of translating everything into language, because the symbolic has a limit and this limit manifests itself and returns symptomatically even and perhaps especially in the primary relation between the daughter and the mother. Although the mother language is a language of contact between body and word, it cannot vaccinate the mother's body against desexualization and the anesthetization of desire to which the patriarchal imaginary had destined it. Our search for symbolic authority can become an accomplice in this desexualization. Although our gratitude toward the mother is a reparatory gesture for the wrongs the mother was subjected to and those she subjected us to, and although this gesture opens onto a positive economy of relationships among women, the real mother's imprint remains and continuously intercepts, in good and evil, the economy of the relationships between one woman and another as well as among women (and with men), as an undecidable factor in our existence. Or rather, it is *the* factor that always reminds us that not everything, in both personal and public existence, is decidable. It is possible that this and other "obscure" aspects of the maternal may require the invention of new practices. To acquire this limit of the maternal potential constitutes, for me at least, an acquisition of freedom as well. Because it is true that without evoking maternal authorization there is no female greatness; but it is also true that if sheltered by an idealized maternal authority female greatness doesn't fly, doesn't risk, and does not even generate.

Translated by Mark William Epstein

NOTES

This chapter is the translation of an edited version of "L'impronta indecidibile," originally published in Diotima, *L'ombra della madre* (Naples: Liguori, 2007), 177–96.
 1. See "I mille rivoli del movimento femminista: Tutto cominciò con lo 'scandalo' della scoperta della madre," *Il manifesto*, 1 June 1979; "È possibile produrre tra donne sfuggendo alla tentazione del rapporto simbiotico con la madre? È possibile rapportarsi a un prodotto 'altro da sé,' negando il fare e disfare quotidiano, l'incompiutezza dell'attività femminile tradizionale?" *Il manifesto*, 24 July 1979.
 2. [Aldo Moro was the president of Christian-Democratic Party. He was kidnapped on 16 March 1978, and then murdered on 9 May by the Red Brigades. This event indelibly marked Italian political history, its institutions and social movements.—Eds.]
 3. For a reconstruction of Florence's "Rosa" collective, even if it is not focused on the mother–daughter relationships that were traversing it, see Anna Scattigno, "*Rosa*: Un gruppo e una rivista," *Memoria* 1–2, nos. 19–20 (1987): 66–83.
 4. Libreria delle donne di Milano and Biblioteca delle donne di Parma, *Catalogo no. 2, Romanzi: Le madri di tutte noi* (Milan-Parma: Privately printed, 1982), 13.

5. See Libreria delle donne di Milano, *Non credere di avere dei diritti* (Turin: Rosenberg & Sellier, 1987). On female authority, the question of the mother, and the relationship between real and symbolic mother, see Lia Cigarini, *La politica del desiderio* (Parma: Pratiche, 1995), 127–84. See also Women's Bookstore Collective, *Sexual Difference: A Theory of Social-Symbolic Practice* trans. Patrizia Cicogna and Teresa de Lauretis (Bloomington: Indiana University Press, 1990). I refer to this text for the description and the meaning of political practices like the relations between women, entrustment, practice of disparity, practice of maternal/female authority, that my essay takes for granted. See also Teresa de Lauretis, "The Practice of Sexual Difference and Feminist Thought in Italy: An Introductory Essay," in *Sexual Difference*, 1–21 and the sharp reading of the text by Linda M. G. Zerilli, *Feminism and the Abyss of Freedom* (Chicago: University of Chicago Press, 2005), 93–123.

6. [The author here refers to Diotima, *L'ombra della madre*.—Eds.]

7. See Manuela Fraire, "Amare al cospetto della madre," *Il manifesto*, 29 October 2006.

8. See Ilvo Diamanti, "Piccoli mostri di provincia," *La Repubblica*, 14 January 2007.

9. On the negative in the relation with the mother and the politics of difference that pivots around it see Diana Sartori, "La tentazione del bene," in Diotima, *La magica forza del negativo* (Naples: Liguori, 2005), 9–33.

10. See Luisa Muraro, *The Symbolic Order of the Mother*, trans. Francesca Novello (Albany: State University of New York Press, 2018), 17–34.

11. "Imprint" and "impression" are terms used by Jacques Derrida in *Archive Fever: A Freudian Impression*, trans. Eric Prenowitz (Chicago: University of Chicago Press, 1996). They designate "the unstable feeling of a shifting figure, of a schema, or of an in-finite or indefinite process" (29). This process is opposed to the rigor of the concept opening it to both memory and the future. It is not a matter of chance that these terms came back to me as connected with the sign of the relation with the mother.

12. See Nancy Chodorow, *The Reproduction of Mothering: Psychoanalysis and the Sociology of Gender* (Berkeley: University of California Press, 1978).

13. See Luce Irigaray, *Speculum of the Other Woman* (Ithaca, N.Y.: Cornell University Press, 1985), *An Ethics of Sexual Difference* (London: Continuum, 2004), and *Sexes and Genealogies* (New York: Columbia University Press, 1993).

14. Muraro, *The Symbolic Order of the Mother*, 77.

15. Muraro, *The Symbolic Order of the Mother*, 1, 98.

16. See my interview "La madre dopo il patriarcato," *Il manifesto*, 28 October 2005, where I raised some issues that I am trying to develop here. The occasion was her *lectio magistralis* upon leaving teaching at the University of Verona. The lecture dealt with a "reelaboration" of *L'ordine simbolico della madre*.

17. See Judith Butler, *The Psychic Life of Power: Theories in Subjection* (Stanford, Calif.: Stanford University Press, 1997).

18. See Luisa Muraro, chapter 2, and my "The Contact Word," chapter 1, in this volume.

19. In addition to the texts by Irigaray I already quoted in note 13, see Margaret Whitford, *Luce Irigaray: Philosophy in the Feminine* (London and New York: Routledge, 1991), 75–97.

20. See Teresa de Lauretis, *The Practice of Love: Lesbian Sexuality and Perverse Desire* (Bloomington: Indiana University Press, 1994).

21. See Angela Putino, *Amiche mie isteriche* (Naples: Cronopio, 1998).

22. "It is precisely the experience of the hysterical body that I am trying to translate into knowledge." Muraro, *The Symbolic Order of the Mother*, 66. See also Luisa Muraro, *La posizione isterica e la necessità della mediazione* (Palermo: Donne Acqua Liquida, 1993) as well as Luisa Muraro's and Zulma Paggi's "Come, quando e perchè Anna O si è trasformata in Bertha Pappenheim," postface to the Italian edition of Lucy Freeman, *La storia di Anna O.*, trans. Adriana Bottini (Milan: Feltrinelli, 1972), 141–70.

23. Putino, *Amiche mie isteriche*, 41–56.

24. In the fall of 2006, in the wake of the death by anorexia of several models, some progressive governments, including the Italian one, introduced laws or protocols and, with the aid of a mass media campaign, also introduced the threshold of size 38 for access to fashion shows. I wrote about it in "I 'willing' anti-anoressia," *Il manifesto*, 21 November 2006.

25. See Louise J. Kaplan, *Female Perversions: The Temptations of Emma Bovary* (New York: Anchor Books/Doubleday, 1992), 266 ff.; George Downing, "La psicoterapia corporea dei disturbi alimentari," in *Sintomi, corpo, femminilità: Dall'isteria alla bulimia*, ed. Francesca Molfino and Claudia Zanardi (Bologna: Clueb, 1999), 253 ff.; Gabriella Ripa di Meana, *Figure della leggerezza: Anoressia, bulimia, psicoanalisi* (Rome: Astrolabio, 1955), 50–51; Massimo Recalcati and Umberto Zuccardi Merli, *Anoressia, bulimia e obesità* (Turin: Bollati Boringhieri, 2006), 49–51.

26. See Recalcati and Zuccardi Merli, *Anoressia, bulimia e obesità*, 43.

27. Recalcati and Zuccardi Merli, *Anoressia, bulimia e obesità*, 49–51.

28. Ripa di Meana formulates this hypothesis via the interpretation of patient's dream, in which the weight the patient has dreamed of is equivalent to the weight differential between her mother and herself. According to Ripa di Meana, the dream expresses the patient's desire to be "the Difference, in other words the quintessence of diversity, pure distinction. That is the most cherished goal, the end to be pursued with authentic fanaticism: I am that weightless remainder that is the difference." *Figure della leggerezza*, 77–78.

29. See Elizabeth Grosz, *Volatile Bodies* (Bloomington: Indiana University Press, 1994), 40.

30. [Here and throughout the rest of this chapter, "talking cure" is in English in the original.—Trans.]

31. See Ripa di Meana, *Figure della leggerezza*, 182 ff.; Recalcati and Zuccardi Merli, *Anoressia, bulimia e obesità*, 104 ff.; Silvia Vegetti Finzi, "L'ideale del corpo morto: Patologia della tarda modernità," in *Sintomi, corpo, femminilità: Dall'isteria alla bulimia*, 80–84.

32. See Ripa di Meana, *Figure della leggerezza*, 32–33; Francesca Molfino and Claudia Zanardi, Introduction to *Sintomi, corpo, femminilità: Dall'isteria alla bulimia*, 27 ff. Molfino and Zanardi also read the passage from hysteria to anorexia as tied to the history of sexual difference and the changes in the relation between the body and the symbolic, and more precisely between a body that separates itself from its internal space and a symbolic that becomes purely *semiotic*, which results in an impoverishment of both the perception of one's bodily self and of the process of symbolization.

33. See Vegetti Finzi, "L'ideale del corpo morto," 61 ff.

34. See *Civiltà e disagio: Forme contemporanee della psicopatologia*, ed. Domenico Cosenza, Massimo Recalcati, and Angelo Villa (Milan: Bruno Mondadori, 2006), vii–viii.

35. "The new forms of unease of civilization are characterized by the presence of the crisis of the word's salvific role and by the tendency toward a push for enjoyment, deadly traits that seem to break down any possible operation of symbolization. We are dealing with a direction of psychoanalytic work that borders on the meaningless opacity of the real." But on the other hand, "the limit of symbolic representation that is highlighted by the 'clinical of the real' is no other than the limit which language as such encounters in its work of endowing the real with meaning: this operation cannot be carried out exhaustively because the real of enjoyment removes itself from a definite casting into symbolic form." Recalcati, "La personalità borderline e la nuova clinica," in *Civiltà e disagio: Forme contemporanee della psicopatologia*, 4–6. The limit of psychoanalysis as talking cure that was highlighted by the new symptoms would simply reveal the limits of the symbolic itself.

36. See notes 31, 32, 33.

37. Recalcati and Zuccardi Merli, *Anoressia, bulimia e obesità*, 19 ff. Slavoj Žižek provides a similar diagnosis in *The Ticklish Subject: The Absent Centre of Political Ontology* (London: Verso, 1999).

38. See Max Horkheimer, "Authority and the Family," in *Critical Theory: Selected Essays*, trans. Matthew J. O'Connell (New York: Herder and Herder, 1972), 47–128; Jessica Benjamin, "Authority and the Family Revisited: or, a World without Fathers?" *New German Critique*, no. 13 (Winter 1978): 35–57.

39. See Elisabeth Roudinesco, *La famiglia in disordine*, trans. Adriana Valle (Rome: Meltemi, 2002), 79. For an analysis of the crisis of the father that partially converges and partially diverges from Roudinesco's, see Manuela Fraire, "Oblio del padre," *Rapsodia* (2011), http://www.rapsodia-net.info/?p=538.

40. Roudinesco, *La famiglia in disordine*, 139 ff.

41. Cigarini, *La politica del desiderio*, 55.

42. Among the most representative see Carole Pateman, *The Sexual Contract* (Cambridge: Polity, 1988); Diotima, *Oltre l'uguaglianza: Le radici femminili dell'uguaglianza* (Naples: Liguori, 1995); Adriana Cavarero, *Corpo in figure* (Milan: Feltrinelli, 1995); Maria Luisa Boccia, *La differenza politica* (Milan: Il Saggiatore, 2002); and Elena Pulcini, *L'individuo senza passioni* (Turin: Bollati Boringhieri, 2001).

43. In this vein I have discussed the reflections on the end of politics in Mario Tronti in my "Eredi al tramonto: Fine della politica e politica della differenza," in *Politica e destino*, ed. Mario Tronti et al. (Rome: Sossella, 2006), 125–43. On the spectrality and melancholy of contemporary politics see Jacques Derrida, *Specters of Marx: The State of Debt, the Work of Mourning, and the New International*, trans. Peggy Kamuf (New York: Routledge, 1994), and its interpretation by Simone Ragazzoni, *La decostruzione del politico* (Genoa: il melangolo, 2006).

44. [Also know as "Legge 40," this law was approved by the Italian government under Berlusconi in 2004. It strictly regulated reproductive technology and research.—Eds.]

45. See Simona Bonsignori, Ida Dominijanni, and Stefania Giorgi, *Si può: Procreazione assistita: Norme, soggetti, poste in gioco* (Rome: Manifestolibri, 2005) and Maria Luisa Boccia and Grazia Zuffa, *L'eclissi della madre* (Milan: Pratiche Editrice, 1998).

46. See Anna Maria Merlo, "Ségolène passa l'esame: 100 idee fra giustizia e ordine pubblico," *Il manifesto*, 13 February 2007.

47. Muraro, *The Symbolic Order of the Mother*, 98.

48. See Chiara Zamboni, "Né una né due: L'enigma di un eccesso nello spazio pubblico," in Diotima, *L'ombra della madre*, 30–32.

PART IV

Thinking with Diotima

And Yet She Speaks!

"Italian Feminism" and Language

ANNE EMMANUELLE BERGER

In "The Contact Word," a piece written in 1998, Ida Dominijanni reflected on the nature and the import of what she called, not "Italian feminism," but "the feminism of the seventies." "The original intuition of the feminism of the seventies," she wrote, namely, "that women were lacking not prostheses so as to resemble men, but needed the words to express themselves starting from their selves instead of from a male imaginary—in other words that the feminine condition is marked more by symbolic than social misery—had already provoked a break, sanctioning the primacy of the word in the politics of change" (chapter 1 in this volume). Dominijanni is a political analyst, a longstanding contributor to the leftist Italian daily *Il manifesto*, and an intellectual companion of the now famous Diotima collective, composed for the most part of Italian feminist philosophers from Verona.[1] She is also a forceful thinker in her own right. For almost two decades now, she has taken on the task of explaining the political meaning of Diotima's work to both an Italian audience and an Anglophone one. With regard to the latter, the Diotima community has also benefited in the United States from the powerful mediation of Teresa de Lauretis, an Italian-born feminist thinker and one of the first proponents of queer theory in the Anglophone world, who introduced their work as well as the work of the Milanese Women's Bookstore collective[2] to an American feminist audience, while engaging in a critical dialogue with them.[3] In the same way as a diverse but limited body of works produced in France in the seventies became known as "French feminism," the reception in America of Diotima's work, starting at the very end of the eighties, has won it the label of "Italian feminism."

Indeed, if the first anthology of *Italian Feminist Thought* published in the Anglophone world as early as 1991 by Paola Bono and Sandra Kemp comprised a variety of authors, not all them related to the Diotima group, the label was largely coterminus with the work produced by these philosophers and their political and theoretical allies or forebears in Italy.[4] This is again evident in a more recent collection entitled *Italian Feminist Theory and Practice*, published in 2002, and of course in the present volume.[5] "Italian feminism" (the label and the intellectual phenomenon it purports to designate) was invented in America before the advent of "Italian thought." But it has obviously received a strong reinforcement and a kind of retrospective validation from the full-blown reception and subsequent invention of the deemed "Italian thought" in the United States. Indeed, if "Italian feminism" is now receiving a belated attention in America, and one that exceeds the precinct of "feminist theory" and feminist intellectual practitioners, as is attested by the present volume, there is no question that the sudden surge of interest in these thinkers is a byproduct of the rise to prominence of "Italian thought." Whereas the previous attempts to bring this body of works to the attention of a large Anglophone intellectual public had largely failed, the branding and marketing of "Italian thought" has succeeded in (re)kindling interest in that work. This in turn raises questions and has consequences, which I will try and address later: is there indeed a commonality of thought between "Italian (male) philosophers" and "Italian feminists"? And how does the current co-reception of "Italian thought" and "Italian feminism" in the American academy affect the intellectual course and the potential relations between the bodies of works and the thinkers these labels serve to index?

THE RISE OF LINGUISTIC FEMINISM

But for the moment, let me return to my initial quotation from "The Contact Word." At the time of the publication of this essay, Italy was in the grips of "Berlusconism,"[6] and American gender and queer theory was just beginning to be read and known in Europe. In that piece, Ida Dominijanni is trying to impress on her readers the scope and farsightedness of one of Luisa Muraro's single-authored and book-length works, *To Knit or to Crochet*, published in 1981. Muraro had previously published a book on witch-hunts in Europe—a focus of major interest for the European feminists of the seventies[7] and a topic that Silvia Federici was to take up again in *Caliban and the Witch*[8]—but *To Knit or to Crochet* may be said to be her first book of "feminist theory" *avant la lettre*. Foreshadowing most of Muraro's subsequent work and in particular *The Symbolic Order of the Mother* (1991), the book, a significant excerpt of which is included in this volume (see chapter 2), relies on Jakobsonian linguistics to undertake two related tasks: it examines the position of women within the symbolic, understood here as a mode of activation of language properties in a particular sociocultural environment, and it launches a critique of what she calls the "hypermetaphoricity regime" of language, a hypermetaphoricity prevalent, according to her, in modern bourgeois capitalist societies and politics, as well as in the high theory that attempted to formalize its features and trends from the beginning of the twentieth century onward. Jakobson used metaphor and metonymy as metatropes to describe what he saw as the general functioning of language. According to his description, all language users, but for those afflicted by pathological speech behaviors,[9] resort to two main types of largely unconscious operations to produce articulated and meaningful speech: an operation of selection among semantic equivalents along a vertical axis of substitution, which he calls "metaphoric," and an operation of combination along a horizontal axis of contiguity, which he calls "metonymic." Thus, speech, for Jakobson, is always already "textual" since it results from the constant weaving together, or, in Muraro's words, knitting, of the two axes. The metaphor of knitting, which connotes a traditional type of women's activity involving the combined use of two needles, refers to the fact that, as Jakobson himself says, both metaphoric and metonymic processes are at work together in normal ordinary speech, even though one may observe the predominance of one over the other in specific cultural contexts or in individual speakers. Even though the excerpt presented in this volume doesn't explicitly say so, one may surmise that crocheting with one needle is considered by Muraro a less satisfying metaphor than knitting for clothing or speech-making, insofar as it indicates an imbalance or a privilege of one axis over the other, namely, in her view, the metaphoric axis.

As tropes, that is, figures of substitution, metaphor and metonymy exemplify the way in which language "replaces" or reinvents the world it symbolizes. Yet, according to Jakobson, metonymy always contains what one might call a referential moment. Take the synecdotal operation, exemplary of metonymic "substitution." In Jakobson's words, the relation of contiguity between, say, a sail and a boat, or a glass and a drink, is an "external one," that is, one that is not based primarily on the internal workings of language but on the observation or experience of reality. In reality, a sail belongs to a boat and that is what prompts the synecdotal use of one for the other. By the same token, it is the shared knowledge or experience of the world that will allow other language users to grasp the trope. In other words, metonymy manages to bring and weave the extralinguistic context into the text. Muraro's argument in favor of the "metonymic" process and resources against what she sees as a cultural drift toward "hypermetaphoricity" is based on this understanding of metonymy. Hers is a call and an attempt to reinforce the link between the word(s) and the world in the face of what she sees as an increasing process of abstraction or "dematerialization of relations" affecting the social and the political world. The "hypermetaphoricity regime" is a symbolic regime whereby "things, facts, bodies, specific experiences are caught in a system of ideal relations," which are relations of equivalence. The two main targets of Muraro's critique of this regime are the politics of formal equality under the law, typical of the way Western democracies approach the problem of social difference(s), and Jacques Lacan's theory of the symbolic, at least as he formulated it before the seventies. The former operates under the assumption of an abstract equivalence between individuals, thus fostering their formal identicalness before the law; the latter insists on the ways in which language severs us from the "realness" of the world, and has promoted the "phallus" to the status of "general equivalent" within the symbolic order.

One could question the binarism of Jakobson's linguistic description and of Muraro's subsequent use of the Jakobsonian conceptual framework. This binarism is typical of, indeed required by, structuralist thinking. One could also remark that the type of analogical reasoning, which it both fosters and relies on (metaphor = selection = paradigm = vertical axis = equivalence versus metonymy = combination = syntagm = horizontal axis = difference, and so on) is always already "metaphorical," inasmuch as it is based on the propensity to link different lexical series and semantic fields through equivalence. But that's not the point I want to make here. What I want to stress before I delve into the details, nature, and scope of Muraro's argument is her thorough participation in the "linguistic paradigm" that dominated European thought in general and European feminism in particular in the seventies. I gather that is what Dominijanni had in mind when she characterized "the feminism of the seventies" as one that called attention for the first time to the fact that "the feminine condition is marked more by symbolic than social misery," one that, again in Dominijanni's formulation, "provoked a break, sanctioning the primacy of the word in the politics of change."

True, *To Knit or to Crochet* was not published in the seventies. The book appeared in 1981 and *The Symbolic Order of the Mother* was published ten years later, roughly at the time of the onset of queer theory in the United States. Furthermore, what I have called the "linguistic paradigm"—an epistemological outlook that has been both identified and relegated to the past under the heading of "linguistic turn" ever since poststructuralism started to be perceived as having exhausted its course or perhaps its attractiveness—cannot be limited to the seventies. The linguistic moment started in fact at the beginning of the twentieth century with the invention of modern linguistics by Ferdinand de Saussure, and it blossomed with the advent of structuralism (in particular structural anthropology and structuralist psychoanalysis), which used linguistics as its major conceptual framework and interpretive grid.[10] Yet, it is fair to say that the full import of the epistemological shift toward both structuralist linguistics and linguistic structuralism was really felt and assessed in the seventies, by Lacan himself, by Jacques Derrida, and by a number of women thinkers who participated in the (self)reflexive turn of structuralism (in)to poststructuralism, while laying the basis for what was to be recognized as "feminist theory" starting in the late eighties. The "word(s)," to use Dominijanni's formula, was indeed the topic of the decade. It is a decade that saw Hélène Cixous cofound with Tzvetan Todorov and Gérard Genette the journal *Poétique*, a journal of literary criticism and theory obviously indebted to Jakobson's own predication of linguistic theory on poetics, while busying herself with the publication of her first "feminist" essays. It is a decade that witnessed Julia Kristeva try to formulate a theory of the maternal at the margins of Lacan's symbolic, and Luce Irigaray start advocating the elaboration of a "female symbolic" in a turn away from, if not against, Lacan; it is the decade, finally, when the group Psychanalyse et Politique, headed by Antoinette

Fouque, founded a publishing house, the Editions des Femmes (1973), and opened the same year a bookstore, the Librairie des femmes, while Muraro herself and a group of women activists from Milan opened shortly afterward the Libreria delle Donne (1975), thus inaugurating the Women's Bookstore Collective I mentioned earlier. In the early to mid-seventies, the opening of these bookstores was considered a major and inaugural political gesture of the women's liberation movement. Who would think today of opening a bookstore, that is, a place to store and advertise women's—or for that matter, any social category's—words or symbolic productions? Who would, moreover, consider such an endeavor a central political gesture and groundbreaking "theoretical practice"?

Muraro's and for that matter Diotima's thought as a whole were indeed shaped by their political experience and intellectual training in the seventies. They started to think and operate in a context that linked what was not yet termed "French feminism" to what was not yet labeled "Italian feminism." I don't think one can understand Muraro's work on the "symbolic order of the mother" or, for that matter, Muraro's, Adriana Cavarero's, or Chiara Zamboni's continued if diverse intellectual investment in the question of language uses, and, specifically, in the "mother tongue,"[11] outside the context of the kind of "linguistic feminism" I have briefly delineated. Muraro, by the way, was first trained in linguistics, as were, for that matter, Kristeva and Irigaray. And Cixous was, and still is, a professor of literature.

This is why, as somebody who began her academic training in the late seventies, who has witnessed the "rise" of transatlantic feminist theory in the eighties and of queer theory in the nineties, and who has only recently started to be acquainted, albeit through sketchy translations, with "Italian" feminist thought and particularly the body of works springing from the Diotima collective, I am struck by the resonance of their work with what has been called poststructuralism. The Diotima community may well have from the start taken its distance from "postmodernism," an intellectual mistrust they definitely share with the thinkers grouped under the banner of "Italian thought";[12] their epistemological tools, the targets of their criticism, and their favorite objects of reflection still smack as it were of poststructuralism. To me, this is a more important aspect of their work and critical intervention than their "essentialism," a charge that has been leveled against most if not all of them by gender and queer theorists, at least those, still few, who have acquired a degree of familiarity with some of their work. True, there is nothing queer about these Italian feminists' thinking; there is no attempt to bend the categories from which they start and within which they operate, to begin with the categories of "woman" and "man," even if it is fair to say that these categories are in no way understood by Muraro, Dominijanni, or Cavarero, to mention only them, as normative categories, and much less so as categories given in advance or determined by "nature," that is, strictly speaking, by birth.[13] Clearly, for Muraro, for instance, the category of woman is primarily "given," that is, molded, by "experience," a central notion in her intellectual vocabulary, and one close, it seems to me, in spirit if not in reference, to Walter Benjamin's understanding of *Erfahrung*. By definition, what experience "teaches" us cannot be given in advance and therefore is not a "given." Moreover, there is no experience that is not informed or constrained to some degree by norms. But what Muraro seems to want to emphasize through this category is the historical nature of "womanhood," in the double sense that it is shaped by historical conditions and that it is lived through by beings at once situated and singular, hence her seemingly indifferent recourse to the singular or the plural when she talks about woman/women. And because experience literally involves a "living through," it is always embodied, which doesn't simply mean "sexed," or even sexual, in predefined or conventional ways. Still, there is indeed no explicit attempt, at least in the works presented in this volume, to link the question of gender and gender identity to that of sexuality and therefore to the history of sexuality (and sexualities). The women featured and imagined (or wished for) by Diotima's work are neither "homosexual" nor "heterosexual," whatever their sexual lives or practices might appear to be. Queer theorists might say, following Monique Wittig, that being self-affirmed "women" and not "lesbians," they do partake in the heterosexual mind frame, whether they claim it or not, whether even their sexual practices involve heterosexual relations or not. And for Teresa de Lauretis, the fact that Muraro in particular leaves the question of desire, and more specifically, the question of the access of women to the position of "subject of desire," conspicuously out of the picture, is highly problematic.[14]

Finally, Diotima doesn't seem to have been much concerned with the issues subsumed under the notion of "intersectionality," namely, with the political and epistemological tensions rising from the complicated intersections of class, race, and gender that have come to the fore of feminist debates since the nineties in both the United States and France. As one of them explains, the Italian context of the seventies didn't lend itself to a consideration of race,[15] a statement that shows how local feminist politics and theory were and perhaps remain, in spite of their internationalist and sometimes universalist outlook. One could say, though, that in their own way and language, the group was profoundly aware of the social and cultural heterogeneity of women. Their criticism of the politics of formal equality was indeed based on the recognition of what they call the "disparity" among women, a disparity that needs to be taken into account and thought through if one wants to pursue a feminist agenda.

I myself find Muraro's and her fellow feminist thinkers' arguments or propositions questionable in several respects, which I will address later. Nevertheless, Muraro's "linguistic" approach to the question of women's oppression,[16] or rather freedom, has led her to articulate a powerful critique of the androcentric view of language and symbolic operations prevalent in structuralist thought and the human sciences the latter helped to shape in the twentieth century. Her critique precedes and resonates in some important aspects with Judith Butler's own criticism of the totalizing and fixed notion of the symbolic one finds in Lacan (albeit not the later Lacan).[17] Before Butler or de Lauretis, Muraro also provided the clearest analysis of the problematic inflection of the Lacanian model by Kristeva, as well as the strongest indictment of the latter's "failed feminism." Moreover, she has proposed a distinctive reformulation of the workings of the "symbolic order," one that has consequences for the understanding of subjecthood (or the process of "subjectivation"), intersubjective relations, and ultimately, perhaps, desire. Finally, if Muraro defined the kind of at once theoretical and practical feminism she advocates as an attempt to foster the social and cultural conditions for the "free existence" of women, rather than as a struggle for equality or the transformation of social categories, there is reason to think that, were they to take place on a meaningful scale, the deep changes in the symbolic function and the subject-positions she tries, with others, to bring about, would indeed result in a redefinition of social categories and identities.

So what is the core of Muraro's argument in her main opus, *The Symbolic Order of the Mother*? How does it fit in the intellectual context I have briefly sketched? But also what significant contribution does she make, and what particular inflection does she give to the critique, initiated in the mid-seventies in both France and the United States,[18] of the peculiar kind of androcentrism exhibited by structural anthropology and psychoanalysis?

AND YET SHE SPEAKS (*E PUR SI PARLA*)

Muraro's argument is deceptively simple. We first learn language, she says, at least usually, through and thanks to our mothers, or whoever occupies their place. Therefore women qua mothers do not only give birth to human beings; they give them language.

What are the stakes of such an apparently matter-of-fact reminder? The fact that mothers, that is, women in their capacity and role as children's caretakers, can and do (also) "give language" and not only milk and "love," is, according to Muraro, forgotten or denied by the androcentric cultural order and its self-authorized interpreters, in all sorts of ways.

Among other things, that is what school, perhaps the greatest and most defining institution of our political modernity, is about, according to Muraro, whose interest in pedagogy combined with her expertise in linguistics lead her from the start to reflect on language acquisition and modes of learning. By becoming the only authorized channel for the teaching of language, starting with children's native language; by treating language, not as an opening to the world but as a set of rules to be learned; by affirming the expertise of the schoolmaster over and against that of the family, that is, mainly, the mother as primary educator; the school may well have contributed to both the demeaning and outright forgetting of the (first) linguistic education dispensed by mothers. Here, Muraro's argument is in line with a long history of complaints by protofeminist women writers and thinkers, who, from the mid-nineteenth century on, expressed worry about the effects the schooling of girls, and even more of boys, with its masculinist ethos and outlook—think of the paramilitary nature of the first *lycées* or *gymnasiums*—had on both the child-mother relation and the mother image. Thus, in *Story of My*

Life, George Sand claimed that in high school, and especially through the learning of Latin and Greek, the "paternal" ancestors of French, boys were taught primarily to hate their mothers.[19]

I will come back to this part of Muraro's argument later. For the moment, I want to dwell on the most explicit charge leveled by Muraro against the linguistic androcentrism of modernity, namely, her charge against Lacan and his epigones. *To Knit or to Crochet* already targeted Lacan, as we have seen, thus inaugurating a long string of feminist criticism of the French psychoanalyst. *The Symbolic Order of the Mother* can be read, as indeed the title of her book invites us to do, as Muraro's most pointed answer to Lacan. Lacan placed language at the core of his theory of subject-formation and its relation to the unconscious. Following and reinflecting both Saussurian and Jakobsonian linguistics in his reading of Freud, he produced a theory of the "symbolic order," that is, the way in which language rules over the subject defined above all as a speaking subject, whereby language acquisition (or more precisely, in Lacanian terms, the entrance into language), the severance from the mother's body, and "castration" understood as a symbolic operation (more precisely, as the very operating mode of the symbolic) are coterminus. Castration determines the different sexual positions of subjects and thus produces the speaking subject as a gendered subject; it ushers the rise of the phallus and the reign of the paternal metaphor, since the *non/nom* of the father thus comes to interrupt forever the child's incestuous enjoyment of the mother's body. This is all very well known, if not always well understood. As I said, Lacan's theory of the inscription of the subject within the symbolic order has given rise to countless feminist counterarguments since the early seventies. He himself significantly altered his view in the decades following his first and most famous pronouncements on the subject. I do not, therefore, want to take this discussion up again. What I want to stress here is what Muraro herself stresses, namely, the fact that, in this scenario, "mothers," hence women, are relegated beyond (and beneath) the symbolic bar, on the side of the Urbody (*das Ding* in Lacanian terms). If the effect of language is to separate children from mothers, that is, from their mother's bodies, if language acquisition hails the onset of "paternal metaphoricity," to paraphrase Muraro, does it mean, then, that mothers, hence women, cannot speak?

If women can't speak, mothers can't give speech. Now, the "symbolic order" doesn't coincide strictly with linguistic ability. Rather, it is what allows language to be meaningful. Perhaps the correct question, then, should be: does it mean that women cannot produce meaning? As absurd as it may sound, at least to those of us who were born female and then agreed to be recognized and to recognize themselves as women, Lacan comes close at times to holding one or the other position. At best, women occupy an eccentric place within the symbolic. More precisely, the place that is marked for them within that order is the place of the absent, the place, Emile Benveniste might have said, of the third person, who/which is strictly speaking a nonperson, since she/it is excluded from the scene of interlocution. "A Woman," claimed Lacan provocatively in *Encore*, "can but be excluded by the nature of things which is the nature of words."[20] Lacan, of course, was not the only one to indulge in such thoughts on the matter. When Freud, addressing an imaginary audience of women in his last conference on "Femininity," told them that they were the riddle "we" (men and male psychoanalysts) speak of, perhaps he meant that women were indeed a riddle for men rather than for themselves, but perhaps he meant also that "women" are indeed by definition the ones who are spoken about between men, rather than the ones who speak.[21] Such a situation of symbolic deprivation would no doubt turn women into riddles for themselves as well. Finally, the inspiration for Lacan's formulations is certainly Claude Lévi-Strauss, whose structural anthropology provided Lacan with a model of how to interpret social and psychological phenomena through the grid of linguistic theory. Lévi-Strauss's theory of the exchange of women that results from the prohibition of incest is based on a linguistic model. Women, he claims in various parts of *The Elementary Structures of Kinship*, are exchanged just like signs are between (male) speakers. At one point, in the concluding part of his work, Lévi-Strauss does acknowledge in passing that women, too, speak, and might even have desire (speaking and desiring are clearly linked in his description). According to him, this additional complication of the model he has taken great pains, and with undeniable efficacy, to put forward, is what accounts for the richness of human interaction.[22] But this doesn't lead him in any way to question his metalinguistic analogy between women and signs, nor the premises of his analysis, namely that men are the subjects and agents of both desire and social interaction, whereas women have structurally been constituted as the objects and means of that interaction.

Kristeva tried to promote in the seventies and eighties both an ethics and a poetics of the maternal through the uncovering of a "semiotic" dimension in language, one that keeps alive, in the gaps of proper symbolization, and bears testimony to one's earliest relation to the mother's body. This primary relation is characterized by not yet formulated affects, not yet mediated drives. Meanwhile, as Muraro reproaches her in *The Symbolic Order of the Mother*, Kristeva accepted the Lacanian framework and its Hegelian model of development. If traces of an archaic bond with the mother could be found in the language of at least some subjects (some women, poets), it is precisely and only as traces of a past. Access to full symbolic competency still involved, according to the early Kristeva at least, the subjection to the paternal law, and the separation from the mother's body. Should such a separation fail, the individual might not attain subjecthood and would risk psychosis, unless he or she became a poet, and found in creative practice a mode of both containment and exploration of the semiotic dimension. The semiotic (dis)order of the mother thus hinders the constitution of the autonomous subject. Its appeal is a regressive one, hence the threatening aspect of the mother's (initial) power. The clear division between the semiotic and the symbolic, their chronological ordering, such that the primary semiotic moment, which characterizes the mother–infant bond, has to be superseded by the symbolic, and maternal attachments by autonomy under the law and in the name of the father, once again leave mothers, and women qua mothers, literally speechless. In this scenario, women as such are incapable of achieving symbolic proficiency outside the traditional oedipal scenario (i.e., the necessary separation from the mother) that is supposed to govern language acquisition. Women qua mothers, reduced to loving/beloved bodies, are unable to promote, much less to bestow, symbolic competency. To use Cavarero's formulation in "Towards a Theory of Sexual Difference," for Kristeva, too, "the mother has a (sweet) voice, but no speech."[23]

To state that women speak or "have" language, and that children can and do, for that matter, learn language and symbolic competency from their mother (or whoever their primary caretaker is), rings, as I said earlier, pretty obvious and deceptively simple. The huge theoretical effort Muraro put into "proving" the case or rather lending it philosophical credentials, may seem, and has seemed to me at times when I read *The Symbolic Order of the Mother*, disproportionate. But the disproportion is itself an indication of what she and other feminist thinkers, particularly of the Diotima persuasion, were coming up against. If Kristeva, considered a feminist by a respectable portion of the Anglophone feminist thinkers of the seventies and eighties, could be seduced by the theories of symbolic mediation prevalent at the time she wrote her most widely read essays, it is because the linguistics-based structuralist approach had an undeniable explanatory power, a power that, moreover, also drew its force from cultural evidence. Because the "symbolic order" was coined in order to name the hard drive, as it were, of cultural production, its theorization provided a highly sophisticated formalization of the workings of culture and social organizations, and consequently offered major insights into the symbolic suppression or demeaning of women. In other words, the theory of women's (internal) exclusion from the symbolic gave a rational basis to masculinist assumptions at work in the social and cultural realm, thus redoubling the exclusion it was supposed to explain. For the same reason, theories of the symbolic are indeed excellent places from which to start analyzing women's age-old foreclosure as agents of language, culture, and history. And because the big theories of linguistic mediation, typical of the structuralist moment, have been both totalizing and all-encompassing theories about culture and subject-formation; because, in order to earn not only the "right to speak," but also the very possibility of being heard, feminist thinkers have had to take to task the whole construct in order to get at its presuppositions, their response, at least Muraro's and her fellow thinkers' response, has tended to yield equally sweeping counterstatements.

The insistence on the cultural, or worst, structural fact of women's internal exclusion from the symbolic order, or, to state it differently, the demonstration of the symbolic operations through which female human beings have come to claim for themselves the symbolic position of object rather than subject of language that marks them as women, has as its corollary the idealization of the (mute) mother as *Ur*-body. One could perhaps say in this sense that Kristeva tried to make the best of what was left or allotted to women within this androcentric logic. The Diotima collective, however, took another intellectual and political path, one which they credit Irigaray for having opened. To my limited knowledge, Muraro and Cavarero in particular, but also Chiara Zamboni, endeavored to restore or rather to lay the theoretical and social conditions for the assumption and recognition of what Muraro calls the "symbolic authority" of the mother. I will address later the question of what the notion of "authority" might involve. Right now, I am trying to account for what I see as a distinctive feature of Muraro's argument, one that sets her apart, it seems to me, from other feminist thinkers of the time, including Irigaray to whom she forcefully (and unusually) claims to be indebted:[24] namely, her downplaying of the necessity to reconnect with one's own and one's mother's "body," a familiar mantra of the women's liberation movement, in favor of the necessity to uphold the mother's symbolic ability to name and shape the world. This is another way of saying that, for Muraro, what is foreclosed, or rather, in this case, denied, by the deemed phallocentric symbolic ordering of culture is not only or not so much the body as indeed the "symbolic authority" of the mother.

In her work, Irigaray has pointed out in various ways the urgent necessity for women to (re)create a female genealogy and reclaim the mother–daughter bond beyond the confines of the oedipal scenario of rejection and rivalry. Starting at the end of the seventies, she began to advocate the creation of another symbolic order, deemed female, one that would be predicated on a different understanding of kinship relations, hence a different practice of familial relations, from the one described and theorized by structural anthropology and psychoanalysis. No doubt Muraro was inspired by Irigaray, in particular by the latter's insistence that women not only speak out, but speak a language of their own, as it were, when she wrote *The Symbolic Order of the Mother*. Yet, when one compares, say, *Sexes and Genealogies*, published in French at the end of the eighties, and Muraro's work, one is struck by a difference in emphasis. In the collection just mentioned, Irigaray devotes one piece in particular to women's relations to "the mother," entitled "Le corps-à-corps avec la mère" (translated painstakingly as "Body against Body: In Relation to the Mother").[25] The piece, written for a conference on "Women and Madness" that took place in Québec in 1980, had already been published in Québec, along with two interviews with Irigaray by Québécois feminists. If Irigaray's lecture is indeed about establishing a new type of relations with our (i.e., women's) mother(s), and finding the words [*paroles*] to name and tend to it, the emphasis is clearly put, as the title indicates, on the body, more precisely on the need, for women, to find their way back, through language, to the body of the mother and its pleasures:

> Our task is to give life back ... to the mother who lives within us and among us. ... We must give her the right to pleasure, to sexual experience, to passion. ...
>
> We also need to find, rediscover, invent the words, the sentences that speak of the most ancient and most current relationship we know—the relationship to the mother's body, to our body—sentences that translate the bond between our body, her body, the body of our daughter. We need to discover a language that is not a substitute for the experience of *corps-à-corps* as the paternal language seeks to be, but which accompanies that bodily experience, clothing it in words that do not erase the body but speak the body.[26]

Interestingly, while or perhaps because Diotima has striven above all to lift women out of "symbolic misery," Muraro and, I think, Cavarero, have been much less interested in the mother's body, and in female pleasures in general, than in the mother's linguistic role, her position as bearer of "knowledge," and, for Cavarero, the ethical dilemma she is facing as a subject.[27] Not that Muraro wants to do away with the body, or, rather, bodies. In the pieces by Muraro and others collected in this volume, there is clearly a warning against the "dematerialization of relations" and an attempt to put language and bodies back in touch, which I will try and address shortly. I suspect rather that staying away from the body and the body question in *The Symbolic Order* is a way for Muraro to avoid the Kristevian pitfall of conflating mother and (mute) body, an intellectual move easy to lapse into as soon as one refers the mother exclusively back to the archaic figure of the infant's caretaker.[28] The speaking mother, or, in Muraro's terms, the authoritative (and literally authorizing) mother, is not, that is, not only, the infant's mother, the forever fantasized object or primary other for the child. As a woman, she is always already a subject for another subject to come: she is a/the woman who comes before me.

Yet the subject, and in particular the female "free" subject, whose path to freedom Muraro and her fellow thinkers have been trying to open in their own fashion, is neither the neo-Hegelian existentialist subject—or ideal subject—of Beauvoirian feminism, who may rise above contingency as she overcomes alienation, nor the neoliberal subject who shares with the former a claim to, or yearning for, full autonomy through self-(re)creation. The subject who recognizes, that is, who remembers and can reclaim the "authority of the mother," is, according to Muraro, a subject who acknowledges her (or his) own fundamental dependency, one who accepts her or his necessary reliance on others. In Muraro's terms, "infantile dependency has actually never ceased. It continues in other forms, through our relation to our material and social environment."[29] Or, in words closer to her main thesis: "I didn't come into the world by myself. I didn't learn to speak by myself."[30]

Here, Muraro's denunciation of the ideology of both subjective and social autonomy, a byproduct of bourgeois modernity that paved the way for the full embrace of neoliberalism in the Western world, is consonant with what some American feminist theorists in the eighties and a number of French theorists starting at the beginning of the twenty-first century have attempted to formulate through a critical investigation of what they have called the ethics and the politics of care. The need for "care," and the varied (although most invariably gendered), complex, and most often unacknowledged forms of its implementation under our "biopolitical regime" points to the limits of the claim to subjective and social autonomy.

But what I want to focus on at this point is the way in which Muraro's alternative view of subject formation, and, in particular, her questioning of the anthropological and psychoanalytical dogma of the subject-instituting "separation from the mother," inflects, and gets reflected in, her understanding of what Lacan would call "the function of language."

THE WORD(S) AND THE WORLD

In *To Knit or to Crochet*, as we have seen, Muraro latches on the figure of metonymy because, in her view, "in metonymy the relation between figural sense and literal sense coincides with a material nexus, which may be spatial, temporal, causal, or of other type" (chapter 2 in this volume). In other words, because, as I remarked before, metonymy has an "external" referent and a contextual impetus, it has the ability to maintain or rather foster the connection with the "material" world. Contiguity names for Jakobson the operating mode of metonymy and ensures continuity with the world. To put it differently, where metaphor represents the transcendence of language vis-à-vis the world, the "horizontalness" of the metonymic operation represents its immanence. In an unusual move within the linguistic paradigm I have briefly delineated, Muraro plays Jakobson against Lacan, whose own understanding of metonymy she vigorously contests. For Lacan, she states in the same piece, "to speak is, originally [one might perhaps better translate: fundamentally—AEB], to metaphorize." And she goes on: "No production of meaning can occur along the metonymic directrix, because metonymy operates between signifiers without overcoming the bar, in a game of references that may either never end or become 'perversely' blocked on the fetish, were it not for metaphor's intervention. Desire is a metonymy" (chapter 2 in this volume). I leave aside for the moment Muraro's indirect indictment of Lacan's notion of desire, predicated as it is, according to her, on an erroneous view of metonymy. What I want to draw attention to for the time being is her attempt or desire to promote not only a theory but also a practice of language that would work against the separation of "words" (or, say, the realm of the word) from the world, to state the case in the broadest terms. By "world" ["*mondo*"], a word and notion she is fond of, Muraro clearly means the material world. More exactly, the notions of "world" and "materiality" are, to say the least, implicated within and by each other in fundamental ways (in Muraro's language/view). Hence a statement like the following one, in *To Knit or to Crochet*: "The insignificance of material relationships, the docile response of bodies to the interpretive word, the phantasmatic mobilization, these are not Lacan's inventions. They are, practically speaking, commonplaces of everyday life" (chapter 2 in this volume). Hence again, Muraro's deploration of the "dematerialization of relations" under the "hypermetaphoricity regime." In this sense, Muraro's thinking, but also Dominijanni's, share in the wishful and generalized materialism of the seventies (one that strived to combine the Marxist historical materialism and a "physical" materialism inherited from the Enlightenment materialists). It is this materialist "wishfulness" that led a number of thinkers of various structuralist and poststructuralist persuasions, up to and including Judith Butler, to insist on what was then commonly called the "materiality of language,"[31] a notion Derrida questioned, without, one has to say, much resonance at the time, when he undertook to deconstruct the "metaphysics of the Sign." For Derrida, the very opposition between ideality and materiality, which underwrites the opposition between the signified and the signifier and therefore the binary structure of the sign, is itself a metaphysical opposition. In particular, the notion of "materiality" itself rests on a notion of "presence," which Derrida's "differance" has striven to undermine. In other words, materialism in this sense, predeconstructive materialism if one wants, belongs to the metaphysical tradition it purports to contest.

But let's continue to unravel the implications of Muraro's interest in metonymy. For Muraro, metonymy, in both its restricted and generalized sense (the latter is what Muraro calls the "metonymic directrix of language"), achieves the feat of replacing without replacing what it stands for, a marvelous and counterintuitive capacity for a trope of substitution. Not surprisingly, the feminist linguist will thereafter attribute this capacity to what she calls the mother tongue [lingua materna], and to it or "her" only,[32] among all the languages a subject may learn to speak in the course of her/his life. "In the metonymic process," she states, "the figurative meaning does not replace the literal one, since they are mutually supportive, nor do words tend to make things superfluous" (chapter 2 in this volume). With and thanks to metonymy, then, "the words" do not make the world disappear by substituting for it. On the contrary, they put us in "contact" with the world, hence Dominijanni's apt formula for it: "the contact word." Such an optimistic view of language's potentiality is definitely at odds with what one could call the "tragic view" (or, in Hegelian parlance, the "negative view") of language upheld by Lacan. For Lacan, as we know, entrance into the "negative" dimension of language marks the constitutive alienation of the subject from his/her body and the latter's severance from the (mute) mother's body. Such severance is nonetheless welcomed because it is inevitable and has important, indeed crucial, secondary benefits, not the least of them being the triggering of desire, which rises from the gap between the "words" and "the world." Language can never "overcome the bar," in Muraro's words, because it is itself the bar that "bars" access to the real. In this sense, language is not the bond maker it appears to be to naive speakers: it is more fundamentally a bond breaker. That is indeed what the business of castration is about: cutting off the speaking subject from the primary drives and original (in)direction of the libido along sharp gender lines, barring access to the other in the very guise of giving access to others.

That is why, in the Lacanian (and Lacanians') narrative, language acquisition tends to be described not as a slow process that involves learning in progressive stages, but as an abrupt stepping into another dimension, almost a traumatic event, which symbolic castration both registers and figures, in its function as a metatrope for language's operation.

There is, then, a connection between Muraro's criticism of the ideology of "autonomy" (a word which means literally "self-naming" or self-regulating) as it relates to a specific cultural and political order, her efforts to downplay or even contradict the neo-Saussurian wisdom regarding language's autonomy from the world (i.e., "things," "bodies," and the socio-historical processes) in favor of a "continuist" model of language/world interaction, and her invitation to reconnect with the mother as language giver and teacher. I will explore this connection further when I examine more closely the tenets of Muraro's (and Zamboni's) eulogy for the mother tongue.

This is not to say, of course, that Muraro means to challenge Saussure's basic assumption regarding the "sign's arbitrariness." I don't think that the arbitrariness of language and linguistic denominations can be questioned, even by her. Rather, what is at stake is the extension given to the Saussurian notion of language's autonomy by a number of thinkers coming from various fields, one that fuels the idea that language severs us irretrievably and in the same thrust from "the mother" and from "the world." The greater the insistence on the symbolic order's autonomous mechanisms, the greater language's apparent or stated immunity from the world. The idea that language is an "autonomous code" obeying its internal logics and disconnected from, or, rather, connected only arbitrarily to, "reality" is what allows language to appear as the great ruler (if possibly unruly itself). To put it differently, autonomy and immunity from the world (i.e., the transcendence of language) are the conditions of language's sovereign power over speaking subjects.

If Muraro manages to enroll Jakobson in more ways than I can expand on here in her challenge to Lacan,[33] there is no question that she is coming up against a formidable adversary. The force of Lacan's formulations and their seductive power can be observed in Judith Butler's own complicated dealings with Lacan's theory of the symbolic order.

I've hinted several times at the unexpected convergences between Butler and Muraro. Both have launched early on an attack against the (structuralist) totalizing and fixed view of the symbolic order, underlining the problems posed by its ahistorical tendency. At what seems like roughly the same time, at least in their writings, both articulated a critique of Kristeva's neo-Lacanian theory of the dual stage of language, pinpointing each in her own way the epistemological and political difficulties arising from Kristeva's consignment of the maternal figure or "stage," as it were, to "unspeakability." Of course, their agendas vastly differed. While Muraro attempted to restore language to mothers as female subjects, what Butler strove to demonstrate in *Gender Trouble* was that what gets consigned to "unspeakability" in or with the early child-mother bond, and therefore what is excluded from intelligibility and the possibility of recognition, is indeed the homosexual bond, and in particular lesbianism. Kristeva clearly describes the "unspoken" or never fully "speakable" pre-oedipal mother–daughter bond, as a/the homosexual moment in the development of the girl, one that needs to be overcome lest the daughter be engulfed in (near) psychosis. (Lacan, in the wake of Freud's remarks on the topic, had indeed linked psychosis and homosexuality in his interpretation of the Schreber case.) In Butler's reading, then, the Kristevian "unspeakable" suddenly takes uncanny and frightening Victorian overtones. At the same time, and strikingly enough, Butler doesn't really contest the predication of the symbolic order on the (paternal) law, at least in "Subversive Bodily Acts," the last section of *Gender Trouble*. What she performs is both an epistemological and logical reversal whereby the "semiotic" might be better understood as an effect of the "symbolic order" rather than as what precedes it, hence as a kind of retrospective fantasy linked to the latter's always already operating order, just as she suggests that sex is an effect of gender. Meanwhile, she leaves all these binary distinctions in place: semiotics/symbolic, maternal/paternal, body/law, sex/gender, etc. The reason is, it seems to me, that, for all her avowed proximity to Michel Foucault and Foucault's notion of the productivity of power, Butler remains drawn (in)to the Lacanian conceptual framework when it comes to thinking about desire and language. Her essay on "The Lesbian Phallus" is a case in point. There, Butler reminds her readers that lesbianism remains firmly located, if perhaps "productively" hence "subversively," within the phallocentric closure, as may indeed be the case for feminism as well, whether the latter likes it or not. For lesbianism, the source and benefit of this location within the phallocentric paradigm is probably primarily libidinal or, say, fantasmatic, rather than epistemological. More importantly for the purpose of my argument here, Butler's understanding of language remains largely inflected by Lacan's, even the early Lacan's theorization of the symbolic order. This accounts in part for her constant moving back and forth between a Lacanian and a Foucaldian conceptual framework in *Gender Trouble*.

Thus, whereas Muraro tries to think of the "order" of language outside the paradigm of the "law" and the latter's conflation with the name of the father,[34] Butler sticks to that paradigm, fully folding language within the "law," even when she insists on the productivity rather than the prohibitive dimension of the latter, and even if, against the early Lacan at least, she thinks of the symbolic order as a reflection of a potentially shifting cultural order, thus promoting culture over and above structure. Language, in this view, is both what forces us and what allows us to make sense within the confines of the dominant cultural order. This may also help explain Butler's almost exclusive focus on the question of "intelligibility," that is, on the question of what conditions or precludes intelligibility in linguistic exchange. The answer is to be found, for Butler as well as for Lacan, at the point where the "law" strikes bodies and renders them legible, linking the production of meaning to the sanction of the cultural order. Only when the (human) "body" is inscribed within the symbolic order, only when it is allowed to make sense, can a body, anybody, be granted subjecthood. Legibility in this sense is coterminus with the validation of an individual's subjecthood, triggering the process of recognition of a subject by another subject.

The shift between "power" and "the law," or between Foucault and Lacan, can be troubling at times, as they start mingling in odd ways, and produce statements such as this one, in the middle of Butler's argument against Kristeva: "By restricting the paternal law to a prohibitive or repressive function, Kristeva fails to understand the paternal mechanisms by which affectivity itself is generated."[35] Here, Butler seems to argue at the same time for the productivity of the law (Foucault), and for the at once logical (or symbolic) and chronological priority of the "paternal law" (Lacan), a law whose "paternal mechanisms" (language, symbolic articulation) even have the power Lacan himself doesn't dare to grant them: the power to "generate affectivity." In other words, the "maternal world" would be nothing in Butler's view but an effect of the "paternal word."

So who is right, might one be tempted to ask? Muraro or Lacan and his heirs, even though the latter may disagree with each other, as we just saw, on important grounds? Is language a bond maker or a bond breaker? Does it alienate us from the world, or can it reconcile us with it? Does it usher the reign of the "father," or does it continue the work of the "mother"? As pressing as it is, since so many theorists have tried to provide an answer, one shouldn't rush to settle the issue. More exactly, the issue cannot be settled. For what we are most certainly dealing with, in all cases including the "Lacan case," are fictions of desire, whatever the source or rather the trigger of desire in human subjects. This is something that, for her part, Butler makes clear enough in *Gender Trouble* since her project is to make trouble for (and in) theory—in this case mostly "French theory"—and feminist theory in particular, by systematically bringing up the question of homosexual desire, that is, by formulating her critique and configuring her objects from the point of view of that desire. Teresa de Lauretis has also lucidly pointed out in her work the ways in which (sexual) fantasy informs and inflects theory, more specifically in her readings of the feminist, and divergent, responses to Kristeva.

But Muraro's view of what language does to and with the speaking subject, and especially the female speaking subject, her view, even, of where speech springs from, is actually more complicated than my description so far indicates. If she seems to want to make the case for language as a bond maker (under the guidance of the mother), as a positive mediation, or, to use her language, as the necessary tool for "restituting" one's concrete and diverse life experience, she is also, as we have seen, fighting against frightening possibilities in that very same language; indeed, ones structurally inscribed within it. Thus, the unavoidable recourse to the metaphoric process can lead to "hypermetaphoricity" when it is excessive. And with hypermetaphoricity the distance between the words and the world increases, their tie threatens to break, ideal relations of equivalence take the place of material relations of difference, "things, bodies, and specific experiences" get alienated in language . . .

and we end up where Lacan started. In other words, there are different kinds of languages in language, different modes of activation of language properties, that yield different, indeed, antagonistic results. And here I am not talking of the obvious fact of natural language diversity on the world scale. Muraro is not interested in language diversity in this sense, no more than Lacan for that matter (and on this level they both part ways with Jakobson). Rather, and to the contrary, she is in fact interested in preserving and promoting one kind of language only, the only kind that can inaugurate and maintain the symbolic order of the mother, resist the metaphoric drift, counter separation and loss, and belie theories of alienation in and through language: (what she calls) the *lingua materna*, the mother tongue.

THE SACRED TONGUE

In *The Symbolic Order of the Mother*, Muraro doesn't simply try to lift women, hence mothers qua women, out of their alleged muteness; she doesn't only try to foster new linguistic relations between speaking subjects: she presses on the "practice" and the symbolic elevation of the mother tongue. Only the mother tongue, it seems, could set off the symbolic revolution Muraro is advocating. But what does Muraro call the "mother tongue"?

The Italian national consciousness (or imaginary) feeds on a well-known mythologizing of the power of the mother tongue, one that is usually traced back and credited to Dante and his decision to write *The Divine Comedy* in his native Tuscan dialect. Dante's promotion of what he himself called "the language of the wet nurse" to the status of literary language over and against the authoritative and written languages of his time precipitated the turning of a hitherto vernacular and mainly oral language into what we now know as Italian. Dante's cultural feat and its political resonance loom large in Diotima's own cultural mythology. Chiara Zamboni calls on Dante in her praise of the mother tongue, and Elisabetta Rasy, a feminist psychoanalyst whom Muraro nonetheless criticizes for her "over-Lacanian" view of language, wrote a book entitled *The Language of the Wet-Nurse*.[36]

Indeed, the very notion of a "mother tongue" only makes sense with regard to non–"mother tongues," namely either vehicular or national languages when the "mother tongue" is equated, as was the case with

Dante, with a local dialect, or languages that involve a breaking away from native speaking conditions, such as "foreign" languages. Yet, in *The Symbolic Order of the Mother*, Muraro is not interested in expounding on the power relations between vernacular and vehicular languages, or in interpreting the defeat or victory of vernacular or regional languages in their bid to become national languages within the framework of nation-states' linguistic policies or power struggles. Rather, she casts the mother tongue in the most general, nonculturally or nonhistorically specific terms (one might say, in structural terms), as the first and primary language learned by the child under the guidance of her/his mother. What distinguishes the first language from all other languages, what sets it apart and above all others, according to Muraro, is that, as I have already hinted at, it has the unique ability of restoring while replacing, hence of replacing without replacing, one's living connection to one's mother and the world. As the primary mediation, the first and only to replace without replacing the mother and the world, the mother tongue is irreplaceable.[37] In Muraro's words, the mother tongue "restitutes, in the process of substituting for it, my oldest and most original experience."[38] "In the strictest sense," she adds later in her opus, "the mother tongue is what results from the exchange between speech and experience, an exchange that is regulated by the mother."[39]

I don't have time to dwell extensively on Muraro's central recourse to the notion of "experience." Suffice it to say that experience involves not only a living through, as I said earlier, but more precisely a living through what "is." Muraro's philosophy of language is clearly embedded, in this sense, in the tradition of onto-phenomenology. I suggested earlier that Muraro's notion of "experience" had Benjaminian overtones in as much as it depends, like Benjamin's, on linguistic mediation. But perhaps her view of language, or more exclusively, the mother tongue, brings her even closer to Martin Heidegger, whose celebration of language as the house of being is tied to his attempt at retrieving the latter's original powers while extolling the virtues of his native tongue.

The ability of the mother tongue or the original language to "state what is" is what confers it what Muraro calls "authority." The mother, she goes on, warrants this authority, being the one who teaches speech. Thus, "the authority of language is inseparable from the mother's authority."[40] "Authority" is a central concept in Muraro's thinking and lexicon.

The word combines the semantic values of originality, precedence, hierarchy, and creation. It evokes the figure of the "author" or "auctor" who "augments" the world (from the Latin verb *augeo*) by adding or bringing something new into it. The *"auctor,"* in this sense, precedes her or his creation and this position gives her or him statutory preeminence over its creation.

To think of mothers not only as language givers, but as having "authority" over the language they "give," suggests that mothers do not simply transmit language. As *"auctore,"* hence "creators" of some kind (they bring the child into the world and they also bring the world to the child through language), they are endowed with godlike features or attributes. It is almost, then, as if they owned language in order to "give it." This of course may be an effect or more precisely a translation of the often strong idealization of the mother of early childhood, in her capacity as all-powerful and oftentimes loving caretaker. But this idealization is transferred over by Muraro to the language mothers speak and teach. As such, it contributes to the sacralization of the mother tongue, a process I will address shortly.

This extolling of maternal "authority" is all the more interesting since Muraro entered politics in the late sixties through the Demau collective, a feminist anti-authoritarian pedagogical league of sorts,[41] which Dominijanni described to me as the first feminist group according to the agreed upon genealogy of Italian feminism. From what I understand, the Demau was one of these "anti-institutional" movements characteristic of the time in the West and particularly strong in Italy (think of the antipsychiatry movement that did lead to the closing of psychiatric hospitals in Italy). It pitted its proponents against the school, the masters, the state, in the name of pedagogical freedom. It is as if Muraro's subsequent participation in the women's liberation movement led her to recast this fight as an attempt to reclaim for mothers the pedagogical power they had been stripped of by the school as a state institution.

In *Emile, ou De l'éducation*, Jean-Jacques Rousseau laid the philosophical groundwork for modern national instruction by trying to imagine the kind of education it would take to turn the child into a citizen. Prior to any content, the first step, according to *Emile*, was to give the (male) child a master, that is, a male master, who would tear the child away from the grips of wet-nurses and other mothers. Far from being authoritative language teachers, the children's early female caretakers, in Rousseau's view, hinder their access to full language competency. Consequently and strictly speaking, for Rousseau, there is no "mother tongue," there is only an "infant tongue," the "babble" that infants themselves teach their caretakers to "speak."[42] Even though Muraro doesn't mention Rousseau's founding text of Western pedagogical modernity, *The Symbolic Order of the Mother* can thus be read as a feminist "Anti-*Emile*."

The symbolic authority mothers exercise and embody is thus something more than just symbolic proficiency. The additional value of symbolic authority over symbolic proficiency marks the qualitative gap between the mother tongue and any sort of language and language learning that comes afterward. "Second" languages, foreign languages, the specialized languages of science, all these languages can never "state what is" because they "replace words with other words," instead of "exchanging speech for experience" or replacing the world without replacing it, as only the first language we learn does. Most pronouncements by Muraro on these "secondary" languages are indeed derogatory, even though, at one point, she compares the ease and pleasure with which one may learn the language of a lover who speaks a foreign language to the pleasures afforded by the learning of the mother tongue. Second languages are not only secondary languages; with them, we risk falling into insignificance, because, detached from what is (the world, the mother who brings it to us), they are literally groundless. They are, we might say in reference to Derrida's analysis of the function of the supplement in Rousseau's work, bad or "dangerous supplements."[43] Only the mother tongue can escape languages' infinite and dangerous substitutability, hence full convertibility into one another; it/her alone can arrest translation, because it alone is irreplaceable.[44]

The exceptionality of the mother tongue points or leads to what I have called its sacralization. The sacrality of the mother tongue is indeed literally avowed in the following statement, taken from the notes Muraro added to the original publication of *The Symbolic Order of the Mother*, on the occasion of its translation in French: "We can undo anything in thought or technologically *save for* our living body and our mother tongue."[45] The double and related exceptionality of one's "living body" and one's "mother tongue" underlines once again the continuity or contiguity of the primary language with the body, such that alone among all languages the mother tongue is indeed a "tongue." What's more, and more to the point, the use of the preposition *"sauf"* in French ("save" in English/*salva* in Italian; remember that Muraro speaks French and reviewed the translation) signals the exceptional granting of symbolic immunity to the living body and the mother tongue. Literally, the living body and the mother tongue are "saved" by virtue of their ontological immunity from symbolic alteration and technical manipulation. Immunity, Derrida claims in "Faith and Knowledge," is a condition, indeed, one of the possible definitions of sacrality, the "sacrum" being, according to Emile Benveniste, what is "isolate[d] from all contact," hence, in Derrida's words, *"unscathed: heilig*, holy, sacred, saved, immune and so on."[46] This is not to say that the philosopher has faith in the immunological power of the sacred. Quite the contrary, he argues that the contemporary attempts at defining and protecting an unscathed, exclusive, proper space, be it that of the family, the nation, or the "linguistic idiom," against what he also calls the "tele-techno-scientific machine," "automatically" entails an "auto-immune" response, hence the possibility of "self"-aggression and desecration.[47] And twice in the course of his meditation on religious violence, he mentions the integrity of "the idiom" as the locus of an immunological phantasy he will further question, if not "destroy" in *Monolingualism of the Other*.[48]

Not surprisingly then, the sacrality of the mother tongue turns its transmission and acquisition into a quasi-religious experience. Indeed, the language of Muraro in *The Symbolic Order* is couched in a religious rhetoric that is both appealing and puzzling. The book is set up as a narrative, which recounts Muraro's intellectual and existential journey toward her discovery of the mother's and the mother tongue's symbolic preeminence and authority. In this respect, it is very much reminiscent of Descartes' *Discourse of Method*. Here is another one, by the way, who extolled the powers of the mother tongue in proto-feminist fashion. Didn't Descartes write the *Discourse of Method* in French, his mother tongue and the not yet authorized language of philosophy, with the stated goal of making himself understood by female readers? Descartes' discovery of the *Cogito*, however, doesn't have the same mystical overtones as Muraro's rediscovery of the onto-theological powers of the mother tongue. Hers is literally a language of religious revelation, as when she states, with anaphoric force, mimicking Saint John's *Apocalypsis*:

I saw the mediating function of language and consented to the possible expression of my whole experience. *I saw* language itself as a restitutive substitute for my earliest and most original experience, that of my coming to life and into the world, in this coincidence between mediation and consent. *I saw* that language is for me the first replacer, and *I saw* that it is, in this capacity, absolutely irreplaceable.[49]

OUR TONGUES WE DO NOT OWE

The exceptionality of the mother tongue, at least as it is construed by Muraro, rests on a number of assumptions that beg questioning.

We do not learn to speak by ourselves, Muraro correctly reminds us. Language comes to us from and through others. It is shared, and it enables forms of sharing while fostering symbolic interdependence among speaking subjects. For all these reasons, it seems difficult to make the philosophical claim that speaking subjects own their language, even when the claim concerns the one language we have received with— and as—the gift of speech. If "I" do not own my language, neither, by the same token, does "my mother." Like any speaking subject, the latter inherits language and participates actively in its transmission. She may even be the primary and most important language teacher under certain social and cultural conditions, as Muraro and other members of the Diotima group insist she is. But she can neither claim for herself nor issue the language she speaks, no more than "I" can or, for that matter, than "my father" can. In this sense, the "authoring" of language by mothers and the "authority" of the mother tongue affirmed by Muraro are but a childish illusion, whose appeal and structure may well have the same roots as the religious illusion described by Freud, with the important difference, of course, that Freud tried to account for the authority of the father figure, while Muraro extols the powers of the mother with a kind of urgency justified by women's symbolic "misery" or debasement.

"I have only one language, and it isn't mine," wrote Derrida provocatively in *Monolingualism of the Other; or, The Prosthesis of Origin*. Derrida's one and only tongue, his alleged mother tongue is not even, he argues, his mother's tongue. For the language Algerian Jews were given or left to speak in Algeria was not "their" language: neither autochthonic or indigenous as Berber languages could be said to be, nor "custom-made" like the Jewish Hispanic dialect called Ladino, French was imposed on the Algerian Jews as a result of a complex colonial history: the history of the Jewish settlements in the Maghreb, and that of the colonial management—and production—of the distinctions between Arabs, Berbers, and Jews under French rule. While expounding on the singularity of this linguistic predicament, Derrida derives from it a general understanding of our linguistic condition. Far from being an exceptional case, the linguistic predicament of Algerian Jews would according to him reveal in both blatant and aporetic fashion the terms underlying our dwelling in language. Such dwelling rests on what one could call an original and infinite expropriation (or, in Derridean terms, "exappropriation") thanks to what Derrida calls "the coloniality of any culture."[50] The coloniality of all or any culture is such that there can never be any natural possession of natural languages, only the more or less violent naturalization of languages' historical imposition.

Lacan stressed the aporetic predicament of the speaking subject who can only say "I" at the cost of submitting her- or himself to the "othering" work of language, and whose self-owning is therefore radically compromised. Moving the argument into the political field, Derrida showed that collective claims to the possession of language(s), were equally ill-thought and politically shortsighted, whatever the scale (local, regional, national) and the rationale (colonialist or anticolonialist) of such claims.

Whether I love my native tongue or hate it, or whether I love and hate it at the same time for personal and ideological reasons, I, woman, man, child, mother, father, other, can never possess it, even when I "master" it.

But do we ever speak one language only? Is language, any language, ever "one," both unique and unified? The sacralization of the mother tongue certainly rests on the assumption of the unity and uniqueness of the "mother tongue." Or perhaps it is the contrary: the sacralization of the mother tongue produces the illusion of its uniqueness and unity. But what if a mother, some mothers, speak and transmit more than one language? Monolingualism, after all, is far from being a universal condition. It is, in fact, a recent byproduct of the development of modern Western nation-states. What would happen, in the case of native or acquired bi- or multilingualism, to the idea that only the single original language has the ability to "restitute experience" and connect us with the world, when other languages (second, foreign languages) only connect words and replace words with words? Against de Lauretis who criticizes Muraro's idealization of the mother figure, Dominijanni asserts in "The Contact Word" that the latter is indeed talking about real mothers, engaged in the daily work of "metonymic symbolization" (chapter 1 in this volume). I'm afraid, however, that de Lauretis is right. If Muraro had in mind real mothers, or the reality of mothering, wouldn't she make room for the possibility of more than one native language and, even more so, for the possibility of more than one early language teacher? Dante himself made the distinction between wet-nurses and "statutory" mothers, according to the child-rearing practices of his time and class. What happens if and when there is more than one infant caretaker? When the wet-nurse, or, say, the/a grandmother and the mother, speak and teach different languages?[51]

Perhaps Muraro is confusing the unicity, for the child, of the mother figure's voice, which can certainly be argued, with the unicity of her speech. Whatever the case, there is no question that, through various philosophical and rhetorical moves, Muraro ends up predicating the exceptionality of the mother tongue on the uniqueness and unity of the mother figure, hence, once again, on a specific cultural configuration (both Catholic and modern bourgeois, like Kristeva's in this respect). If Muraro allows for the plurality of women, if she even insists quite rightly on "disparity" among women, when it comes to mothers, she drops the "s," as she does in the title of her main opus, which pits the generic Mother over and against the generic Father of Lacan. And she ends up doing what she claims she wants to fight against: "metaphorizing" mothers, producing and extolling an ideal and unified figure through the erasure of concrete differences, a figure that lends itself in *The Symbolic Order of the Mother* to unqualified celebration. Once again, it is in Muraro's afterword to her book that one finds the clearest indication of her yielding to this perhaps unavoidable "metaphorical" temptation: "Ce qui vient avant une femme, c'est la mère, il n'y a pas d'autre nom" ["What comes before a woman is the mother, there is no other name"] she writes in both apodictic and aphoristic fashion. Note the loaded grammatical distinction between the use of the indefinite article when she speaks of " [a] woman" and the use of the definite or generic article—

the mother—when it comes to (and from) the mother. Stating that there is no other name for "mother" (the being and the word) than "mother" brings to mind the religious phrase of Islamic monotheism: there is no other God than God. "The mother" thus shares with God the gift of linguistic exceptionality whereby the name "mother" becomes a quasi-proper name, irreplaceable and tautological, as it were: absolute.

One could also ask what happens to the notion of the unconscious when (metonymic) language, in the guise of the mother tongue, protects us from loss and separation (from both the mother and the world) and gives us back again and again the world the mother has opened for us. Doesn't the psychoanalytical notion of "the unconscious," with its attending assumptions (the repression of drives, the erring of desire) entail some form of alienation from, or (forced) renunciation of, the primary sources of "jouissance" dispensed by an archaic mother figure?

On another level, and to go back to the question of the mother tongue's double immunity from the world's destructive drives and from language's metaphorical drift, isn't it paradoxical that the mother tongue qua immune language is precisely the one and only deemed capable of putting us in touch (or, as Dominijanni says, in contact) with the world? Doesn't the ability to grant or make contact with the world, and to "restitute" experience, imply losing or relinquishing one's immunity, and taking the infinite risk of alteration in/by the world?

Finally, doesn't the very notion of [the] "mother tongue" (or, for that matter, the wet-nurse tongue)—a catachretic and indeed synecdotal formula to which English native speakers (at least in the West) generally prefer the gender-neutral "native language"—rely on a traditional division of roles along gender lines in the care of children? True, this certainly corresponds to real and vastly predominant practices. And there is nothing wrong, quite the contrary, with starting from real conditions and reinterpreting them, when one has a political agenda for transformation. But doesn't the emphasis put on the "mother" in this way tend to reify that division?

HINTS OF THE COMMON

In lieu of a conclusion, let me now return to my initial question: (how) does what has come to be recognized as "Italian feminism" fit in the contemporary Italian intellectual landscape?

In "Wounds of the Common," a paper published in a special issue of *Diacritics* devoted to "Contemporary Italian Thought" in 2009, Dominijanni faults such philosophers as Roberto Esposito on the one hand and Antonio Negri on the other for having failed to take into account the "sexual differential" in their conceptualization of "community" or "multitude."[52] It is not clear whether the "wounds of the common" exposed by Dominijanni are the wounds inflicted by sexual difference, and the philosophy of sexual difference devised by Italian feminists, to both the political community and the contemporary theories of community, or whether they are not also the wounds suffered by the Italian feminist philosophers themselves, whose efforts at imagining and putting into practice alternative forms of community haven't been fully acknowledged by their male counterparts. What Dominijanni's reproach and argument show, at any rate, is that she, along with the women philosophers she is in a sense speaking for, has read the Italian thinkers that make up the bulk of "contemporary Italian thought."

Like some of these thinkers and from the start, if through different paths, the Diotima collective has indeed criticized the shortcomings of Western democracy, its juridical formalism and abstract individualism, as well as its complicity with, or dependence on, late capitalism. Like them, the group has focused on the question of the possibility of "community" today. Like them again, as Dominijanni argues in "The Undecidable Imprint," the Diotima collective has tried to address contemporary biopolitics and contributed to the theory of biopower. It first did so unknowingly, as it were, since raising the double question of sexual difference and sexual politics necessarily meant encountering the problem of the political treatment of "life" (*bios, zoe*) in one guise of the other; and it has done so in explicit terms, ever since the Diotima collective started questioning the overlooking of feminist thought by "Italian philosophers." As Dominijanni remarks in the same essay, the latter's focus on biopolitics should have led them to encounter the philosophy of sexual difference and to take it into account. Yet they didn't.[53] Finally—and, for somebody affiliated with the French "poststructuralist" moment, this is particularly striking—both "Italian feminists" and "Italian philosophers" have shared from the start a distrust or dislike for what they call "postmodernism" and its alleged "nihilism," even though, as I said earlier, the Diotima collective is clearly indebted to, and embedded in, poststructuralist thinking in the most rigorous sense. At the same time, its emphasis on "origin(s)," "experience," being, and truth shows that, like Esposito for instance, it remains faithful, contrary to a number of deemed "postmodernist" thinkers, to the project of "Western metaphysics."

There are then, a number of hints of a common ground between "Italian feminists" and "Italian philosophers." Yet, there is no question that between them, the dialogue has gone largely one way, at least until the very last few years.

Dominijanni's diagnosis of wounds in the common Italian intellectual and political body, suggests, as I said earlier, both a rift and a gap in the community, be it the political community, real and imagined (present or wished for), or the intellectual community that tries to think about it. Is the "wound" an accurate metaphor for the political and intellectual situation Dominijanni is trying to account for? I do not know how to answer and can only remark that it connotes bodily life and vulnerability—a feminine response, perhaps, to this intellectual partition— while gesturing toward Esposito's philosophy of immunity and his interpretation of biopolitics. For my part, I see "Italian philosophers'" lack of responsiveness toward "Italian feminists" as a sign of relative indifference, a still rather "common" attitude among male intellectuals toward their female counterparts, as much as one would want to resist this cursory reference to alleged sexual affiliation. This indifference, however— and the ignorance it breeds—may well have been compounded by Diotima's intellectual as well as political separatism. The Western women's liberation movements of the seventies all advocated at one point or another, and on various levels (political, pedagogical, sometimes sexual), some sort of separatism, in more or less sophisticated ways. But the Diotima collective is the only one, to my knowledge, to have both theorized and practiced intellectual separatism with rigor and constancy. Under the guidance of Muraro (or so it seems), they insisted on drawing their intellectual food from female thinkers almost exclusively, and they framed their arguments with regard to the latter. This was, in their view, a means of creating a female intellectual genealogy, which parallels and complements the female symbolic genealogy the "symbolic order of the mother" is supposed to enable. Such intellectual separatism may be questionable, and is likely to be untenable in the long run. But given the overwhelming tendency, not the least among feminist theorists and scholars, to consider women thinkers, even the most prominent of them, as epigones, secondary sources, and copies of their (male) masters, the endeavor is worthy of consideration. To give just one example, the very fact that Alice Jardine decided to sidestep the work of the so-called French feminists in her book on the iconic function of "woman," "femininity," and "sexual difference" in contemporary French theory; the fact that she focused exclusively on various French (male) masters (most prominently Lacan, Derrida, Deleuze, and Jean-François Lyotard) on the grounds that all the women thinkers of the time were but disciples and imitators of the former, may be an extreme case of the pervasive phallocentric bias among women themselves, but it's a telling case, coming from a recognized American feminist critic in the mid-eighties.[54] It is this type of entrenched intellectual habit that the Diotima collective endeavored to fight against, which is also why it directed its attention mainly to other feminists' intellectual work as well to women's rather than men's response to their own work.

Up to recently, then, Italian feminist philosophy hasn't had much influence on, and has had little share in, the course of Italian intellectual life and "contemporary thought." But with the reception and construction of "Italian thought" in the United States, things may be changing. Ida Dominijanni was among the featured guests at the major conference on "Contemporary Italian Thought" and the question of the "Common" organized at Cornell University by Tim Campbell, a prominent American Italianist, in 2010. A two-volume issue from *Diacritics* followed, which included "Wounds of the Common," Dominijanni's indirect address to "Italian philosophers." Esposito has shown a sustained interest in the work of Donna Haraway, a prominent American feminist biologist and theorist. But the philosopher doesn't directly engage the work of other Western feminist thinkers closer to home (an immunitary precaution?), who have used like him the example of pregnancy, in various and sometimes contradictory ways, to try and address a number of questions at once biological, biopolitical, and ethico-ethological. At least he hadn't at the time he wrote *Immunitas: The Protection and Negations of Life*.[55] Perhaps then, Esposito will now be compelled to gesture in the direction of "Italian feminists" in his current project on the specificity of Italian thought. Perhaps.

Whatever the case, the current reception of "Italian thought" and the belated reception of "Italian feminism" is blurring the neat lines of the now authorized and dominant narrative of the intellectual history of our Western present. This narrative tells the story of a double supersession: that of the "linguistic turn" by the "political turn," and, on the side of feminism, that of feminist theory by queer theory. With the recent publications, in English, of various works by Diotima's current and former affiliates, the question of language has come back to haunt the turn to politics and ethics. With Judith Butler's partial shift away from a politics of equality and plurality toward an ethics of alterity, as well as with her recent attempts to formulate a political theory based on the problem of symbolic and corporeal vulnerability, previously unforeseeable or unnoted connections with Diotima's political outlook, in particular its criticism of formal democracy and the politics of autonomy, are now traceable, even beyond the dialogue that has been ongoing for a number of years by now, between the American feminist philosopher and Adriana Cavarero.

With Diotima as well as with other Italian philosophers, there may be no end to metaphysics. As far as the former is concerned, there is also an endurance, through unexpected connections and original pathways, of poststructuralist feminism. The latter hasn't said its last word.

NOTES

1. In a thoughtful email exchange I had with Dominijanni in the spring of 2015 after she had read the present contribution, she stressed the fact that Diotima was not simply a "compact group" but a "differential community" made up of singular women involved in collective research and linked by the common history of women. She therefore suggested that I refrain from using the word "group" (a word I had carelessly used in the first version of this essay) when mentioning the Diotima collective. I gladly defer to Ida's request and thank her for her informative remarks and suggestions.

2. The Milan collective predates the formation of Diotima but is close to it in outlook.

3. One should also mention the role of *differences*, the "journal of feminist cultural theory" founded in the early nineties by Naomi Schor and Elizabeth Weed. Intended as a welcoming American forum for French feminisms and theory, the journal has been a central broker of the dialogue between North American feminism(s) and European feminisms. It has played a major role in the introduction of "Italian feminist thought" to an American audience, featuring

pieces by de Lauretis on the topic as well as important contributions by Rosi Braidotti and Adriana Cavarero. The latter was one of the founding members of Diotima in 1983 until she parted ways with the collective in the early 1990s.

4. Paola Bono and Sandra Kemp, eds., *Italian Feminist Thought: A Reader* (Oxford: Basil Blackwell, 1991).

5. Graziella Parati and Rebecca J. West, eds., *Italian Feminist Theory and Practice: Equality and Sexual Difference* (Madison, N.J.: Fairleigh Dickinson University Press, 2002).

6. In 1998, Berlusconi, who had won the 1994 general elections, was no more prime minister but he returned to power in 2001 and remained in power, but for a short period of time, until 2011.

7. Among many other examples, a group of French feminists founded a feminist literary journal named *Sorcières* (Witches) in 1975. The journal lasted until 1982.

8. Silvia Federici, *Caliban and the Witch: Women, the Body, and Primitive Accumulation* (Brooklyn, NY: Autonomedia, 2004).

9. It is actually the study of different forms of speech disturbances that led him to formulate his view of language. See Roman Jakobson, *Child Language, Aphasia, and Phonological Universals* (The Hague: Mouton, 1968), first published in 1941.

10. On this topic, see Jonathan Culler's groundbreaking study, *Structuralist Poetics: Structuralism, Linguistics, and the Study of Literature* (London: Routledge and Kegan Paul; Ithaca, N.Y.: Cornell University Press, 1975).

11. In Italian as well as in French, one speaks of "maternal language" (*lingua materna/langue maternelle*), preferring the less substantive epithet "*materna*" to the name of, and reference to, the mother per se. It seems to me, however, that Muraro does want to promote the substantive link to the/a mother, at least in *The Symbolic Order of the Mother*. See my remarks below.

12. On this question, see my section "Hints of the Common."

13. As language teaches us, it is its "native" quality that defines the naturalness of the "natural": the notion of "nature" comes from the Latin verb "nascior, natus sum," which means to be born.

14. Teresa de Lauretis, *The Practice of Love: Lesbian Sexuality and Perverse Desire* (Bloomington: Indiana University Press, 1994), 181–90.

15. I believe the remark was made by Muraro herself even though I cannot find the reference anymore. The remark was made in answer to the question of the apparent lack of "racial" or ethnic diversity of the collective at the time. Indeed, Italy in the seventies was overwhelmingly white, much more so than (neo)colonial France, for instance.

16. As mentioned shortly after, Muraro starts with the question of the conditions of women's freedom rather than with the (factual) problem of their oppression.

17. For another forceful American feminist critique of the Lacanian symbolic order, see also Nancy Fraser, "The Uses and Abuses of French Discourse Theories for Feminist Politics," in *Revaluing French Feminism: Critical Essays on Difference, Agency, and Culture*, ed. Nancy Fraser and Sandra Lee Bartky (Bloomington: Indiana University Press, 1992), 177–94.

18. I am thinking among others of Luce Irigaray's *Speculum of the Other Woman* published in French in 1974, followed by the English translation, *This Sex Which Is Not One*, in 1977, or of Gayle Rubin's famous piece, "The Traffic in Women: Notes on the Political Economy of Sex" (1975).

19. George Sand, *Story of My Life: The Autobiography of George Sand*, group translation (Albany: State University of New York Press, 1991), 118.

20. Jacques Lacan, *On Feminine Sexuality: The Limits of Love and Knowledge (1972–73), Encore: The Seminar of Jacques Lacan, Book XX*, trans. Bruce Fink (New-York: W. W. Norton, 1999), 69.

21. Sigmund Freud, "Femininity," in *The Standard Edition of the Complete Psychological Works of Sigmund Freud*, ed. and trans. James Stratchey (New York: W. W. Norton, 1965), 130–67.

22. "Woman could never become just a sign and nothing more, since even in a man's world she is still a person, and since in so far as she is defined as a sign she must be recognized as a generator of signs. . . . Each woman preserves a particular value arising from her talent, before and after marriage, for taking her part in a duet. In contrast to words, which have wholly become signs, woman has remained at once a sign and a value. This explains why the relations between the sexes have preserved their affective richness, ardour and mystery which doubtless originally permeated the entire universe of human communications." Claude Lévi-Strauss, "The Principles of Kinship," in *The Elementary Structures of Kinship*, rev. ed., trans. James Harley Bell and John Richard von Sturmer (Boston: Beacon Press, 1967), 496.

23. Adriana Cavarero, "Towards a Theory of Sexual Difference," in *The Lonely Mirror: Italian Perspectives on Feminist Theory*, ed. Sandra Kemp and Paola Bono (New York and London: Routledge, 1993), 200. The forceful criticism of Kristeva's delineation of the "maternal realm" by the Diotima collective shows once again that the conflation of "French feminists," and the reduction of the feminist thinkers of "sexual difference" to one and the same intellectual position doesn't make much sense. Feminist theories of sexual difference were and remain as varied and potentially at odds with each other as are the various brands of gender and queer theory.

24. The repeated claims of indebtedness toward the work of Irigaray by the Diotima collective and Muraro in particular are all the more striking as this is an unusual attitude among feminist thinkers, at least of that generation. As far as I know, Irigaray herself hardly ever acknowledges, in her writings, the work of her feminist forebears but for sketchy mentions of Simone de Beauvoir, and she

refers even less frequently to the work or existence of her feminist contemporaries. The serious attempt by Diotima to devise an entirely female intellectual genealogy and to foster a feminist intellectual community stands in sharp contrast to that general trend.

25. Luce Irigaray, *Le corps-à-corps avec la mere* (Montréal: Editions de la Pleine Lune, 1981).

26. Luce Irigaray, *Sexes and Genealogies*, trans Gillian C. Gill (New York: Columbia University Press, 1993), 18–19.

27. See, for instance, Cavarero's 2008 interview in *differences*, where she describes the mother as "an ethical figure," "facing a decision to wound or not to wound, to care or not to care." Adriana Cavarero and Elisabetta Bertolino, "Beyond Ontology and Sexual Difference: An Interview with the Italian Feminist Philosopher Adriana Cavarero," *differences* 19, no. 1 (2008): 142.

28. It is as if the muteness of the infant was projected onto the mother, a clear indication that most discourses on "the mother" are indeed held from the (small) child's perspective.

29. Luisa Muraro, *L'ordre symbolique de la mère*, trans. Francesca Solari and Laurent Cornaz (Paris: L'Harmattan, 2003), 66. Here and throughout, in my translation from the French.

30. Muraro, *L'ordre symbolique de la mère*, 121.

31. See, for instance, Judith Butler, "The Lesbian Phallus," in *Bodies That Matter: On the Discursive Limits of 'Sex'* (New York and London: Routledge, 1993), 67–70.

32. Italian, like Latin, is a gendered language. Because language, *"lingua"* in Italian, is gendered feminine, it makes it easier to think of it as relating to some feminine or female source of utterance.

33. Jakobson's understanding of language processes is indeed more nuanced than Lacan's in several respects. If Lacan claims the priority of structure over culture(s), Jakobson has always exhibited a great sensitiveness to what he calls, in "Linguistics and Poetics," the "temporal dynamics" that affect the speakers' relation to language(s). See Roman Jakobson, "Closing Statement: Linguistics and Poetics," in *Style in Language*, ed. Thomas A. Sebeok (New York: Wiley, 1960), 352. He has shown a deep recognition of the way in which particular historical conditions are registered by languages and influence speech patterns. He has consistently insisted on the ways in which various "cultural models" and "personal styles," or what Muraro might call "specific experiences," inflect language uses. Careful to weave together a synchronic and diachronic approach to linguistic phenomena, he too can be said to be using two needles. In any case, Lacan's and Muraro's divergent readings and uses of Jakobson clearly show that structuralism is not the monolith it is sometimes taken to be.

34. Muraro, *L'ordre symbolique de la mère*, 88. In French: "Que la normativité de la langue traduise l'autorité de la mère, cela se voit à ceci: elle s'exerce non

comme une loi, mais comme un ordre—ordre vivant plus qu'institué. L'ordre linguistique en effet ne se maintient pas par l'observation rigide de règles, mais par une incessante transformation qui lui permet de se reformer malgré et même grâce aux innombrables irrégularités de nos façons de dire." ["The ability of language to produce norms is a function of the mother's authority. Indeed, language's normativity makes itself felt not so much as a law but as a command, as a living rather than an instituted order. The linguistic order doesn't perpetuate itself thanks to the rigid application of rules, but through ceaseless transformation. Thus it can maintain itself not in spite of but thanks to the numerous irregularities of our ways of speaking." —My translation].

35. Judith Butler, *Gender Trouble: Feminism and the Subversion of Identity* (New York and London: Routledge, 2008), 116.

36. See Elisabetta Rasy, *La lingua della nutrice* (Roma: Edizioni delle Donne, 1978), 22, and Muraro's commentary in *L'ordre symbolique de la mère*, 146.

37. Muraro, *L'ordre symbolique de la mère*, 86.

38. Muraro, *L'ordre symbolique de la mère*, 86.

39. Muraro, *L'ordre symbolique de la mère*, 96.

40. Muraro, *L'ordre symbolique de la mère*, 51.

41. The acronym stands for "Demystification of Patriarchal Authoritarianism."

42. On Rousseau and the question of the mother tongue, see my piece "The Popularity of Language: Rousseau and the Mother Tongue," in *The Politics of Deconstruction: Jacques Derrida and the Other of Philosophy*, ed. Martin McQuillan (London: Pluto Press, 2007), 98–115.

43. See Jacques Derrida, ". . . That Dangerous Supplement . . . ," in *Of Grammatology*, trans. Gayatri Chakravorty Spivak (Baltimore: The Johns Hopkins University Press, 1976), 141–64. See also the many pronouncements by Muraro regarding such "foreign" languages as what she calls "conventional language" or even the exchange of money, considered as a form of semiotic exchange. Muraro, *L'ordre symbolique de la mere*, 96 and 103.

44. "Les premiers mots, en effet, ne remplacent pas d'autres mots, ils remplacent les choses, oui, mais sans rien mettre à leur place." ["The first words indeed do not replace other words, they replace things without, as it were, putting anything in their place."] Muraro, *L'ordre symbolique de la mere*, 81. Muraro continues, a few pages later: "J'ai vu [. . .] la langue comme substitution restitutrice de mon expérience la plus ancienne et la plus originale, celle de ma venue à la vie et au monde. J'ai vu que pour moi la langue est la première qui-vient-à-sa-place, et je l'ai vue, en cette fonction, absolument irremplaçable." ["I saw language as the restitutive substitute for my earliest and most original experience, the experience of my coming to life and into the world. I saw that language is for me the first replacer and I saw that, in this capacity, it was absolutely irreplaceable."] Muraro, *L'ordre symbolique de la mere*, 86.

45. Muraro, *L'ordre symbolique de la mere*, 134; my emphasis.

46. Jacques Derrida and Gianni Vattimo, eds., *Religion*, trans. David Webb et al. (Stanford, Calif.: Stanford University Press, 1996), 46.

47. "The reaction to the [tele-techno-scientific] machine is as automatic (and thus machinal) as life itself. Such an internal splitting, which opens distance, is also peculiar or 'proper' to religion, appropriating religion for the 'proper' (in as much as it is also the *unscathed*: *heilig*, holy, sacred, saved, immune and so on), appropriating religious indemnification to all forms of property, from the linguistic idiom in its 'letter,' to blood and soil, to the family and to the nation. This internal and immediate reactivity, at once immunitary and auto-immune, can alone account for what will be called the religious resurgence." Jacques Derrida, "Faith and Knowledge," in *Religion*, 45–46. For a critical reading of Derrida's notion of "auto-immunity" that nonetheless builds on his insights into the "immunologics" of the so-called religious discourse, see Roberto Esposito, *Immunitas: The Protection and Negation of Life*, trans. Zakiya Hanafi (Cambridge: Polity Press, 2011); see in particular "The Katechon," 53–57.

48. Derrida, "Faith and Knowledge," 53.

49. Muraro, *L'ordre symbolique de la mère*, 86.

50. Jacques Derrida, *Monolingualism of the Other; or, The Prosthesis of Origin*, trans. Patrick Mensah (Stanford, Calif.: Stanford University Press, 1998), 39. Translation modified.

51. On the issue of the at once political, cultural, and psychological import of infant care by several, socially heterogeneous female caretakers, see, for instance, Rita Laura Segato, *L'Oedipe noir: Des nourrices et des mères* (Paris: Petite Bibliothèque Payot, 2014).

52. See "Wounds of the Common," in *Contemporary Italian Thought (2)*, ed. Tim Campbell, Sergia Adamo, and Lorenzo Fabbri, *Diacritics* 39, no. 4 (Winter 2009): 137.

53. More exactly, what has been lacking on the part of Italian male thinkers, again according to Dominijanni, is not so much proper acknowledgment but rather an active response to Diotima's philosophical and political propositions. Indeed, as Dominijanni stressed in her response to me, Roberto Esposito has published all the Diotima's books in the series he heads at the Liguori publishing house. And Toni Negri designated Luisa Muraro as one of the three most important Italian philosophers of the twentieth century, the other two being Antonio Gramsci and Mario Tronti.

54. Alice Jardine, *Gynesis: Configurations of Woman and Modernity* (Ithaca, N.Y.: Cornell University Press, 1985).

55. Roberto Esposito, *Immunitas: The Protection and Negations of Life*, trans. Zakiya Hanafi (Cambridge: Polity, 2011).

Origin and Dismeasure

The Thought of Sexual Difference in Luisa Muraro and Ida Dominijanni, and the Rise of Post-Fordist Psychopathology

ANDREA RIGHI

In his work *Living Thought: The Origins and Actuality of Italian Philosophy* (2012), Roberto Esposito argues that, beginning at least with Machiavelli, a constitutive trait of Italian philosophy consisted in bypassing the "necessarily negative tones" of contemporary thought, which after the so-called linguistic turn seems capable of "affirm[ing] itself only by negating itself," for "once the possibility of thought, and therefore also of action, becomes dependent on the transcendentality of language, it is as if the philosophical experience were continuously sucked into the same entropic vortex it seeks to escape."[1] In this perspective, the source of any space of order—language, society, and so on—vanishes into the dark night of negativity. According to Esposito, this is the typical retrospective effect of an immunizing logic that, protecting the coherence of a system "against the self-dissolutive risk of the partaking-in-the-commune," usually characterizes "origin—the original community . . . so negatively, as primeval chaos or a state of nature, that there is no question about the need to bar it."[2] The best Italian philosophy instead is characterized by a *living-thought* that critically engages with origin and draws from it not a paralyzing and static perspective, but the energy typical of beginning [*cominciamento*] and its originating force.

Looking at Italy from a distance—not only at its society, but also at its cultural production—one thing that continuously strikes me is how the country enjoys falling into a provincial image of itself. This is a common phenomenon. Under the gaze of foreign eyes people tend to reenact an exaggerated representation of their autochthony. Although Esposito's idea of distinguishing Italian philosophy as driven by the problem of life seems a simple and thus brilliant intuition, one may think that it runs the abovementioned risk. Especially in the U.S. context, it risks, in other words, attaching to the various philosophies produced in the peninsula the typical flavor of *Italianness* that is so successful abroad: the vigorous, quasi-animal but charming and innocuous representation that Hollywood usually welcomes.

Here, however, we should avoid the benevolent critique that dismisses this philosophical attempt simply because it exoticizes an irreducible form of cultural production. As a matter of fact, we should read the expected reproach of essentialism on the backdrop of an ideology, constructivism, which, maintaining that whatever exists is constructed and mediated socially, forecloses materiality and its dialectics. Contrary to what it seems, this sort of *provincialization* of Italian philosophy should be taken instead to its extreme degree. In other words, today's task is showing how its marginality, or particularity, has deep social motives and in fact captures a specific historical configuration of modern biopolitics. As our times are marked by subsumption of the whole personhood in the work process—think of cognitive work or the care work typical of the sphere of reproduction—it is precisely this biopolitical configuration that brings the issue of life (and its origin) to the foreground.[3] Thus divesting Italian philosophy of its supposed claims of universality and framing it from the specific angle of the presentness of origin and its amorphous threat-force is an audacious enterprise, one that could free Italian philosophers from the traditional imperative of writing first and foremost historiography.[4]

In his genealogy of this philosophy of life, one current of thought that Esposito hastily mentions is feminism. I would argue that far from being just another example of Italian living-thought, the voices that constitute the plurality of Italian feminisms disclosed the precondition for that very practice. In other words, their *different* and *autonomous* theoretical stance should have a sort of logical precedence over any genealogy of life-philosophy. Isn't in fact the patriarchal order established precisely on a set of (immunizing) devices that neutralize and dominate the specific feminine power of procreation? Isn't patriarchy a macroscopic case of *excluding inclusion* typical of the dialectic of immunization?[5] To put it in straight materialist terms: as the main agents of the work of reproduction, women inhabit a concrete social-natural ambit where capital and labor fight over a strategic item: the production of life—what Marx called labor power. This is why groups like Lotta Femminista, a neo-Marxist branch of Italian feminism, investigated the family as a (hidden) center of production of labor-power, disclosing how the latter constituted both the matrix of their subordination and a platform for rebellion. Others, such as the Milan-based collective called Demau (Demystification of Patriarchal Authoritarianism), privileged a psychoanalytical approach that deconstructed the patriarchal organization of the sphere of reproduction, thus elaborating an anti-institutional and antiauthoritarian critique that was highly influential for the 1968 movement. But it is probably the Diotima community in Verona that more extensively interrogated the issue of life and its origin from the autonomous perspective of sexual difference.

Women's relation to procreation is complicated. Although praised as an exceptional gift, historically their capacity to reproduce life has been regarded as the emblem of their oppression. It is presumably this closeness with nature that made her inferior to man, as the latter, claiming for himself an exclusive role in public life, moved civilization forward. The Diotima community aimed at disparaging this powerful masculine discourse that precluded any positive instantiations of an autonomous feminine dimension. It did so by reverting what was considered a sign of inferiority into the locus of *authority*. So it engendered a theory and a set of practices that shaped a different configuration of psychic and social life that they called the maternal symbolic.[6]

Looking at the thought of a prominent intellectual of the community, Luisa Muraro, in the next pages, I will explore the ways in which the thought of sexual difference worked out key elements of Lacanian psychoanalysis, and thought through the problem of origin and its symbolic organization from a female point of view. In this sense, I will show how the notion of the maternal symbolic embodies a fundamental aspect in the deconstruction and critique of what Esposito calls the "secularization paradigm" and its dubious "historical fulfillment of the originary genetic nucleus" of life.[7] Next, I will discuss the new challenges that the maternal symbolic faces, drawing on the insights from Ida Dominijanni's work. Her reflection on the notion of *sexed subjectivity* in light of the transformations of the organization of labor—post-Fordism—in the so-called *society of enjoyment* is crucial to sketch the criticalities of contemporary psychopathology as well as its most promising elements of conflict.[8]

THE SOCIAL SPLIT OF HUMANITY AND SEXUAL DIFFERENCE

The translation of the power to procreate into a curse, into a pluri-secular form of disfranchisement and expropriation, rests on a common assumption: the physiological difference between men and women. This difference defines procreation as a biological destiny for women, disciplining their processes of subject formation. Italian feminism turned around this notion and transformed it into a political practice. To fully appreciate the valence of this move, let us approach the problem of the difference between sexes from an anthropological point of view, and then move to its psychoanalytic significance. Here the question is: what is the most defining characteristic in the physiological dimension of sexuality across genders?

The first distinction we must draw is not one between genders, but between species, that is, between the animal and the human. As Mina Davis Caulfield noted, "almost all our living relatives" show "physiological cues, triggers to arousal for both females and males that effectively limit sexual behavior to the periods of maximal probability for impregnation."[9] Humans, on the contrary, do not experience a specific sexual season and copulate independent of natural cycles. The loss of a sexual season, that is, the *loss of estrous cycles* where female and male respond to sexual cues, seems to be the result of the evolutionary change that occurred in the transition from ape to human (although it is also true that some primates copulate regardless of their mating season). A whole set of repercussions proceeds from this assumption and constitute the foundations of what is commonly known as sociobiology. Donna Haraway has demonstrated how historically this discipline "has been central in the development of the most thorough naturalization of patriarchal division of authority in the body politic and in reduction of the body politic to sexual physiology."[10]

Silvia Vegetti Finzi, a psychologist and militant in the Italian women's movement, stated that the woman is a "domesticated animal" (the absence of estrous is usually a characteristic that mammals develop in captivity). Furthermore, for a woman "the loss of estrous does not simply imply asynchrony with respect to natural cycles . . . but also estrangement with respect to her own body and desire."[11] If for men the consequences of this primary alienation seem straightforward—the detachment from procreative ends creates the conditions for a socio-symbolic experience of sexuality—for women the matter is more complex. Women's sexuality is still molded by reproductive processes, but since she simultaneously engages in nonprocreative activities, it is also directed toward a nonspecified goal. This goal is a point of great disagreement. If it is defined as the taking care of herself and her progeny, that is, as sexual favors in exchange for protection, the conclusion is a social Darwinism upholding an implicit patriarchal view of society. If it is defined as an autonomous and liberating enjoinment, a neo-libertine call for authenticity usually is at stake. Is this ambiguity between sexuality as women's self-determination (protection, pleasure) and contemporaneously as their overdetermination (procreation) the genuine difference between men and women?

Slavoj Žižek argues that at the bottom of Jacques Lacan's *formulae of sexuation*—that is to say at the core of the positions the subject assumes with respect to reality—resides the problem of the primary difference that is implicit in the loss and/or lack of estrous. Lacan's inquiry in fact examines the passage "from animal coupling led by instinctual knowledge, regulated by natural rhythms, to human sexuality possessed by an eternalized desire" qua the emergence of the symbolic order.[12] This transformation cannot be articulated through a linear causal transformation. It is a derangement, a rift that breaks an established pattern. As with natural selection, this radical split illustrates the typical paradox of necessity. Necessity is always *retrospective*. At a certain point in time something new emerges, yet this emerging contains two contradictory characteristics: it must be *thought* as something that it did not exist before and, simultaneously, as something that was already posited and necessary for existence. This is the true nonteleological ratio of Darwin's evolutionism: "contingent and meaningless genetic changes are retroactively used . . . in a manner appropriate for survival," thus "temporality here is future anterior, that is, adaptation is something that always and by definition will have been."[13]

The extinction of a regulated, overdetermined sexuality qua reproduction becomes a *lack*, a gap that transitions humankind into a new territory. This lack, however, should never be thought as a limitation, but as an absence that gives rise to a new openness. For instance, the unhooking of the sexual act from its biological base opens up a great variety of nonreproductive practices that fuel "the development of shared and learned behavior and symbolic communication."[14] In this new field *both* genders inhabit their biological base in a more reflective way. "Sexual pleasure—for instance—which originally signaled that the goal of procreation was achieved, becomes an aim-in-itself."[15] Detached from rigid natural patterns, sensuous pleasure is now invested with a whole set of meanings and values, becoming the object of social negotiations. Sexuality is thus already on the human side of the rift. Its biological base is thoroughly complicated, traversed by social constructions and symbolizations.

I believe that this is the most natural element we can capture at the bottom of sexuality: the *grafting* on the biological base of sexuality as a social complex. It would be pointless to look for something more natural in the institution of sexuality apart from the grafting, which retrospectively bears witness to its necessity. It is the self-positing work of humankind that in relation with (e.g., influencing and responding to) a complex and fluctuating environment experiences morphological changes. Morphology is self-causing. Sexuality is part of this set of self-transformative activities in dialectical relation with environs. Any archaic animal residue still informing women's sexuality bears testimony to concrete historical arrangements. In a society where reproduction is crucial and those who perform that job are powerless, the pseudo-natural pressure of sexuality as procreation will hold sway. So the specific positions that males and females assume regarding sexuality—their different goals (pleasure or procreation) and the scrutiny of their imbalances—follow existing social organizations and their conflicts.

THE LACAN-ŽIŽEK TAKE ON THE FORMULAE OF SEXUATION

Historicizing the symbolic forms (e.g., patriarchy) that organize the biological base is central to the engendering of a new politics of sexuality. Adriana Cavarero, for instance, traced this occultation back to ancient Greek myths. Particularly in Hesiod's myth of creation, she reads the mark of male domination "translating birth into the negative meaning of the beginning of death, the uterus into a container of evils . . . and all those other figures of misogynous culture that follow on the centralizing of the male as the universal subject of thought and language."[16] But the claim feminists make is also that the discipline that studied these symbolic economies, psychoanalysis, contributed to the preclusion of a genuinely direct expression and construction of women's symbolic unity, that is, what they called the maternal symbolic. The French scholar Luce Irigaray, who is very influential among the Diotima group, argued that a key concept in Freud and Lacan, the *phallus*, is nothing less than the masculine expropriation of the relation to origin and of the desire for and as origin.[17] "We know," Cavarero argues, "that corporeal facts . . . are the raw material of the symbolic elaboration that expresses their signification."[18] Hence the task is to signify this sexual difference in a productive, nonstatic way.

To show how the philosophy of sexual difference outlined the configuration of the maternal symbolic I propose to go back to Lacan by way of Žižek. The Slovenian psychoanalyst is in fact particularly interesting for us as he does not propose a monolithic rendering of Lacan, but rather he looks at Lacan's work as a "succession of attempts to seize the same persistent traumatic kernel."[19] As Žižek notes: "In so far as sexual difference is a Real that resists symbolization, the sexual relationship is condemned to remain an asymmetrical non-relationship in which the other, our partner, prior to being a subject, is a Thing."[20] By recognizing the transcendental nature of woman as other we deploy this asymmetry. According to Lacan, two different gender modalities exist that are expressed in his famous formulae. The feminine is limitless, but at the same time not totalizable (not-whole); the masculine instead is universal and definite, but founded on exception (*phallocentrism*). Žižek argues that this symbolic placement crops out a factor elevating it to an absolute condition. This is what he calls "humanization at its zero-level" that is, "the elevation of a minor activity into an end-in-itself" that has the same features of a "deadly excess of enjoyment as the goal in itself."[21] Symbolic communication emerges out of this background as a barrier that mediates this form of *jouissance* without ever subsuming it completely. It is important to notice that this is a specific kind of "animalized" jouissance, an obsessive form of enjoyment that we will find also at work in post-Fordism.

Key to the formulae of sexuation is the "fundamental Hegelian paradox of reflexivity."[22] Žižek argues that "if the subject is to emerge, he must set himself against a paradoxical object that . . . cannot be subjectivized," that is "a piece of flesh that the subject has to lose if he is to emerge as the void of the distance towards every objectivity."[23] Men and women respond to this impasse in different ways and this justifies their different location with regards to Lacan's schema. It is in Seminar XX, *Encore*, that Lacan lays out a complex topology, or logical space of sexual difference.[24] Here Lacan begins with man in order to work out woman's position. The masculine side of the formula defines a relationship between him as a barred subject and reality: $—a. We said that the subject must emerge in opposition to an object. Žižek argues that this happens through the interpellation of another subject (an *Other* which is usually the mother) who addresses the infant.[25] When the subject responds to this puzzling demand s/he establishes her or his conditions of possibility and, departing from her or his presymbolic state, begins positing her- or himself as someone *for* somebody. This is the first step to initiate a process of subjectification that inaugurates the entrance of the subject into the symbolic order. Hence, according to Lacan, and contrary to what we commonly think, we don't begin as subjects, but as object for a subject, for somebody else. Fantasy is the proper name for this work that sustains subject formation, that is to say, for a procedure that offers a "way for the subject to answer the question of what object he is in the eyes of the Other."[26] Responding to this demand (the demand of the Other) is an activity an individual will carry on for the rest of her or his life.

Yet as this asymmetry characterizes our subjectivity, it also marks our inconsistency. This means that the subject is hollow. In other words, inside our head (or our heart) there is no little replica of ourselves in charge of the operations, because we are born out of a request of/from the Other. This is why Lacan bars the S of the subject ($). This vacuous essence of the self reflects also the early perceptions that infants have as they begin to realize their individuality. In the so-called mirror stage, the infant composes her or his "dispersed erogenous zones into the totality of a unified body."[27] The symbol of this limitation, the *phallus*, delimits (or castrates) the subject and in so doing it also provides the future structure of reference for his desire. It becomes a signifier of a signified that cannot be fulfilled. Here desire is articulated in both its *transitive* meaning, as desire *for* the Other, and its *causative* meaning, as the desire for the recognition *by* the Other. What is paramount here is desire's relational structure. This rapport can be extinguished only when the radical difference between subject and Other is foreclosed as in the abovementioned case of the zero-level jouissance.

Moreover, the response (fantasy) the subject fabricates cannot be taken as something positive, either. In the formula ($—a) the subject establishes through his fantasy a relation with the Other, which Lacan calls the *objet petit a*. The *objet petit a* is a sort of structural mechanism that feeds on itself, comprising various levels: "Object a is simultaneously the pure lack, the void around which the desire turns and which, as such, causes the desire, *and* the imaginary element which conceals this void, renders it invisible by filling it out."[28] A good example Lacan uses to illustrate the structure of the *objet petit a* is that of the book that goes missing from a library bookshelf. The book's absence is visible and—if we take for granted the physical impossibility of retrieving the volume—it now constitutes its presence. Thus for Lacan, those individuals located in a masculine position are continuously caught in the reproduction of this phantasmatic object. As he writes, this man "is unable to attain his sexual partner, who is the Other, except insomuch as his partner is the cause of his desire."[29] But the cause of his desire is simply a fantasy, a filler of a void that cannot be filled.

This vacuous matter is not proper to the male only. According to Žižek, it is in *Encore* that Lacan revises his previous position, concluding that the symbolic order too is inconsistent. Prior to the 1960s, Lacan believed that "the Name-of-the-Father *qua* the central signifier . . . guarantee[d] the consistency of the symbolic field."[30] In other words, the structure of reference constituted by the symbolic order was based on an exception, a principle ensuring from the outside the coherence of the symbolic field. In *Encore*, however, Lacan affirms that "there is no Other of the Other."[31] Here Lacan stages a negation that works at two levels. The first negation (*there is no Other*) implies that the symbolic order is not founded on a determinate transcendent element that defines it—for instance the famous Freudian idea of Moses as the non-Jewish father of the Jews. The second (*there is no Other of the Other*) implies that the threshold of the symbolic is split open, operating as a fragmented border not defining what is in and what is out, but rather generating an infinity of points.[32]

It is at this extremity that we encounter the woman. As Lacan argues, "Woman is that which has a relationship to that Other... in the most radical sense."³³ Her position reflects the very structure of the boundaries of the symbolic field, borders that rely on a groundless basis. Therein we encounter her epistemological significance. Her position is expressed by the following formula: S—($\bar{A}$). S here stands for the signifier, as she too is part of the symbolic field. While she inhabits the zone of indistinguishability of the borders, she is certainly not stuck into a pre-symbolic stage. Yet, as she replicates the same infinite structure, she is also in direct relation with the Other ($\bar{A}$) to the extent that, as a transcendent exception, it does not exist. Here the figure of the hysteric, as Žižek notes, better explains the female defiance of the symbolic inscription. Stormed by paradoxical requests, the hysteric personality is caught up in a masquerade that ultimately shows how behind these radically contradictory performances there is no subject. Thus the hysteric acts out the properly bottomless configuration of any subjectivity that is not completely subjected to the fantasy of a self-centered subject. In Žižek's interpretation the woman retains a fundamental epistemological value insofar as she constitutes a transcendental condition. Accordingly, any positive determination of her essence, what he calls "the pre-symbolic eternally Feminine" is useless and gives rise in fact to "a retroactive patriarchal fantasy."³⁴

In this regard Žižek but also other eloquent interpreters of *Encore*, like Ellie Ragland, maintain that, for however traumatic or fragmentary, it is the phallus that regulates the symbolic position "vis-à-vis difference."³⁵ The woman instead—and this is a productive and positive difference that Žižek censures—entertains a special relation to jouissance for, as she escapes the phallic function, she is also simultaneously able to "take a certain distance from the *all* of the master discourse."³⁶ Man, on the other hand, has access to phallic jouissance, which hinges on some prop (the partial *objet a*) that momentarily satisfies the subject only to make him begin his search again. This fantasy propels a series of attempts that are multiple, continuous but also determined and mostly serialized. On the contrary, whoever occupies the feminine position does not follow recursive phallocentric logic, but s/he operates on an economy of desire based on "quantitative infinity."³⁷ For Žižek this is a transcendental position, one that functions as a limit and does not allow the coming into being of a subject; so while he installs her in the throne of the transcendental, Žižek denies her access to a positive subjectification.

LUISA MURARO: THE MATERNAL SYMBOLIC AND THE FUNCTION OF FIXATION

With Lacan and Žižek we flew high on the wings of philosophy and theoretical conceptualization. By paying attention to more concrete life experiences, the Diotima group asks instead a series of more basic questions. If we take for granted Lacan's topology and the epistemologically superior position of the woman, is it actually true that she falls outside the domain of symbolic communication? Moreover, is it true that because of this peculiar relationship with the symbolic she becomes incapable of "free signification" and thus of expressing "a symbolic order of difference"?[38] And most important, is it true that that deep, all-comprising love and tenderness of infancy must be severed by the enigma of the Other and the following castration?

My argument is that the feminist revision of the psychoanalytic framework is based on two fundamental points. One is historical and disputes the configuration of the symbolic order as it has been delineated in the modern age. The second has an ontological objective and challenges Lacanian thought by taking to its full consequences the scheme of sexuation. We may assess these points in light of the work of Luisa Muraro, beginning from a very simple, intuitive question she raises. It regards the relationship between the infant and her or his mother, but what is at stake here is also the hidden structure that lies behind the transcendental priority of women.

For what we have said so far, there seems to be a discrepancy between the symbolic as a structure that guarantees signification and the process of learning our native language as a concrete activity. Muraro points out that "we learn to speak from the mother or from the one in her place. We learn to speak not in addition to something or as a supplement but as an essential part of the vital communication we have with her."[39] In effect, even if language cuts through our symbiosis with the environment as a foreign medium and castration provides access to our future social interactions, this event entails a long period of apprenticeship. But in Lacan, as well as in Žižek, this seems to happen in a transcendental laboratory where moves, responses, and dynamics are determined by abstract laws.

On the contrary, in everyday living experience, it is usually the mother who carries out this linguistic labor by establishing an expansive relationship with the creature she gave birth to. This is a powerful and vital dimension. Why does it have to be severed? Muraro does not refuse the reality of the symbolic, which is objective and historically true, but argues that these theorizations only show us the particular point of view of the masculine social order.[40] Accordingly, the "symbolic order must begin to establish itself (otherwise it will never establish itself) in the relationship with the mother, and . . . the 'break' separating us from her does not correspond to a necessity for the symbolic order."[41]

The repressing or foreclosing of a *maternal* genealogy of signification is due not only to a male-dominated society, but also to a lack of theorization, where with the term *theory* Muraro recalls the Greek definition of *theorein*, that is, to "look at." This incapacity to look at or show the logic and the role of a different maternal symbolic is what the thought of sexual difference strove to produce. Here we come to the metaphysical argument. I come to believe that the notion of the maternal symbolic that the Diotima group elaborates is not in disagreement with Lacan and the definition of woman as a nonwhole; rather it represents a full development of its contents. Let us go back again to Lacan. As he notes, the woman's position appears contradictory by standard logic only if framed in the context of a set theory based on a *finite* field. If the latter is *infinite*, however, "the not-whole [cannot] impl[y] the existence of something that is produced on the basis of a negation," but rather it implies that of an "indeterminate existence." The couplet "indeterminate existence" connects the idea of an open variability (*indeterminate*) to its concrete and individual actualization (*existence*). Indeterminate existence visualizes the idea of a split boundary, one in which the field, instead of being limited, grows as through a graph, or a series of variations. This is how, Lacan concludes, "woman is truth," but as such "one can only half-speak of her."[42] Muraro articulates her full structure giving form to Lacan's (precluded) truth by reconsidering the concept of *fixation*. Instead of an obsessive behavior caused to the persistence of an attachment to a libidinal level, Muraro transcends its pathological blockage, rescuing a structural value, that of a principle able to organize the maternal dimension.

Why does Muraro focus on fixation? Doesn't this approach clash with standard feminist theory that depicts repetition and sameness as the typical results of phallocentrism? According to Muraro fixation does not exactly entail the repetition of the same. A different (structurally more fundamental) kind of circularity displaces the endless replacement of the *objet petit a*. The concept of fixation is linked to *substitution* in such a way that in the former "something of the primordial relationship with the matrix of life" is kept that actually enables any chain of substitutions.[43] It is the permanence of an archaic trait that we inherited as infants: a presentness of the world that develops out of the first indistinctive feeling that newborns have before any proper symbolic individuation. In the so-called presymbolic stage, this powerful and all-encompassing experience accompanies the subsequent individualization and actually supports the child's capacity to relate with any ambit of her or his life experience. The radical point that Muraro makes is that our tendency to reactivate that configuration of being is precluded by the symbolic order, which allows its functioning only through the displaced object. But this attachment to the matrix of life constitutes an original horizon of sense that is necessary and that presents a clear maternal lineage.

Going beyond the masculine symbolic, this capacity engenders, moreover, an alternative form of signification. I said that fixation implies substitution, but substitution here does not mean exchanging something *for* something else. This substitution is also "restitution," for we never replace "the mother with something *other* from her." But how is it possible? Don't we reach a sort of impasse where the presence of the original blocks any growth, any change? Muraro argues that the mother has a "symbolic predisposition" to substitution as any "woman can become mother or not, and, in any case, always remains the daughter of her mother, so that any natural mother is already a substitute."[44] Hence the maternal symbolic takes the form of a plane in which the symbolic order represents only a regional area ruled by deterministic (phallocentric) sets of laws. The plane instead is the immanent field of possibilities of the phenomenal world. The difficulty in conceptualizing it, Muraro argues, "can be solved if we manage to think 'a substitution without substitutes' for the mother in agreement with the structure of the maternal continuum. This is possible because a 'substitution without substitutes' exists: it is the language we speak." Here words, she continues, "do not substitute for other words. Certainly they 'substitute' for things, but without putting anything in their place."[45]

The famous opposition between metaphor and metonymy that Muraro rethinks in her work *Maglia o uncinetto* (1998) better illustrates this point.[46] The masculine symbolic order organizes its field and ensures coherence through analogies, through resemblances among different objects that refer back to a common denominator: the phallus. So substitution here means the return of the same (the phallus). The variants that grow in the maternal contínuum, on the other hand, follow a different logic, one that is marked by its sexual constituency. The woman's relation to her sexual organs underscores the importance of interiority and contiguity—the lips of the vagina being here the primal referent. Metonym, in fact, follows "dynamics of the near and not of the proper, movements coming from the quasi contact between two unities hardly definable as such."[47] Metonym brings together what is close, thus expressing relations, vicinities among things or facts that happen to be already there. Metonym, thus, provides a more open and differential economy, which is horizontal and contingent. This is why fixation qua substitution-restitution is compared to language, for it represents the deployment of what Ferdinand de Saussure conceived of as a linguistic system: an infinite syntagmatic field of associations *in presentia*.

Within this phenomenal plane, subjectification bears no nostalgia for an original, because that *origin* is already inscribed in the fabric that sustains its form of life. Where psychoanalysis saw an empty whole, the blind spot of subjectivity, feminism discovers infinite fullness: the diagram of maternal fullness. Psychoanalysis in fact constructs the idea of the sayable, of what can be determined or better signified, basing its configuration on the inaccessibility of the symbolic order, the barred subject, and so on. But beyond this limited field, there stands also truth (and Lacan acknowledged it) with its indeterminate configuration. Yet, this duality cannot be reconciled as we can look at truth only from the point of view of the symbolic. Feminism instead turns the argument around and discovers a differential consistency that gives back a material and expansive dimension of being where nothing is lost.

In this perspective the figure of the hysteric changes radically. Hysteria is not simply the typical female masquerade behind which one finds the inconsistency of a positive subject. This fundamental gap actually shows how the hysteric is tied to the Other, her object of love, "as nourishment of her own feeling."[48] This Other is the mother. Yet being too close to her, the hysteric refuses any substitution. In other words, she does not recognize "that the substitution is restitution."[49] The cure for this extreme case of fixation consists precisely in language. The *talking cure* developed by psychoanalysis, and its successive adoption among feminists through consciousness-raising meetings—in Italian *presa di coscienza e di parola*—was a means to practice a relationality between women beyond the masculine occlusion. It offered a way of being together that was communal and differential like speech. This is the true meaning of the symbolic maternal order: not a limitation but a possibility to populate being, not simply a theory to give form to a socio-symbolic configuration for women but its actual creative transformation as a living dimension. In conclusion, in the context of the patriarchal society, the maternal symbolic defined a political practice that dialectically turned what looked like a cause of oppression into a source of authority and strength.

POST-FORDIST PSYCHOPATHOLOGY, IDA DOMINIJANNI, AND THE PROBLEM OF INTERNAL ROTATION

The rise of post-Fordism brought forward new dynamics that put into question some of the principles of the theory of the maternal symbolic. The economic and the symbolic order usually go hand in hand, and this is all the more true today when the hegemony of a neoliberal ideology coexists with the faltering of the law of the father and its symbolic order. The two are not disconnected. Just as the symbolic order of the father, with its privileges and interdictions, melts into thin air, society too loses its traditional vertical structures and customary norms. Similarly, in post-Fordist production we experience a destructuring of the organization of work that produce zones of indistinguishability. Consider, for instance, the unification of labor place and living space, the indiscernibility between labor time and nonlabor time or between consumption and production, and the dissolving of a standard of measurement to remunerate immaterial work.[50]

Our experiential dimension of life changes drastically as well. Think of the vast and always new choice of products available on the market and how consumerism solicits countless modes of self-realizations, lifestyles, and so on. This technical use of pleasure is embedded in the very being of the modern individual and constructs life as a boundless, but private and serialized, field of experience. The chief consequence here is that the notion of desire has now collapsed in the function of enjoyment, which is private, repetitive, and excessive as the subject disposes of the object of pleasure precisely as a thing.[51] This is the libidinal face of post-Fordism; this is the lucrative disorder of the society of enjoyment. In the lack of measure of post-Fordism we perceive the thriving of an animalized form of jouissance, one that is caught in an obsessive circulation due to the lack of a symbolic intervention.

What happens to the thought of sexual difference in this context? This is a tough question because the core of the theory of the maternal symbolic was elaborated in the wake of the patriarchal discourse and did not directly assess the techniques of power at work in post-Fordism. The problem is that these new economic mechanisms also seem to reflect in a distorted way some tenets of sexual difference. As Ida Dominijanni rightfully pointed out, the maternal symbolic cannot be thought as something monolithic; there is always a *negative* residuum that escapes and that the maternal symbolic "needs to continuously reelaborate and rework" (chapter 7 in this volume). The positive expression of the maternal does not erase the presence of what she calls "an imprint . . . an *impression* of the constantly returning origin," and thus complicates the primary relationship with the matrix of life and desire (chapter 7 in this volume). For one of the astonishing results of the affirmation of the theory of sexual difference is that woman's sexuality has progressively desexualized itself. Paradoxically, she argues, "the more the mother became a sexed figure of origin, of female speech and authority, the more her sexuality vanished" (chapter 7 in this volume).

The question we need to ask is: what happened to the relation with the Other under post-Fordist biopolitical control of the masses? The eclipse of desire in favor of enjoyment and its compulsive pattern of repetition points toward the category of fixation that was central in Muraro's analysis. Dominijanni gestures toward this issue when acknowledging that in post-Fordism a shift occurs from the centrality of the hysteric figure to that of the anorexic. In her view, it is now the anorexic who bears testimony to a general disorder in our processes of symbolization. As she notes: "If hysteria is the symptom that accompanied women's entry into modernity and which feminism responded to politically, anorexia can then be seen as not only the symptom of a female resistance to a hedonistic and consumerist postmodernity, but also as an unforeseen and paradoxical effect of ... the feminist symbolic revolution" (chapter 7 in this volume). In what sense is anorexia replacing the hysteric position? Hysteria is tied to modernity as the latter is defined by the patriarchal order, where the absolute transparency and consistency of phallocentrism begins to falter but still keeps society under control. As we said, through the masquerade, women registered and gave form to the ontological reality of a saturated attachment to the mother as the object of love. Based on a strict exclusionary principle of order, the patriarchal order did not allow such dissent and thus forbid these comportments. In its extreme pathological form, hysteria is a neurosis caused by interdiction.

This symptom cannot hold sway in today's society of enjoyment, whose salient features are narratives that command systematic satisfaction instead of injunctions to defer and repress desires. In such a context, individuals are pushed to realize themselves under the command of enjoyment, thus following patterns that are properly psychotic. In psychosis, in fact, the subject's responses and actions are literally absorbed by the pressure of the Real, for the symbolic has lost its morphological capacity to structure reality. The postmodern individual thus lives in a hallucinatory dimension, where these hallucinations are manifestations of the Real. As Massimo Recalcati affirms, if in neurosis one can detect "a symbolic return of the Real repressed through the apparatuses of the subconscious, in psychosis there is a symbolic collapse and a return to the Real as such, without any symbolic mediation."[52] Hence the fixation, the compulsive repetition typical of psychosis.

The anorexic girl (but the same holds for the male) is caught in this psychotic loop, only she projects it onto her body. Dominijanni argues that the anorexic is confronted by an overwhelming presence that she identifies with the figure of the mother: "the desexualized body of the anorexic" refuses the talking cure that was so effective with hysteria and "presents itself as an identitarian given, a nonsymbolizable return of the real" (chapter 7 in this volume).[53] This residuum resists symbolization and seems to produce "discontinuity from the maternal, a female difference from the mother to which space and meaning should be given" (chapter 7 in this volume). It is in this conflicting relation with origin that we catch a glimpse of the heuristic potentiality of the anorexic in post-Fordist psychopathology. On the one hand, she is the result of decades of struggles in which sexual difference wrestled its spaces of affirmation out of the masculine foreclosure. On the other, with her mute protest she also crops out the criticalities of the maternal continuum in the context of post-Fordist dismeasure. The anorexic embodies a more critical position than other common psychotic figures of our time such as, for instance, the cocaine addict or the workaholic. Perfectly functional to the post-Fordist imperative of performance and self-entrepreneurship, both those figures enthusiastically commit themselves to the pattern of reiteration while they dissipate and exhaust their being. On the contrary, the anorexic nightmare of the disciplinary control over the body implies sufferance and pain. These are evidences of a stubborn refusal; they are markers of an implicit unruliness to the injunction of enjoyment.

If we look at the anorexic from a slightly different angle, beyond the return of the Real qua mother, we also perceive a dangerous attack to the category of *fixation* as an organizing principle. The circularity of the substitution-restitution seems saturated by a movement that lost its capacity of mediation/innovation. But isn't this blockage again a symptom of the socioeconomic transformations of post-Fordism? Isn't this the effect of the technical organization of excess produced by immaterial work? In effect, a post-Fordist society does not need a coherent structure of reference. Its key words are: deregulation, decentralization, flexibility but also social cooperation in the guise of network-based production. Thus neoliberalism recognizes the openness of the field and controls it horizontally and molecularly, from the inside of the very individuals that populate it. Through a compulsive reiteration to work and consume more psychotic comportments proliferate that internalize this form of control as former restrictions or limitations—among which basic social rights typical of a liberal democracy—are progressively dissolved.

So psychosis is not an individual pathology: it is the whole socioeconomic infrastructure that organizes it. Consider, for example, a common trait of our life: *self-exploitation*. This phenomenon is tied to the passage from the Fordist figure of the wage-worker to the post-Fordist notion of human capital and immaterial labor. Here, the worker—leaving behind rights and the infrastructure guaranteeing personal social services—is supposed to prosper in the market by realizing her or his full potentiality.[54] As Andrea Fumagalli notes, "The self-employed worker subsumes wage laborer and entrepreneur: his remuneration is strictly dependent on the self-exploitation of his or her laboring skills and the negotiating power that the latter has on the market."⁵⁵ Be it a lucky and prosperous enterprise or a less fortunate one, one that struggles daily with precarious incomes, the self-employed worker needs continuously to invest in herself or himself by developing skills, knowledge, capacities as if they were economic assets. Alienation here seems to disappear as the worker comes into being precisely by profiting from her or his own valorization. Yet this also means that labor becomes indistinguishable from nonlabor, from life. Obviously this merging engenders an inexhaustible dynamism, an excess. Post-Fordism feeds on this excess and cannibalizes it by inciting laboring practices that it ultimately expropriates—and the financialization of the real economy (its speculation and cyclical crisis) is but the most blatant example.⁵⁶ Thus self-realization blurs into mere survival; efficiency and performance lead to the dissolution of bodily and mental energies. Therein the immaterial laborer assumes onto herself or himself an unlimited form of command that follows a psychotic behavior.

Neoliberalism foments and disciplines our present dismeasure and disaggregation, producing a final form of dissipation that impacts the human, but also the social and certainly the ecological life of the planet—if we consider our pending environmental catastrophe. Thus the anorexic represents both the effect and the critique of these short-circuits. In other words, she is a *symptom*. In her challenge, one can detect the contours of a future "subject of difference that emerges—not by accident—with the decline of the identitarian subject, accelerat[ing] the deconstruction and crisis of the latter without nihilistic or auto-annihilating results."⁵⁷

In this sense, Dominijanni tries to create a new turn to the thought of sexual difference, one that echoes Esposito's idea of a *rotation*. After the reactivation of the fault line of the plane of life through a critical elaboration—in our case the maternal symbolic—one must work on its "internal rotation," turning it "from a defense barrier against the outside to a process of differential transformation of the very subjects it identifies."⁵⁸ Hence if Muraro, especially in her *L'ordine simbolico della madre*, deploys sexual difference through the recovery of the fullness of the maternal continuum, in the society of enjoyment the latter must undergo a new torsion, one in which fullness assumes its radically differential and self-reflexive premises. This implies reinforcing the idea that sexual difference is to be conceived as a productive practice that gets resignified in the collective dimension of today's society. In addition, the chain of substitution-restitution must reinvigorate its circulatory and generative capacity, avoiding relapses in a saturated restitution of the mother while simultaneously creating order.

As we said, post-Fordism exploits the excess of social cooperation intensively and internally, for it works through the psychotic drive to a self-consuming recursivity. The problem is to give measure to the immeasurable respecting its ethic, in other words finding a distribution that connects two sides of the same question: the finite of singularity and the infinite spectrum of its variation. This would be the eternally contingent and historically concrete *fixture* of a new concept of *fixation*. This is why Dominijanni warns that the real *concrete* mother, the source of love but also conflict and pain, will never be completely subsumed by the maternal continuum. It is important to keep that singular person in front of us and continue to interrogate and renegotiate our specific relationship with her. This emphasis on the concrete, historical condition of the maternal is also a response to the desexualization of the mother. Hence Dominijanni urges us to take into account the father as well. What is the economy of desire that relates him to the mother and the daughter? How do we resignify these relationships in the context of the faltering of patriarchal figures of power?

At a theoretical level the materiality of sexual difference must be safeguarded as well. Hence sexual difference must play itself out so that its *undecidable* nature, its being an *imprint* more than a symbol, as Dominijanni notes, becomes a reflexive supplement. Somewhere Lacan said that the unconscious lives in the temporality of the *not yet*. The interval between the now of the symptom, its origin and its meaning, allows us to dispose of it as a manifestation, as an always looming possibility for the emergence of a singularity. Doesn't this virtual dimension offer the most productive way to think about the presentness of origin in our life, to project the constituent capacity of beginning into the architectonic of the now? This is the sort of reflective difference that Dominijanni calls "Venus's strabismus." Hence we should "keep a sort of cross-eyed view on the present, both on the best and the worst of our present," because this distorted perspective "can preserve us from delusions of omnipotence and from considering female freedom as a progressive or definitive conquest, which is not subject, as it indeed is, to counterthrusts, backlashes, regressions."[59]

This is a good methodological tip. It is an example of *good* dialectic, one that men should entertain as well as they discuss how to renegotiate their masculinity and their desire in light of the decay of the symbolic order and the rise of psychotic forms of enjoyment. Men too should begin by recognizing the distinguishing traits of their symptomatology. And while performing this analytical work, we should all remember the structural connection that binds the symbolic to the economic: men and women alike. If, in fact, contemporary capitalism puts to work our *bios*—that is, our corporeal and psychic dimension—it is there that political practices should uncover the potentials for tomorrow's decisive conflicts. I believe the key question that still remains open for both sexes is how to overturn the biopolitical ordering of excess in our society. In other words, how to reappropriate the potentiality of dismeasure, developing the promises of freedom it lodges. It is, once again, the old Marxist question of how to turn forms of vassalage into triggers of liberation.

NOTES

This is a revised version of "Origin and Dismeasure: The Thought of Sexual Difference in Luisa Muraro and Ida Dominijanni, and the Rise of Post-Fordist Psychopathology," originally published in *ResPublica: Revista de Pensamiento Politico* 29 (2013): 35–56.

1. Roberto Esposito, *Living Thought: The Origins and Actuality of Italian Philosophy*, trans. Zakiya Hanafi (Stanford, Calif.: Stanford University Press, 2012), 7.
2. Esposito, *Living Thought*, 258.
3. Today's centrality of life creates that paradoxical temporality at work in any evolutionary theory for which ideas elaborated in a distant past can be fully comprehended only in the now. Far from being a teleological ratio, this means that residues of the past acquire relevance for us in our act of interrogating them from our present condition. On the causes behind the turn to life see Antonio Negri, "The Labor of the Multitude and the Fabric of Biopolitics," *Mediations* 2 (2008): 8–25; Andrea Righi, *Biopolitics and Social Change in Italy: From Gramsci to Pasolini to Negri* (New York: Palgrave Macmillan, 2011); and Paolo Virno, *A Grammar of the Multitude*, trans. Isabella Bertoletti, James Cascaito, and Andrea Casson (New York: Semiotext[e], 2004).
4. The weight of tradition and the typical Crocean approach to culture force Italian philosophy departments to work almost exclusively on the history of philosophy. In this sense, the prominence of life and the thought it generates can be innovative only insofar as this perspective maintains a clear non-idealistic direction. That is, if it does not fall into the trap of constructing a positive (laudatory)

representation and instead stares at the different material developments that are produced. Thus, in drawing a genealogy of living-thought, one must also be keen to foreground its reactionary degenerations. Consider, for instance, the group of intellectuals gathered around Strapaese who played a key cultural (and political) role during fascism as it constituted a strong, unitary image of Italianness built on autochthony, local folklore, and mostly violence. If one examines the editorials that Mino Maccari wrote for the magazine *Il selvaggio* (the herald of the Strapaese group) or other writings by Giovanni Papini, it becomes clear how their similar attention to nature gave rise to a pure masculine affirmation of the right of force and violence in every ambit of life. It is in fact paramount to explore the power dynamics and the social conflicts that lie behind any presumably atemporal, ahistorical return to the centrality of nature. See Andrea Righi, *Italian Reactionary Thought and Critical Theory: An Inquiry into Savage Modernities* (New York: Palgrave Macmillan, 2015).

5. See Massimo Donà, "Immunity and Negation: On Possible Developments of the Theses Outlined in Roberto Esposito's *Immunitas*," *Diacritics* 36, no. 2 (2006): 57–69.

6. As Ida Dominijanni argues, if "what a woman suffers from is being put into the world without a symbolic placement," the political task becomes "speaking her sexual difference and giving it social existence." See her "Radicality and Asceticism," in *Italian Feminist Thought: A Reader*, ed. Paola Bono and Sandra Kemp (Cambridge: Basil Blackwell, 1991), 129.

7. Esposito, *Living Thought*, 261.

8. See Todd McGowan, *The End of Dissatisfaction? Jacques Lacan and the Emerging Society of Enjoyment* (Albany: State University of New York Press, 2004).

9. Mina Davis Caulfield, "Sexuality in Human Evolution: What Is Natural in Sex?" *Feminist Studies* 2 (1985): 344–45.

10. Donna Haraway, "Animal Sociology and a Natural Economy of the Body Politic, Part I: A Political Physiology of Dominance," *Signs: Journal of Women in Culture and Society* 1 (1978): 26. See also the second part of the article, "Animal Sociology and a Natural Economy of the Body Politic, Part II: The Past Is the Contested Zone: Human Nature and Theories of Production and Reproduction in Primate," *Signs: Journal of Women in Culture and Society* 2, no. 1 (1978): 37–60.

11. Silvia Vegetti Finzi, "L'animale femminile," in *Verso il luogo delle origini*, ed. Centro Documentazione Donna di Firenze (Milan: La Tartaruga edizioni, 1992), 56. From here on all translations from Italian are mine.

12. Slavoj Žižek, *Interrogating the Real* (London: Continuum, 2006), 73.

13. Žižek, *Interrogating the Real*, 99; this is also what John Bellamy Foster calls Marx's logic of emergence of Darwinism. See *Marx's Ecology: Materialism and Nature* (New York: Monthly Review Press, 2000), 230–36.

14. Caulfield, "Sexuality in Human Evolution," 353.

15. Slavoj Žižek, *Organs without Bodies: On Deleuze and Consequences* (New York: Routledge, 2004), 141. In a recent writing on this matter, Žižek further clarifies this point stating that in the derailment of sexuality, the latter "changed in its very substance: it is no longer the instinctual drive to reproduce, but a drive that gets thwarted as to its natural goal (reproduction) and thereby explodes into an infinite, properly meta-physical, passion." This is how "culture retroactively posits/transforms its own natural presupposition" and "denaturalizes nature itself." Žižek, "Hegel, Sex, and Marriage," *Lacanian Ink*, no. 37 (2011): 113–14.
16. Adriana Cavarero, "Thinking Difference," *Symposium*, no. 2 (1995): 126.
17. Luce Irigaray, *Speculum of the Other Woman*, trans. Gillian C. Gill (Ithaca, N.Y.: Cornell University Press, 1985), 33.
18. Cavarero, "Thinking Difference," 125.
19. Slavoj Žižek, *Metastases of Enjoyment: Six Essays on Woman and Causality* (London: Verso, 1994), 173.
20. Žižek, *Metastases of Enjoyment*, 108.
21. Žizek, *Organs without Bodies*, 142–43.
22. Žižek, *Metastases of Enjoyment*, 105. See, for instance, Toril Moi, "From Femininity to Finitude: Freud, Lacan, and Feminism, Again," *Signs: Journal of Women in Culture and Society* 3 (2004): 841–78.
23. Žižek, *Metastases of Enjoyment*, 33.
24. See François Regnault, "Introduction to *Encore*," *Lacanian Ink*, no. 37 (2011): 47–55; Ellie Ragland, *The Logic of Sexuation: From Aristotle to Lacan* (Albany: State University of New York Press, 2004).
25. This is also one of the main points in which post-Lacanian feminism departs from the current developments of Lacanian thought, thus superseding it. For psychoanalysis the prohibition of the Thing, which, coincidentally, is also the Maternal Thing, is the unavoidable mechanism that gives access to the symbolic field. See Massimo Recalcati, *Il complesso di Telemaco: Genitori e figli dopo il tramonto del padre* (Milan: Feltrinelli, 2013).
26. Žižek, *Metastases of Enjoyment*, 177.
27. Žižek, *Metastases of Enjoyment*, 128.
28. Žižek, *Metastases of Enjoyment*, 178.
29. Jacques Lacan, *On Feminine Sexuality: The Limits of Love and Knowledge* (New York: W. W. Norton, 1999), 80.
30. Žižek, *Metastases of Enjoyment*, 173.
31. Lacan, *On Feminine Sexuality*, 81.
32. Yong Wang makes a similar argument with reference to social system in "Agency: The Internal Split of Structure," *Sociological Forum*, no. 3 (2008): 481–502.
33. Lacan, *On Feminine Sexuality*, 81.
34. Žižek, *Metastases of Enjoyment*, 151.
35. Ragland, *The Logic of Sexuation*, 183.

36. Ragland, *The Logic of Sexuation*, 182.
37. Žižek, *Interrogating the Real*, 65.
38. Ida Dominjianni, "L'eccedenza della libertà femminile," *Motivi della libertà* (Milan: Franco Angeli, 2001), 50, 52.
39. Luisa Muraro, *The Symbolic Order of the Mother*, trans. Francesca Novello (Albany: State University of New York Press, 2018), 40.
40. Muraro, *The Symbolic Order of the Mother*, 43.
41. Muraro, *The Symbolic Order of the Mother*, 41.
42. Lacan, *On Feminine Sexuality*, 103.
43. Muraro, *The Symbolic Order of the Mother*, 53.
44. Muraro, *The Symbolic Order of the Mother*, 52.
45. Muraro, *The Symbolic Order of the Mother*, 59.
46. See Luisa Muraro, *Maglia o uncinetto: Racconto linguistico-politico sulla inimicizia tra metafora e metonimia* (Rome: Manifestolibri, 1998).
47. Irigaray, *Speculum of the Other Woman*, 111.
48. Muraro, *The Symbolic Order of the Mother*, 56.
49. Muraro, *The Symbolic Order of the Mother*, 59 [modified].
50. Immaterial work implies the employment of all aspects of one's personality and thus escapes the quantitative measurement used under Fordism: wage labor. Here one can see the two side of the problem: on the one hand the force and creativity of the new laborer, on the other the fact that the limited and exploitative dimension of wage labor constitutes the only safeguard against her or his starvation.
51. See Jodi Dean, *Blog Theory: Feedback and Capture in the Circuits of Drive* (Malden, Mass.: Polity, 2010) Massimo Recalcati, *L'uomo senza inconscio: Figure della nuova clinica psicoanalitica* (Milan: Raffaello Cortina Editore, 2010) and *Forme contemporanee del totalitarismo* (Turin: Bollati Boringhieri, 2007).
52. Recalcati, *L'uomo senza inconscio*, 16.
53. On the clinical significance of the anorexic see also Massimo Recalcati, *Elogio del fallimento: Conversazioni su anoressie e disagio della giovinezza* (Trento: Edizioni Erikson, 2011).
54. See Michel Foucault, *The Birth of Biopolitics: Lectures at the Collège de France 1978–1979*, trans. Graham Burchell (New York: Palgrave Macmillan, 2008), 229. I discuss the issue of self-exploitation in more detail in "The Ontological Experience of Absolute Presence: Sebastiano Timpanaro and the Groundwork for a Critique of Late Hyper-Idealism," *Annali d'Italianistica*, no. 32 (2014): 515–20.
55. Andrea Fumagalli, *Bioeconomia e capitalismo cognitivo: Verso un nuovo paradigma di accomulazione* (Rome: Carocci, 2007), 142.
56. See Andrea Fumagalli, ed., *Crisis in the Global Economy: Financial Markets, Social Struggles, and New Political Scenarios* (Los Angeles: Semiotext(e), 2010). On the exploitative dimension of immaterial labor in itself see Matteo Pasquinelli,

Animal Spirits: A Bestiary of the Commons (Rotterdam: NAi Publishers/Institute of Network Cultures, 2008).

57. Ida Dominjianni, "Heiresses at Twilight," *the commoner*, no. 11 (2006): 102.

58. Esposito, *Living Thought*, 261.

59. Dominjianni, "Venus's Strabismus: Looking at the Crisis of Politics from the Politics of Difference," *Iris*, no. 2 (2010): 182.

Mother Degree Zero; or, Of Beginnings

An Afterword on Luisa Muraro's Feminist Inaptitude for Philosophy

CESARE CASARINO

It is perhaps because to think about the mother is to think about beginnings that beginning to write about the mother is especially difficult. Everything begins for us with the mother, after all, and the mother, thus, turns beginning into a problem for thought.

It is not a coincidence that in the extraordinary first chapter of *The Symbolic Order of the Mother*—titled "The Difficulty of Beginning"—Luisa Muraro grapples with this difficulty head-on: the difficulty of beginning to write anything at all.[1] "I wanted to write concerning a topic about which it seemed to me I had both something to say and the desire [*voglia*] to say it, but I was not able to begin," she explains in the opening sentence.[2] The decision itself to begin writing has the effect of "throwing" her "thoughts into disarray [*disordine*]," "so that"—she continues—"I find myself struggling among different choices, uncertain about how to proceed, easy prey to the most unpredictable changes of mind, and forced, hence, to begin all over again several times and to go on amid a thousand uncertainties."[3] And, finally, she concludes the first page thus: "This piece of writing would not have been an exception; only that, this time, thinking and rethinking, from one change of mind to another, the starting point became precisely this, namely, to interrogate the difficulty of jump-starting and bringing to completion an endeavor made of words."[4] Starting with this interrogation, the rest of the first chapter of *The Symbolic Order of the Mother* unfolds like a bildungsroman of sorts, as Muraro recounts and reflects on her difficult apprenticeship in philosophy.

The following pages may be thought of as a commentary on this bildungsroman, as notes on the margins of this admirably self-reflexive, candid, and courageous document that is not afraid of running the risk of falling into and even drowning in the quicksands of the confessional the better to bear witness to the difficulty of thinking and writing. In this afterword—as a way of providing an open-ended, provisional, inconclusive conclusion to *Another Mother*—I will focus on the first chapter of *The Symbolic Order of the Mother*: I will follow, encapsulate, and dwell upon the main episodes of the apprenticeship that took Muraro in, through, and, ultimately, outside philosophy altogether. I will assume basic knowledge and understanding of Muraro's theory of the maternal symbolic, which the previous chapters of this volume have articulated as well as engaged and grappled with: rather than reiterating, explicating, defending, or refuting, I am primarily concerned here with learning from Muraro in order to rethink the question of beginnings in and for philosophy.

If Muraro's apprenticeship in philosophy was difficult, that was due precisely to the problem of beginnings: it was to find a solution to this problem that the young Muraro turned to the study of philosophy in the first place. Muraro tells us that she turned to philosophy in search of not merely any kind of beginning but specifically a logical beginning. "If I must say not just anything but that which demands to be said by me, then I shall have to proceed logically, and the beginning of a work whose property it is to be logical shall have to be logical in turn. Such a beginning, in other words, shall have to be a beginning not only de facto but also de jure, so that nothing essential may be presupposed to it and so that everything shall have to follow in its wake, effortlessly."[5] Such a beginning—Muraro reasoned—would create a seamless agreement and perfect correspondence between her, the things that demanded to be said by her, and the words that she used to say them, thereby dispelling all those doubts, uncertainties, and hesitations that plagued her as soon as she had decided to start writing. Hence philosophy: all great philosophers articulated, exemplified, and made a wonderful display of such beginnings in their works, and, further, it seemed as if the primary aim of philosophy itself was to teach the lesson of the fundamental—indeed, foundational—importance of a logical beginning. And yet the lesson did not take, the student did not learn, the doubts remained, the student continued to struggle. . . . Was there something wrong with the lesson, or with the student, or both? It seems to me that Muraro's answer to this question is: both, yet neither. It was not so much that there was something wrong both with the lesson and with the student—there was, but that was not the point. More importantly, neither was the lesson relevant for the student, nor did the student have any aptitude for the lesson. I will return to this missed encounter and relating nonrelation between lesson and student that I call *inaptitude*. For the moment, I want to focus first on the fact that such a missed encounter does not explain the student's prolonged and abiding attraction, devotion, attachment to philosophy: a frustrating and damaging cathexis, after all, still constitutes an expression of desire, still holds an unfulfilled promise. What was, what is, the promise—indeed, the lure—of philosophy?

It is this promise, this lure, and, most importantly, the breaking of its spell, that occupy Muraro in her first chapter. Zigzagging her way to and fro in the history of Western philosophy, indifferent to scholarly etiquette such as chronology or boundaries (e.g., the boundaries of the classical branches of metaphysics), Muraro brushes past G. W. F. Hegel (the *Science of Logic* and the *Encyclopedia*, from which the title of her first chapter is taken),[6] John Locke (*An Essay Concerning Human Understanding*), Plato (Book VII of the *Republic*), Parmenides, and, above all, Edmund Husserl (*The Crisis of European Sciences*) and René Descartes (*Discourse on Method* and *Meditations on First Philosophy*), noting the high premium they all place on a logical beginning understood as first principle, and examining the two prime metaphors for such a beginning (i.e., beginning as germ and beginning as foundation, both indicating that philosophy develops from within itself and builds on itself, ex nihilo). Their vast differences notwithstanding, all these philosophers—according to Muraro—share in positing a logical beginning by oversimplifying the starting point to the highest degree and by subtracting or eliminating *tout court* most of that which is there where and when one starts to philosophize: philosophers never start from that there, which is nothing other than "given reality"—and this is justified by alleging that reality is often deceptive and is hence the locus of falsehoods of all sorts, and by arguing that in order to be logical a beginning must not contain anything that may be false, lest it invalidate the ensuing philosophical construction. In short, philosophy teaches that to philosophize one has first to bracket off everything that is "normally present."[7] Muraro writes: "It seems to me that the entire history of Western philosophy transmits this lure: it's a promise of joyous rapture, of elevation above everything and everybody."[8] Clearly, this is the lure of transcendence—and this lure attracted her, fascinated her, and kept her firmly under its spell, even though it did not bear the desired fruits.

In the midst of such reflections, Muraro tells us a story of her student days at the University of Leuven. She was undecided between studying logic and studying linguistics, eventually chose the latter, and—after several months of eager and intense research—presented her work to a linguist, who seemed perplexed by what she had produced. His laconic comment was: "You should start from the most recent literatures; you can always go back and look at the beginnings later, if necessary."[9] For a student who had spent months studying exclusively Ferdinand de Saussure—convinced that if she started from the very beginning she would not only understand but also automatically know all the rest—these words were nothing short than a thunderbolt, as they flew in the face of a firmly held conviction that had seemed obvious up until that point. But what disconcerted Muraro even more was the—at first very faint—intuition of just how right these words were, far more than her teacher could have imagined, as they revealed the nature of her impasse: "I start from the beginning because I don't know how to start from where I am, and that is so because I am nowhere."[10] Muraro does not tell us what this condition of being nowhere entails. It is not far-fetched, however, to hear resonating implicitly in this poignant sentence a formulation Muraro uses repeatedly throughout *The Symbolic Order of the Mother*, namely, "symbolic disorder" [*disordine simbolico*, also translatable as "symbolic confusion" or "symbolic disarray"]: for Muraro, this formulation perfectly captures and expresses the condition par excellence of women within patriarchy.

Importantly, it is when Muraro distills the moral from this student-days story that the mother makes her first appearance in the entire book:

As it is often the case, what attracted me and what blocked me was the same thing in the end. I was attracted to philosophy because I wanted to achieve symbolic independence from given reality. I did not want my mind to be at the mercy of contingent and unforeseen events. But I was not able to achieve this goal because the philosophy that was able to provide me with shelter from the capricious sway of the real was at the same time—as I would finally understand—the very philosophy that turned me against my mother, whose work I judged, implicitly, to be badly made, deformed. I wanted to go to the very beginning of things in order to understand and to understand myself, and instead I was going against my mother.[11]

Elsewhere, Muraro defines "symbolic independence" as, "roughly, the ability to say 'I' even when, materially, I am a we or an impersonal entity"—adding that she sought such "symbolic independence" in philosophy as a "remedy to her symbolic disorder," without knowing she was doing so and without being able to find it.[12] As Ida Dominijanni astutely points out in an essay included in this volume—"The Contact Word"—the crucial intuition of Italian feminism in the 1970s was that "the feminine condition is marked more by symbolic than social misery," or, in other words, that what women lacked was "not prostheses so as to resemble men" and that what they needed, rather, was "the words to express themselves starting from their selves instead of from a male imaginary" (chapter 1 in this volume). Expressing oneself with words that start from oneself is implicitly posited by Dominijanni as the beginning of a solution to the problem of symbolic misery and hence, presumably, as the beginning of "symbolic independence." What Muraro makes clear in the passage quoted above, however, is that to begin an "endeavor of words" starting from oneself—that is, starting from the most immediate given reality—cannot constitute "symbolic independence" for the simple reason that the latter is the hallmark of a male imaginary whose foundation is the parthenogenetic fantasy of eliminating given reality and its intrinsic element of contingency from any starting point whatsoever. Put differently, Muraro's symbolic misery consisted precisely in her desire for symbolic independence from given reality: far from one constituting the solution to the other, symbolic independence and symbolic misery are one and the same. Suddenly to insert the mother here—

at this point in her story and in her argument—is tantamount to throwing a wrench into the machine of the male imaginary: the mother breaks this tautological merry-go-round (in which running away from symbolic misery and running after symbolic independence only brings one back to the starting point) and radically reconfigures both independence and the symbolic, by positing the former (i.e., independence) not at all as the opposite but as the explicit acknowledgment and affirmation of a presupposed, insurmountable, and everlasting dependence on given reality, and by positing the latter (i.e., the symbolic) as being constituted in and through such a dependence in the first place. The appearance of the mother at this point in the chapter has the effect and the function of showing that what the male imaginary construes as symbolic independence is nothing other than symbolic dependence and, indeed, symbolic debt. (Here, it is important to reiterate that, as Andrea Righi and I pointed out in the introduction to this volume, "mother" in Muraro is always a relational concept: put differently, Muraro implicitly posits dependence and debt as constitutive of social relations.)

The male imaginary and its fantasies, however, are not really Muraro's concern here and throughout *The Symbolic Order of the Mother*. Indeed, one of the most striking and symptomatic features of this book is its relative indifference to the male imaginary, including an indifference to producing a critique of it. Continuing to draw the moral of her story, Muraro explains, in fact, that going against the mother was not exactly what philosophy taught her but was nonetheless what she learned from philosophy: hostility toward the mother was the meaning that doing philosophy had taken on for her. Muraro writes:

> The reason for this is that, without my being aware of it, there was within me an obscure aversion to the author [*autrice*] of my life—an aversion that philosophy managed to revive. Philosophy and that obscure sentiment came to form a vicious circle. The more I sought symbolic independence, the more my uneasiness, awe, and fear of given reality grew. It is likely that my first inclination toward philosophy was not innocent. It is likely that from the very start I was driven unknowingly by a will to invalidate maternal authority and maternal work. . . . The vicious circle . . . found its point of closure precisely on this deformed figure of the mother. I felt and acted as if the woman who had brought me into the world was the enemy of my

symbolic independence and as if such independence would entail necessarily my separation from her and her very end. This way of thinking is common to many women.[13]

Notably, the fact that this way of thinking is common also to many men and is constitutive of the male imaginary is not what is at stake here. Undoubtedly—Muraro points out—the history of Western philosophy, much like the entire culture of which it is integral part, may be understood as an incessant attempt to invalidate the mother and as the manifestation of a profound rivalry with the authority and the work of the mother. Muraro notes, for example, how Plato's allegory of the cave functions as metaphor of a second birth (i.e., a birth from the cave into a world explicitly governed by a political conception of justice and of truth that wishes to supersede and to substitute itself for another symbolic order that Plato calls the realm of generation and presents as intrinsically unjust and deceitful); further, Muraro notes how this metaphor exerts a profound influence on ancient, medieval, and modern thought, including on the phenomenological *epoché*. Here, Muraro returns to some of the central concerns of her earlier *To Knit or to Crochet? A Political-Linguistic Tale on the Enmity between Metaphor and Metonymy* by remarking on how this process of invalidation of the mother is hardly distinguishable from the process of metaphorization itself: in both cases "this process consists of transferring the attributes of the work and power [*potenza*] of the mother to cultural production (such as science, law, religion, etc.), thereby stripping and reducing her to opaque and deformed nature above which the subject (of knowledge, of law, of belief, etc.) must rise himself so as to dominate her."[14] Muraro continues: "I see now that the realm of generation and the natural world which philosophers talk about is not nature at all—whether good or bad nature, ordered or chaotic nature; it is, rather, the possibility of another symbolic order that does not strip the mother of her qualities."[15] The debt Muraro owes to Luce Irigaray's critique of phallogocentrism in the history of Western philosophy is evident in these passages, and this is a debt Muraro acknowledges here and elsewhere.[16] But—and here lies one of the most important differences between Muraro and Irigaray—such a critique is for Muraro at once accurate to some degree, necessary to some extent, yet altogether beside the point. *The Symbolic Order of the Mother* is not a work of critique.[17]

The critique of philosophy serves as the steppingstone for another and more important project, which eventually revises such a critique by turning it on its head.[18] Muraro writes: "I run the risk of redoing against philosophy what I did against my mother, imputing to her as a lack that which she cannot be and as an excess that which she cannot not be, so as to rise above my own lacks and my own excesses. And I run the risk also of being cursed to repeat this process indefinitely, going in circles and restarting always all over again, without ever reaching symbolic independence, because I lack a logical beginning.... Might such an effect [of going against the mother] be imputable more to a bad use of philosophy than to philosophy as such?"[19] In a sense, this passage absolves philosophy, as well as reaches beyond and swerves away from its critique: as we learned earlier, after all, the student's aversion to the mother preceded her attraction to philosophy. Philosophy—Muraro seems to be implying—is just what it is and does just what it does: there may not be much point in chiding it either for what it cannot be or for what it cannot not be; the point is what one does with it. The point, in other words, is the "use of philosophy" (and the Wittgensteinian echo in this deployment of "use" here is unavoidable).[20] In this context, philosophy and its phallogocentrism are much more a symptom than a cause. In a crucial passage that deserves to be quoted at length, Muraro explains:

> If I look at the works of the great philosophers, I almost think that the problem truly may amount to the bad use of philosophy at the hands of people (women, me) who have no aptitude for it [*che non è dotata per essa*]. Great philosophers speak in such a beautiful manner, dive into the deepest waters of doubt (it's Descartes's image) without drowning in them, and remerge reenergized and regenerated just a few pages later (this is the case for Descartes, while others take longer); they plan and realize radical and vast deconstructions from which nothing is saved, even though they are always superbly assisted by language in such deconstructions; they sift through the data of their historical context, selecting or discarding according to infallible criteria; they detach themselves from given reality without ever losing track of and contact with it; likewise, they detach themselves from tradition but not from its nourishment (in this case I have in mind especially the relation between Christian philosophers and ancient

Mother Degree Zero; or, Of Beginnings 311

Greek philosophers); and they do all this while showing no hint of being perturbed in the least by the phantasms of retribution of maternal power [*potenza*]—a power [*potenza*] that I accuse them of silencing after having imitated it and after having stripped it bare.

When it comes down to it, these men show a capacity for symbolic weaving—in their use of language, as well as in their relations with the thought that preceded them and with present reality—which I lacked (I am reminded of the episode in Leuven) and which now I know they cannot but have learned from their familiarity with the matrix of life. They show that they frequented it and that they learned her art. . . . But this is not what they teach. They do not teach the capacity for symbolic weaving that they learned in their relation with the mother, and perhaps they do not even know how to teach it. They received it thanks to a historical privilege that they seem to believe was a gift fallen out from the sky or a natural attribute of theirs. Patriarchal society, in which philosophy developed, nurtures and takes care of the love between mother and son as its most precious good. It is the hearth in which all great desires blaze and burn, the kitchen of sublime endeavors, the workshop of the law. Everything seems to start there. If there is something that I envy men—and how not to envy it!—it is this culture of love of the mother in which they are raised. This is the practical foundation and live germ from which philosophical discourses develop. . . . But philosophers do not realize this. They ignore the historical privilege of male children and hide the origin of their knowledge with ideal foundations. They love a mute mother, whose work they present as an image and approximation of their own work, thereby upending the order of things. . . . If I do not seem to have a nature that is suitable for philosophy, on the other hand, this too needs to be seen not as a misfortune visited upon me from above or as a defect of nature but as a historical condition. I was born in a culture in which love of the mother is not taught to women. And yet it is the most important knowledge, without which it is difficult to learn all the rest and to be original at something.[21]

Irony? Sarcasm? If the tone of the first paragraph of this quotation seems to be one of irony occasionally laced with more than a hint of sarcasm; if the tone of the first paragraph, in other words, seems to express an implicit mode of critique, the rest of this passage leaves both irony and critique firmly behind. Far from being ironic, jocular, or coy, Muraro's

inaptitude for philosophy demands to be taken literally and seriously—
and some provisional conclusions may be drawn from this.

The first implication is that this inaptitude for philosophy finds its
deepest roots not in philosophy but in that "patriarchal society, in which
philosophy developed." Such inaptitude, in other words, has its source
in patriarchy's generalized and active preemption of women's "love of
the mother." Importantly—lest we attribute essentialism to this line of
argumentation—such a love for Muraro is not immediate or spontaneous but is something that is taught and learned and hence is also "knowledge" ("I was born in a culture in which love of the mother is not taught
to women. And yet it is the most important knowledge, without which it
is difficult to learn all the rest.". . .). I will return to this overlap of learning, love, and knowledge shortly. Here, I want to draw attention to one
of the important implications of this passage, namely, that women's love
of the mother—due to its inherent possibility of a different symbolic
order—may be far more dangerous for patriarchy than that "historical
privilege" which goes by the name of Oedipus. This may also explain why
the preemption of women's love of the mother and the oedipal interdiction appear and function very differently in patriarchal culture: the former is as "mute" as the mother that men love; or, put differently, the
preemption of women's love of the mother is far less broadcasted and
publicized than the far more garrulous and noisier oedipal interdiction—
for the latter, after all, ignites, fuels, and, indeed, teaches and prescribes
men's love of the mother as the essential ingredient for the production
and reproduction of patriarchy and its symbolic order in the first place.[22]
If men's love of the mother is produced and incited precisely by being
forbidden and repressed, women's love of the mother is not even negated:
it is not repressed, disavowed, or foreclosed, because any of these types
of negation would in effect produce it. Women's love of the mother,
rather, is "not taught"—it is preempted, forestalled, forever held in abey-
ance, because it cannot be thought in any form, not even in the form
of negation, within patriarchy. Unthought and unthinkable, it is, quite
simply, not in the realm of the possible: killed even before being born, it
is something that could have been but wasn't—a miscarriage, at best. In
the context of a discussion of Sigmund Freud, Muraro emphasizes the
distinction between the girl's initial attachment to the mother and the

love of the mother that typically does not follow such an attachment: differently from Freud—who posits the girl's initial attachment already as love and who claims that this love later turns into hatred due to the forcible and inevitable separation from the mother—Muraro claims: "In actuality, this is not a transformation of love into hatred; rather, this is a lack of knowing how to love—a lack because of which the initial attachment goes bad and becomes like a sore that never heals."[23] It is here, in this perpetually festering wound, that women's love of the mother remains preempted and unrealized. And it is here, in this lack of maternal love and knowledge, that the inaptitude for philosophy and for much else is born always already stillborn.

The second implication, however, crucially modifies the first. The second implication, in fact, is that this inaptitude for philosophy is the proverbial blessing in disguise. This inaptitude consists in an inability to formulate and produce a beginning understood as first principle, a beginning that subtracts and eliminates given reality, in short, a beginning construed as the "ideal foundation" which great philosophers use to "hide the origin of their knowledge" and to bury "the practical foundation and live germ from which philosophical discourses develop." It is legitimate, thus, to question Muraro's frank declaration of envy: "If there is something that I envy men—and how not to envy it!—it is this culture of love of the mother in which they are raised." Surely, it is possible to envy something and not want it at one and the same time. It strikes me that this is the case with Muraro: she may well envy all this—and yet this is precisely not what she wants. I believe the passage quoted above makes abundantly clear that there is a structural asymmetry and difference between men's love of the mother and women's love of the mother. Men's love of the mother is that oedipal love of a "mute" mother that enables, among other things, great philosophers first to imitate and learn from "the matrix of life" and then to represent that matrix as "an image and approximation of their own work, thereby upending the order of things"; this is love, in other words, as experienced at the specular, imitative, projective, and narcissistic level of the imaginary. Muraro, on the one hand, does consider this type of love to constitute a figuration of the pre-oedipal from the retroactive standpoint of a definitionally oedipal symbolic order (and here she is in agreement with the likes of Jacques Lacan and Julia

Kristeva), and, on the other hand, does nonetheless understand this love as the "practical foundation" of a specifically patriarchal conception of the symbolic that needs to refract and distort such a foundation precisely as a retroactive figuration of the pre-oedipal in order to preclude the emergence of another symbolic order (and here she parts company not so much with Lacan but certainly with Kristeva, as it becomes explicitly evident in later chapters of *The Symbolic Order of the Mother*).[24] Men's love of the mother is an imaginary fantasy, yes—but a fantasy that bears the marks of the real, which is why it has very real, very productive effects.[25] This is not Muraro's fantasy, however. Her fantasy is unproductive because it is, as it were, too real—as it is stuck in a festering wound. The first chapter of *The Symbolic Order of the Mother* chronicles the process of going through this other fantasy.

Ultimately, Muraro's inaptitude for philosophy—namely, her inability to produce a beginning that is logical to the degree to which it eliminates given reality—is an inaptitude for patriarchy and its symbolic order *tout court*, is an eminently feminist inaptitude. If and when realized, women's love of the mother transforms the very idea of a logical beginning and incepts and sets in motion another logic altogether: indeed, women's love of the mother can only be love of a beginning that is logical to the extent to which it starts there where one is—in given reality, in that mess which is the middle of things. (It is crucial to note that for Muraro given reality is never absolutely immediate: Muraro reiterates the unavoidable presence and necessity of mediation—language, above all—throughout her work. To start in the middle is to be in mediation.)[26] The logical beginning begins not from the very beginning, not from a mythical origin; it begins right here, right now. Far from constituting a mirage of origins, Muraro's mother is not ab ovo: she is, rather, in medias res. Neither phallic nor castrated, neither excess nor lack, neither a minus nor a plus, Muraro's mother is a zero: mother degree zero.[27] (In a different terminology—one that, much like the terminologies of the great philosophers cited by Muraro, does not acknowledge the mother and yet may not be incompatible with such an acknowledgment—this zero degree of being that Muraro does not hesitate to call "being-being,"[28] this "outside" that is more "internal" than any inside,[29] this ontological-maternal principle that never ceases to produce both life and language in and through and with us, would be called "the plane of immanence," which is, by definition, the at once prephilosophical and nonphilosophical condition of possibility of philosophy).[30]

Muraro writes:

> Suddenly I realize that the beginning I was looking for is right in front of me: it is to know how to love the mother. I am certain that this is it because no other beginning is possible for me: only this one, in fact, breaks the vicious circle and lets me out of the trap of a culture that, by not teaching me how to love my mother, also deprived me of the strength necessary to change this very culture, thereby leaving me only with the strength to complain, indefinitely.
>
> But how will I learn? Who will teach me? The answer is simple: the necessity and need in which I exist shall teach me—a need so great and so instructive that I have already learned, that I already not only know what this knowing how to love the mother is but also discover that it had always been in me and that it had always aided me in my search for order that will be able to give me symbolic independence. What else, in fact, was this always increasing difficulty of beginning if not an incentive to continue to search till I would find the true beginning? . . . This is how the difficulty of beginning was solved and how I found the logical beginning of my research. It is a poorer beginning than the one demanded by the sternest philosophies characterized by beginning-as-foundation.[31]

The logical beginning is never left behind and is always already there. This poor beginning is rich at once in life and language, in love and knowledge.[32] But Muraro's sudden discovery that the logical beginning had been staring at her in front of her face all along, her sudden realization that (her aversion to her mother notwithstanding) she had always known how to love her mother, is not a spiritual illumination, mystical epiphany, or transcendent miracle. On the contrary, the suddenness and apparent ease of the discovery presupposes a difficult struggle, a political struggle: "I found the way out not thanks to philosophy but thanks to women's politics. It is from this politics that I learned in a very precise manner that to exist in freedom a woman needs, symbolically, maternal power [potenza], much like she needed it materially to come into the world."[33] Tucked away as an aside somewhere in the middle of the first chapter of *The Symbolic Order of the Mother*, this startling revelation is mentioned in passing and never again commented upon or further elaborated. It turns out that what broke both the spell of philosophy and the vicious circle of philosophy was something outside philosophy, namely, feminist politics. Elsewhere, Muraro triumphantly declares: "I assert that knowing how to love the mother constitutes symbolic order."[34] It is by virtue of this rallying cry that Muraro's feminist inaptitude for philosophy constitutes another mother for philosophy, is an other philosophy. And now we can finally truly begin.

NOTES

1. Luisa Muraro, *L'ordine simbolico della madre* (Rome: Editori Riuniti, 2006), 3–15; my translation throughout. *L'ordine simbolico della madre* was first published in 1992.
2. Muraro, *L'ordine simbolico della madre*, 3.
3. Muraro, *L'ordine simbolico della madre*, 3.
4. Muraro, *L'ordine simbolico della madre*, 3.
5. Muraro, *L'ordine simbolico della madre*, 4.
6. "The difficulty of beginning" is a quotation from Hegel's *Encyclopedia*. G. W. F. Hegel, *The Encyclopedia Logic*, trans. T. F. Geraets, W. A. Suchting, and H. S. Harris (Indianapolis: Hackett, 1991), 24.
7. Muraro, *L'ordine simbolico della madre*, 5.
8. Muraro, *L'ordine simbolico della madre*, 6.
9. Muraro, *L'ordine simbolico della madre*, 7–8.
10. Muraro, *L'ordine simbolico della madre*, 8.
11. Muraro, *L'ordine simbolico della madre*, 8.
12. Muraro, *L'ordine simbolico della madre*, 108.
13. Muraro, *L'ordine simbolico della madre*, 8–9.
14. Muraro, *L'ordine simbolico della madre*, 10.
15. Muraro; *L'ordine simbolico della madre*, 11.
16. See, among other places, Muraro, *L'ordine simbolico della madre*, 10–11 and 108–9, as well as Muraro, *Maglia e uncinetto: Racconto linguistico-politico sulla inimicizia tra metafora e metonimia* (Rome: Manifestolibri, 1998), 111.
17. Muraro states explicitly that the critique of philosophy is not her project at several points in *The Symbolic Order of the Mother*. See, for example, Muraro, *L'ordine simbolico della madre*, 109.
18. Arguably, much like Muraro, Irigaray too eventually turns away from the critique of phallogocentrism in order to embark on different projects, best exemplified by her later work (such as, for example, *Between East and West: From Singularity to Community*, *The Way of Love*, and *Una nuova cultura dell'energia: Al di là di Oriente e Occidente*). It is also arguable, however, that Irigaray's most

important contributions consist in her early work of critique and that her later work suffers from regrettable flights into transcendence and from a lack of attentiveness to symbolic processes—almost as if the entire question of the symbolic, including the possibility of a different symbolic order, is the baby thrown away with the bathwater of phallogocentrism. Muraro, on the other hand, has never lost sight of the question of the symbolic precisely due to the fact that her project consists in theorizing, practicing, and materializing this other symbolic order that she calls the symbolic order of the mother.

19. Muraro, *L'ordine simbolico della madre*, 11.
20. The locution "use of philosophy" occurs, among other places, on p. 12 of *L'ordine simbolico della madre*. Muraro discusses Ludwig Wittgenstein's thought at several points in her work; see, for example, *L'ordine simbolico della madre*, 110–11.
21. Muraro, *L'ordine simbolico della madre*, 12–13.
22. The intuition that, far from posing a threat to patriarchy, Oedipus is indispensably productive for and of patriarchy was perhaps one of Jacques Lacan's most important discoveries (and certainly one of his discoveries that proved to be most useful for feminist philosophy). See, for example, this succinct statement in *Seminar XI*: "even by basing the origin of the function of the father on his murder, Freud protects the father." Jacques Lacan, *The Four Fundamental Concepts of Psychoanalysis: The Seminar of Jacques Lacan Book XI*, ed. Jacques-Alain Miller, trans. Alan Sheridan (New York: W. W. Norton, 1998), 59.
23. Muraro, *L'ordine simbolico della madre*, 14.
24. See the third chapter of *L'ordine simbolico della madre*, titled "La parola, dono della madre" [The word: The mother's gift]. Muraro, *L'ordine simbolico della madre*, 37–51, and especially 43–46. If I say that Muraro does not completely part ways with Lacan on this point that is because Lacan, late in life, started acknowledging the mother as the foundation of the symbolic order as well as referring to the question of maternal language; see, for example, a rare interview given by Lacan in 1970 and excerpted in Françoise Wolff's film *Jacques Lacan Parle*. I am grateful to Dylan Mohr for having drawn my attention to this film.
25. On this point, see also Slavoj Žižek on the presence and function of the real in ideology. Slavoj Žižek, "The Real in Ideology," *PsychCritique* 2, no. 3 (1987): 255–70.
26. See, for example, Muraro, *L'ordine simbolico della madre*, 67.
27. It may seem odd to make recourse to such a conceptual and linguistic turn of phrase—i.e., "mother degree zero"—here and in the title of this afterword, given the thorough and compelling critique Muraro undertakes of the notion of a zero degree in rhetoric, structural linguistics, and in other discursive fields (see, for example, the section titled "Degree Zero" in the excerpt from *To Knit or to Crochet?* in chapter 2 in this volume). My usage of this expression is not meant to counter Muraro's critiques of it—i.e., as if I claimed that she,

ultimately, does and says the very opposite of what she argues. Rather, my claim here is that the zero degree I am invoking has very little to do with the notion Muraro rightly and correctly criticizes: whereas that notion in rhetoric and linguistics sooner or later reveals itself to be a mask behind which we find hidden familiar notions of norm and normality—e.g., as in a zero degree of language from which rhetorical tropes deviate—what I am calling zero degree is a determinate way of conceiving of beginnings, in which the beginning is different from origin or norm, and in which the beginning is always already there in "given reality," and not as some sort of static background to reality but as its dynamic ontological principle that one may or may not actively engage with, which engagement, or lack thereof, begets a variety of results. As Andrea Righi and I point out in the introduction to this volume, after all, "mother" in Muraro is not an inert and mute notion; it is, rather, a relational one, namely, a concept that expresses a certain type of onto-epistemological relation (which, like all relations, may or may not occur, may occur badly or well, may be established but weakly rather than strongly, etc.). This is why, shortly, I will compare what I call "mother degree zero" to the plane of immanence; see also note 32 below.

28. Muraro, *L'ordine simbolico della madre*, 41.

29. Regarding the principle of linguistic communication, Muraro writes: "According to this principle, which is the authentic motor of the primary structure of knowledge, sayability has no limits but only rules; in fact, it has only one rule, which is immanent to sayability itself: to acknowledge the necessity of mediation. . . . This principle turned my going outside myself into the equivalent of rediscovering the internal more internal in me." Muraro, *L'ordine simbolico della madre*, 67.

30. I am referring to Gilles Deleuze's as well as Gilles Deleuze and Félix Guattari's concept of the plane of immanence. See, among other texts, *What Is Philosophy?*, 35–60, and especially 40–42 (for their characterization of the plane of immanence as at once "prephilosophical" and "nonphilosophical" condition of possibility of philosophy) and 58–59 (for their characterization of the plane of immanence as "an outside more distant than any external world because it is an inside deeper than any internal world"). Let me add that the comparison between Muraro's "mother" and Deleuze and Guattari's "plane of immanence" is warranted also by the fact that knowledge in both cases—i.e., knowledge of the mother, knowledge of the plane of immanence—entails active production of that which is known without, for that, falling into the trap of believing that there is nothing outside the epistemological discourse that enables us at once to know and to produce that which we know. Much like for the plane of immanence in Deleuze and Guattari, the mother in Muraro is not simply there: she needs to be made, but by a subject who is willing and able to be made—i.e., radically undone and then transformed—in turn. On this point, see also how the plane

of immanence needs to be produced anew by each and every philosopher, as well as how this production is radically transformative for the philosopher in question: Deleuze and Guattari, *What Is Philosophy?*, trans Hugh Tomlinson and Graham Burchell III (New York: Columbia University Press, 1996), 39–40, 41–42.

31. Muraro, *L'ordine simbolico della madre*, 13–14.

32. There is another philosopher who, much like Muraro, dares to bring love and knowledge together in a nexus that constitutes the highest point of his onto-epistemology: I am thinking of Baruch Spinoza, who posits a third and highest kind of knowledge beyond both imagination and reason, which he calls intuition, which is a knowledge *sub quadam aeternitatis specie*, under a certain species of eternity, and which constitutes what he refers to as *amor intellectualis Dei*, intellectual love of God—a love that, adjectival modifier notwithstanding, is also fully material and corporeal, as Spinoza makes clear at several points in Part Five of his *Ethics* (see, for example, Proposition 29 and its proof in Part Five). Besides the fact that Muraro is not at all averse to engaging with the question of God (and, more generally, with the question of the divine) understood as nexus of love and knowledge from the standpoint of sexual difference—see, for example, her compelling *Il Dio delle donne* [The god of women] (2003), but see also her *Lingua materna, scienza divina: La filosofia mistica di Margherita Porete* [Maternal language, divine science: Margherita Porete's mystical philosophy] (1995)—in the passage quoted above Muraro describes the discovery of the fact that she had always known how to love the mother in ways that are uncannily similar to the ways in which Spinoza describes the achievement of the third kind of knowledge: among other things, what is especially similar in both accounts is the temporality that characterizes this discovery and achievement (i.e., one does not discover X but, rather, one discovers that X had been there always already even though it is its discovery that nonetheless actualizes and materializes X), which is the temporality of an experience of the synchronic from within the diachronic, or, in Spinoza's terminology, an experience of eternity from within duration or time; compare the above passage, for example, with the Scholium to Proposition 33 of Part Five of the *Ethics*. It would take me further afield to explain how and why Muraro's love-knowledge of the mother is akin to Spinoza's third kind of knowledge also in terms of its relation to other kinds of knowledge, how and why, in other words, Muraro's love-knowledge of the mother constitutes, much like Spinoza's third knowledge, at once a cleavage between (tendentially metonymic) imagination and (tendentially metaphoric) reason, as well as, hence, a combinatory short circuit between the two. On this question, see the excerpt from Muraro's *To Knit or to Crochet* in chapter 2 in this volume. In any case, the productivity of this most misogynist of philosophers for feminist philosophy is well known: one thinks here of Rosi Braidotti, Moira Gatens, Elizabeth Grosz,

Genevieve Lloyd, and many others. Although Muraro's thought differs significantly from the thought of these feminist thinkers who explicitly engage with Spinoza (and who are themselves quite different from one another), and although Muraro does not mention Spinoza anywhere in the works examined in this volume, the points of contact between Muraro and Spinoza are both numerous and crucial, and they constitute the topic of another essay I am writing.

33. Muraro, *L'ordine simbolico della madre*, 9.

34. Muraro, *L'ordine simbolico della madre*, 21.

Contributors

ANNE EMMANUELLE BERGER is distinguished professor of French literature and gender studies at Paris 8 University (Vincennes Saint-Denis) and heads the research unit LEGS (Laboratoire d'études de genre et de sexualité, CNRS/Université Paris Lumières Paris 8). She is a specialist of nineteenth-century French literature, twentieth-century French thought, epistemology, intellectual history of the field of gender and sexuality studies in the Western world, the politics of language(s), and the relations among literature, philosophy, and politics. She is the author of *The Queer Turn in Feminism: Identity, Sexuality, and the Theater of Gender*, and *Scènes d'aumône: Misère et poésie au XIXe siècle*.

CESARE CASARINO is professor of cultural studies and comparative literature at the University of Minnesota. He is the author of *Modernity at Sea: Melville, Marx, Conrad in Crisis* (Minnesota, 2002), coauthor (with Antonio Negri) of *In Praise of the Common: A Conversation on Philosophy and Politics* (Minnesota, 2008), and coeditor of *Marxism beyond Marxism*. His essays on literature, cinema, and philosophy have appeared in *Angelaki*, *boundary 2*, *Critical Inquiry*, *Diacritics*, *differences*, *October*, *Paragraph*, *Parallax*, *Qui Parle*, and *Raritan*. He is senior editor of *Cultural Critique*.

IDA DOMINIJANNI is a philosopher, political theorist, essayist, and journalist. An editor and columnist at *Il manifesto* for decades, she is a member of the Diotima community of women philosophers and of the Center for the Reform of the State (CRS) in Rome. She taught political theory at Roma Tre University in Rome and the University of Siena and was a fellow at the Society for the Humanities of Cornell University, Ithaca, New York, in 2014–15. She is the author of *Il Trucco: Sessualità e biopolitica nella fine di Berlusconi* and *Motivi della libertà*.

MARK WILLIAM EPSTEIN has translated numerous books, including Davide Tarizzo's *Life* (Minnesota, 2017).

LUISA MURARO is a philosopher and leading theorist of the thought of sexual difference in Italy. A cofounder of the Libreria delle donne di Milano (1975) and of the Diotima community of women philosophers, she taught at the University of Verona and at the University of Barcelona. She is the author of *L'anima del corpo, Autorità, Il Dio delle donne, L'ordine simbolico della madre, Lingua materna scienza divina: Scritti sulla filosofia mistica di Margherita Porete, Guglielma e Maifreda: Storia di un'eresia femminista*, and *La Signora del gioco*.

ANDREA RIGHI is assistant professor of Italian studies and coordinator of the Italian studies program at Miami University. He is the author of *Italian Reactionary Thought and Critical Theory: An Inquiry into Savage Modernities* and *Biopolitics and Social Change in Italy: From Gramsci to Pasolini to Negri*. He is coeditor with Mark Epstein and Fulvio Orsitto of *TOTalitarian ARTs: The Visual Arts, Fascism(s), and Mass Society*.

DIANA SARTORI is a member of the Diotima community of women philosophers and the editor-in-chief of Diotima's online journal *Per amore del mondo*. She is a coauthor of several volumes published by Diotima (*Femminismo fuori sesto, La festa è qui, Potere e politica non sono la stessa cosa, La magica forza del negativo*, and *Oltre l'uguaglianza*) and of multiauthored books such as *Esercizi di filosofia al cinema* and *Lo spazio della scrittura: Letterature comparate al femminile*.

CHIARA ZAMBONI is associate professor of theoretical philosophy at the University of Verona and cofounder of the Diotima community. She is author of *L'inconscio può pensare?, Pensare in presenza: Conversazioni, luoghi, improvvisazioni, Parole non consumate, La filosofia donna: Percorsi di pensiero femminile*, and *Interrogando la cosa: Riflessioni a partire da Martin Heidegger e Simone Weil*.

Index

Accame, Lorenzo, 24, 78–79, 82, 117n21
Addio Lugano bella (film), 160
Adorno, Theodor, 7, 27n13
affidamento. *See* entrustment
Agamben, Giorgio, 12, 24, 110–12
Ahmed, Sara, 9
All'inizio di tutto: La lingua materna [At the beginning of everything: The maternal language] (Diotima collective), 24–25
Almodóvar, Pedro, 201n3
Amiche mie isteriche (Putino), 218–19
anorexia, 220–22, 232n24, 233n32; post-Fordist psychopathology and, 293–97
Antigone's Claim: Kinship between Life and Death (Butler), 9
antiracist theory, patriarchy and, 13–15
aphasia, Jakobson's discussion of, 37, 123, 149–54, 272n9
Arendt, Hannah, 8
Augustine, Saint, 159
Auschwitz, poetry and, 7, 27n13
Aut aut (journal), 33, 36, 62n6
authenticity, 47, 162–63, 281
authority: of maternal symbolic, 15, 18, 24, 37, 50, 177, 183, 188, 196, 198, 216, 226–27, 250, 279–80, 308; of mother language, 218, 260–64, 292
autonomy, ideology of, 252–59
axis of selections, metaphor and metonymy and, 37, 43, 50, 68–71, 239–40

Bachofen, Johan Jakob, 176
Badiou, Alain, 3–4
Balibar, Étienne, 13
Barthes, Roland, 61n5
Baubo, myth of Demeter and, 164–65, 168
Baudelaire, Charles, 141
Baudrillard, Jean, 38, 58
Beauvoir, Simone de, 273n24
"Before the Law" (Kafka), 134–35
beguines, language used by, 139–40
Benjamin, Walter, 65n42, 140, 184, 243, 260
Benveniste, Émile, 147–48, 247, 263
Berardi, Franco (Bifo), 12
Berlin Childhood around 1900 (Benjamin), 140
Berlusconi, Silvio, 56, 234n44, 238–39, 272n6
Bifo. *See* Berardi, Franco
biopolitics: black feminism and, 14–15, 29n28; bodies and, 220–21; formulae of sexuation and, 282–87;

323

in Italian feminist discourse, 12, 16, 227–30; post-Fordist psychopathology and, 292–97; sexual difference and, 280–82; shadow of the mother and, 186–92
black feminist theory, mythology of matriarchy and, 14–15, 29n28
Black Sun (Zamboni), 156n17
Boccia, Maria Luisa, 175
bodies: body language and, 143–45; language and, 216–17; metaphor and metonymy and, 95–98, 252–59; mother tongue and, 262–64; souls and, 92–95; symbolic order and, 98–104
body politic, eclipse of the mother and, 177
Bonhoeffer, Dietrich, 146
Bono, Paola, 34, 238
boundaries: in maternal language, 137–40; sexual difference and, 140–45
Braidotti, Rosi, 34, 61n3, 319n32
Brown, Wendy, 207n59
Bühler, Karl, 127–28
Butler, Judith, 8–9, 156n19, 208n64, 271; on Lacan's symbolic order, 255–56; on language, 244, 253–59; on politics and power, 167, 179–80

Caliban and the Witch (Federici), 239
"Californian ideology," 59
Calvino, Italo, 58
Campari, Maria Grazia, 159
Campbell, Timothy, 270
Canetti, Elias, 137
capitalism: praxis of sexual difference and, 15–26; social order and, 90–92
care ethics and politics, 252, 276n51
"Caspoggio debate," 212–13
Castells, Manuel, 188
Catalogo giallo [Yellow catalogue], 212–15
Caulfield, Nina Davis, 280

Cavarero, Adriana: Italian feminism and, 242–43, 271, 274n27; sexual difference and, 177, 248, 250–51, 282–83
Chan-Wook, Park, 209n72
Child Language, Aphasia, and Phonological Universals (Jakobson), 149–54
children: Chomsky on linguistic behavior of, 150–52; language acquisition in, 133–34, 149–50; loss of maternal language in, 137–38, 245–52; Muraro's discussion of language in, 19; Piaget on language learning in, 152; symbolic order in education of, 39, 97–98, 104–6, 274n28; verbal language acquisition in, 141–42
Chomsky, Noam, 42, 74, 148, 150–54, 158n41
Cigarini, Lia, 159, 225–26
Cixous, Hélène, 140, 241–42
coherence, in language, 145–48
Collin, Françoise, 163
colonialism, language and, 264–65
communication: linguistics and, 318n29; maternal language and, 137–40; politics and, 55–60
Communist Manifesto, The (Marx and Engels), 9
Confessions (Rousseau), 100
conformism, 44–46, 48
Conrad, Joseph, 179, 204n29
contagion, diffusion by, 93–95
context, language and, 104–9
contiguity, similarity and, 84
contract theory, eclipse of the mother and, 177
corpo sociale selvaggio. See wild social body
"correlationism," 5
Crisis of European Sciences, The (Husserl), 148, 305
"Cultural Criticism and Society" (Adorno), 27n13

culture, 264–65; differentialism and racism and, 21–22; in Italian philosophy, 297n4; language and, 41–42, 150–54, 246–52, 274n33; mother tongue in, 259–64

Dalla Costa, Mariarosa, 12
Dante Alighieri, 259–60, 266
Davis, Angela, 14
Dean, Jodi, 191, 207n63
de Lauretis, Teresa, 40, 64n42, 237, 243–44, 258, 266
Deleuze, Gilles, 26, 224–25, 270, 318n30
Demau (Demystification of Patriarchal Authority) collective, 13, 261, 275n41, 279
De Mauro, Tullio, 134–35
Demeter, myth of, 164–65, 176
Derrida, Jacques, 3, 231n11, 241, 263, 276n47; Dominijanni's discussion of, 38, 61n5, 62n18; French feminism and, 270; on language, 253–54, 264–65; on Rousseau, 262; on sacrality, 263–64
Descartes, René, 90, 263–64, 305, 310
Dietz, Mary, 209n74
differences (journal), 271n3
Diotima collective: *affidamento* [entrustment] in, 20–21; contemporary debates in, 25–26; Dominijanni and, 237, 261, 268, 271n1, 276n53; founding and mission of, 10–15, 29n30, 274n24; Italian feminism and, 242–45, 268–71; maternal symbolic and work of, 18–26, 249–52, 287–91; publications by, 28n21; research on the negative in, 162; sexual difference and, 15–26, 273n23, 279–80
Di Quinzio, Patrice, 177
Discourse on Method (Descartes), 263–64, 305
Di Stefano, Christine, 178

Divine Comedy, The (Dante), 259
division of labor, symbolic production and, 104–9
Dolto, Françoise, 25, 136–38, 143, 149
Dominijanni, Ida, 10, 16, 23–26; Italian feminism and, 237–38, 241–45, 261, 268–70, 271n1, 276n53, 307; on materiality of language, 253–59; on Muraro's work, 25, 159–60, 238–45, 266; post-Fordist psychopathology and work of, 292–97; on sexed subjectivity, 279–80

Eco, Umberto, 107
Editions des Femmes (publishing house), 242
Elementary Structures of Kinship, The (Lévi-Strauss), 247–48
Emile, ou De l'éducation (Rousseau), 261–62
Encore (Lacan), 247, 284–86
Encyclopedia (Hegel), 305
Engels, Friedrich, 9
entrustment [*affidamento*], 20–21, 213, 231n5
equality, metaphorization of, 106–9
Erfahrung, Benjamin's discussion of, 243
Esposito, Roberto, 12, 268–70, 276n53, 277–80, 295
Essay Concerning Human Understanding, An (Locke), 305
essentialist philosophy, 51; Diotima community and, 242–45; Muraro and, 19
"ethical act," 190, 207nn61–62
Ethics (Spinoza), 319n32
evolutionary theory, centrality of life in, 297n3
exchange: language and, 122–28; Lévi-Strauss's theory of, 247–48
experience: language and, 148–54, 274n33; metaphor and, 105–9; mother tongue and, 260–64;

post-Fordist psychopathology and, 291–97; "silenced experience," 110–14
extralinguistic reality, 110–14

Fachinelli, Elvio, 44, 225–26
faith: Kant's discussion of, 90–91; trust and, 147–48
"Faith and Knowledge" (Derrida), 263, 276n47
family, 8–9, 224–25
fathers and fatherhood: marginalization of, 224–25; Muraro's discussion of, 160–68; symbolic order and, 181–85, 203n16, 257–59. *See also* patriarchy
Federici, Silvia, 12, 239
Feltrinelli Opuscoli series, 33–34
female freedom, eclipse of mother and, 180–85, 188–92
feminism: Anglophone, 26n1; difference in, 166–68; Diotima community and, 10–15; eclipse of the mother in, 175–81; French, 237, 242, 270, 271n3, 272n7, 273n23; Italian (*see* Italian feminism); maternal symbolic in, 17–18; motherhood in, 1–5, 26n1; politics and, 5–6, 211, 225–30; psychoanalysis and, 159–68, 287–91
fetishism, Freud's discussion of, 78–79
Feyerabend, Paul, 24; on Greek cosmology, 71–72
"fides," trust and, 147–48
Finzi Vegetti, Silvia, 280
fixation function, maternal symbolic and, 287–91, 296–97
Flax, Jane, 178, 183, 191, 193
force, symbolic order and relations of, 121–22
Fortunati, Leopoldina, 12
Foucault, Michel, 4, 12, 17, 122; Dominijanni's discussion of, 37, 41, 46; Freud and Lacan and, 62n18; genealogical analysis of, 64n42; on power, 256–57
Fouque, Antoinette, 241–42
Fraire, Manuela, 33–34, 61n2
Frankfurt School, 188, 207n60
Frazer, James, 84
Freud, Sigmund, 3, 24, 256, 264; on condensation and displacement, 83–84, 87; Derrida's discussion of, 62n18; on fetishism, 78–79; on ghost and the mother, 198; on hysteria, 165–66, 220, 222–24; Lacan's interpretation of, 68, 90–92; Muraro's discussion of, 37, 40–44, 82, 312–13; on oedipal father, 189, 223–24; *phallus* in theory of, 283, 285; signifier and work of, 85–86; symbolic order and work of, 222–23, 246–48
Fumagalli, Andrea, 294

Galileo Galilei, 82, 111–12
Gatens, Moira, 319n32
gender theory, 51; education and learning and, 245–52; humanity's split with sexual difference and, 280–82; Italian feminism and, 238–45; Lacan's signifier and, 89; language and, 274n32
Gender Trouble (Butler), 256–58
Genette, Gérard, 241
Golden Bough, The (Frazer), 84
grammar, language and, 135–36, 143–45
Greek mythology: sexual politics and, 282–83; symbolic production in, 71
Green, André, 25, 162–63, 165, 167
Grosz, Elizabeth, 61n5, 319n32
Guattari, Félix, 224–25, 318n30
Guillaumin, Colette, 14

Haraway, Donna, 65n51, 270, 280
Hegel, G. W. F., 305
Heidegger, Martin, 3–4, 37, 41–42, 53, 144–45, 260

Hesiod, 282–83
historical truth, narration and, 100–104
History of the Langobards (Paul the Deacon), 100
Hölderlin, Friedrich, 149–50
hooks, bell, 14
Horkheimer, Max, 223, 225
humanity, sexual difference and, 280–82
Husserl, Edmund, 110, 148, 305
hypermetaphoricity regime: bodies and, 101–4; division of labor and, 105–9; imitation and, 109–14, 116; on materiality of language, 253–59; Muraro's concept of, 24, 38–39, 44–60, 127–28, 239–45, 258–59; narration and, 98–104; symbolic production and, 47, 92–95
hysteria: maternal symbolic and, 216–30, 232nn24, 28, 233n32, 290–91; modernity and, 292–97; Muraro's discussion of, 165–66; sexuation formula and, 286–87

Iacchus, myth of Demeter and, 165
identity politics, sexual difference and, 51, 53–60
Il Dio delle donne [The god of women] (Muraro), 319n32
Il manifesto (newspaper), 58, 159, 211, 237
Il selvaggio (magazine), 297n4
imitation: hypermetaphoricity and, 109–14; women's mimicry as, 113–16
immanence, 253; plane of, 26, 314, 318n27, 318n30; of the symbolic,19, 21, 24, 289
Immunitas: The Protection and Negations of Life (Esposito), 270–71
imprint, of maternal symbolic, 215–16, 231n11, 296–97
Indo-European Language and Society (Benveniste), 147–48

Intellectual and Manual Labor: A Critique of Epistemology (Sohn-Rethel), 90
intelligibility, Butler's concept of, 257–59
Interpretation of Dreams, The (Freud), 83–84
intersectionality, Italian feminism and, 244–45
Iraq, atrocities in, 7
Irigaray, Luce, 3–4, 8, 204n37; analysis of matricide by, 175–76; Diotima community and, 10–11, 242, 273n24, 283; on Lacan, 52; maternal symbolic and, 241–42, 250–52, 316n18; on mimicry, 113–15, 156n20; Muraro and, 24, 64n36, 216, 218, 273n24, 309; political praxis of sexual difference and, 15–17, 61n6; on social body, 103, 183
Islamic State of Iraq and Syria (ISIS), 7, 13
Italian feminism: *affidamento* [entrustment] in, 20; current issues in, 12–15, 267–71; Diotima community and, 10–11, 237–38; genealogy of, 261–64; language and, 237–71; political praxis in, 15–26; sexual difference politics and, 181, 277–82; women's relationships and, 214–30
Italian Feminist Theory and Practice (ed. Parati and West), 238
Italian Feminist Thought (ed. Bono and Kemp), 238
Italian philosophy: culture and, 297n4; feminist theory and, 12, 261–64, 276n53; Muraro's feminism and, 303–16; provincialization of, 277–80
Italicus massacre (1974), 44, 62n21

Jacques Lacan Parle (film), 317n24
Jakobson, Roman: on aphasia, 123, 149–54, 272n9; on Freud, 83–84;

hypermetaphoricity and work of, 92–95; Lacan and, 82–89, 246; on language, 71–74, 274n33; on linguistics, 148–54, 239–45; on metaphor and metonymy, 37, 40–42, 52, 54, 68–71, 84–89, 116n2, 252–59; Muraro's discussion of, 24, 67–116; structural linguistics and, 74–77; symbolic order and work of, 99–104; zero degree concept and, 77–82
Jardine, Alice, 270
Joan of Arc, 113
Jones, Kathleen, 177
Joyce, James, 42, 141
Jung, C. G., 83, 190

Kafka, Franz, 134–35
Kant, Immanuel, 4–5, 7, 90–91
Kantorowicz, Ernst, 59
Kemp, Sandra, 238
knowledge, pleasure and, 37
Kore, myth of, 176
Kristeva, Julia, 8, 17, 25, 204n37, 257–59; Diotima's critique of, 241–42, 256, 273n23; Dominijanni's discussion of, 41–42; Muraro and, 63n25, 244, 266, 313–14; on poetry, 141–42, 155n17; on semiotics of maternal body, 178–80, 204n30, 248–49, 251
Kuhn, Thomas, 41

labor: Italian feminist discourse on, 12–13; merging of nonlabor with, 291–97, 300n50; symbolic production and division of, 104–9
Lacan, Jacques, 3, 17, 24; Butler and, 256–57; Dominijanni's discussion of, 40–43; on fatherhood, 161; feminist revisions of, 287–91, 299n25; formula of sexuation in, 281–87; French feminism and, 270; Freud and, 62n18; on ghost and the mother, 198; Kristeva and, 248–49; on language, 139–40, 241–42, 246–52, 254–59, 274n33, 317n24; on metaphor and metonymy, 68–71, 82, 116, 253–59; Muraro and, 254–59, 313–14; on patriarchy and oedipal discourse, 317n22; on phallocentrism, 283–87; on psychoanalysis, 86–89, 104; signifier discussed by, 82–89, 118n41; structural linguistics and, 241; on subject formation and the unconscious, 158n39, 246; on symbolic order, 52, 89–92, 244, 246–52
Lacombe Lucien (film), 115
Lady Windermere's Fan (Wilde), 4
lalingua/lalangue, Lacan's concept of, 139–40
La magica forza del negativo [The magical force of the negative] (Diotima collective), 173–75, 181–82
"La mère morte" [The dead mother] (Green), 162
language: body and, 216–17; boundary crossings and, 140–45; colonialism and, 264–65; fear of subversion and, 94–95; Feyerabend's concept of, 71–72; frequentation in, 123–28; imitation and, 110–14; Italian feminism and, 237–71; Kristeva's dual stage theory of, 256; limits and infinite opening in, 137–40, 151–54; living experience of, 148–54; maternal symbolic and, 24–26, 133–54, 272n11; metaphorization of, 102–4; mother tongue and, 259–64; Muraro's discussion of, 37–38, 41–42, 245–52, 314–16; Piaget on, 148, 152–54; politics and transformation of, 47, 55–60; rhetorical dimensions of, 74–77; rules and use of, 134–35, 198–99; sacred tongue and, 259–64; social institutions and, 90–92; Woolf's discussion of, 124–28; zero degree in, 78–82. *See also* mother tongue

Language of Psychoanalysis, The (Laplanche and Pontalis), 79
Language of the Wet-Nurse, The (Rasy), 259
language-reason, Muraro's discussion of, 48–49
Laplanche, Jean, 79, 209n77
La signora del gioco (Muraro), 164
Lautréamont, Comte de, 141
learning, loss and, 138–40, 149–54, 245–52
"Legge 40," 227–28, 234n44
Leibniz, G. W., 153–54
L'erba voglio [The grass I want] (bimonthly), 44–45
"Lesbian Phallus, The" (Butler), 256–57
Les mots et les choses (Foucault), 122
"L'étourdit" (Lacan), 140
"Let's Spit on Hegel" (Lonzi), 13
Lévi-Strauss, Claude, 37, 247–48, 273n22
Librarie des femmes (bookstore), 242
Libreria delle donne (bookstore), 25, 206n50, 212–13, 242
Lingua materna, scienza divina: La filosofia mistica di Margherita Porete [Maternal language, divine science: Margherita Porete's mystical philosophy] (Muraro), 319n32
linguistics: Chomsky on, 150–54; communication and, 318n29; feminism and, 238–45; Jakobson on, 148–54; Kristeva's discussion of, 141–42; living experience of language and, 148–54; metaphor and metonymy and, 68–71; Muraro's "linguistic paradigm" and, 241–45; philosophy and, 3–4; Piaget on, 148, 152–54; signifier in, 85; symbolic representation and, 54–60. See also structural linguistics
Living Thought: The Origins and Actuality of Philosophy (Esposito), 277
Lloyd, Genevieve, 320n32

Locke, John, 305
L'ombra della madre [The shadow of the mother] (Diotima collective), 25, 174–75
Lonzi, Carla: Diotima community and work of, 10–13; on sexual difference, 15–16, 47–49, 52
L'ordine simbolico della madre (Muraro). See *Symbolic Order of the Mother, The*
L'Orsaminore (journal), 33, 61n2
Lotta Femminista, 279
Luce Irigaray: Philosophy in the Feminine (Whitford), 64n36
Lyotard, Jean-François, 84, 270

Maccari, Mino, 297n4
Mach, Ernst, 41
Machiavelli, Niccolò, 176–77, 277
Maglia o uncinetto (Muraro), 290–91
Mallarmé, Stéphane, 141
Malle, Louis, 115
Marazzi, Christian, 65n50
Marx, Karl, 9, 41, 279, 298n13
Marxism: Dominijanni's discussion of, 33; feminist reproduction politics and, 177, 279–80; Italian feminism and, 13, 24
Maso, Pietro, 39
Mateen, Omar Mir Seddique, 6–7, 27n11
materiality: of language, 253–59; of sexual difference, 296–97; social order and, 89–91
"*Mater mortifera*" (Cigarini), 225–26
maternal continuum, 218–19
maternal language, 18–25, 37, 42–44, 49–51
maternal symbolic: authority of, 279–80; Diotima community discourse on, 14, 18–26; Dominijanni's discussion of, 211–30; in feminist scholarship, 17–18; "fides" and fabric of, 145–48; language and, 24–26, 133–54; limits and infinite

opening and, 137–40; living experience of language and, 148–54; Muraro's discussion of, 287–91, 303–16; patriarchy and, 181–85; post-Fordist psychopathology and, 291–97; psychoanalysis and maternal language and, 156n18; race and, 14–15, 29n28; sacred tongue and, 259–64; sexual difference and, 282–87; symbolic order and, 246–52
matricide, feminist scholarship on, 175–80, 204n30, 214–15
meaning: children's production of, 19; hypermetaphoricity and, 112–14; language and, 146–48; metaphor and generation of, 86–89, 95–98; translation of, 117n3
media, politics and communication and, 56–60
Meditations on First Philosophy (Descartes), 305
Meillassoux, Quentin, 5
Meneghello, Luigi, 137
metalinguistics: Jakobson's discussion of, 73–74; words and things and, 123–28
metaphor: hypermetaphoricity and, 92–95, 239–45; Jakobson on, 37, 40–42, 52, 54, 68–71, 84–89; Lacan's discussion of, 83–89; metonymy and, 38–39, 56–60, 67–71, 290–91; Muraro on necessity of, 95–98; rhetoric and, 74–77; symbolic production and competition with metonymy, 71–74; zero degree and, 77–82
metaphoric directrix, 68–71, 73–74, 93–95, 104
metonymic directrix, 68–71, 73–74, 253–59
metonymy: contiguity and, 252–59; hypermetaphoricity and, 38–39, 92–95, 239–45; Jakobson on, 37, 40–42, 52, 54, 68–71, 84–89; Lacan's discussion of, 83–89; maternal language and, 218–19; metaphor and, 56–60, 67–71, 290–91; mimicry and, 115–16; Muraro's discussion of, 35–36, 41–42, 52–53, 67; psychoanalysis and, 42–43; rhetoric and, 74–77; self-conscientization and, 125–28; symbolic production and, 71–74, 266; words and things and, 122–28; zero degree and, 77–82
mimicry, women's use of, 113–16, 156n20
misogyny, patriarchal culture and, 7–8
"monad," Leibniz's concept of, 153–54
monism, Muraro's philosophy as, 20
Monolingualism of the Other (Derrida), 263–66
Moro, Aldo, 211, 230n2
Moses, Freudian concept of, 285–86
Moses and Monotheism (Freud), 189
mother and motherhood: in academic discourse, 1–5; dead mother complex and, 159–68; eclipse of, 173–81; as environment, 121–28; maternal language and, 24–26, 133–54; patriarchal culture and role of, 8; political praxis of sexual difference and, 16–26; race and sexuality and, 14–15; returning to, 173–75
mother–daughter relationship: maternal symbolic and, 17–26, 250–51; myth of Demeter, 160, 164–68; patriarchal erasure of, 176
mother–son relationship, 160, 198–201, 210n82
mother tongue: exceptionality of, 264–67; Muraro's concept of, 259–64, 272n11
Mountain Meadows massacre (1857), 6

multilingualism, 262–66
Muraro, Luisa: on aphasia, 63n22; Berger on, 25; on conventional language, 275n43; Diotima community and, 10, 239–45, 269–71; Dominijanni on, 25, 33–60; on duplication of being, 19; on exceptionality of mother tongue, 264–67; on Kristeva's work, 248–49; Lonzi's work and, 47–49; on maternal language, 37–38, 41–42, 245–52; on maternal symbolic and fixation function, 287–91; on metaphor and metonymy, 56–60; on motherhood, 2–5, 8, 11, 24–26, 215–16; on nihilism, 19; philosophy and feminism of, 303–16; political activism of, 261–64; and sacred tongue, concept of, 259–64; on sexual difference, 277–97; "symbolic order of the mother," theory of, 5–6, 16–26, 239–45, 256–59; translation of Irigaray by, 10–11

Narcissisme de vie, narcissisme de mort (Green), 162
narration, symbolic order and, 98–104
negative: feminist scholarship on the, 162, 173–75, 181–85; maternal symbolic and the, 214–30
Negri, Antonio, 12, 268, 276n53
neoliberalism: Diotima's discourse on sexual difference and, 21–22; Muraro's rejection of, 252; post-Fordist psychopathology and, 291–97
Nietzsche, Friedrich, 37, 41, 107, 187, 189–90
Non credere di avere dei diritti (Libreria delle donne di Milano), 213
normality, 79–82

objet petit a, 285–87, 289
O'Brien, Mary, 177, 203n16

Of Woman Born: Motherhood as Experience and Institution (Rich), 1
Old Boys (film), 209n72
On the Way to Language (Heidegger), 144–45
Order of Things, The (Foucault), 41
Oresteia (Euripides), 159, 176
Other: 189–92; maternal symbolic and the, 290–91; post-Fordist psychopathology and the, 292–97; sexuation and the, 284–87

Papini, Giovanni, 297n4
Parmenides, 305
Pasolini, Pier Paolo, 39
passive pulsions [*Trieb*], 136–37; signification and, 141–43
Pateman, Carol, 176
patriarchy: death of, 187–92; eclipse of the mother in, 176, 181–92; immunization dialectic and, 278–80; Italian feminist discussion of, 12–13, 29n30; misogyny and, 7–8; motherhood and, 4–5, 17–26; Muraro's discussion of, 45, 216–18; philosophy linked to, 312–13; postpatriarchy discourse and, 185–91, 206n50, 207n63, 209n73; praxis of sexual difference and, 15–26. *See also* fathers and fatherhood
Paul the Deacon, 100
Persephone, myth of Demeter and, 164–65
phenomenology, queer theory and, 9
philosophy. *See* Italian philosophy
phonemes, 149–54
Piaget, Jean, 148, 152–54
Piazza Fontana massacre (1969), 44, 62n21
Pitkin, Hannah, 176–77
Plato, 305, 309
Poétique (journal), 241
poetry: Kristeva's discussion of, 141–42, 155n17; linguistic theory

on poetics and, 241–45; maternal language and, 144–45, 149–54
politics: communication and, 55–60, 65n45; eclipse of the mother in, 175–81, 185–92; end of, 238n43; feminist discourse on motherhood and, 5–6, 211; historical change and, 35–36; hypermetaphoricity and, 44–47; maternal symbolic and, 46–47, 49–50, 211–30; metonymy and, 53–60; praxis of sexual difference and, 15–26; psychoanalysis and, 43; women's, 163–68, 228–30
Politics of Reproduction, The (O'Brien), 177
Pontalis, Jean-Bertrand, 79
poor schema [schema povero], Dominijanni's discussion of, 41–42
post-Fordism, 22; Muraro's discussion of, 35; sexual difference and, 277–97
post-oedipal discourse: mother in, 2–5; neoliberal governmentality and, 22–23; patriarchy and, 317n22; symbolic order of the mother and, 17–18; violence against women and, 8
postpatriarchy discourse, 185–92, 206n50, 207n63, 209n73
poststructuralism, Diotima community and, 242–45, 268–71
power: Butler's discussion of, 179, 256–59; genealogy of, 10–11, 29n30; imitation and, 111–14; maternal relationship and, 156n19, 210n83; of mother tongue, 259–64; Muraro on, 105; neoliberal governmentality and, 22–23
Prosthesis of Origin, The (Derrida), 264–65
Proust, Marcel, 137, 155n8
Psychanalyse et Politique (group), 241–42
Psychic Life of Power, The (Butler), 156n19, 179

psychoanalysis: feminism and, 159–68, 287–91; Lacan's discussion of, 86–89, 104; maternal language and, 156n18, 216–30, 233n35; Muraro's discussion of, 42–44; rhetoric and, 78–82; symbolic order and, 91–92
Pulse nightclub shooting (2016), 6–7, 13, 27n11
Putino, Angelo, 217–19

queer theory: Italian feminism and, 237–38, 241–45, 271; kinship and, 8–9

racism: cultural differentialism and, 21–22; Italian feminism and, 244–45, 272n15; patriarchy and, 13–15
"radical evil," Kantian concept of, 207n62
Ragland, Ellie, 286–87
Rasy, Elisabetta, 259
rationality: Kant's discussion of, 90–91; politics and, 46
reality: contingency of, 161; extralinguistic reality, 110–14; post-Fordist psychopathology and, 293–97; symbolic order and, 121–28
Recalcati, Massimo, 293
representation: hypermetaphoricity and, 38–39; juridical-political, 54–60
repression, eclipse of mother and, 177–81
reproduction: eclipse of the mother and, 175–81; Italian feminist discourse on, 12–13; marginalization of father and, 224–25; materiality of, 279–80; mother function and, 8–9; sexual difference and, 280–82
reproductive technologies, 175, 202n5
Republic (Plato), 305
Retractationes (Augustine), 159
Revelli, Nuto, 39

Revolution in Poetic Language (Kristeva), 141–42, 155n17
rhetoric: metaphor and metonymy and, 68–72, 75–77; norms and, 79–82; psychoanalysis and, 78–79; scientific language and, 81–82
Rhétorique générale (Group Mu), 75–77, 80, 82
Rich, Adrienne, 1, 204n37
Ring, The (film cycle), 185, 205n44
Ripa di Meana, Gabriella, 232n28
Room of One's Own, A (Woolf), 24, 124–25
"Rosa" collective, 211, 230n3
Rose, Jacqueline, 8, 28n14
Rossanda, Rossana, 6in2, 159
Rosselli, Amelia, 164
Roudinesco, Elizabeth, 223–25
Rousseau, Jean-Jacques, 100, 176, 261–62
Rovatti, Aldo, 34
Royal, Ségolène, 228
Rubin, Gayle, 9

Sand, George, 246
Sartori, Diana, 10, 28n18, 64n39, 204n31, 231n9; on maternal vs. masculine symbolic, 25; on violence and patriarchy, 22–23
Saussure, Ferdinand de, 3, 37, 42, 68, 122, 241, 255, 290, 306; Lacan and, 84–85, 246
Sbrogiò, Adriana, 164
Schmitt, Carl, 54, 65n43
Schor, Naomi, 271n3
Science of Logic (Hegel), 305
scientific language: hypermetaphoricity and, 107–9; linguistics of, 148–54; metaphor and, 104; rhetoricity of, 81–82, 117n27
self-conscientization, 125–28
self-consciousness, feminism and, 47–48
self-exploitation, post-Fordist psychopathology and, 294–97

semiotics: boundaries of language and, 142–45; Butler's discussion of, 256–59; Kristeva's discussion of, 178–80, 204n30, 248–49; social order and, 103–4; symbolic order and, 155n16
Sexes and Genealogies (Irigaray), 250–52
sexual difference: boundary crossings and, 140–45; Diotima collective on, 14–15, 242–45; Dominijanni's discussion of, 33–34; humanity and, 280–82; Italian feminism and, 10, 181, 242–45; maternal symbolic and, 133–54, 217–18; Muraro's discussion of, 40–60; political praxis and, 15–26, 40–41, 222–30; post-Fordist psychopathology and, 277–97, 292–97; terminology of, 9; Woolf and, 124–25
sexuation, formula of, 282–87
Shadow Line, The (Conrad), 179, 204n29; the maternal and, 181, 186–87, 198, 201
shadow of the mother: ghosts and demons and, 192–201; Sartori's discussion of, 173–92
signification: Derrida's metaphysics of the Sign and, 254; Kristeva's discussion of, 141; maternal genealogy of, 288–91
signifier: imitation and, 116; metaphor and metonymy and, 82–89
"silenced experience," 110–14
sincerity, language and, 146
slavery, reproduction and, 14–15
social order: hypermetaphoricity and, 92–95; language and, 143–45; symbolic order and, 89–92, 95–98, 101–4; women's relationships and, 214–30
Sohn-Rethel, Alfred, 24, 41, 90
Solari, Francesca, 160–62, 165
Sollers, Werner, 141
Sorcières [Witches] (journal), 272n7

Sottosopra (journal), 58, 159
speculative realism, 5
Speculum of the Other Woman (Irigaray), 15
speechlessness [mutismo], 122–28, 188–92
Spillers, Hortense, 14–15, 29n28
Spinoza, Baruch, 319n32
Stein, Gertrude, 42
Stoic philosophy, 4
Story of My Life (Sand), 245–46
Strapaese group, 297n4
structural linguistics, 3; Jakobson's discussion of, 74–77, 240–45; Muraro's discussion of, 39–44, 240–45
subalternity, context and metaphorization and, 104–9
subject and subjectivity: Dominijanni's sexed subjectivity and, 279–80; Lacan's theory of, 284–87; language and role of, 151–54, 158n39
substitution: fixation and, 289–91; metaphor and, 74–77
subversion, social order and fear of, 92–95
suffering, in language, 145–48
Symbolic Order of the Mother, The [L'ordine simbolico della madre] (Muraro), 10, 17, 25, 27n2, 159–68, 216–19, 229–30; Dominijanni's discussion of, 37, 49–50; Italian feminism and, 239, 241–45; Lacan critiqued in, 246–52; maternal language and, 245–52, 266–67; philosophy and feminism of, 303–16; sacred tongue in, 259–64; sexual difference in, 295–97; translations of, 274n34, 275n44
"symbolic order of the mother," theory of, 16–26
symbolic order/symbolic production: Butler's discussion of language and, 255–59; competition of metaphor and metonymy in, 71–74; division of labor in, 104–9; "fides" and fabric of, 145–48; ghosts and demons and, 192–201; historical change and, 34; hypermetaphoricity and, 47, 92–95; imitation and, 109–14; Jakobson's discussion of, 68–71, 74–77; Lacan's concept of, 55, 84–85, 87–92, 244, 246, 317n24; maternal language and, 134–54, 221–30; Muraro's discussion of, 52–60, 242; narration and, 98–104; politics and, 46–47, 49–50; reality and, 121–28; semiotics and, 155n16; sexual difference and, 16–26; shadow of the mother and, 185–92; social order and, 89–92, 97–98; words and things and, 121–28
synecdoche, metonymic substitution and, 70, 240
syntagm, 68

talking cure, 221–23, 232n30, 233n35; Muraro's interpretation of, 290–91, 293
Tarrying with the Negative (Žižek), 207n62
technology, politics and, 59–60, 65n51
Terranova, Tiziana, 65n51
textuality, metaphor and metonymy and, 68–71, 239–40
Theory of Language (Bühler), 127–28
"therapeutic work," Muraro's discussion of, 160–62, 165, 228–30
things, words and, 121–28
Three Guineas (Woolf), 24, 124–25
Ticklish Subject: The Absent Centre of Political Ontology, The (Žižek), 167–68
Todorov, Tzvetan, 75–76, 80, 241
To Knit or to Crochet? A Political-Linguistic Tale on the Enmity between Metaphor and Metonymy (Muraro), 24; contiguity discussed in, 252–59; critique of Lacan in, 246–52; Dominijanni's discussion of, 33–37,

40, 43–45, 47, 49–60, 238–45; philosophy discussed in, 309–10; zero degree in, 317n27
Totem and Taboo (Freud), 84, 189
"Towards a Theory of Sexual Difference" (Cavarero), 248
Tractatus Logico-Philosophicus (Wittgenstein), 41, 91, 105
trust, maternal language and, 145–48
Tulsa race riot (1921), 6

United States: European feminism and, 271n3; Italian feminism and, 270–71
"universals of form," Chomsky's concept of, 150–54

Vegetti Finzi, Silvia 184, 205n39, 280–81
vernacular language, mother tongue and, 259–64
Via Dogana (journal), 206n50
Vienna Circle, 3
violence: by mothers, 214–15; neoliberal governmentality and proliferation of, 22–23; against women, 7–8, 28n14, 206n51
Virno, Paolo, 12, 22
Volver (film), 185, 201n3

Wahl, François, 88
Wahl, Jean, 24
Weed, Elizabeth, 271n3
Weheliye, Alexander G., 29n28
Weil, Simone, 122, 158n40
What Is Philosophy? (Deleuze and Guattari), 318n30
Whitford, Margaret, 64n36
Wilde, Oscar, 4
wild social body [*corpo sociale selvaggio*]: Dominijanni's discussion of, 36, 38–39; maternal order and, 23
Winnicott, Donald E., 121–28
witch-hunts, feminist scholarship on, 238–39, 272n7

Wittgenstein, Ludwig, 3; Dominijanni and, 37, 39, 41; on language, 19, 310; maternal symbolic and, 24, 198, 208n66, 209n81; Muraro's discussion of, 317n20; on power, 104–5; symbolic order and, 91
Wolff, Françoise, 317n24
women: Freud's discussion of, 247; as imitators, 113–16; Lacan's signifier and, 89, 118n41, 246–47, 286–87; Lévi-Strauss's theory of exchange and, 247–48; passive pulsions [*Trieb*] of, 136–37; semiotics of language and, 142–45
"Women and Madness" (1980 conference), 250–52
Women's Bookstore Collective (Milan), 20, 212, 237, 242, 271n2
Woolf, Virginia, 24, 122–25
words: maternal language and memory of, 138–40; Muraro on language and, 253–59; things and, 121–28
"wounded attachments," maternal symbolic and, 197–98, 207n59
Wounded Knee massacre (1890), 6
"Wounds of the Common" (Dominijanni), 268, 270
Wynter, Sylvia, 29n28

Yazidi women, ISIS massacre of, 7, 13

Zamboni, Chiara, 10, 23–25, 28n18, 63n32; on maternal language, 242, 250, 255; on mother tongue, 259; on patriarchy, 187–91; on shadow of the mother, 194–95
zero degree: metaphor and metonymy and, 77–82; rhetoric and, 75–77, 317n27
Žižek, Slavoj, 206n57, 207nn58–62, 208n64, 225; Freud and, 189–91; maternal symbolic and, 25, 198, 286–91; on power, 167–68; on sexual difference, 281–85, 299n15